D0489080

THE UNIVERSITY
of LIVERPOOL

Physical Interventions and the Law

Legal issues arising from the use of physical interventions in supporting children, young people and adults with learning disabilities and severe challenging behaviour

Professor Christina M Lyon and Alexandra Pimor

This report is funded by:

The Loddon School

British Cataloguing in Publication Data

A CIP record for this book is available from the Public Library

ISBN 1 904082 73 4

© 2004 Professor Christina M Lyon and Alexandra Pimor

Published by:
British Institute of Learning Disabilities
Campion House
Green Street
Kidderminster
Worcestershire DY10 1JL

Telephone: 01562 723010
Fax: 01562 723029
E-mail: enquiries@bild.org.uk
Website: www.bild.org.uk

Please contact BILD for a free publications catalogue listing BILD books, reports and training materials.

DISCLAIMER

Every effort has been made to ensure that the information contained in this report is correct, or at least is a reasonable interpretation. However, the reader should bear in mind that a report of this nature is likely to contain some errors; that the law constantly changes and is anyway subject to inherent uncertainties; and that individual disputes possess their own unique set of circumstances and facts. The time of finalising the writing is March 2004.

COPYRIGHT PROTECTION

Acknowledgements

Professor Lyon and Alexandra Pimor would like to acknowledge here the contributions made by a wide range of individuals and organisations, who could be described as experts in the field of working with those with learning disabilities who also present with severely challenging behaviour. They include individual service users and their advocate groups as well as those who engage in the training of staff who work with service users and their families. It should be noted that a number of individuals who made specific contributions to particular parts of the text are acknowledged at that part of the text and are not referred to again here for reasons of space. Nevertheless, the authors would like to take this opportunity to thank them all for their help. The use of physical interventions to respond to the severely challenging behaviour of those with learning disabilities is not generally an approach which gains much support, *except* as a *last* resort when all other non-aversive approaches have been tried and have failed, and when there really is no alternative. That is the approach with which the authors of this report would agree. Even then, there are many professionals, carers and service users who feel that the use of physical interventions is counter-productive. This report echoes the calls for more research to be done on the service user's perspective on the use of physical interventions.

The authors feel it necessary to stress the critical importance of training and being equipped with the right skills before anyone seeks to use physical interventions and the duty to provide such training on the part of the employers of those who work in this field. This duty is now heavily stressed in the *Code of Practice for Employers of Social Care Workers*, published in September 2002 by the Social Care Councils in England and Northern Ireland, the Care Council in Wales and the Scottish Social Services Council. Those who are self-employed working in this field are under an identical duty.

Among those groups and individuals whom the authors would particularly like to thank are: various officials at the Department of Health and the Department for Education and Skills, who gave of their time and advice so freely; John Harris and all the staff at BILD (British Institute of Learning Disabilities); George Matthews and all the staff at Team-Teach; David Leadbetter and all the staff at CALM Training; Graeme Brady and Andy McDonnell and all members of staff at Studio 3; Gary O'Hare of the National Control and Restraint General Services Association; Patrick Crawley, Trevor Dickens and Margaret Townley, Training Officers with Nottingham City Social Services for giving Professor Lyon privileged access to such staff and service users; Professor David Allen, Consultant Clinical Psychologist, Bro Morgannwg NHS Trust and Professor of Intellectual Disability at the University of Swansea; Marion Cornick of the Loddon School, Hampshire; Vanessa Muir of the Devon Partnership National Health Service Trust; a number of other medical personnel, including consultants, who know who they are but who wished to remain anonymous and provided us with a number of examples of difficult situations involving those with challenging behaviour; Steve Hyland; various subscribers to the Mental Health Policy Forum run by Neil Morris of the Learning Disabilities Foundation; members of VOICE UK; and finally, Anne Morris of the University of Liverpool

Law School for reading and commenting upon the Employer's Liability sections, although any errors of law remaining throughout the text are entirely the authors' responsibility.

Finally, the authors would both like to acknowledge the huge debt of gratitude owed to the former and current Personal Assistants for the Centre for the Study of the Child, the Family and the Law at the University of Liverpool: Collette Smith, and Clare Dickinson, who so ably produced the manuscript for the final copies of this report and the parents and carers guide.

Contents

Preface   Professor Chris Jones, University of Liverpool   xi

Part I: Introduction

1   **Introduction and essential background**   **3**

    Introduction   3

  1.1 Scope and coverage of this 2004 report and the parents and carers guide   3

    1.1.1 Coverage of adults and children   3

    1.1.2 Coverage of the major UK jurisdictions   4

    1.1.3 The meaning and significance of the terms 'common law', 'primary legislation' and 'secondary legislation', 'Guidance' and 'Circulars'   4

  1.2 Impact of new legislation   6

    1.2.1 The human rights legislation   6

    1.2.2 The Care Standards legislation and the Codes of Practice   6

    1.2.3 Changes to education legislation and policy Guidance   7

    1.2.4 Changes to children's legislation   8

    1.3 The impact of earlier legislation and policy Guidance and the creation of inspection bodies   8

    1.3.1 The impact of the three pieces of children's legislation   8

    1.3.2 The creation of the local authority Inspection Units   8

    1.3.3 The National Care Standards Commission   9

    1.3.4 The Commission for Social Care Inspection   9

    1.3.5 The creation of the Children's Rights Director and Commissioners for Children's Rights   9

  1.4 The mythology of the Children Act 1989 in England and Wales   10

    1.4.1 The impact of the 1994 MHF documents on that mythology in England and Wales   10

  1.5 The new focus on the needs of each individual   10

  1.6 The benefits of considering the impact of the law in informing the practice and policy of different agencies   11

  1.7 The 2004 documents   11

2   **Definitions, key concepts and the interpretation of terminology**   **12**

    Introduction   12

  2.1 The definition of a 'child' and of an 'adult'   12

    2.1.1 The definition of a child   12

    2.1.2 The definition of an adult   13

  2.2 Learning disability and learning difficulty   14

  2.3 Challenging behaviour and severely challenging behaviour   15

  2.4 Restrictive and non-restrictive physical interventions   18

  2.5 The concept of positive handling   20

  2.6 The key concepts of civil and criminal liability   21

2.7 The key concepts of justifications and the defence of lawful excuse   22

2.8 The concept of significant harm in relation to children contrasted with the concept of abuse as used in relation to vulnerable adults   22

2.9 The concept of parental responsibility   25

2.10 Definitions of carer, unpaid carer, care worker, care provider for adults and social care worker   46

2.11 The welfare principles   48

    2.11.1 The statutory provisions on the paramountcy principle   48

    2.11.2 The welfare checklist   48

2.12 Applying functionally and specifically appropriate criteria when assessing care and control   49

2.13 The influence from the children's legislation of the key concepts of parental responsibility, and the safeguarding of the child's welfare by doing what is reasonable in all the circumstances of the case   50

Part II: Challenging behaviours

3   **Challenging behaviours: causes and prevention strategies**   **55**

    Introduction   55

3.1 The term 'challenging behaviour'   55

3.2 Forms of challenging behaviour   55

3.3 Causes of challenging behaviour   57

    3.3.1 Biological   57

    3.3.2 Learnt behaviour   58

    3.3.3 Ecological   59

    3.3.4 Means of communication   61

    3.3.5 Care giver's belief, perception and behaviour   61

3.4 Staff training   64

3.5 Prevention strategies   66

    3.5.1 Feeling-based model of prevention   66

    3.5.2 Management strategies for challenging behaviours   67

    3.5.3 The best strategies – applied behaviour analysis   67

4   **Responses to challenging behaviour focusing on physical interventions**   **69**

    Introduction   69

4.1 Challenging behaviour and best practice   70

    4.1.2 The legal implications of reactive management strategies   70

4.2 Physical intervention   70

4.3 The use of medication as an intervention   76

    4.3.1 Medical treatment and issues of consent and capacity   76

    4.3.2 Consent and capacity to give such consent   77

    4.3.3 Forms of consent   83

    4.3.4 Consent to medical treatment and the Human Rights Act 1998   83

4.4 Control and restraint   84

4.5 Restraining garments   85

4.6 A consideration of Guidance issued by the Department of Health in respect of the Permissible Forms of Control in Children's Residential Care – Circular 93/13   85

    4.6.1 Introduction and background   85

4.7 The provisions of s.550A Education Act 1996 and DfES Circular 10/98 –
The Use of Force to Control or Restrain Pupils   92

4.8 Good practice   100
     4.8.1 Taking Care, Taking Control   100
     4.8.2 Clear Expectations, Consistent Limits   101

4.9 Detention of pupils outside school hours   103

4.10 Duties on local education authorities and schools to safeguard and promote
the welfare of children   105

PART III: Employer's responsibilities

5   **Employer's responsibility in England and Wales**   **109**
     Introduction   109

5.1 Criminal vicarious liability   109

5.2 Employer's civil liabilities   109
     5.2.1 Civil vicarious liability   110
     5.2.2 Employer's liability   114
         5.2.2.1 Common law duties   114
     5.2.3 Statutory duties   120
         5.2.3.1 Health and safety related matters *(applicable to Scotland
as well)*   121
         5.2.3.2 Health and Safety at Work Act 1974   122
         5.2.3.3 Management of Health and Safety at Work Regulations 1999   123
         5.2.3.4 The Manual Handling Operations Regulations 1992   124
         5.2.3.5 Risk assessment   125
     5.2.4 Employer's responsibility to provide P.I. training   130

5.3 Violence at work   132
     5.3.1 Risk assessment   132
     5.3.2 National Task Force on Violence Against Social Care Staff   134

6   **Employer's responsibility in Scotland**   **136**
     Introduction   136

6.1 Vicarious liability   136

6.2 Employer's liability   139

Part IV: The law in England and Wales
     Introduction   **143**

7   **Criminal law**   **145**
     Introduction   145

7.1 Offences against the person   145
     7.1.1 False imprisonment   145
     7.1.2 Common assault   146
     7.1.3 Battery   147
     7.1.4 Section 47 OAPA 1861 – Assault Occasioning Actual Bodily Harm   147
     7.1.5 Section 20 OAPA 1861 – Malicious Wounding or Inflicting Grievous
Bodily Harm   148
     7.1.6 Section 18 OAPA 1861 – Wounding/Causing Grievous Bodily Harm
with Intent   149

7.2	Homicide – understanding the elements		149
	7.2.1	Murder	151
	7.2.2	Voluntary manslaughter	152
	7.2.3	Involuntary manslaughter	156
7.3	Defences		157
	7.3.1	Consent	157
	7.3.2	Necessity	158
	7.3.3	Duress of circumstances	159
	7.3.4	Lawful correction	160
	7.3.5	Self-defence	162
	7.3.6	Mistake	163
	7.3.7	Common law and statutory power to detain the insane	163
	7.3.8	Prevention of a breach of the peace	165
	7.3.9	Prevention of a crime	166

8 Civil law **167**

Introduction 167

8.1 Assault 168
8.2 Battery 168
8.3 False imprisonment 169
8.4 Negligence 169
    8.4.1 Elements of the tort of negligence 169
        8.4.1.1 Duty of care 169
        8.4.1.2 Breach of duty 171
        8.4.1.3 Damage and causation 173
            8.4.1.3.1 Nervous shock 173
            8.4.1.3.2 Omissions 173
    8.4.2 Defences 173
        8.4.2.1 Volenti non fit injuria 173
        8.4.2.2 Self-defence 174
        8.4.2.3 Contributory negligence 174
        8.4.2.4 Necessity 175
        8.4.2.5 Statutory authority 175
        8.4.2.6 Illegality 175
        8.4.2.7 Inevitable accident 176
        8.4.2.8 Mistake 176

9 Human rights law **177**

Introduction 177

9.1 Articles especially relevant to physical interventions (2, 3, 5, 7, 8, 10, 14 and 17) 177
9.2 Impact of each article 179
9.3 Application 184
    9.3.1 Private individuals and public bodies 184
    9.3.2 Public authority 184
    9.3.3 Victim 184
9.4 Procedure and remedies 185
    9.4.1 Procedure 185
    9.4.2 Remedies 185
    9.4.3 The courts' interpretation 186

Part V: The Law in Scotland

10	**Criminal Law**	**191**
	Introduction	191
10.1	Non-sexual offences against the person	191
	10.1.1 Assault	191
	10.1.2 Culpable and reckless conduct	193
	10.1.2.1 Cruel and barbarous treatment and cruel and unnatural treatment	193
	10.1.2.2 Causing real injury	193
	10.1.2.3 Reckless injury	194
	10.1.2.4 Recklessly endangering the lieges	195
10.2	Homicide	195
	10.2.1 Murder	195
	10.2.2 Culpable homicide	196
	10.2.2.1 Involuntary culpable homicide	196
	10.2.2.2 Voluntary culpable homicide	197
10.3	Defences	197
	10.3.1 Reflex actions	197
	10.3.2 Self-defence	197
	10.3.3 Provocation	198
	10.3.4 Diminished responsibility	201
	10.3.5 Necessity	202
	10.3.6 Coercion	203
	10.3.7 Lawful force	203
	10.3.8 Common law power to restrain a lunatic	205
11	**Civil law in Scotland**	**206**
11.1	Delictual liability	206
	11.1.1 Introduction	206
	11.1.2 The law of delict	207
11.2	Intentional delicts	208
	11.2.1 Assault	208
	11.2.1.1 Defences	210
	11.2.2 Injuries to liberty	210
	11.2.2.1 Defences	211
	11.2.3 Fear and force	211
11.3	Unintentional delict	211
	11.3.1 Negligence	211
	11.3.1.1 Duty of care	211
	11.3.1.2 Breach of duty of care	214
	11.3.1.3 Standard of care	215
	11.3.1.4 Causation of harm	217
	11.3.2 Defences	218
	11.3.2.1 Volenti non fit injuria	218
	11.3.2.2 Contributory negligence	218
	11.3.2.3 Joint fault	219
11.4	Professional liability	219
11.5	Adults with Incapacity (Scotland) Act 2000	221
	11.5.1 Scope of AWI(S)A 2000	221
	11.5.2 Key definitions	222

	11.5.2.1	Adult	223
	11.5.2.2	Incapable/incapacity	223
	11.5.2.3	Intervention	223
	11.5.2.4	Medical treatment and physical intervention	224
	11.5.3	Assessment of (in)capacity	224
	11.5.4	Liability under the AWI(S)A 2000	226
	11.5.4.1	Limitation of liability	226
	11.5.4.2	Section 83(1) AWI(S)A 2000	227
11.6	Rights, Risks and Limits to Freedom – Guidance for the Use of Restraint		228
	11.6.1	Defining restraint	228
	11.6.2	General principles	230
	11.6.3	Direct physical restraint	232
	11.6.4	Direct mechanical restraint	233
	11.6.5	Locking the doors	233
	11.6.6	Medication restraint	234

12 Human rights law in Scotland **235**
Introduction 235
12.1 Human rights and criminal law 235
12.2 Human rights and medical law 237

Part VI: Case studies

13 Case studies **241**
Introduction 241
13.1 Carer and employer's legal position 241
13.2 Medical treatment, consent and human rights 243
13.3 Carer victim of assault, self-defence 244
13.4 Parental right to reasonable chastisement 246
13.5 Incident recording 246
13.6 Physical restraint and assault 247
13.7 Physical restraint, therapeutic purposes 248
13.8 Therapeutic treatment, Article 3 HRA 1998 248
13.9 Physical intervention, policies and prevention 249
13.10 Environmental changes, seclusion, false imprisonment 250
13.11 Violence against carers and defences 250
13.12 Parental right to reasonable chastisement 252
13.13 Physical restraint and assault 252

Appendix A **255**
Introduction 255
Feedback on physical intervention training with a physical intervention training organisation 255

Appendix B: Glossary of terms **259**

Bibliography **283**

Index **293**

Preface

Professor Chris Jones

The Impact of the 1994 report entitled *Legal issues arising from the care and control of children with learning disabilities who also present with severe challenging behaviour* and the Parents and Carers guide of the same name.

P.1.1   In 1992 the Mental Health Foundation commissioned Professor Lyon to undertake some work looking at the legal issues arising from the care, control and safety of children with learning disabilities who also presented with severe challenging behaviour. The purpose of that work was to look specifically at a range of legal issues arising from the provision of services to such children as well as from the use of physical interventions in providing for the care of such children. At the time, she was serving on the Foundation's Committee looking at services for children with learning disabilities and severe challenging behaviour. In 1997, that Committee was to produce its own report on the poor state of services for such children in England and Wales entitled *Don't forget us* in which Professor Lyon also wrote the chapter on legal issues. It had emerged very strongly in the course of that Committee's work that there were a huge number of myths concerning the legitimacy of the use of physical interventions springing up as a result of the implementation, in October 1991, in England and Wales of the Children Act 1989.

P.1.2   As Alan Jefferson noted in his Foreword to Professor Lyon's 1994 report:

> 'these myths concerning the types of care and control which could be offered to provide for the safety of such children developed as a result of people's imperfect understanding of what the Children Act actually provided and which children were actually specifically included within the Act's provisions. Professionals, parents and carers, in giving evidence to the Committee, also revealed a great deal of uncertainty and deep-seated concern about both the legality of the measures to which they might on occasion have to resort in difficult situations and about their potential liability in both criminal and civil law. It was widely acknowledged even by officials at the Government departments involved that what limited central government guidance existed contained no explanation of the legal implications of actions which were being advised and indeed in some cases openly acknowledged this to be the case. This could be seen most clearly in the Department of Health Guidance on Permissible Forms of Control of Children's Residential Care issued in 1993.'

(This Guidance is again examined in detail at para 4.6 of this report.)

P.1.3   For this reason, as Alan Jefferson noted, the Committee decided in 1992 to ask Professor Lyon to produce guidance, which would enable everyone providing such care to be more certain about the legal implications of Government guidance as well as of then current and emerging practices. Two years after being commissioned to produce both a full *Research,*

Policy and Guidance Report and a Parents and Carers guide, the two documents were published in 1994 by the Learning Disabilities Committee of the Mental Health Foundation, later to become the Foundation for People with Learning Disabilities.

P.1.4 The influence and impact of the 1994 documents were very considerable and took all of those involved, especially Professor Lyon's colleagues at the Mental Health Foundation, by surprise. The Mental Health Foundation was constantly having to order reprints of the report even as late as 1999. Even more interesting was the warmth of the welcome extended to the two documents by Government bodies such as the Department of Health and the Department for Education and Skills. Departmental representatives on the MHF Committee had been intensely sceptical that such guidance could be produced since, in their experience, government lawyers, like local authority lawyers, had been very loath to give advice on such issues.

P.1.5 The impact of the 1994 documents can be seen most clearly today both in a number of documents of guidance produced by the British Institute of Learning Disabilities, the work of training organisations, and in the content of the Department of Health and Department for Education and Skills' own 2002 *Guidance on the Use of Restrictive Physical Interventions for Staff working with Children and Adults who display Extreme Behaviour in Association with Learning Disability and/or Autistic Spectrum Disorders*, which is the subject of detailed examination in Chapter 4 at para 4.2.2. Thus, several paragraphs and examples given throughout the current DfES/DoH Guidance are derived from the 1994 documents, for example, in the underlying principles at page 4, and at paras 3.3, 3.5; 4.1; 6.1; 8.1 and 8.2; 9.1; 9.3; 10 generally, 11,12 and 13.The 'TINA' approach, that of resorting to physical interventions only when 'there is no alternative' was indeed used first by Professor Lyon as it was the short name by which she had been known since childhood. She therefore first used it in training in 1981 to suggest the 'TINA' approach now used by a variety of trainers across the country. In addition, the recently proposed Mental Incapacity Bill for England utilises many of the approaches first put forward by Professor Lyon in the 1994 documents, which were largely based on established principles of child law. Thus, the 'best interests' approach (clause 4), combined with the 'substituted judgement test', (clause 4(2)(c)(ii) and (d) and the 'checklist of factors', (clause 4(2)) to be considered by those making decisions in respect of those with mental incapacities, all to be found in Part I of the Mental Incapacity Bill, draw extensively on such principles. Originally, Professor Lyon entered discussions with David Ellis at the Department of Health to ensure that when the new Guidance emerged, this report, which is intended to aid in its interpretation, would be immediately available. Indeed at one stage, the Department expressed an interest in funding the production of both the report and the parents and carers guide.

P.1.6 Unfortunately, David Ellis informed Professor Lyon in late 2000, that due to a shortage of resources, funds to support the production of a new report and guidance were not available from central government. John Harris at the British Institute of Learning Disabilities then gathered together a consortium of funding bodies to finance the production of this new report on *Physical Interventions and the Law* and the new *Parents and Carers Guide to Physical Interventions and The Law*. Clearly Christina and Alex Pimor, her Research Assistant in the Centre for the Study of the Child, the Family and the Law here at the University of Liverpool, owe a huge debt of thanks to John Harris and the Funding Consortium. Without them stepping in to fund this important work it could not have been produced.

P.1.7 Christina had originally estimated that this work would take approximately six months from the date of starting work in July 2002. The demands, however, involved in producing a work seeking to cover the principal legal jurisdictions of the United Kingdom especially Scottish law, which is so very different from English, Welsh and Northern Irish law and the need to obtain real life examples from a range of parents, professionals and service users meant the work could only be finalised in December 2003. Working with Christina and Alex in the Centre has meant that I have had a close opportunity to observe the painstaking efforts in which they have engaged to ensure that this work will be of the greatest value possible to those who support children, young people and adults with learning disabilities and challenging behaviour. I commend this work to all those who work with and support such children, young people and adults.

Professor Chris Jones

Professor of Sociology, Social Policy and Social Work, Department of Sociology, Social Policy and Social Work, Co-Director of the Centre for the Study of the Child, the Family and the Law, University of Liverpool

PART 1

Introduction

Chapter 1

Introduction and essential background

Introduction

This chapter sets out to delineate the scope and coverage of the new report emphasising that it will cover both adults and children. It also seeks to delineate the jurisdictional coverage of the document, the meaning of certain terms used to describe different types of law, legislation, Guidance and Circulars, the impact of the introduction since 1994 of key pieces of UK-wide legislation such as the Human Rights Act 1998, the Care Standards legislation, the Health and Social Care (Community Health and Standards) Act 2003 as well as the impact of other legislation in the different jurisdictions in such areas as child protection and education.

1.1 Scope and coverage of this 2004 report and the parents and carers guide

1.1.1 Coverage of adults and children Even when the first version of this work, entitled *Legal issues arising from the care control and safety of children with learning disabilities who also present with severe challenging behaviour,* was published by the Mental Health Foundation in 1994 it was recognised that much of the law discussed within that volume was of equal, if not of even greater, relevance to adults. Much of the case-law used within that first research report and upon which the companion *Parents and Carers Guide* of the same name was based, was case-law involving adults. Few, if any, of the cases primarily concerned children. This was why it was a great shame, in retrospect, that those first two documents were seen as applying almost exclusively to children and young people. Indeed, Professor Lyon spent several years in correspondence with groups all over the country reassuring them that the guidance was equally applicable in all cases involving adults with learning disabilities, who also presented with severe challenging behaviour, as it was to children. The only exceptions to this were those passages dealing specifically with such issues as the provisions of the Children Act 1989 and guidance issued by the Department of Health directed at those looking after children in a range of different professional settings. Critically, as was noted in the Preface, such principles as the 'welfare paramountcy principle' and the 'welfare checklist' to be found within the children's legislation were seen, as a result of the 1994 documents, to be of immense value in informing best practice approaches to dealing with the problems posed by adults with learning disabilities presenting severe challenging behaviour. The influence of such concepts in the 1994 documents can also be seen in the 2002 Guidance issued by the DfES and DoH, and in the current work being done on the production of *Model Policies for Local Education Authorities and for Special Schools on the Use of Physical Interventions for Pupils with Severe Behavioural Difficulties,* and these principles are discussed again in this report at paras 2.11 ff.

The 1994 MHF documents analysed a wide range of guidance produced by such bodies as the Special Hospital Authority and the Codes of Guidance produced under the Mental Health Act

1983, which were exclusively concerned with adults. Accordingly, when this new report and guidance were being planned, the intention was that these should be volumes which could equally be used by those supporting adults as well as children and young people.

1.1.2 Coverage of the major UK jurisdictions The 1994 documents only covered the law relating to England and Wales, but now the coverage has been widened to include coverage of the law in Scotland, which has a part of Part III as well as the whole of Part V to itself, as it is in many ways very different. In some areas of legislation, Scotland has followed on after England and Wales and then its legislation dealing with the same issues represents an improved version of that applicable in England and Wales. This is very evident in the Children (Scotland) Act 1995, which is much more compliant with the demands of the United Nations Convention on the Rights of the Child 1989 than its English and Welsh counterpart. Northern Ireland legislation, when the Assembly has not sat or is suspended, has tended to be fully debated by the UK Parliament and generally copies English legislation, while certain allowances are made for the different institutions such as the Health and Social Services Boards which operate in that country. It thus has its children's legislation in 1995 in the form of the Children (Northern Ireland) Order 1995, which has all the defects of the Children Act 1989. (These issues are all discussed at length in Chapter 2.) The substantive law of torts and crime in Northern Ireland in this area is very much the same as in England and Wales. There are differences, however, in criminal procedure in the courts in that Northern Ireland does not have a judge sitting with a jury in criminal cases but just a judge, and in the body charged with the task of prosecuting offences, the Public Prosecution Service for Northern Ireland. Where there are substantial differences, or important provisions are being noted, these are pointed out and discussed. For example, in relation to parental responsibility and the law relating to children, there is considerable mention made in Chapter 2 of the Children (Northern Ireland) Order 1995, and the Children (Scotland) Act 1995 is also dealt with in detail in Chapter 2.

1.1.3 The meaning and significance of the terms 'common law,' 'primary legislation', 'secondary legislation', 'Guidance' and 'Circulars' The term 'common law' is generally used by lawyers to encompass such law as has been established and developed by the courts in their decisions over hundreds of years. Where decisions are made by the higher courts illuminating and explaining the approach to be taken, for example in expanding upon the meaning to be given to a well-established legal concept such as the 'duty of care' or in the interpretation of phrases used in statutes such as the meaning of 'likely to suffer significant harm' in s.31 Children Act 1989, then such decisions will be referred to as laying down a 'precedent' which must usually be followed. That is why in a work of this nature there is constant reference both in the text and in the footnotes to the decisions of the higher courts reported in the various different law reports.

The term 'legislation' is used to designate law which has been passed by Parliament directly (sometimes referred to as 'primary legislation') or by a Secretary of State or other government officer under 'delegated powers' (sometimes referred to as 'delegated' or 'secondary legislation'). Thus, many lawyers use the phrases 'primary' and 'secondary' legislation when writing about or discussing various types of law. The authors of this report have tried to avoid using such terms but when the term 'primary legislation' is used in other works, it is used to signify actual statutes passed by the Westminster Parliament through its normal processes such as, for example, the Children Act 1989, the Children (Northern Ireland) Order 1995 and the Children (Scotland) Act 1995, which are discussed at some length in this work. Since devolution, the Scottish Parliament has had the power to enact primary legislation whereas the Welsh Assembly only has powers to make 'secondary' or 'delegated' legislation relating to Wales and to make recommendations to the Westminster Parliament about primary legislation which affects Wales. In the case of Northern Ireland when there is no functioning Assembly due to suspension of the provisions of the Northern Ireland Act 1998, and prior to its coming into existence, then the relevant legislation may be referred to as Orders in Council, and will be designated as an Order, for example, the Children (Northern Ireland) Order 1995.

All statutes ie all primary legislation, will have been debated and discussed in various stages through Parliament and will have been subjected to detailed parliamentary scrutiny. Only after having been passed by both Houses of Parliament and being signed by the Queen is the statute enacted. It will only become law when the Commencement dates for implementation are indicated by Parliament.

The term 'secondary' or sometimes 'delegated legislation' is used to signify the fact that the power to make Rules or Regulations in certain areas has been delegated by Parliament to the relevant Secretary of State. The power is 'delegated' in recognition of the fact that the Secretary of State concerned and/or the relevant Government department have the necessary detailed knowledge in these areas and that it would not be appropriate to take up Parliamentary time debating the very many different Regulations and Rules required to give effect to the detail of what is contained in the statutes. Thus, for example, the power to make regulations governing the provision of private fostering is delegated to the Secretary of State for Health under the provisions of the Children Act 1989 (s.67(2)) and the power to make Rules of Court dealing with how applications to court should be made under the Children Act 1989 is delegated to the 'relevant authority' in England and Wales, usually the Department for Constitutional Affairs. (s.93 CA 1989) Before the delegated legislation drawn up by the relevant body comes into force, it must be 'laid before Parliament' ie a copy put in both Houses of Parliament for several days so that members are given an opportunity to signify whether or not a vote is required. Where no vote is required the delegated legislation comes into effect by negative resolution or, if a vote is required, it will come into force after a vote in favour.

In addition, the relevant Secretary of State or body such as The Scottish Executive may from time to time issue 'Guidance'. Such Guidance does not have the force of law in any of the principal jurisdictions of the UK and thus is not, in law, mandatory. The general principle which can be stated, however, is that in any of the jurisdictions such Guidance should be followed unless there are very good reasons to justify non-compliance such as would constitute a good excuse by the courts. This can be seen from specific legislative provisions which do deal with the status of Guidance. Thus, where such Guidance is issued to local authorities by the Department of Health in England and Wales, it is treated as Guidance issued under s.7 Local Authority Social Services Act 1970. As such 'it does not have the full force of statute, but should be complied with unless local circumstances indicate exceptional reasons which justify a variation'.[1] Each piece of Guidance stresses this fact usually in their Prefaces under the heading 'The Status and Content of this Guidance' (see for example the Preface to *Working Together to Safeguard Children* (DoH, 1999)). The courts have from time to time given an explanation of the role of such Guidance. In the case of <u>*R v Islington London Borough Council ex parte Rixon*</u> in 1996, the High Court judge, Mr Justice Sedley, stated that 'local authorities have to follow the path charted by the Secretary of State's guidance with liberty to deviate from it where the local authority determines on admissible grounds that there is good reason to do so but without the freedom to take a substantially different course'. Where such a deviation occurs and an

---

[1] At page viii *Working Together to Safeguard Children* (DoH,1999)

action arising from this is taken in the courts, then the local authority would have to defend its actions by producing evidence to support its case. It should also be noted that just because the local authority has followed to the letter the Guidance issued, this does not mean that such a course of action will automatically be deemed by the courts to have been the correct or the best one to pursue. Thus, in the foreword to *An Introduction to the Children Act 1989*,[2] the Department of Health acknowledged very clearly that 'the government is not entitled to give an authoritative interpretation of the law as ultimately any interpretation is a matter for the courts'.

Other guidance in the form of other documents or 'Circulars' may be issued by various government departments from time to time and extensive reference is made in this work to Circulars issued for example by the Department for Education and Skills as it is now. One such example would be DfES Circular 10/98 – *Section 550A of the Education Act: The Use of Force to Control or Restrain Pupils*. Circulars do not have the status of guidance issued under s.7 Local Authority Social Services Act but where the advice given is not followed then this might give rise to censure in any case which might be taken in the courts. Again, were such a situation to be considered by the courts in any of the jurisdictions, then very exceptional reasons would have to be provided in order to justify departure from the terms of such Circulars or other documents issued by any government department or body. Matters of interpretation of phrases used in legislation which such Circulars may seek to explain, however, such as, for example whether a particular action constitutes 'reasonable force' have to be left to the courts to determine, as was made clear in the *Introduction to the Children Act 1989*.[3]

1.2 Impact of new legislation

1.2.1 The human rights legislation Probably the single most important piece of legislation to impact on this area of work across all the major jurisdictions of the United Kingdom has been the Human Rights Act 1998 (hereinafter the HRA 1998). This Act implements directly into UK law many, though not all, of the rights conferred by the European Convention for the Protection of Human Rights and Fundamental Freedoms 1951 (hereinafter the ECHR). The HRA 1998 came into force across the whole of the UK on October 2 2000, although the provisions of the ECHR had already been brought into effect on 1 July 1999 in both Scotland and Wales under the terms of the Government of Scotland Act 1998, s.100, and the Government of Wales Act 1998, s.106. The importance of the Human Rights Act 1998 is such that this merits entirely separate chapters being devoted to it. (see Chapters 9 and 12)

1.2.2 The Care Standards legislation and the Codes of Practice Of no less importance, however, has been the passing of Care Standards legislation and the creation of the various Care Standards authorities across all the jurisdictions. Thus, the General Social Care Council for England began its work on 1 October 2001, at the same time as the Northern Ireland Social Care Council, the Scottish Social Services Council and the Care Council for Wales. Critically, the issuing of the new Codes of Practice for Social Care Workers and Social Care Employers, contemporaneously in all the jurisdictions in September 2002, is a development to which many more should pay close attention since they are now of binding legislative effect and impose very high standards of care not only on workers but also and very significantly upon employers. Most employers, but also employees, have failed to appreciate the very real significance of these

---

[2] *An Introduction to the Children Act 1989*, (DoH) (HMSO)(1990)
[3] *Ibid*

documents in all the jurisdictions and they do so at their peril. In particular, Part 3 of the *Code for Employers of Social Care Workers* imposes upon employers the duty to provide 'training and development opportunities to help social care workers to do their jobs effectively and prepare for new and changing roles and responsibilities'. Equally, para 6.1 of the *Code for Social Care Employees* demands that employees 'must meet relevant standards of practice and work in a lawful, safe and effective way'. Para 6.8 requires the worker to 'undertake relevant training to maintain and improve their knowledge and skills'. This, of course, presupposes that the employer has made available the necessary training to support those who work with children, young people and adults with learning disabilities who present severely challenging behaviour. In the course of our work we met with a number of employees from agencies sometimes referred to as 'bank staff', who had had no relevant training to equip them with the skills which might be necessary in working with such service users, such as the use of physical interventions as a measure of last resort. Such staff were, they told us, resorting to the use of physical approaches but had never received any relevant training in the use of physical interventions, as required by the latest DfES/DoH Guidance.[4]

1.2.3 Changes to education legislation and policy Guidance

1.2.3.1   Since the production of the 1994 documents, developments within the education field have proceeded apace. Later the same year, two DFE Circulars were issued which dealt with the issues of physical restraint of children in schools. Thus, in DFE Circular 8/94, it was stated that 'in extreme cases which while rare do occur, a teacher might have to physically restrain a pupil to prevent him or her causing injury to themselves, the teacher or another pupil'. In DFE Circular 9/94 on *The Education of Children with Emotional and Behavioural Difficulties* it was accepted that on rare occasions there was no alternative to restraining pupils physically in the interest and safety of themselves or others. But the Circular advised that where restraint was used, it should be done with only 'the minimum of force and only where it is likely to succeed'. The purpose of such restraint was to restore safety and as the Circular advised 'brief periods of withdrawal away from the point of conflict into a calmer environment may be more effective for an agitated child than holding or physical restraint'. The type of restraint being considered here was often in relation to children with learning disabilities and challenging behaviour. Thus, as the Circular also advised, any child who required such complex or repeated physical management should have a prescribed written 'handling policy', which became known generally as a 'positive handling policy'. That Circular also made reference to the Department of Health Circular 93/13 *Guidance on Permissible Forms of Control in Children's Residential Care* examined in detail at para 4.6 in Part II of this report.

1.2.3.2   The next important development was the passage of the new section 550A of the Education Act 1996. This was inserted by the passing of the Education Act 1997 in the dying days of the Conservative administration over the Easter period of 1997 when few MPs were still left in the House of Commons. The new s.550A Education Act 1996, implemented on 1 September 1998, provides that a 'member of staff at a school is able to *use such force as is reasonable in all the circumstances of the case* to prevent a pupil from committing any offence, causing personal injury to, or damage to the property of any person including the pupil himself, or engaging in any behaviour prejudicial to the maintenance of good order and discipline at the school or among any of its pupils, whether that behaviour occurs during a teaching session or

---

[4] *Guidance on the Use of Restrictive Physical Interventions for Staff Working with Children and Adults who Display Extreme Behaviour in Association with Learning Disability and/or Autistic Spectrum Disorders* issued by both the DfES and the Department of Health in July 2002

otherwise'. Physical restraint can thus be used whether the pupil is on the school premises or elsewhere on a school trip and restraint can be exercised by any member of the school staff, including laboratory assistants and dinner-time supervisors or volunteers, if authorised to do so by the headteacher. These provisions are examined in more detail in Chapter 4 at para 4.7 together with the very important accompanying Circular entitled *Section 550A of the Education Act 1996: The Use of Force to Control or Restrain Pupils* (DfES Circular10/98) which was issued when the provision was implemented on 1 September 1998. It was recognised by all working in both the educational and health fields that some co-ordination was now required in relation to any Guidance which might be issued dealing with the use of physical restraint in relation to those children and adults with severe challenging behaviour. The resulting *Guidance on the Use of Restrictive Physical Interventions for Staff Working with Children and Adults who Display Extreme Behaviour in Association with Learning Disability and/or Autistic Spectrum Disorders*, issued by both the DfES and the Department of Health in July 2002, is examined in detail also in Chapter 4 (see para 4.2.2). A further amendment to the Education Act 1996 was made by the insertion of section 527A, which requires local education authorities to develop and publish behaviour support plans in relation to the education of those pupils with behavioural difficulties (this was supported by Circular 1/98). Supplementary guidelines for local education authorities and special schools on the specific issue of drawing up policies on the use of restrictive physical interventions is now provided in a Circular, issued by the DfES as this report was going to print, entitled *Guidance on the use of restrictive physical interventions for pupils with severe behavioural difficulties* LEA/264/2003. (This Guidance is available online at www.dfes.gov.uk/sen) Finally, further legislation in the education arena of potential relevance to this work includes s.131 Schools Standards and Framework Act 1998 (s.16 Standards in Scotland's Schools Act 2000), which prohibit corporal punishment in all educational establishments, and s.175 Education Act 2002 which imposes a general duty on all schools to safeguard and promote the welfare of all children in their care.

1.2.4 Changes to children's legislation   In addition to those very significant pieces of legislation and guidance within the education field, there has also been amending legislation in the form of the Adoption and Children Act 2002 affecting the Children Act 1989 as it operates in England and Wales. The legislation is noted at the relevant parts of this document.

1.3   The impact of earlier legislation and policy Guidance and the creation of inspection bodies

1.3.1   The impact of the three pieces of children's legislation   The Children Act 1989 was implemented in October 1991, in England and Wales, followed by the passing of the Children (Scotland) Act 1995 and the Children (Northern Ireland) Order 1995 and their implementation in 1996. These pieces of legislation caused many professional and informal carers, as well as parents, to review the care practices (particularly in respect of control and restraint) which they employed when working with children with learning disabilities who also presented severe challenging behaviour. The Acts and their associated guidelines did not, however, address the specific needs of this group of children and neither did the Department of Health Circular LAC (93) 13, *Guidance on Permissible Forms of Control in Children's Residential Care* issued by the Department of Health in England in 1993 (see para 4.6).

1.3.2 The creation of the local authority Inspection Units   The three different pieces of children's legislation had brought about an increase in the monitoring of the care being offered, particularly in residential settings throughout the 1990s. The responsibilities of managers were clarified and in England and Wales newly-created 'arm's length' Inspection Units of Social Services Departments were given statutory inspection duties. These developments took place in the context of concerns arising out of a number of national 'scandals' about the quality of care provided in children's homes and residential schools. Public opinion had, on the one hand, expressed anxiety about ill-treatment of children in 'repressive' care regimes while, almost simultaneously, criticising authorities for failing to contain children regarded as a danger to themselves or others. It was in this climate, and because of uncertainty as to what extent policy guidance about standards and practice applied to children with learning disabilities and severe challenging behaviour, that the 'ground rules' for this monitoring by the Inspection Units had to be established.

1.3.3 The National Care Standards Commission   The task of such inspections, together with responsibility for monitoring the care of all children and adults who receive day or residential care, passed from 1 April 2002 to the National Care Standards Commission and its regional offices under the Care Standards Act 2000. Similar responsibilities had been laid upon corresponding bodies in Wales, Scotland and Northern Ireland. The NCSC was, however, criticised for being a weak and ineffective body in England. This was partly as a result of its failure to address many of the difficult issues in the provision of care all over the country, but also as a result of the lack of co-ordination between it and the Social Services Inspectorate (SSI), and the Joint Social Services Inspectorate (JSSI) and Audit Commission Review Team (ACRT).

1.3.4 The Commission for Social Care Inspection   From 1 April 2004, the NCSC will be replaced by the Commission for Social Care Inspection (CSCI) under the provisions of the Health and Social Care (Community Health and Standards) Act 2003. The new body, the CSCI, will combine the work of the NCSC, the SSI, the JSSI and ACRT. The Stakeholder Information Pack entitled *Making social care better for people* issued by the CSCI[5] emphasises that it will, however, be a completely new organisation, not simply a bolting together of pre-existing roles and that its remit will be greater than anything seen before in social care. It goes on to state[6] that 'bringing together the inspection and regulation of all social care services into one place will result in a rational integrated approach to the assessment of social care services. And one which will provide a complete picture of social care; locally and nationally; in adult services and children's services; for local councils, voluntary and private providers; for government; and for people who use the services'. Whether the new body can deliver on these promises remains to be seen.

1.3.5 The establishment of the Children's Rights Director and Commissioners for Children's Rights   The Care Standards Act 2000 also introduced the office of the Children's Rights Director for England and the Children's Rights Commissioner for Wales, while Scotland has introduced such a Commissioner as the result of the enactment of the Commissioner for Children and Young People Act 2003. While the Care Standards Act 2000 had provided for the establishment of a Children's Rights Commissioner in Wales, the powers given by the Westminster legislature were felt to be too restrictive in not allowing individual children to make complaints to the Commissioner. The Welsh Assembly then extended the powers of the Welsh Commissioner to allow individual children to refer issues of concern to them by enacting the Children's Commissioner for Wales Act 2001. The Welsh Commissioner, Peter Clarke, has been in post for two years. Provision has also been made by legislation for the Northern Ireland Children's Rights Commissioner by the Commissioner for Children and Young People

---

[5]   Issued by Denise Platt, Chair and the Shadow Commission for Social Care Inspection, 31 October 2003, and see www.doh.gov.uk/csci

[6]   At page 1

(Northern Ireland) Order 2003 and under this legislation individual children can refer matters directly to the Commissioner. The Northern Irish Commissioner, Nigel Williams, took up office in September 2003. The Government in England has acknowledged that the much weaker position of the Children's Rights Director in England (a post occupied by Roger Morgan since April 2002) needed to be addressed. It has now provided for a Children's Rights Commissioner in clauses 1 to 5 of the Children Bill 2004, which was introduced in the House of Lords on March 4, 2004, although at present the Bill does not allow individual children to refer their cases to the Commissioner. The Secretary of State for Education has stated that he will keep the position under review as the Bill makes its way through Parliament and if it is the general opinion that the powers need to be widened in order to protect children then provision to allow them to refer their cases directly to the Commissioner will be inserted in the Bill.

1.4 The mythology of the Children Act 1989 in England and Wales

A number of 'myths' had grown up by 1994 in England and Wales about 'what the Children Act would allow' in respect of the use of physical interventions. Those often owed more to individual beliefs than the law, though sometimes there were attempts to legitimise them by vague references to 'fundamental human rights'. It was hardly surprising that many parents, carers and other professionals sought clarification from the MHF Committee when it was hearing evidence about exactly what they were 'allowed' to do when supporting children presenting these difficulties.

1.4.1 The impact of the 1994 MHF documents on that mythology in England and Wales

As Alan Jefferson noted in his Foreword to the 1994 research report, 'by providing detailed guidance about the impact of criminal, civil and public law provisions in England and Wales, as well as a detailed explanation of the provisions of the Children Act 1989', he hoped that the report would 'offer an invaluable point of reference for those people, who were anxious to avoid care practices, which might have led to criticism from official bodies or might have given rise to legal action'. He expressed the view that the 1994 report would 'be of immense value and relevance to educational and care staff in residential facilities, social workers, psychologists, general practitioners and other health care professionals and to people who were responsible for the regulation of the care being offered to children with learning disabilities and challenging behaviour'. Alan Jefferson also stated that the main report 'considerably assisted in the determination of policy and good care practice in the handling of challenging behaviour across a range of services in England and Wales'. He noted that 'the documents, however, make it clear that there could be no "checklists" of absolutes in respect of acceptable and unacceptable practices'. The defences, which were offered in those documents as potential justifications of particular care practices, Jefferson felt were inextricably linked to the assessment and continuing review of what was 'reasonable' for an individual child in his or her individual circumstances.

1.5 The new focus on the needs of each individual

Jefferson further noted that 'the focus on the needs of each child provided an essential bridge between an approach based on a strict interpretation of the "letter of the law" and a practical, reasonable approach, which took into account the realities and difficulties of providing appropriate care for this group of children'. For this reason, Jefferson stated that the documents would be and had been 'welcomed by those people who remained uncertain about and were anxious to test the validity of their care practices'. Such a process, he stated, was 'further helped by the identification, within the material, of a number of broad principles which should have governed the determination of an appropriate balance between control and freedom in respect of each child for whom care was being provided. It is the intention of these documents to provide a focus on the needs of each individual, whether child, young person or adult.'

1.6 The benefits of considering the impact of the law in informing the practice and policy of different agencies

Jefferson was also of the view in 1994 that 'by providing a clearer understanding of the impact of "The Law" (not just of the Children Act 1989), the 1994 documents informed individual practice and facilitated the formulation of appropriate policy and procedural guidelines for individual facilities and agencies'. 'Considering the implications of the law,' he stated, 'helped the resolution of some of the conflicting expectations, which could occur where care was routinely shared between formal and informal carers. Such a detailed consideration of the law,' Jefferson suggested, also 'performed the important function of challenging some of the myths, which had developed about acceptable practice in the care of children with learning disabilities who also presented severe challenging behaviour'. Finally, Jefferson was of the view that 'even though the documents were drawn up by reference to the needs of those looking after children they had a very considerable beneficial effect in terms of helping those who sought to provide for the care of those children as they made the transition into adulthood'. In addition, the 1994 documents also provided assistance to those parents and adult children who were performing the task of looking after their adult relatives with learning disabilities, who also presented with severe challenging behaviour. Since these new documents are drawn with reference *both* to the needs of adults *and* children we can specifically endeavour to meet the needs of all those who might now seek guidance from within these pages.

1.7 The 2004 documents

These new documents deal principally with the provisions of the law in all the UK jurisdictions, having some bearing upon the legality and legal implications of the use of physical interventions practised on both adults and children engaging in challenging behaviour. Thus, it is not appropriate to devote the same amount of time and space to a detailed discussion of the Children Act 1989, particularly those parts relating to the provision of services, as was the case in the 1994 documents. This report, nevertheless, has to deal at some length with the relevant law relating to parental responsibility and child protection as it is in all of the UK jurisdictions. It seeks to incorporate the implications of the implementation of the Human Rights Act 1998 as well as the potential relevant law when physical interventions are used in England, Wales and Northern Ireland, which are broadly very similar. There are separate sections in chapters and an entire part of this work devoted to the relevant law in Scotland, which is very different from the other three jurisdictions. It is simply not possible, nor even appropriate in this work, to include the sort of discussion on services provided under two countries' legislation in a work with these new expanded foci. The CA 1989 has been in force in England and Wales for some 12 years since October 1991, and the Mental Health Foundation also published in 1997 its report entitled *Don't Forget Us*. Sadly, many of the problems identified in that report are still being faced today by parents of children with learning disabilities, who present severe challenging behaviour. Similarly the problems identified in the *Mansell Report* in 1993 are still experienced by the families of adults with learning disabilities who present severe challenging behaviour.

Chapter 2

Definitions, key concepts and the interpretation of terminology

Introduction

This report is concerned with giving advice about the legal issues arising from the use of physical interventions, primarily to professionals and carers, who might seek to work in partnership with the families of children or adults with learning disabilities, who engage in severely challenging behaviour. This chapter is therefore a key one in the context of the whole report, and needs to be read before the rest of the report will make sense. It is also very long, dealing as it does with all aspects of parental responsibility and the principles affecting the exercise of such responsibility. This is dealt with in such detail because the principles will, in many cases, continue to be applicable into adulthood for those whose mental capacities do not enable them to participate in any way in decisions being made in their interests. The chapter, thus, deals with different legal definitions used commonly throughout the report such as the definitions of: 'adult', 'child' and 'abuse' in the context of vulnerable adults; and 'significant harm', which is a term employed in legislation in relation to children but also in government Guidance in relation to adults. It also deals with the meaning and interpretation to be given to key concepts employed within a range of legal documents such as: the notion of 'physical interventions'; the concept of criminal and civil liability; the definitions of 'carer', 'unpaid carer', 'care worker' and 'social care worker'; the 'welfare paramountcy' principle, the 'best interests' principle, and the 'substituted judgement' test. It seeks to explain the interpretation by the courts of different terms. The terms 'learning disability' and 'severe challenging behaviour' for example are not legal terms, nor are they necessarily universally accepted. Many people may seek to argue with them. It has, however, been necessary in producing this report to adopt a readily-identifiable phrase which could be seen as communicating clearly the group of children, young people and adults being discussed. What follows, therefore, is an amalgam of an explanation of the 'legal' definitions and other terms used in this report and guidance and an indication of some areas of potential disagreement with such definitions, terms and key concepts. Some definitions which are very specific, for example in relation to health and safety at work matters, or to Scottish civil law, are discussed at the relevant points in the chapters dealing with those issues and are not included here. A Glossary of Terms is, however, included at the end of the report for easy reference purposes. (See appendix B)

2.1 The definition of a 'child' and of an 'adult'

2.1.1 The definition of a child The law in England, Wales, Scotland and Northern Ireland adopts an essentially chronological approach to the definition of 'child'. Thus, in civil law in England, Wales, Northern Ireland and Scotland the term 'child' is used either to:

- denote the legal capacities attributable to such a person, or

- denote a relationship between two people.

In Scottish law there are further clear delineations between the capacities of children between 12 and 16, and those over the age of 16 but under 18 (see post at 2.9). For the purposes of this report the definition adopted in the Children Act 1989 has been used, except where Scottish law specifically provides otherwise, as dealt with in this chapter. Apart from the law relating to parents and their children, Scottish law is dealt with separately now in Part V of this report. Section 105(1) Children Act 1989 (the relevant applicable law in England and Wales) and Article 2 Children (Northern Ireland) Order 1995 define a child as being 'a person under the age of 18'. The Children (Scotland) Act 1995 similarly defines a child as being a person under the age of eighteen years for the purposes of Part 1 of that Act. (s 93 (2) (b)) That Part deals with the Scottish law relating to the exercise of parental responsibilities in respect of children and the position of children, who are made the subject of private law applications between the parents.

2.1.2 The definition of an adult   Interestingly, until comparatively recently none of the jurisdictions had statutes which contained any definition of the term 'adult' although the Family Law Reform Act 1969 provided in England and Wales for the reduction of the age of majority from 21 to 18. Section 1 (1) provides that, since 1971, a person attains 'full age' on attaining the age of 18 instead of on attaining the age of 21. The Age of Majority Act (Northern Ireland) 1969 made identical provision for Northern Ireland and in Scotland, the provisions of Sections 1 (1) and (2) of the Age of Majority (Scotland) Act 1969 provided for the same age of majority. In Scotland, however, further changes were effected to the law on capacity of minors to enter into transactions by the Age of Legal Capacity (Scotland) Act 1991. This provided that generally children under 16 would have no capacity to enter into binding transactions, except of a kind commonly entered into by persons of his age and circumstances, and on terms which are not unreasonable. (Thus, for example one would expect a seven-year-old to be able to buy sweets and comics, and a seven-year-old can operate a National Savings account.) The general incapacity imposed in section 1 was subject to certain major exceptions such as the power to make a will (conferred on those 12 and over (by s.2(2)), to consent to adoption, (again conferred on those age 12 and over (by s.2(3)) and the right to consent to medical treatment, conferred (by s.2(4)) much more widely on those who are deemed 'capable of understanding the nature and possible consequences of the procedure or treatment'. Thus, for example, a five-year-old may give consent to an eye test. The Act provided, however, that those over 16 would have a general capacity to enter into transactions of a more legally binding nature such as contracts for the supply of goods and services. This approach of assuming that those over the age of 16 had general capacity to enter into transactions in Scotland was then adopted in the Adults with Incapacity (Scotland) Act 2000 and in section 1 of that Act both the terms 'adult' and 'incapacity' were for the first time defined. The term 'adult' is thus defined in s.1(6) of that Act as meaning for the purposes of that Act anyone who has attained the age of 16 years. It should be emphasised that the definition of adult is only provided for the purposes of this Act, and thus cannot be taken to define 'adult' for any other purposes in Scottish law. (see for further detail on this Part V Chapter 11.)

It should be noted that in England and Wales the Care Standards Act 2000 provides a circular definition of 'adult' in section 121. Thus it provides that 'adult' means 'a person who is not a 'child', and then immediately defines a 'child' as meaning 'a person under the age of 18'.

2.2 Learning disability and learning difficulty

Learning disability is a preferred alternative term for such older expressions as 'mental handicap' or 'mental retardation', which are considered to be socially stigmatising. Nowadays, 'learning disability' is the widely accepted term, although some parents, carers and other professionals, as well as people with a learning disability would rather use the term 'learning difficulty', although this has the very specific legal definition provided in the education legislation in s.312 Education Act 1996. (see below)

The White Paper *Valuing People* defines a learning disability as including 'the presence of:

- a significantly reduced ability to understand new or complex information, to learn new skills (impaired intelligence), with;

- a reduced ability to cope independently (impaired social functioning);

- which started before adulthood, with a lasting effect on development'.[7]

The White Paper emphasises that the term 'learning difficulty' is not to be confused with 'learning disability', and that 'learning difficulty is a term more widely used in education legislation, in which its definition has a broader scope'.

The term 'learning disability' can be defined potentially by reference to two Acts of Parliament, although neither of these statutes actually use the phrase 'learning disability'. The Mental Health Act 1983, which is essentially a statute dealing with the reception, care and treatment of mentally disordered patients in hospitals, provides a definition of 'mental impairment' which may then be used to determine the necessity for the assessment or treatment of patients. The definition is provided in section 1 of the Act, and this defines 'mental impairment' as a 'state of arrested or incomplete development of mind, which includes significant impairment of intelligence and social functioning'. The definition goes on to identify issues of conduct which may be associated with the condition but in looking at the definition of learning disability it is not necessary at this stage to consider the behavioural element of the definition. In addition to providing a definition of 'mental impairment', the Act also provides for a definition of 'severe mental impairment', to which those dealing with learning disabilities may also refer. Thus, section 1 of the Act provides further that 'severe mental impairment' means 'a state of arrested or incomplete development of mind which includes severe impairment of intelligence and social functioning'. This definition also deals with issues of associated conduct, which may have relevance when looking at challenging behaviour.

It should be emphasised that, in considering the definition provided in the Mental Health Act (1983), one is looking merely to statutory aids in coming to some sort of accepted definition of learning disability.

The other statute, which could be seen as providing a far more acceptable definition of 'learning disability', nevertheless defines this in terms of a 'learning difficulty'. This is to be found in s.312 of Part IV Education Act 1996, which provides that 'a child has a learning difficulty if:

(a) he has a significantly greater difficulty in learning than the majority of children of his age,

---

[7] *Valuing People: A New Strategy for Learning Disability for the 21st Century*, A White Paper, Department of Health March 2001

(b) he has a disability which either prevents or hinders him from making use of educational facilities of a kind generally provided for children of his age in schools within the area of the local education authority, or

(c) he is under the age of five and is, or would be if special educational provision were not made for him, likely to fall within paragraph (a) or (b) when of or over that age'.

Section 312 (3) further adds that 'a child is not to be taken as having a learning difficulty solely because the language (or form of the language) in which he is, or will be, taught is different from a language (or form of a language) which has at any time been spoken in his home'.

The particular focus of this report and guidance is, of course, on the combination of learning disabilities and severe challenging behaviour. Some children and adults who come within the scope of this report and guidance will have milder learning disabilities than others, while a number of the children and adults will have very severe learning disabilities and may communicate non-verbally. For this reason, this report has tended to assume a quite severe level of learning disability in addition to the severely challenging behaviour in order to give the fullest possible advice. This advice will therefore have to be appropriately interpreted if one is dealing with a child or adult with lesser learning disabilities and greater capacities of learning and communication. This would particularly be the case in relation to, for example, issues of consent to medical treatment.

2.3 Challenging behaviour and severely challenging behaviour

2.3.1   The term 'challenging behaviour' is used to describe an individual's behaviour which represents a 'challenge' to themselves, their environment (both people and property) and/or society in general. Such behaviour may be classified as 'seriously challenging' where there is perceived to be a greater risk of the individual's behaviour potentially harming himself, others, or damaging property, or where it is perceived as representing a greater challenge to the capacities of those who have to deal with both the behaviour and its consequences. The use of such terms, however, does not refer to an intrinsic 'wrongness' with the person presenting the challenge, but is rather reflective of a situation which is defined and interpreted by social factors.

Severe challenging behaviour has been defined by Emerson *et al*[8] as:

> *'Behaviour of such intensity, frequency or duration that the physical safety of the person or others is placed in serious jeopardy or behaviour which is likely to seriously limit or deny access to the use of community facilities. Ordinarily, it would be expected that the person would have shown the pattern of behaviour that present such a challenge to services for a considerable period of time. Severely challenging behaviour is not a transient phenomenon.'*

---

[8]   Emerson E, Barrett S, Bell C, Cummings R, Hughes H, McCool C, Toogood A, Mansell J, *The Special Development Team; Developing Services for People with Severe Learning Difficulties and Challenging Behaviour,* University of Kent, Institute of Social and Applied Psychology (1987) as adapted and used in the Mansell Report *(Services for People with Learning Disabilities and Challenging Behaviour or Mental Health Needs,* HMSO, London (1993))

2.3.2 This definition provided by Emerson *et al* in 1987 was quite extensively relied upon, although not everyone has universally agreed with it. Emerson further refined this definition in 1995, when he defined challenging behaviour as:

> *'culturally abnormal behaviours of such an intensity, frequency or duration that the physical safety of the person or others is likely to be placed in serious jeopardy, or behaviour which is likely to seriously limit use of, or result in the person being denied ordinary access to ordinary community services'.*[9]

Before the term 'challenging behaviour' was used, the term 'problem behaviour' had gained wide currency, and many people preferred the term 'challenging behaviour' as being less stigmatising. Some of the parents responding to draft copies of the 1994 *Guide for Parents and Carers*, thus, perceived the term 'problem behaviour' as importing some element of blame and also as being stigmatising. In some areas of the country the views of some parents on this have apparently been considered and a number of organisations refer to their specialist teams or units as 'additional support teams' or 'additional support units' rather than 'challenging behaviour units' or 'challenging behaviour teams'.

2.3.3 The Committee on Services for Children with a Learning Disability and Severely Challenging Behaviour, established by the Mental Health Foundation in 1993 and which finally reported in 1997[10] adopted a rather more expanded working definition of severely challenging behaviour, which many of those working in the field found more acceptable. Thus, this Committee defined severely challenging behaviour as:

> *'Behaviour of such an intensity, frequency, or duration that the physical safety of the person or others is likely to be placed in serious jeopardy, or behaviour which is likely to seriously limit or deny access to and use of ordinary community facilities or impair a child's personal growth, development and family life. It should be emphasised that such behaviour represents a challenge to services and that definitions are therefore based on social judgements (what challenges one service or institution may not challenge another) and definitions must be considered in context.'*

2.3.4 Many of those responding to the Committee's working definition of 'challenging behaviour' responded very positively to that working definition and felt that it represented an improvement on that provided by Emerson *et al*. Yet others felt that it was not appropriate to use such labels to describe behaviour and preferred to see each child described individually.

2.3.5 Some of the parents involved in the preparation of the 1994 research report also felt that the Emerson definition failed to identify sufficiently the challenge to the family represented by the child's behaviour, and the very considerable stresses and strains which the child's behaviour might impose on the family's physical and mental well-being as well as their own participation in social and community activities.

The three main points emerging from both Emerson's and the Committee's definitions are that:

1. A challenging behaviour is not a clinically defined condition. It is determined by reference to social standards and subjective criteria/factors.

---

[9] Emerson E, *Challenging Behaviour Analysis and Intervention in People with Learning Disabilities*. Cambridge: Cambridge University Press 1995
[10] The Mental Health Foundation, *Don't Forget Us – Children with Learning Disabilities and Severe Challenging Behaviour*, 1997, p.12

2. The behaviour represents a physical threat to people and/or to property;

3. The threat can be sufficient to prevent an individual from enjoying 'normal' access to, and use of, community services.

Since the qualification of an individual's behaviour as challenging is dependent on context, Cullen suggested the expression 'interactional challenge', instead of challenging behaviour, arguing that 'behaviour is the result of the individual interacting with their environment. Labelling a "behaviour" as challenging adds little more to our understanding of how that behaviour functions in the person adapting to their world. Referring to interactional challenges alerts those working to support the individual to the necessity of looking beyond the person, often to others in their immediate environment.'[11]

Many carers also prefer not to use the term 'challenging behaviour', because it implies that the challenge only originates from the individual with a learning disability and that other factors such as the environment or other people involved have not been taken into consideration. There is an effort by those in health and social services to only use the term sparingly or use the expression 'labelled as having challenging behaviours/needs' instead. As one health professional put it[12] 'this is not a term I tend to use, as often the difficulty is that of miscommunication or lack of facilities to enable a person to be able to communicate'.

Despite the real difficulty surrounding the issue of definitions and the fact that challenging behaviour is not a clinical diagnosis, a survey conducted by Emerson et al[13] suggested that between 5–15% of people who are labelled as having a learning disability seem also to present some form or other of challenging behaviour.

It could be argued that 'a challenging behaviour' is not so much a condition of the individual with a learning disability as a description of how the carers perceive the individual's behaviour in a given situation. The notion of challenging behaviour can be said to be an umbrella term covering a wide range of behaviours and behavioural issues which may be distinguished on a case-by-case basis.

For instance, the Additional Needs Net[14] defines challenging behaviour in a school setting as 'any form of behaviour that interferes with children's learning or normal development; is harmful to the child, other children or adults; or puts a child in a high risk category for later social problems or school failure. (. . .) [It] is acknowledged to be any form of behaviour that causes concern to teachers'.[15]

An individual presenting a behaviour, the purpose of which is either not obvious to a support worker or other observer, can represent a challenge for the carers if the latter would qualify the behaviour as 'abnormal', inappropriate, or useless because it appears to have no purpose or to be dangerous. The RNIB[16] thus stated that 'stereotypical behaviour (repetitive action or

---

[11] Cullen C, *A Review of Some Important Issues in Research and Services for People with Learning Disability and Challenging Behaviour*, www.scotland.gov.uk/ldsr/cullen.pdf, October 1999, p.3 and 4.

[12] From a letter written to the Centre for the Study of the Child, the Family & the Law in response to a call for participation in the research project for practitioners' and carers' views on this subject, 18 November 2002

[13] Emerson E, Kiernan C, Alborz A, Reeves D, Mason H, Swarbrick R, Mason L & Hatton C, *The prevalence of Challenging Behaviors: a total population study; Research in Development Disabilities*, 2001

[14] www.additionalneeds.net/ is a website which provides information for teachers (in pre-, primary and secondary school) and for parents who want to know more about additional needs.

[15] www.additionalneeds.net/Challenging_Behaviour/whatis.htm

[16] Royal National Institute of the Blind, www.rnib.org.uk/, provides information and support to anyone who has a visual difficulty.

behaviour which does not appear to serve any useful purpose) is often regarded as "challenging behaviour".'[17]

From the reading of various literature, including publications (Cullen 1999,[18] *Don't Forget Us*,[19] *Learning Disabilities – The Fundamental Facts*,[20] and *Promoting Well-Being and Preventing Challenging Behaviour*[21]) and web pages on Challenging Behaviour (such as the NHS National Electronic Library for Health – Learning Disabilities,[22] the RNIB,[23] West Midlands Learning Disability Group[24] and the Scottish Office Social Work Research Findings No.26[25]), it appears to be quite difficult to agree on one single, clear and all-inclusive working definition of the term 'challenging behaviour'.

The present report translates the notion of 'challenging behaviour' into an amalgam of the various sources mentioned above since, in a sense, they complement one another. Moreover, the report also considers the fact that a challenging behaviour can be more precisely or particularly described by the actual forms it can take.

The types of behaviour focused upon in this report and set out in the case studies in Chapter 13 of this report have been produced as a result of consultation with a range of parents, carers and professionals involved in supporting such children, young people and adults as well as with the children, young people and adults themselves. It is acknowledged that these represent only a small sample of the type of behaviours which might be deemed to be severely challenging. One of the serious consequences of a child, young person or adult with learning disabilities demonstrating severe challenging behaviour, however, is that there is an increased likelihood that some form of restrictive physical intervention will be practised.

2.4 Restrictive and non-restrictive physical interventions

2.4.1   A restrictive physical intervention is defined as 'involving the use of force to control a person's behaviour and can be employed using bodily contact, mechanical devices or changes to the person's environment'.[26] The idea is that there may be some kind of resistance exercised by the person to whom the force is applied. Non-restrictive physical interventions which do not involve the use of force may, the Department of Health, suggests, include such measures as assisting a person in walking.[27]

There are various forms of physical intervention, for instance:

- blocking someone's path by restraining them by the arm or by using a barrier. An example of this would be someone stopping a child running into the road;

---

[17] www.rnib.org.uk/multdis/chall.htm#P2560 175221
[18] supra, n.4
[19] supra, n.3
[20] Emerson E, Hatton C, Felce D and Murphy G, the Foundation for People With Learning Disabilities, 2001
[21] Lally J, Manchester Learning Disability Partnership 2002
[22] http://minerva.minervation.com/ld/challenging/
[23] supra, n.9
[24] www.ldbook.co.uk/Chapter_1.htm
[25] www.scotland.gov.uk/cru/documents/rf20-00.htm
[26] *Guidance on the Use of Restrictive Physical Interventions for Staff working with Children and Adults who display Extreme behaviour in Association with Learning Disability and/or Autistic Spectrum Disorders*, DfES and DoH July 2002
[27] See Table at para 3.1 of the Guidance.

- preventing someone from leaving an area against their will, eg preventing someone from jumping out of a window;

- using devices, materials or equipment to limit a person's mobility. An example of this would be using a mechanical restraint to keep someone in a wheelchair.

All such interventions may constitute the offences of assault, assault and battery, or false imprisonment or, in more serious cases, may constitute the offences of inflicting grievous bodily harm, causing grievous bodily harm with intent, and where death occurs, manslaughter or murder. (See for the detailed discussion of all these offences Chapter 7, covering England, Wales and Northern Ireland and Chapter 10 covering Scotland.)

It should be emphasised therefore that this report and guidance focuses on legal issues arising out of the use of 'restrictive physical interventions',[28] or 'restraint'.[29] For the purposes of this report generally the terms 'physical intervention' or 'restrictive physical intervention' will be employed since these are the preferred terms used by the DoH and the DfES. Guidance issued by the Mental Welfare Commission for Scotland in Scotland has used the term 'restraint'. The analysis in this report should not in any way, however, be seen as seeking to encourage the employment of such techniques, when this would not be appropriate from the perspective of all those engaged in providing for the support of children, young people and adults with learning disabilities and severe challenging behaviour.

2.4.2   There is a wealth of literature dealing with positive behaviour management programmes. Much pioneering work has been done in this country by training organisations and BILD, which is now recognised by the DoH as having a role both in accrediting organisations which use, as well as those which train people in the use of physical interventions. Early intervention initiatives in partnership with the families of children with learning disabilities and challenging behaviour have also emerged from both Social Services and Education Authorities.[30]

2.4.3   This report and guidance for parents and carers should not be seen in any way therefore as advocating or approving the use of more restrictive methods of control and care. It is to be hoped that such practices will only be used where there is no alternative (the so-called TINA situations) as a measure of last resort, as the least detrimental alternative, for the shortest possible time and only where it can be shown that it has been done with the child's, young person's or adult's welfare being regarded as the paramount consideration. One of the problems with the use of restrictive physical interventions, particularly when central government implicitly recommends the use of such procedures through the issuing of Guidance on the subject, (see particularly the analysis of these pieces of Guidance in Chapter 4) is the dearth of research both in terms of the effectiveness of such interventions and their negative impact on service users.[31] Indeed, it may be that further much-needed research would demonstrate that the use of restrictive physical interventions may, with many service users, be completely counterproductive.

---

[28] The term used by the DfES and the DoH in their Guidance issued for England, see above note 21.

[29] Mental Welfare Commission for Scotland-*Principles and Guidance on Good Practice in caring for Residents with Dementia and Related Disorders and Residents with Learning Disabilities where consideration is being given to the use of Physical Restraint and other limits to Freedom* (2002) discussed in detail at para 11.6

[30] (For further detail on this, see the Report of the Mental Health Foundation's Committee on Services to Children with a Learning Disability and Challenging Behaviour, *Don't Forget Us* (MHF(1997).

[31] For just how little research of this nature has been conducted, see Peter Baker *Best Interest? Seeking the views of Service Users* in *Ethical Approaches to Physical Interventions* ed Allen D, BILD (2002)

2.5 The concept of positive handling

Positive handling is a term used by the DfES and others to describe a whole plan which has been devised for the child, young person or adult, which may incorporate physical intervention strategies but which may also include other systems of rewards as reinforcement of good behaviour. Team-Teach has defined positive handling plans as 'the agreed strategies (non-verbal, verbal and physical) that aim to support the individual, providing them with a sense of security, safety and acceptance, allowing for recovery and repair, facilitating learning and growth for all involved'.[32]

It is also clear that the term positive handling is used by others such as those in education, health and social services as an alternative term to the term 'physical intervention' because it does not have the same negative connotations as the term 'physical intervention' and is seen as being more acceptable both to those supporting children and young people with learning disabilities and severe challenging behaviour and to their parents. It should be stressed that the two terms do not however mean the same thing. Thus, positive handling generally refers to a whole plan whereas physical intervention refers to the specific intervention or restraint, which is only part of a positive handling plan. The term 'positive handling' is used in para 8.2 of the DfES Circular on *Physical Interventions* where it is stated that 'in schools, the possible use of restrictive physical interventions, as part of a broader educational or therapeutic strategy, will be included within the pupil's *Positive Handling Plan*' but no further indication is given there of the meaning of this term as understood by the DfES. Appendix 1 to that Guidance, however, includes the letter on the Use of *Positive Handling Strategies* from Chris Wells at the DfES, which was sent out on 24 April 2001 to Chief Education Officers. The purpose of that letter was to update Chief Education Officers on work which the DfES had been taking forward since the initial consultation on the guidance. This was eventually published with the title *Guidance on the Use of Restrictive Physical Interventions for Staff working with Children and Adults who Display Extreme Behaviour in Association with Learning Disability and/or Autistic Spectrum Disorders*. Interestingly, Chris Wells refers to that consultation as 'the consultation on guidance *to promote positive handling strategies* for pupils with severe behavioural difficulties'. The whole of the rest of the letter goes on to make it clear however that what is being discussed is the use of 'physical force', and that term or the term 'force' or 'reasonable force' is used no less than 11 times in the letter. While this is perhaps understandable when describing the provisions of s.550A Education Act 1996 and Circular 10/98, it is perhaps regrettable that the DfES cannot be consistent in the use of the various terms which it uses to describe 'physical interventions'. The letter only uses the term 'physical interventions' instead of 'force', when mention is made of: the work being done with the DoH to produce the joint guidance on the 'use of *physical interventions* with children and adults with learning disabilities'; the request which had been made to BILD to 'work up model *physical intervention* policies for LEAs and schools'; and, very significantly, when mention is made of the need to refer whole LEA policies to Area Child Protection Committees to 'ensure greater consistency and safety when using *physical intervention* with children with severe behavioural difficulties'. (p. 26)

Attached to the letter from Chris Wells is some Guidance entitled *Agreeing Procedures for the Use of Physical Force on Pupils*, (at pp. 27–31) which he says 'takes into account the responses to the promoting *positive handling strategies* consultation'. This Guidance runs to some five pages which in the first 11 paragraphs makes extensive reference to the use of 'physical force',

---

[32] In Team-Teach training manuals since 1997, as advised by George Matthews of Team-Teach in an email 29 June 2003

then uses the term 'physical intervention' in paragraph 12, and then reverts to the term 'physical force' in the remainder of the guidance. Where is there any reference to the substance of this 'positive handling' strategies consultation upon which this document is said to be based? It would be helpful if the Department developed a consistent and rational approach to the different terms it is using in all its documents, especially where questions of interpretation may subsequently be raised in courts of law.

2.6 The key concepts of civil and criminal liability

2.6.1 The protection of individual liberty is fundamental to our society and this is reflected by the law. Any action which infringes upon the freedom of an individual, *without lawful excuse*, may incur criminal and civil liability. In seeking to determine whether criminal or civil liability has been incurred by any individual, it will have to be established that a criminal offence or a civil wrong has been committed. It is therefore appropriate to ask what is meant by the terms criminal offence and civil wrong, and to consider also the notion of *lawful excuse*.

2.6.2 What is a criminal offence? A developed civilised society will generally provide that certain types of conduct will not be acceptable and will provide for that conduct to be unlawful through its criminal law. The criminal law of England and Wales is made up of offences to be found either in statutes passed by Parliament, or in judge-made or customary law referred to as the 'common law'. Where any person therefore engages in any sort of conduct which has been designated a criminal offence, if the police are notified they will then investigate and consider charging the individual concerned with the particular criminal offence. If the circumstances surrounding the commission of the alleged offence cause the police (and Social Services where they have been consulted) difficulties, they may pass the matter on to the Crown Prosecution Service, or in Scotland the Office of the Procurator Fiscal or in Northern Ireland the Public Prosecution Service (the Government departments responsible for prosecuting an offence through the courts) for its advice. An example of this would be a case of suspected assault or battery against a child with learning disabilities who also presents severe challenging behaviour, The Crown Prosecution Service (or in Scotland, the Office of the Procurator Fiscal or in Northern Ireland, the Public Prosecution Service) will then consider all the circumstances of the case and will pay special attention to whether these disclose that there was a lawful excuse for the actions giving rise to the consideration of charges by the police.

2.6.3 What is a civil wrong or tort? The same circumstances which give rise to the possible prosecution of an individual under the criminal law may also amount to the commission of a civil wrong, sometimes referred to as a 'tort' or in Scotland a 'delict'. If a civil wrong arises out of the same conduct, then the individual may find that as well as being prosecuted by the police, the victim takes an action in the civil courts, for example for assault and battery, and claims 'damages', a sum of money by way of compensation for the injuries received.

It should be pointed out that even where the Crown Prosecution Service, (the CPS) in England and Wales, the newly-named Public Prosecution Service for Northern Ireland, (the PPSNI) (replacing the former Department of the Director of Public Prosecutions) in Northern Ireland, or the Procurator Fiscal's Office in Scotland, decide not to proceed with a criminal prosecution, an action may still be taken by the victim (or his parents or carers on his behalf) in the civil courts. In many situations, the conduct being complained of may not be serious enough to constitute the commission of a criminal offence, although it may still give rise to an allegation of a civil wrong and a claim in damages for the wrong which has been perpetrated.

2.7 The key concepts of justifications and the defence of lawful excuse

2.7.1 There will be some situations in which parents or carers of children, young people and adults with learning disabilities who also present severe challenging behaviour technically commit criminal and/or civil offences. This may come about in an attempt to provide adequate care, control and safety of their children, be they under 18 or adults, or to provide for the safety of other persons.

2.7.2 The law does however, recognise that in certain situations justification may exist for engaging in conduct which might otherwise give rise to criminal or civil liability and this justification is generally referred to as the defence of *lawful excuse*. An example of such a justification or raising of the defence of *lawful excuse* would be that the child, young person or adult would otherwise harm himself or others, and the parent or other carer has had to take preventative action which would without such *lawful excuse* have given rise to criminal or civil liability.

Considerable concern has been generated all over the UK by those supporting children, young people and adults with learning disabilities who also present severe challenging behaviour as to the circumstances in which their actions in attempting to safeguard such individuals or others might be deemed to constitute a *lawful excuse* in answer to any allegations of civil or criminal wrongdoing against the children, young people or adults. Parents or carers omitting to take such safeguarding action could be the subject of severe censure for failing to act as a responsible parent or carer. In extreme cases they may be the subject of a criminal prosecution for neglect or exposure to serious risk or harm in relation to children under s.1 of the Children and Young Persons Act 1933 or s.12 Children and Young Persons (Scotland) Act 1937, as well as the possible removal of the child from her family pursuant to s.31 of the Children Act 1989, Article 50 Children (Northern Ireland) Order 1995, or s.52 Children (Scotland) Act 1995, and to a prosecution for assault in the case of an adult. Since the essence of such parental action is *the responsible exercise of parental responsibility,* this is central to what would be considered to be their defence of *lawful excuse.*

2.8 The concept of significant harm in relation to children contrasted with the concept of abuse as used in relation to vulnerable adults

A Significant harm

2.8.1 It would be wrong to say that there will never be circumstances when those caring for children with learning disabilities who also present severe challenging behaviour may be guilty of exposing the child to the suffering, or the likelihood of suffering, 'significant harm'. Where there are such suspicions on the part of social services, then they are obliged by s.47 CA 1989, Art 56 C(NI)O 1995 and s.56 C(S)A 1995[33] to make investigations in a range of circumstances to enable them to determine whether any action should be taken to safeguard a particular child.

2.8.2 Professional evaluation and assessment of actions and risks The options open to social services will vary according to the degree of risk to the child and the assessment of the extent to which those with parental responsibility are able and willing to co-operate in any plans

---

[33] See para 2.1.1 for the full titles of each of these statutes.

for continuing assessment and support. The Guidance issued by the Department of Health for England and Wales in 1991 on *Children with Disabilities* (Volume 6 Guidance on the Children Act 1989) (DoH, 1991) points out at paragraph 15.3 that other authorities such as housing, education and health are required to provide relevant information unless this could be regarded as unreasonable in the circumstances (section 47 (10) CA 1989, Art 66 CNIO 1995 and s.56 CSA 1995). Under section 47 (4) CA 1989, Art 66 (4) and s.56(4) and (6) CSA 1995 social workers should try to see the child in the course of the investigative process unless they are satisfied that they have available to them sufficient recent information. Local authority social services may then be prompted into action which may result in them convening a child protection conference, to which the parents and other carers of the child should be invited. The convening of such a child protection conference will usually take place where the circumstances surrounding the concerns for the child's well-being are not of an emergency nature. Where it is considered necessary to take urgent action, a child protection conference may well follow on from the actions of social workers in applying to the appropriate courts for an emergency protection order.

2.8.3 What is meant by the term 'significant harm'?

2.8.3.1   Both the convening of a child protection conference and an application for a protection order in Scotland under the provisions of CSA 1995 or an emergency protection order in England, Wales and Northern Ireland under s.44 CA 1989 and Art 60 CNIO 1995 (hereinafter referred to as an EP0) will be based on a consideration of whether the child is deemed to be suffering, or is likely to suffer, *'significant harm'*. For these purposes *'harm'* is defined in s.31 CA 1989, and Art 50(2) CNIO 1995 but not in the Children (Scotland) Act 1995 as meaning the *'ill-treatment or the impairment of health or development **including any impairment resulting from seeing or hearing the ill-treatment of another'*;[34] and *'development'* is defined as meaning 'physical, intellectual, emotional, social or behavioural development'; and 'health' is defined as meaning 'physical or mental health'. Section 31(9(b) CA 1989 and Article 50 CNIO 1995 go on to define 'ill-treatment' as 'including sexual abuse and forms of ill-treatment which are not physical'. The provisions continue with s.31(10) CA 1989 and Art 50 (3) CNIO 1995 providing that 'where the question of whether harm suffered by a child is significant turns on the child's health or development, his health or development shall be compared with that which could reasonably be expected of a similar child'.

2.8.3.2   When assessing the quality of care, control and safety being offered to children with learning disabilities who also present severe challenging behaviour, the comparison which therefore has to be made is with an 'objectively' similar child. Professionals must therefore be aware, yet again, that they must apply the functionally appropriate standards relevant to the developmental age of the child. (see para 2.12) Furthermore, parents have a responsibility to ensure that local authorities have fulfilled their duty in the provision of services to the family under s.17 CA 1989, Art 18 CNIO 1995, and s.22 CSA 1995 and also of those expanded services provided under Schedule 2 CA 1989, and Schedule 2 CNIO 1995. Scottish law makes no such supplemental provision.

---

[34] Words in bold inserted in s.31(9) by the Adoption and Children Act 2002

B Abuse of vulnerable adults

2.8.4 As is suggested in the DoH Guidance[35] issued with regard to the protection of vulnerable adults from abuse, the use of physical intervention is always accompanied by the risk of physical or psychological injury, financial damage or emotional trauma due to the potential abuse which may have resulted. The notion of abuse is defined in the DoH Guidance *No Secrets* as 'a violation of an individual's human and civil rights by any other person or persons',[36] and in particular, physical abuse is said to include 'hitting, slapping, pushing, kicking, misuse of medication, restraint, or inappropriate sanctions'.[37]

Physical intervention implies the presence of a potential risk of harm; therefore any use of force for restraint, restriction and control purposes that is unnecessary and disproportionate is a form of abuse, and thus entails a potential breach of the law and a potential breach of an individual's human rights.

Physical intervention can become abuse when it is used in order to force an individual to comply with rules or with somebody else's wishes; when it is deployed because there is a staff shortage, or because it is the easiest option for the person employing the force; when the force used is not commensurate with the situation at hand; and when the force will cause injury.

According to the Foundation for People with Learning Disabilities, there are an estimated two million people with either a mild or severe learning disability in the UK. A survey conducted by Mencap suggests that 23% of adults with learning disabilities are subjected to physical abuse.[38]

Section 80(6) of the Care Standards Act 2000 defines a vulnerable adult as:

'(a) *an adult to whom accommodation and nursing or personal care are provided in a care home;*

(b) *an adult to whom personal care is provided in their own home under arrangements made by a domiciliary care agency; or*

(c) *an adult to whom prescribed services are provided by an independent hospital, independent clinic, independent medical agency or National Health Service body'.*

No Secrets makes it clear in addition that a vulnerable adult is 'someone over the age of 18' 'who is or may be in need of community care services by reason of mental or other disability age or illness and who is or may be unable to take care of him or herself, or unable to protect him or herself against significant harm or exploitation'.[39] In *No Secrets* therefore the Department of Health has considerably expanded on the statutory definition in the Care Standards Act 2000 and it is strongly urged by the authors of this report that this definition should be incorporated into statute for the greater protection of all vulnerable adults.

---

[35] Department of Health, *No Secrets: Guidance on developing and implementing multi-agency policies and procedures to protect vulnerable adults from abuse*, 2000
[36] supra n.35, para 2.5
[37] supra n.35, para 2.7
[38] *Living in Fear*, London: Mencap, 1999
[39] supra n.35, at paras 2.2 and 2.3

2.9 The concept of parental responsibility

Introduction

2.9.1   The concept of parental responsibility is one of the pivotal concepts of each of the three principal pieces of legislation governing the civil law relating to children within the United Kingdom. The law in England and Wales is governed by the Children Act 1989, in Scotland, by the Children (Scotland) Act 1995, and in Northern Ireland, by the Children (Northern Ireland) Order 1995. The provisions dealing with parental responsibility are almost identical in England, Wales, Scotland and Northern Ireland, although obviously to be found in different 'Sections', or 'Articles' as they are termed in the legislation in Northern Ireland, and therefore the discussion which follows concentrates on the provisions of the Children Act 1989. There will not be a separate discussion of the provisions in Northern Ireland since these are the same and to do so would involve needless repetition. A note will, however, be made in the course of such discussion of the relevant Northern Ireland Article numbers in brackets after the Section reference to the Children Act 1989, in order to enable readers to access those provisions most relevant to them.

2.9.1.1   In Scotland, the position is slightly different, since there the legislators took the opportunity presented by new legislation to bring Scottish law more closely into line with the demands of the United Nations Convention on the Rights of the Child. Thus, the C(S)A 1995 includes provisions requiring the parents of a child to: provide guidance and direction in accordance with the evolving capacities of the child; (s.1(1)(b) C(S)A 1995)(Article 5, UNCRC) to listen to the views of the child in all major decisions affecting them; (s.6 SCA1995)(Article 12, UNCRC) and to maintain contact with the child if living apart from the child (s.1(1)(c) C(S)A 1995, Article 9, UNCRC). Despite some differences with regard to the greater definition of roles and responsibilities, many of the provisions are again the same and so wherever possible reference will simply be made in brackets to the corresponding provisions of the Children (Scotland) Act 1995, in brackets after the Children Act 1989 reference, in the same way as with Northern Ireland. Thus, for example, the provisions dealing with the equal responsibility under the law of married parents which are respectively: section 2 of the Children Act 1989, section 3 of the Children (Scotland) Act and Article 5 of the Children (Northern Ireland) Order 1995, will appear in the text in brackets linked to the discussion as (CA 1989, s.2; CSA 1995, s.3; CNIO 1995 Art 5).

2.9.1.2   The concept of parental responsibility is particularly important when considering the duty of parents to provide for the care and control of their children under the age of 18. It assumes even greater importance in the minds of those parents who are responsible for providing for the care, control and safety of children with learning disabilities and severe challenging behaviour. It is critical, therefore, that the provisions of the Children Act 1989, (hereinafter the CA 1989) and the corresponding provisions of the Children Scotland Act 1995 (hereinafter the SCA 1995) and the Children Northern Ireland Order 1995 (hereinafter the CNIO 1995), dealing with parental responsibility are understood and that is the purpose of this section.

2.9.1.3   All three pieces of legislation provide that both married parents of a child should have joint and equal parental responsibility in respect of their child or children (CA 1989, s.2; CSA 1995, s.3; CNIO 1995 Art 5). Unmarried fathers do not obtain automatic parental responsibility but the legislation provides for different procedures to be followed which will allow for the conferring of parental responsibility on an unmarried father. (s.4 CA 1989; ss. 4 and 11

CSA 1995; Art 7 CNIO 1995) Under recent amending legislation which applies to England and Wales, the most straightforward means of the natural father acquiring parental responsibility is the registration of the child's birth by the unmarried father together with the child's mother and the provisions allowing for this were implemented on 1 December 2003. (See s.4 CA 1989 as amended by the Adoption and Children Act 2002.) Having set out who is entitled to exercise parental responsibility, the legislation further provides for the delegation of responsibility at the determination of the parent (see further s.2 CA 1989; s.3(5) CSA 1995; Article 5 CNIO 1995) and also provides for a standard of care to be exercised by any person other than a parent, who is looking after the child. (see s.3(5)CA 1989; s.5(1) CSA 1995; Article 6(5)CNIO 1995). In Scotland interestingly, specific provision is also made to allow such a person caring for the child to 'give consent to surgical medical or dental treatment or procedures in those circumstances where the child is not able to give such consent on their own behalf', *and* where 'it is not within the knowledge of such person that a parent of the child would refuse to give the consent in question' (s.5(1)(a0 and (b) CSA 1995).

2.9.1.4 The Children Act 1989 and the CNIO 1995 define what is meant by the phrase 'parental responsibility' (s.3(1) CA 1989 and Art 6 CNIO 1995) but do not seek to provide a list of such responsibilities since it has been argued that such a list would be unduly restrictive and hamper the development and recognition of new responsibilities.[40] (See Law Com. No. 172, 1988 Report on Guardianship and Custody at para. 2.1) In Scotland, there is a limited attempt in s.1 CSA 1995 to define what is meant by 'parental responsibility' by reference to: safeguarding and promoting the child's welfare, providing appropriate direction and guidance, maintaining personal relations and direct contact with the child, and acting as the child's legal representative. Somewhat confusingly, given that the intention of the legislation was to move over to an emphasis on the concept of parental responsibility and away from the notion of parental rights, there is in section 2 CSA 1995 another limited attempt this time to define 'parental rights' by reference to: the right to have the child living with him or her or otherwise to regulate the child's residence; controlling, directing or guiding the child's upbringing; maintaining personal relations and direct contact with the child; and acting as the child's legal representative. All of these provisions are examined in some detail hereafter, and consideration is also given to the issue of how the notion of parental responsibility may be interpreted when focusing on the actions of parents or other carers seeking to provide for the care, control and safety of children and young people under the age of 18 with learning disabilities who also present challenging behaviour.

2.9.2 Who is a parent?

2.9.2.1 The parents of a child are either the biological parents, ie the child was produced from the female mother's egg and male father's sperm and carried by the female mother, or they are people who are treated as the mother and father as defined by the Human Fertilisation and Embryology Act 1990. The provisions of this Act apply across all the jurisdictions. Section 27 (1) of that Act defines a mother as: 'the woman who is carrying or has carried a child as a result of the placing in her of an embryo or of sperm and eggs and no other woman is to be treated as the mother of the child'.

Section 28(2) states that a father is a man who is married to the mother and did not object to the placing in her of the embryo or the sperm and eggs or to her insemination.

---

[40] See Law Commission Report No.172 Review of Child Law: Guardianship and Custody (HMSO, 1988)

Section 28(3) makes the same provision as above but for an unmarried couple. No other man is to be treated as the father of the child.

2.9.3 What does parental responsibility mean?

2.9.3 (a) The statutory definition of parental responsibility

2.9.3 (a) 1   The term 'parental responsibility' is entirely the creation of statute, although the phrase was generally reckoned to be encompassed within the terms 'parental rights and duties', 'parental powers and duties', or 'the rights and authority of a parent' which was the confusing variety of terminology current in the common law and in statutes up to the enactment of the Children Act 1989. Not only were these terms inconsistent with one another but the Law Commission in England (the Government body specifically charged with the task of recommending reform of the law) had earlier commented that 'it can be cogently argued that to talk of "parental rights" is not only inaccurate as a matter of juristic analysis but also a misleading use of ordinary language'.[41] In its Report on Guardianship and Custody, the Law Commission was concerned that, because of the continued use of such terms, the law did not *adequately* recognise that parenthood is a matter of *responsibility* rather than of rights, a view gaining increasing currency in Europe at the time.[42] Thus the Council of Europe stated that:

> *'the term "parental responsibilities" describes better the modern concept according to which parents are, on a basis of equality between parents and in consultation with their children, given the task to educate, legally represent, maintain, etc their children. In order to do so they exercise powers to carry out duties in the interests of the child and not because of an authority which is conferred on them in their own interests.'*

2.9.3 (a) 2   Accordingly, the Law Commission in England, and the Law reform bodies of Scotland and Northern Ireland recommended the introduction of the concept of 'parental responsibility' to replace all the ambiguous and misleading terms previously employed in statutes. In the English Law Commission's view the use in statutory provisions of the term 'responsibility' would reflect the everyday reality of being a parent and emphasise the responsibility of all who are in that position.[43]

The Commission sought to clarify the principal purpose behind the change of nomenclature thus:

> *'The parental claim can be recognised in the rules governing the allocation of parental responsibilities, but the content of their status would be more accurately reflected if a new concept of "parental responsibility" were to replace the ambiguous and confusing terms used at present. Such a change would reflect the everyday reality of being a parent and emphasise the responsibility of all who are in that position.'*[44]

2.9.3 (a) 3   The Law Commission also quoted with approval from the House of Lords in *Gillick v West Norfolk and Wisbech Area Health Authority* 1986,[45] the statement of Lord Scarman to the effect that 'Parental rights are derived from parental duty and exist only so long

---

[41] para 4.18 Law Commission Report No.118 Illegitimacy (HMSO, 1982)
[42] See Council of Europe Recommendations on Parental Responsibilities, 1984
[43] See above at note 34 at para 2.4
[44] See above at note 34 at para 2.6
[45] [1986] AC 112

as they are needed for the protection of the person and property of the child' (per Lord Scarman in *Gillick*) and the Commission also noted that 'the House of Lords has held that the powers which parents have to control or make decisions for their children are simply the necessary concomitant of their parental duties'. This, said the Law Commission, 'confirms our view that to talk of parental "rights" is not only inaccurate as a matter of jurisdiction analysis but is also a misleading use of ordinary language'.[46] The Government accepted the English Law Commission's recommendation, which was echoed by the Law reform bodies for both Northern Ireland and Scotland.[47] It was thus intended that 'parental responsibility' should become the pivotal concept of the three pieces of legislation. Scottish law, however, as has been noted above, introduced some detailed definitions of both parental 'responsibilities' and confusingly parental 'rights' in the CSA 1995.

2.9.3 (a) 4 The statutory definition of parental responsibility for England, Wales and Northern Ireland

For England, Wales and Northern Ireland, parental responsibility is defined as:

> *'all the rights, duties, powers, responsibilities and authority which by law a parent of a child has in relation to the child and his property' (s.3(1)CA 1989; Art 6(1) CNIO 1995.)*[48]

It should be noted that neither the CA 1989 nor the CNIO 1995 actually define these rights, duties, powers and responsibilities, and while the Law Commission did not feel compelled to provide any greater definition, it did note that:

> *'some might find it attractive ...The concept of "parental responsibility" can be defined by reference to all the incidents, whether rights, claims, duties, powers, responsibilities, or authority, which statute and common law for the time being confer upon parents ... It would be superficially attractive to provide a list of these changes from time to time to meet differing needs and circumstances ... It must also vary with the age and maturity of the child and the circumstances of each individual case.'*[49]

Family Law textbook writers have over the years compiled lists of what might be included within such notions, and it is proposed simply to note here those rights and duties which have been included on such lists, so that readers may be clear as to the range of duties and responsibilities to which parents and others who may be granted parental responsibility might be subject.

2.9.3 (b) The possible list of parental responsibilities derived from other statutory provisions Thus the potential, but it should be noted not necessarily exhaustive, list of those

---

[46] See above at note 34 at para 7.16

[47] See the Scottish Law Commission in its Discussion Paper No. 88 *Parental Responsibilities and Rights* at para 2.1: 'Parenthood would entail a primary claim and a primary responsibility to bring up the child. It would not, however, entail parental "rights" as such'.

[48] Reference may usefully be made to a number of articles which have been written on the subject of parental responsibility since its introduction in UK law and these include: J Roche *Children Act 1989 Once a Parent, Always a Parent* [1991] Journal of Social Welfare and Family Law (JSWFL) 345; J Eekelaar *Parental Responsibility: State of Nature or Nature of the State* [1991] JSWFL, pp 37-51; N Lowe *The Meaning of Allocation of Parental Responsibility* [1997] Volume II International Journal of Law, Policy and the Family 192

[49] Law Com no 172 at para 2.6.

duties, rights, powers and responsibilities, which may be said to be derived from a range of statutory provisions and from common law include:

(i) The duty to register the child's birth and to give the child a name

Parents have a duty within six weeks to register the child's birth and the child's names as provided for in England and Wales by s.2 Births and Marriages Registration Act 1953, in Northern Ireland by the Births, Deaths and Marriages Registration (Northern Ireland) Act 1956 and in Scotland by the Registration of Births, Deaths and Marriages (Scotland) Act 1965.

(ii) The duty to protect the child and to provide for the child's care and upbringing

This duty can be found from within the provisions of the criminal law which make it an offence punishable with up to ten years in prison to wilfully assault, ill-treat, neglect, abandon or expose a child in a manner likely to cause him unnecessary suffering or injury to health (Children and Young Persons Act 1933, s.1(1); Children and Young Persons (Scotland) Act 1937, s.12); and in the civil law child protection provisions of s.31 Children Act 1989 (Art 57 CNIO 1995, s.50 CSA 1995) which provide for the removal of children suffering or likely to suffer from significant harm where this is attributable to the failure by the parents to provide a reasonable degree of parental care. (See para 2.8 for a much more detailed discussion of the concept of 'significant harm'.)

It should also be noted that the duty to protect the child can extend to a duty to protect the child from publicity. Thus in _Re Z_ 1995,[50] the Court of Appeal held that where a parent owes a duty of confidentiality to the child, for example in respect of medical treatment or in respect of the child's education, a decision to waive confidentiality is an incident (ie a term meaning one of the parental powers) of parental responsibility. Accordingly, an injunction was upheld restraining a parent from publicising by way of a film which would have identified the treatment which the child had received at a unit specialising in the treatment of children with special educational needs.

(iii) The parental 'right' or 'power' to discipline a child

The existence of this right or power receives legislative support from the provisions of Section 1(7) Children and Young Persons Act 1933 in England, Wales and Northern Ireland, giving parents the ability to raise the defence of 'reasonable chastisement' to any charge of assault. The parent must, of course, prove that the punishment administered is 'reasonable', and also that it does not breach the right of the child 'to be free from cruel, inhuman or degrading treatment or punishment' under the now implemented provisions of the European Convention on Human Rights (see Schedule 1 Article 3 Human Rights Act 1998). (For its application in UK law see _A v UK_ 1998,[51] in which it was held that the UK had failed to protect the child from punishment in breach of Article 3, in this case being beaten on the legs with a garden cane so as to draw blood requiring medical attention, and see also _Z v UK_ 2001,[52] in which the parents' treatment of their five children exposing them to appalling living conditions, harsh punishments and near starvation at times was held to breach Article 3.) The parent is, however, characterised as having the 'right' to administer 'reasonable lawful chastisement' on their child. It should be

---

[50] [1995] 4 All ER 961
[51] [1998] 2 FLR 959 ECHR
[52] [2001] 2 FLR 431

noted however that cultural differences are no defence, as seen from the cases of _R v Derriviere_ 1969[53] and also _Re H_ 1987[54] (for further discussion on this, see post and see also Lyon, CM _Loving Smack – Lawful Assault – A Contradiction in Human Rights, Social Policy and the Law._[55]) It should also be noted that as a result of the Court of Appeal Criminal Division's decision in _R v H_ 2001[56] juries must now be directed in accordance with the decision of the European Court in _A v UK_ 1998[57] and thus when considering whether the parent's chastisement can be considered reasonable the jury must consider:

i)   the nature and context of the defendant parent's behaviour;

ii)   the duration and frequency of that behaviour;

iii) the physical and mental consequences in respect of the child;

iv) the age and personal characteristics of the child;

v)   the reasons given by the defendant parent for administering the punishment.

It is particularly important that those parents or carers delegated by parents providing for the care, control and safety of children and young people with learning disabilities, who also present severe challenging behaviour appreciate the implications of these criteria, so that it will rarely if ever be appropriate to administer corporal punishment to such a child or young person, both because of the child's personal characteristics and because of the mental consequences for someone who may not even be able to appreciate that they have done anything wrong.

The position in Scotland is now rather different from that in the rest of the UK. In 2001, the Scottish Executive had proposed legislation to outlaw all forms of corporal punishment of children under three and 16 or over and the use of any implements whatsoever in the corporal punishment of children. In September 2002, however, it indicated that it was reconsidering as a result of negative public reaction to its original proposals. Ultimately, however, the Scottish Assembly enacted section 51 of the Criminal Justice (Scotland) Act 2003, which came into force on 27 October 2003, and which repeals section 12(7) of the Children and Young Persons Act 1937. Section 51 then provides a list of factors to which the court must have regard in determining whether a parent can claim that their action in punishing a child is a 'justifiable assault' carried out in exercise of a parental right or of a right derived from having care of the child. These factors are those which the European Court of Human Rights determined should be followed by UK courts in _A v UK_ in interpreting what could be regarded as 'reasonable' when considering the nature and degree of chastisement meted out by parents, and which are now followed by the courts in England and Wales. (See those set out in the preceding paragraph.) In addition, section 51 (3) provides that the defence of 'justifiable assault' is not available to a parent or others having charge or care of the child where the action includes or consists of: a blow to the head; shaking; or the use of an implement. These actions are therefore outlawed. Section 51 (4) also provides that children 16 and over cannot be the subject of the parental right to physical punishment.

While parents currently retain the power to inflict lawful chastisement on their children, although this has been restricted in Scotland, as set out above, as a result of s.131 School

---

[53] (1969) 53 Cr App R 637
[54] [1987] 2 FLR 12
[55] published by the Institute of Public Policy Research, June 2000
[56] [2001] 1 FLR 580
[57] [1998] 2 FLR 959

Standards and Framework Act 1998, corporal punishment has no longer been permissible in any educational setting in England and Wales, whether public or private, since September 1 1999. The defence, previously available to teachers of 'reasonable chastisement' is thus no longer available in either civil proceedings, (this right was removed for teachers in state schools in 1986) or (as a result of s.131) in any criminal proceedings taken against teachers in any sort of school. (In Scotland the directly comparable provision is s.16 Standards in Scotland's School Act 2000.) Parents also cannot give permission for teachers or any other member of the staff at a school in the UK to use corporal punishment even where the parent believes that it is their right to be able to do so. (See _Williamson v Secretary of State for Education_ 2003[58])

(iv) Parent's duty to ensure that the child attends school

The emphasis here is on the parent's duty under the provisions of s.7 Education Act 1996. This provides that it is the responsibility of a parent to ensure that a child between the ages of five and 16 receives efficient full-time education suitable to his age, ability and aptitude and to any special educational needs he may have, whether by going to school or otherwise. In Scotland the responsibility is imposed on parents in respect of school age children by virtue of s.30 Education (Scotland) Act 1980 and s.31 defines school age as being between the age of five and 16 years of age.

The child's attendance at school can be enforced using such means as: a court issuing an attendance order under the Education Act 1996 s.437 requiring the child to be registered at a school, backed up by the issuing of a summons where the parents fail to comply with the order; or where the child is registered at a school, but is not attending regularly, by the parents being found guilty of the offence of failing to secure the regular attendance of a child at school under the provisions of s.444 Education Act 1996. The maximum sentence for a parent found guilty of such an offence is now six months' imprisonment and not as previously a fine. It should be noted that children of school age and particularly older girls as can be seen from the relevant case-law on the subject, cannot be kept at home to look after other family members when the mother is ill, at work, or away. (see _Jenkins v Howells_ 1949.[59]) Similar provisions with regard to the making of attendance orders exist in Scotland by virtue of sections 38 and 39 Education (Scotland) Act 1980 as amended.

The importance of Article 2 of the First Protocol European Convention on Human Rights should be noted in relation to both children and adults with learning disabilities presenting severely challenging behaviour. This provides that 'no person shall be denied the right to education and that state provision of education and teaching should be in conformity with parents' religious and philosophical convictions'. The UK however entered a reservation that the right to education was to be 'subject to the efficient use of resources' and this should be carefully noted. Many had hoped in the field of special educational needs that the provisions of Article 2 of the First Protocol could be used to press for much better provision for both children and adults with learning disabilities presenting severely challenging behaviour, but because of this reservation, which was the only one entered by the UK upon incorporation of the European Convention on Human Rights within the UK law (by the Human Rights Act 1998), such has not proved to be the case.

---

[58] [2003] 1 FLR 726
[59] [1949] 2 KB 218

It should also be noted that the impact of the condition that teaching should be 'in conformity with the parents' religious and philosophical convictions' is in reality very limited. Thus, in the case of _Kjeldsen, Busk, Madsen and Pedersen_ 1986,[60] the parents of Danish primary school children, who were objecting to their children receiving sex education on the basis of this right, were overruled as the court held that to uphold their right would be in conflict with the basic right of the child to receive education. In the case of _R on the application of Williamson v Secretary of State for Education and Employment_ 2003[61] the Liverpool Christian Fellowship School supported by 40 other schools in the UK sought to maintain the right of parents to give permission to teachers at their children's schools to administer corporal punishment in accordance both with their right to have the child educated in accordance with their religious and philosophical convictions (Protocol 1 Article 2 ECHR) and also in pursuance of their right to freedom of religious expression and beliefs (Article 9 ECHR). It was determined that the parents could not maintain either of these rights in order to support their claim that they should be allowed to give permission for the teachers at their children's school to be able to administer corporal punishment in contravention of s.131 School Standards and Framework Act 1998. Thus, parents will be unsuccessful if they attempt to argue that certain behaviour modification techniques should be used on their child or young person in school or any other educational setting because those techniques are based on their religious and philosophical convictions, or are in furtherance of their right to expression of their religious beliefs.

(v) The parental power to determine the child's religious upbringing

The parental power to determine the child's religion has to be set against the child's increasing maturity. Where the child is old enough to make his own decisions about his religious views then under the provisions of both Articles 8 and 9 of the ECHR, the law requires that those views should be upheld. In Scotland, it is presumed that a child aged 12 and over is presumed to have the capacity to make such a decision for himself and for children under that age, the law provides that the parents must consult with the child before making any major decision concerning him (Children (Scotland) Act 1995, s.6).

(vi) Parental duty to provide and parental power to consent to medical treatment – the position in England, Wales and Northern Ireland

It is a parental duty to provide adequate medical care for a child and failure to do so may result in criminal liability under the criminal law provisions set out above under (ii) Duty to protect. (See Children and Young Persons Act 1933 s.1, _R v Senior_ 1899,[62] and Children and Young Persons Scotland Act 1937, s.1.) Where there is a disagreement between parents over whether the child should be given medical treatment then resort may be made to a specific issues order under s.8 CA 1989, Article 8 CNIO 1995, or s.11(2)(e) CSA 1995. The provisions of Family Law Reform Act 1969 s.8(1) should be noted in that in England, Wales and Northern Ireland, the consent of a 16-year-old can be accepted in place of the consent of the parent. It should also be noted that the mature younger child is also able to consent to treatment on the principles laid down in the _Gillick_ case. (see _Gillick v West Norfolk and Wisbech Area Health Authority_ 1986[63])

---

60 (1986) 1 EHRR 711
61 [2003] 1 FCR 1
62 [1899] 1 QB 283
63 [1986] AC 112

Where parents are refusing consent therefore, the child's consent may override their refusal. It should be noted, however, that if the parents are consenting and the child is refusing treatment recommended by the doctors, the parents' consent is likely to be that which is acted upon. Any one parent with parental responsibility may give such consent under the provisions of s.2(9) CA 1989 and Art 5(6) CNIO 1995 but where persons with parental responsibility disagree over such treatment then it will be advisable to refer the decision to the courts. It should also be noted that the courts are inclined as part of the exercise of their inherent parental jurisdiction to override a child's objections to treatment even when he does have sufficient understanding and has reached the age of 16. The courts start with a preference for respecting the child's views but will not allow the child to die or probably suffer serious harm through lack of treatment, more especially if the illness could be said to be distorting the child's judgement. This was seen in the cases of _Re W_ 1993[64] and in _Re M_ 1999.[65] The girl in _Re M_ was aged 15 at the time of the proposed operation and was opposed to having an operation which would give her a new heart as she felt that this would mean that she would lose her soul. The judge paid full attention to her views and visited her in hospital in order to listen to her. He felt however that her views were based on an imperfect understanding of science, and that she was not fully able to appreciate the consequences of her refusal. Accordingly, he ordered the operation to proceed. It should be noted that a person with parental responsibility, including a local authority holding a care order on the child, can also override the child's views, as seen in _Re KW & H (Minors – Consent to medical treatment)_ 1993.[66]

Where both parents and the child are refusing to give consent the court may, through the exercise of its inherent jurisdiction, even overrule statutory provisions which were intended to give the child the power to refuse such treatment. This was seen in the case of _South Glamorgan County Council v W and B_ 1994.[67] There a 15-year-old girl exercised her right under s.38 CA 1989 to refuse her consent to a court-ordered psychiatric examination. The local authority got around her valid statutory refusal by applying to the High Court for a direction that the examination should be proceeded with as it was in the girl's paramount interests (for a discussion of the paramountcy principle see para 2.11.1). Mr Justice Douglas Brown in the High Court granted the direction thus overruling the girl's exercise of her statutory right. That decision followed a well-established trend of cases where the courts have sanctioned blood transfusions for children in the face of religious objections by the parents and sometimes the religious objections of both the parents and the child as seen in _Re S_ 1993[68] and _Re E_ 1993.[69] In _Re S (A Minor) (Consent to Medical Treatment)_ 1994,[70] the girl aged 15 was refusing treatment, as was her mother, a Jehovah's Witness, but the court ordered that the operation should proceed (See also _Re L_ 1998[71]).

Further Guidance, which repeats much of what has been set out above, is provided with respect to the legal position of children and young people providing consent to medical treatment in the Department of Health's _Reference Guide to Consent for Examination and Treatment_.[72] As far as children who lack capacity are concerned, and this may include children with learning disabilities, then the document advises that parents can give such consent but they themselves

---

[64] [1993] Fam 64 CA
[65] [1999] 2 FLR 1097
[66] [1993] 1 FCR 240
[67] [1994] 1 FLR 574
[68] [1993] 1 FLR 386
[69] [1993] 1 FLR 386
[70] [1994] 2 FLR 1065
[71] [1998] 2 FLR 810
[72] Department of Health 2001 at pages 16–19.

must 'have capacity, must be acting voluntarily and must be appropriately informed'. It further states that 'the power to consent must be exercised according to the "welfare principle": that the child's welfare or best interests must be paramount. The *Reference Guide* also points out that 'even where a child lacks capacity to consent on their own behalf, it is good practice to involve the child as much as possible in the decision making process'.[73]

The position in Scotland

Under s.1 Age of Legal Capacity Scotland Act 1991 all those over the age of 16 and not suffering from any mental disability (s.1(3)(b)) have full legal capacity to enter into any transaction which includes the ability to consent or to refuse consent to any medical procedure or treatment. In Scotland the legislators have put the effects of the <u>Gillick</u> case into statutory format for those who are under 16 so that the position there is arguably much clearer. Thus, under s.2(4) Age of Legal Capacity (Scotland) Act 1991 it is provided that:

> '*A person under the age of 16 years shall have legal capacity to consent on his own behalf to any surgical medical or dental procedure or treatment where, in the opinion of a qualified medical practitioner attending him, he is capable of understanding the nature and possible consequences of the procedure or treatment.*'

It has been suggested that the word 'procedure' is used to cover an examination, blood donation, and the fitting or prescribing of contraceptives as well as ordinary treatment. It has also been pointed out that the question of whether a child has a sufficient level of understanding is left to doctors and health care professionals in order to protect them and that the level of understanding required will obviously vary with the treatment proposed. Thus, it is suggested that a child of eight can readily understand and consent to the bandaging of a bleeding knee but only much older children would have sufficient judgement to weigh up the advantages and disadvantages of cosmetic surgery.[74] Again, in relation to children with learning disabilities it may, or may probably, be the case that they would not be deemed to have such legal capacity depending on the severity of the learning disability and the nature of the procedure for which the consent is being sought. Finally, it should be pointed out that the 1991 Act did not affect a Scottish parent's entitlement to give consent on behalf of his or her child or the right of a parent to be involved in consultations about medical procedures proposed for his or her child.

(vii) The parental right to consent to marriage

Under the provisions of the Marriage Act 1949, as amended by the Children Act 1989, it is the responsibility of each person with parental responsibility to give consent where a child of 16 or 17 is proposing to get married. It should however be noted that if a marriage does take place without the appropriate consents then, if both parties are 16 and over and there is no other impediment, for example there is no suggestion that either party lacks the necessary capacity, the marriage will, nevertheless, be valid.

(viii) The parental power to arrange for the child to leave the country

It is a parental responsibility to decide whether a child may leave the country (ie the UK) either temporarily or permanently. The Crown requires the consent of a parent before issuing a

---

[73] Ibid at page 18 para 9
[74] See David Nicholls – *Current Law Statutes Annotated* 1991 Vol 2 at p50/3

passport to a child under 16. Since parental consent to the issue of a passport is required, it follows that consent for the child's emigration is essential from those with parental responsibility. Since 5 October 1998 the child must be issued with his own passport, and the alternative of adding the child's name to a parent's passport is no longer available. The Passport Agency has published clear guidance on the circumstances in which it will not grant passport facilities to children where there are objections. An objector can ask the agency not to issue a passport where a court in the UK has made certain orders such as a prohibited steps order or a residence order under the CA 1989 and in the case of a residence order if the objector is the person in whose favour the order was made.

In the absence of a court order, an objection can be heard from the mother if she and the father have not been married, or from the police where they have notified the Passport Agency of their intention to exercise their power of arrest under the Child Abduction Act 1984. If an objection is lodged the Agency cannot compel surrender of the child's passport. The most it can do is to note the child's name for a period of 12 months, so that if, during that time, the passport should come into its possession the Agency could then act on the objection.[75]

The High Court has an inherent power to order the surrender of a passport, which is held by a person who the court fears might remove the child. Since the purpose of surrender is to protect the child's interests, the power also extends to foreign passports (see _Re AK_ 1997[76]).

Where there is an order in force prohibiting or restricting the removal of the child from the jurisdiction, the court which made the order may require surrender of the child's passport. Moreover, a parent, who in breach of a residence order, removes his child from the jurisdiction may be ordered to surrender his own passport until he purges his contempt by arranging for the child to be returned (see _Re A (Return of passport)_ 1997[77]).

(ix) Representation of a child in legal proceedings

Under the law in England, Wales and Northern Ireland a parent has the right to act as 'next friend', and a duty to act as 'guardian ad litem' (technical term meaning guardian to the dispute) of a child in legal proceedings. Certainly, the court gives preference to a parent to act in those capacities and will generally only substitute another person if the parent is shown to have acted improperly and against the child's best interests or alternatively has decided not to act at all (see _Kinnear v DHSS_ 1989[78]).

In Scotland, the position is clearly governed by statute as the provisions of both Sections 1 and 2 CSA 1995 clearly provide that it is both a parental right and a parental responsibility to act as the child's legal representative. It should be noted however, that in proceedings under CA 1989 or CNIO 1995 where these are taken by the State in the form of care and supervision order proceedings under these statutes, the child will be made a separate party from the parents and be entitled to separate legal representation and will have a court-appointed children's guardian who is, in effect, an experienced social worker (s.41 CA 1989 and Art 60 CNIO 1995).

---

[75] See Practice Direction [1986] 2 FLR 89
[76] [1997] 2 FLR 569
[77] [1997] 2 FLR 137 CA
[78] [1989] Fam Law 146

In private law proceedings under the CA 1989 and CNIO 1995, such as applications made by parents for s.8 orders, the child is not automatically made a party although the case can be ordered to benefit from the child being made a separate party and benefiting from representation provided by CAFCASS (the Children and Family Courts Advisory and Support Service). The child can also seek to instruct her own solicitor where she seeks leave to make an application for a Section 8 order. The Children Act 1989 provides that the child has the right under s.10(8) of the Act to apply to the court for leave to be allowed to make an application for any of the orders under s.8 and the child will be allowed to proceed provided he or she is deemed to be of sufficient age and understanding, and will seek to instruct his or her own solicitor. (Under the provisions of ss.41 and 93 Children Act 1989 as amended by Adoption and Children Act 2002, the Lord Chancellor is given additional powers to make new rules of court providing for a much wider group of children to be designated as 'parties' to private law proceedings and to be accorded rights to separate representation but as yet no rules of court have been made and no date set for implementation of wider rights to party status in children in private family proceedings.)

(x) Power to appoint a guardian of a child

A parent may by will, by deed, or by any document which is signed by the parent in the presence of two witnesses, provide for the appointment of a guardian for the child to act in the place of the parent after his or her death (see CA 1989 s.5, CSA 1995, s.7 and Article 160 CNIO 1995).

(xi) Administration of the child's property

A parent has a right to administer and deal with a child's property in exactly the same way as any guardian of the child would (see Children Act 1989 s.3(2) and (3), CSA 1995 s.7(1),CNIO 1995, s.6(2) and (3)).

(xii) Agreement to a child's adoption

Subject to the power of the court to dispense with the parent's agreement on specified grounds the parent's agreement is a pre-condition to the making of an order for the adoption of his or her child – see Adoption Act 1976, s.16(i) and (ii) and Adoption NI Order 1987 Art 16(i) and (ii) and Adoption (Scotland) Act 1978. (Note: these provisions will be changed by the new Adoption and Children Act 2002 amendments but no date has yet been set for implementation of the new provisions.)

(xiii) Parent's duty to maintain

Under the provisions of the Domestic Proceedings Magistrates' Courts Act and the Matrimonial Causes Act 1978 both parents were equally liable to maintain any children of their family. However, the provisions of the Child Support Acts 1991 and 1995 (which apply across all the jurisdictions) supersede this liability to maintain by providing that both parents, whether or not they have parental responsibility, are liable to financially support their children. That is assessed and enforced through the Child Support Agency, leaving only a residual jurisdiction for the courts, and both parents are expected to co-operate in enforcing one another's liabilities. Generally most parents will provide for their duty to support the child by providing a home for the child rather than by seeking to pay someone else to look after the child.

(xiv) The right to bury or cremate a deceased child

The case of <u>R v Gwynedd County Council ex parte B</u> 1992[79] established that it is the parents of a child, even where the child has been living with foster parents for a long time, who have the absolute right to arrange for the burial or cremation of their child.

Comment

These then are some of the rights, duties, powers and responsibilities which may be encompassed within the phrase 'parental responsibility' as used in the three statutes. Such lists were not provided in any of the statutes but have had to be drawn up by reference to the many duties, powers and responsibilities contained within a range of statutory provisions as well as in common law.

2.9.3.6   The actual definitions provided in Sections 1 and 2 Children (Scotland) Act 1995
As noted earlier, however, Scottish law goes rather further in seeking to define within the statute to a greater, though still limited extent, both the concepts of parental responsibilities and parental rights. Thus, the Children (Scotland) Act 1995 actually provides respectively for in section 1 – parental responsibilities and in section 2 – parental rights. In addition, Scottish law requires through the provisions in s.6 that parents should consult their children on all major decisions affecting them.

Thus s.1 Children (Scotland) Act 1995 provides

1   (1) *Subject to Section 3(1)(b) and (3) of this Act, a parent has in relation to his child the responsibility –*

   (a) to safeguard and promote the child's health, development and welfare;

   (b) to provide, in a manner appropriate to the stage of development of the child –

      (i) direction

      (ii) guidance,

      to the child;

   (c) if the child is not living with the parent, to maintain personal relations and direct contact with the child on a regular basis; and

   (d) to act as the child's legal representative, but only in so far as compliance with this section is practicable and in the interests of the child.

   (2) *'Child' means for the purposes of –*

   (a) paragraphs (a), (b),(i), (c) and (d) of subsection (1) above, a person under the age of sixteen years.

   (b) paragraph (b) (ii) of that subsection, a person under the age of eighteen years.

---

[79] [1992] 2 All ER 317 CA

(3) The responsibilities mentioned in paragraphs (a) to (d) of subsection 1 above are in this Act referred to as 'parental responsibilities'; and the child, or any person acting on his behalf, shall have title to sue, or to defend, in any proceedings as respects those responsibilities.

(4) The parental responsibilities supersede any analogous duties imposed on a parent at common law; but this section is without prejudice to any other duty so imposed on him or to any duty imposed on him by, under or by virtue of any other provision of this Act or of any other enactment.

Section 2 provides that:

2 (1) Subject to section 3(1) (b) and (3) of this Act, a parent, in order to enable him to fulfil his parental responsibilities in relation to his child, has the right –

(a) to have the child living with him or otherwise to regulate the child's residence;

(b) to control, direct or guide, in a manner appropriate to the stage of development of the child, the child's upbringing;

(c) if the child is not living with him to maintain personal relations and direct contact with the child on a regular basis; and

(d) to act as the child's legal representative.

(2) Subject to subsection (3) below, where two or more persons have a parental right as respects a child, each of them may exercise that right without the consent of the other or, as the case may be, of any of the others, unless any decree or deed conferring the right, or regulating its exercise, otherwise provides.

(3) Without prejudice to any court order, no person shall be entitled to remove a child habitually resident in Scotland from, or to retain any such child outwith, the United Kingdom without the consent of a person described in subsection (6) below.

(4) The rights mentioned in paragraphs (a) to (d) of subsection (1) above are in this Act referred to as 'parental rights', and a parent, or any person acting on his behalf, shall have title to sue, or to defend, in any proceedings as respects those rights.

(5) The parental rights supersede any analogous rights enjoyed by a parent at common law; but this section is without prejudice to any other right so enjoyed by him or to any right enjoyed by him by, under or by virtue of any other provision of this Act or of any other enactment.

(6) The description of a person referred to in subsection (3) above is a person (whether or not a parent of the child) who for the time being has and is exercising in relation to him a right mentioned in paragraph (a) or (c) of subsection (1) above; except that, where both the child's parents are persons so described, the consent required for his removal or retention shall be that of them both.

In fulfilling his/her parental responsibilities, Scottish law further provides under s.6 that:

6 *(1) A person shall, in reaching any major decision which involves –*

(a) his fulfilling a parental responsibility or the responsibility mentioned in section 5(1) of this Act; or

(b) his exercising a parental right or giving consent by virtue of that section, have regard so far as practicable to the views (if he wishes to express them) of the child concerned, taking account of the child's age and maturity, and to those of any other person who has parental responsibilities or parental rights in relation to the child (and wishes to express those views); and without prejudice to the generality of this subsection a child twelve years of age or more shall be presumed to be of sufficient age and maturity to form a view.

(2) A transaction entered into in good faith by a third party and a person acting as legal representative of a child shall not be changeable on the ground only that the child, or a person with parental responsibilities or parental rights in relation to the child, was not consulted or that due regard was not given to his views before the transaction was entered into.'

2.9.3.4 What are the duties of a person with the care of a child?   It should be noted that s.3(5) CA 1989 and Article 6(5) CNIO 1995 provide that 'a person who does not have parental responsibility for a particular child but has care of the child may, subject to the provisions of the Act, do what is reasonable in all the circumstances of the case for the purpose of safeguarding or promoting the child's welfare'. This provision is compared in a detailed discussion with a similar provision in s.5 Children (Scotland) Act 1995 at para 2.9.3.17.

2.9.3.5 What does the notion of parental responsibility represent?   As John Eekelaar, a leading academic commentator on the law, observed shortly before implementation of the Act, parental responsibility can represent two ideas: one, that parents must behave dutifully towards their children; and the other, that responsibility for child care belongs to parents, not the State (see Parental Responsibility: State of Nature or Nature of the State 1991 *Journal of Social Welfare and Family Law* p. 37 at p. 38-39). Both these ideas are important and both were embodied in the Children Act 1989. The former idea was encapsulated first by the Lord Chancellor of Great Britain, Lord Mackay, who said in December 1988 when introducing the Children Bill in the House of Lords, that the concept of 'parental responsibility':

'emphasises that the days when a child should be regarded as a possession of his parents, indeed when in the past they had a right to his services and to sue on his loss, are now buried forever. The overwhelming purpose of parenthood is the respon-sibility for caring for/and raising the child to be a properly developed adult both physically and morally.'

This comment was echoed by the Department of Health's Introductory Guide to the Children Act which stated that the phrase 'parental responsibility':

'emphasises that the parent's duty is to care for the child and to raise him to moral, physical and emotional health is the fundamental task of parenthood and the only justification for the authority that it confers.' (Introduction to the Children Act 1989, published by HMSO, 1989, at para 1.4)

2.9.3.6 Who holds parental responsibility? In s.2 CA 1989, Art 5 (1) CNIO 1995 and s.3(1) CSA 1995, it is provided that where a child's father and mother were married to each other at the time of his birth (or where they marry each other subsequently), they shall each have parental responsibility for the child. Where the child's mother and father were not married to each other at the time of his birth and have not married subsequently, then it is provided that the *mother alone* has automatic parental responsibility for the child (s.2(2)(a) CA 1989, Art 5(2) CNIO 1995, and s.3(1)(a) CSA 1995). It is provided that the father shall not have parental responsibility for the child unless he acquires it (s.2(2)(b) CA 1989) by:

- the making of a formal written agreement in the prescribed form, which is then registered with the Principal Registry in London, or the equivalent offices in Edinburgh and Belfast (in accordance with s.4CA 1989, Art 7 CNIO 1995, and s.4 CSA 1995);

- *or* by obtaining a court order giving him parental responsibility under s.4 CA 1989, Art 7(1) CNIO 1995 and s.11 CSA 1995;

- *or* by obtaining a residence order providing that the child should live for at least a part of the time with the father, which then by virtue of s.12(1)CA 1989, Art 12(1) CNIO 1995, and s.11 CSA 1995, requires the court also to make an order under s.4, CA 1989, Art 7 CNIO 1995 and s.11 CSA 1995 giving him joint parental responsibility with the child's mother.

In addition under the provisions of the Adoption and Children Act 2002, Section 4 has been further amended to allow for an unmarried father to obtain parental responsibility by registering the child's birth but as at March 2003 these provisions have yet to be implemented although indications have been given that this should occur in late 2003 to 2004.

2.9.3.7 The effect of other persons acquiring parental responsibility Very importantly, s.2 CA 1989 (Article 5 CNIO 1995 and s.3 CSA 1995) also makes it clear that not only can more than one person have parental responsibility at the same time (s.2(5)CA 1989 Art 5(4) CNIO 1995), (and clearly where a child's parents are married this will be the norm) but also that a person does not cease to have responsibility because someone else acquires it (s.2(6)CA 1989, Art 5(5) CNIO 1995). This requires further explanation. Thus, where a child's parents are married to each other then, as seen, *both* hold parental responsibility. If the child's parents were to divorce then again *both* parents would continue to hold parental responsibility and the fact of divorce will make no difference to this, although the actual exercise of day-to-day responsibilities may well fall upon the person with whom the child is living. That parent may then form another relationship and marry again and the person whom they marry may obtain a residence order that confers parental responsibility on the holder.

2.9.3.8 The position of step-parents The mere fact of marriage to a child's parent does not confer any of the legal status or incidents (ie rights, duties, powers and responsibilities) of parenthood. Although the parent's partner is often referred to as the child's step-parent this is not a legal status and confers no legal rights or responsibilities. In many situations, however, the step-parent may well be assuming a very important role in the child's life and in some cases, and sometimes for very good reasons, the parent who is not caring for the child may have limited contact with the child. Where this is the case the step-parent may well wish to consider applying for a 'residence order' under the provisions of Section 8 Children Act 1989. Alternatively, once the new provisions of section 4A Children Act 1989 are implemented, step-parents will be able to make a 'parental responsibility agreement' with the agreement of everyone who holds parental responsibility, or they will be able to make an application to the court for a parental responsibility order under s.4A Children Act 1989 as inserted by the Adoption and Children Act 2002.

2.9.3.9 Definition and effects of making a residence order   A 'residence order' is merely an order settling the arrangements to be made as to the person with whom the child is to live. (s.8 CA 1989, Art 8 CNIO 1995, s.11(2)(c) CSA 1995.) Such orders will most commonly be made on the divorce or relationship breakdown of the child's parents, although the general philosophy underlying the CA 1989, the CNIO 1995 and the CSA 1995 is that such orders should not be made, unless it can be shown that 'making the order is better for the child than making no order at all' (s.1(5) CA 1989; Art 3(5) CNIO 1995 and s.11(7)(a) CSA 1995). Most commonly, in divorce or relationship breakdown situations, the children will go to live with one parent or the other but this is not always the case, and a residence order may be made in favour of an aunt or grandmother if the court is persuaded for some reason that this would be better for the child. Where such an order is made in favour of any person who is *not* the parent or guardian of the child concerned that person shall have parental responsibility for the child while the residence order remains in force (s.12(2) CA 1989). The effect of the making of such an order is therefore to confer upon that person all the rights, duties, powers and responsibilities which, by law, the parent of a child has in relation to that child (see s.3(1) CA 1989). Where a residence order made in favour of someone who is *not* a parent is subsequently revoked by a court, this has the effect also of terminating that person's parental responsibility.

2.9.3.10 Holders of parental responsibility   It must be emphasised very strongly however that, as a result of s.2(6) CA 1989, Art 6 (4) CNIO 1995 and s.3 CSA 1995, the mere fact that *someone else* has acquired parental responsibility does not mean that others holding such responsibility *cease* to hold it. Thus, in the example of the divorce situation given above, although the court making a s.8 CA 1989, Art 8 CNIO 1995, or s.11(2) CSA 1995 residence order would need to have been convinced that the order in favour of the child's step-parent was in the child's paramount interests, it is merely conferring the status of the holder of parental responsibility on *an additional person*. The order does *not* have the effect of removing parental responsibility from existing holders. Indeed, the only ways in which a parent, be they the mother or father, of a marital child can lose parental responsibility is by reason of the death of the child or by the making of an adoption, or freeing for an adoption, order under the provisions of the Adoption Act 1976. (When the Adoption and Children Act 2002 is implemented, which is not likely until late 2004 or early 2005 freeing for adoption orders will be replaced with the new placement orders. (s.21 Adoption and Children Act 2002) The court cannot, under the provisions of the CA 1989, make an order depriving a *marital* parent of parental responsibility.

2.9.3.11 The vulnerability of the unmarried father's position   The unmarried father of a child, however, is in a much more vulnerable position in that a court order, or a parental responsibility agreement made under s.4 CA 1989, Art 7 CNIO 1995 and s.4 CSA 1995, giving an unmarried father parental responsibility can, in fact, be revoked. This is done by an order of the court made on the application of any person who has parental responsibility for the child, or, with the leave of the court, the child himself. It should be noted that it is extremely rare for a court to make such a revocation order, and there is in fact only one reported case where this has occurred. This was the case of _Re P_ 1995[80] where the unmarried father with parental responsibility had been guilty of the most appalling acts of sadism against his young son and

---

[80] [1995] 1 FLR 1048

upon the mother's application for an order revoking the parental responsibility agreement reached between them after his birth, the court granted the order.

2.9.3.12 Circumstances in which the making of a residence order will be deemed appropriate It should also be pointed out that there may be situations in which other significant adults in a child's life may deem it appropriate, with the consent of the child's parent, to apply for a s.8 CA 1989, Art 8 CNIO 1995 or s.11 CSA 1995 residence order. This might arise, for example, if the child's mother is very young or is seriously ill and the child, for these or other similar reasons, is living with a near relative such as an aunt or grandparents. The courts have already determined, under the CA 1989, that it is right and proper that, in such circumstances, the grandparent or other near relative will need to be able to give permission for the child to go on school trips, to have vaccinations, to receive dental treatment, and to have any necessary medical treatment and that, in such circumstances, it is clearly in the paramount interests of the child that a s.8 residence order should be made which has the effect of conferring parental responsibility on the person with whom the child is living and who is having to make such day-to-day important decisions (seen in _B v B_ 1993[81]).

2.9.3.13 The ability to exercise parental responsibility independently It should be emphasised that once possessed of parental responsibility, _each_ holder of responsibility can continue to exercise it by him/herself without the need to consult any other holder (s.2(7)CA 1989, Art 5 (6) CNIO 1995 and s.3 CSA 1995) subject only to the overriding condition that he or she must not act incompatibly with any existing court order (s.2(8)CA 1989, Art 5(7) CNIO 1995, s.3(4) CSA 1995). Thus, the consent of only one holder of parental responsibility is required for any step taken in relation to the child which merely needs the consent of one parent. This covers most events in a child's life, such as medical procedures, including the administration of medicines properly prescribed by a doctor. This is, therefore, a particularly important rule which was drawn up to allow _each_ parent, but especially the one with whom the child lives, or who is actually providing the daily care for the child, to perform that task and make decisions without having to consult with, and obtain the consent of, the other parent. The other parent may, of course, object but anyone acting on the consent or authorisation of the one giving consent will be protected at law if there is any dispute as to whether a particular course of action should have been adopted. The parent who wishes to prevent something being done bears responsibility for taking the matter to court, and not the other way around. The Law Commission felt this to be the most sensible and practical way to ensure that children were properly looked after and that those delegated the task of providing for their care should know where they were, and feel comfortable acting on the basis of the consent of one parent.

2.9.3.14 Exceptions to the general principle allowing independent action Two limitations to the general principle allowing independent action should however be noted. Firstly, the rule in s.2(7) CA 1989, s.2(2) CSA 1995 or Art 5(6) does not affect any statutory provision requiring the consent of more than one person in a matter affecting the child, for example to his/her marriage or adoption or placement order for adoption. Secondly, the fact that a person has parental responsibility does not entitle him to act in any way which would be incompatible with an order about the child made under the 1989 Act (s.2(8) or s.2(2) CSA 1995 or the 1995 Order (Art 5(7)). Thus, where there is an order that the child should live with his mother and attend a special needs unit for children with severe challenging behaviour, then his father cannot decide that he is going to send him away to boarding school. Alternatively, if there

---

[81] [1993] 1 F.C.R. 21

is an order of the court (which might be in the form of a specific issue order under s.8 CA 1989) that the child attends a special therapeutic activity on a particular day, the parent cannot change this unilaterally.

2.9.3.15 Delegation of parental responsibility   Under the CA 1989, the CSA 1995 and the CNIO 1995, it is further provided that a person who has parental responsibility for a child may not surrender or transfer any part of that responsibility to another but may arrange for some or all of it to be met by one or more persons acting on his behalf (s.2(9) CA 1989, s.3(5) CSA 1995 and Art 5(8)). That other person might be a teacher, carer, child-minder or baby-sitter, or indeed as the Act goes on to provide 'someone who already has parental responsibility for the child' (s.2(10) CA 1989, s.3(5) CSA 1995, Art 5(9) CNIO 1995). It should be noted that the making of any such arrangement does not affect the liability which the parent may have for failing to meet his own responsibility for the child. Thus, the parent may still be liable for neglecting his child if, knowing the child has both severe learning disabilities and challenging behaviour, she chooses an inadequate baby-sitter or child-minder, who could not reasonably have been expected to cope with such a child (see further _Lancashire County Council v B_ 2000[82]).

In such a situation, the parent may be deemed to have criminally neglected the child, or otherwise to have exposed the child to risk, under the provisions of Section 1 of the Children and Young Persons Act 1933 (see Part IV). Providing substitute carers with proper information about the child whom they are looking after is thus a facet of the 'responsible' exercise of parental responsibility. In addition to incurring criminal liability, the potential for civil liability would arise if any injury befell the child of a third party (eg another child placed with the child minder or the child minder's own child). If such injury occurred as a result of the child minder not being aware of how to cope with a child with learning disabilities, who also presents severe challenging behaviour, and not being aware that the child actually experienced such problems then the parents might be sued for damages (by analogy with the cases of _W v Essex County Council_ 2000[83] and _A v Essex County Council_ 2003[84]). In practice, most parents would not be insured against such risks and therefore it would not be considered worthwhile bringing an action against them, more particularly if the action were being considered on behalf of their own child. The parents of another child to whom injury has been caused, may however feel it worth their while pursuing legal action in anticipation of recovering even a small award for damages to compensate their child for any injuries received and any consequential additional costs.

2.9.3.16 What can be encompassed within the delegation of parental responsibility?
Given that s.2(9) and the other corresponding provisions provide that a person with parental responsibility may arrange for some or all of that responsibility to be met by one or more persons acting on their behalf, what may be encompassed within such an arrangement? This will clearly be of crucial importance in relation to substitute carers of children with learning disabilities who also present severe challenging behaviour. For behaviour modification techniques, which have been agreed upon in partnership between professionals, such as the Community and Mental Health Support teams and parents to be successful, these should be consistently maintained. Thus, responsible parents would be expected to delegate the responsibility for engaging in such techniques to child-minders or babysitters. If there has,

[82] [2000] 1 FLR 583
[83] [2000] 1 FLR 657
[84] (2003) Times 26 January

nevertheless, been some recognition that on occasions more restrictive techniques have to be employed and the Commission for Social Care Inspection, which is now the body responsible for registering the child-minder, points out that these are in conflict with Department of Health Guidance relating to child-minding and day care provision (see Volume 2, *Family Support, Day Care and Educational Provision for Young Children*, HMSO, London 1991) what might then happen? The local Commission for Social Care Inspection officer will consult with the CAMHS team but if the officer is unconvinced by their explanation, concluding that the techniques employed are in conflict with a whole range of DfES/DoH advice concerning control of children, (although it should be noted that these were almost entirely drawn up by reference to children without learning disabilities, see paras 4.6 to 4.7) then further steps will need to be taken. The officer informs the child-minder that either she refrains from using the agreed levels of restraint in situations of extreme outbursts or she will be de-registered as an 'unfit person' to be a child-minder (see s.71(7)(a) CA 1989).

The position then resembles very closely that of <u>Sutton London Borough Council v Davis</u> 1994,[85] in which Mrs Anne Davis appealed to the High Court against the local authority's decision to de-register her as a child-minder because, with the agreement of the child's parents, she had disciplined the child in her care by smacking. Sutton LBC had sought to argue that Mrs Davis's actions conflicted with Guidance issued by the Department of Health which purported to extend the ban on corporal punishment in state schools to 'any other parties within the scope of this guidance', which specifically dealt with child-minding and day-care provisions. Since Mrs Davis refused to change her approach, the local authority argued that this was now in clear conflict with the Guidance and she should, in consequence, be deemed 'unfit' to be a child-minder and be de-registered. The magistrates at first instance allowed Mrs Davis's appeal against the decision to de-register her and this approach was confirmed in the High Court Family Division before Mr Justice Wilson, who warned against local authorities elevating what was only 'Guidance' from the Department of Health into inflexible policy, since courts were possessed of the powers to review such an approach.

While many people, including the lead author of this report, were very concerned at the substance of the Davis decision, the DoH has subsequently changed its Guidance and child-minders are not now allowed to use smacking as an appropriate form of punishment in relation to any child in their care. Child-minders must also seek specific advice in relation to their care of children with learning difficulties who also present severe challenging behaviour. If, for example, a child is excluded from the care of the child-minder because in the absence of being able to use appropriate restraint to control explosive outbursts, the child-minder feels unable to care for the child, then this cannot in any way be described as being in the 'paramount interests' of the child. The child-minder should seek to discuss fully the types of approaches that the parent is using at home if she is proposing to adopt them and should contact the relevant CAMHS team to check that such approaches have been agreed with professionals concerned with the child and his or her family.

A failure to follow such a course of action to provide the child minder, nursery school or school support workers with the essential advice and Guidance may mean that the child might be excluded from a child minding, nursery or school setting. This will mean that the child is excluded from all the benefits which this entails, including the company and stimulation of other children and adults, and is forced to remain at home in the company of his or her parents, who are now denied the much-needed break derived from the child attending school. Inevitably,

---

[85] [1994] 1 FLR 594

the pressures on the parents will then build up to such an extent that some will be unable to cope. Such care is unlikely to be able to compete with the quality of care and education being offered previously by the combination of the parents and the school. Who has gained anything in these circumstances and how could this result be described as being in the *paramount interests* of the child?

2.9.3.17 The position of persons without parental responsibility but with care of the child   The CA 1989, the CNIO 1995 and the CSA 1995 give further statutory expression in UK law to the notion of a person who is not a parent possessing certain powers or responsibilities in relation to a child who is in their care. (Further examples include: the duty under the Education Act 1996 in England and Wales, and the Education (Scotland) Act 1980, to ensure that a child in one's care receives full-time and efficient education up to the age of 16, and the responsibility to ensure that any child in one's care is not exposed to any harm or risk of harm under the provisions of the Children and Young Persons Act 1933 or the Children and Young Persons (Scotland) Act 1937.)

Under s.3(5) CA 1989, and Article 6(5) CNIO 1995, it is provided that:

> '*A person who:*
>
> *(a) does not have parental responsibility for a particular child, but*
>
> *(b) has care of the child,*
>
> *may (subject to the provisions of this Act) do what is reasonable in all the circumstances of the case for the purpose of safeguarding or promoting the child's welfare.*'

Under section 5 (1) CSA 1995 it is provided in very similar terms that:

> '*It shall be the responsibility of a person who has attained the age of 16 years and who has the care or control of a child under that age, but in relation to him has no parental responsibility, to do what is reasonable in all the circumstances to safeguard the child's health, development and welfare.*'

It should be noted that in the CSA 1995 provision, however, it states clearly that it is a 'responsibility' imposed on the person giving such care. In the English, Welsh and Northern Irish provisions, however, it states that such a person 'may do what is reasonable in all the circumstances of the case' and the 'duty' as such has to be implied from other provisions. The Scottish provision is also much wider in that it covers not only safeguarding the child's welfare but also expressly mentions the child's health and development. These are not mentioned in the other jurisdictions' provisions, although it can be argued that the term 'welfare' embraces the other two concepts fully.

The extremely inadequate definition of *parental responsibility* offered by the legislation in all the jurisdictions has already been noted in this part and its special implications for those looking after children with learning disabilities who also present severe challenging behaviour has also been discussed. The notion of what it is *reasonable* to expect someone who is looking after such a child to do in order to *safeguard and promote that child's welfare* must logically be considered in the context of that discussion. It must, therefore, be the case, that those looking after a child, in whatever context, 'may', not 'must', do what is reasonable in all the circumstances of the case, although the 'must' is probably implicit in the provisions. This means that such a person has to do all that a responsible parent would be expected to do. This would include all such action as a parent might be expected to take to prevent the child harming himself or others, or exposing himself or others to harm. The provisions as drafted imply that such a person should therefore take such action and this is reinforced by the obligation under the criminal law that they must not wilfully assault or ill-treat the child or abandon or expose the child to harm. Where the person looking after the child fails to take action in accordance with these obligations, then they might then be guilty of an offence under the CYPA 1933 or the CYPA (Scotland) 1937. (see earlier for the discussion under 2.9.3(a) (2)).

2.10 Definitions of carer, unpaid carer, care worker, care provider for adults and social care worker

A carer, other than a parent or other person with parental responsibility, in the context of this work is a person who is involved in providing for the care, control and safety of children, young people and adults with learning disabilities presenting severe challenging behaviour. 'Carer' could thus encompass day-centre workers, residential workers, paid respite carers, health workers, employees of voluntary organisations and of local authority social services departments, and many would thus be defined under the Care Standards legislation as 'social care workers' (see next page for a full explanation).

An **unpaid carer** (which may well include parents and other relatives, who may thus qualify for assistance under the Carers (Recognition and Services Act) 1995) is someone who has not entered into a contract to care for another, or is not providing such care as a volunteer for a voluntary organisation. Under s.1(1) of that Act, a carer is someone who provides or intends to provide (on an unpaid basis (ss.3) which excludes those who are contractually providing care or doing so as a volunteer on behalf of a voluntary organisation) a substantial amount of care on a regular basis for the relevant person (ie the person in need of care). An unpaid carer has also been described in DoH Guidance as someone who looks after 'a relative or friend who needs support because of age, physical or learning disability or illness, including mental illness'.[86]

A **care worker** is defined in Section 80(2) Care Standards Act 2000 as:

> '(a) an individual who is or has been employed in a position which is such as to enable him to have regular contact in the course of his duties with adults to whom accommodation is provided at a care home;
>
> (b) an individual who is or has been employed in a position which is such as to enable him to have regular contact in the course of his duties with adults to whom prescribed services are provided by an independent hospital, an independent clinic, an independent medical agency or a National Health Service body;
>
> (c) an individual who is or has been employed in a position which is concerned with the provision of personal care in their own homes for persons who by reason of

---

[86] Caring About Carers, http://www.carers.gov.uk/whatis.htm, April 2003, DoH. According to this website, there are approximately 5.7 million people who fit this definition in Great Britain today, although the General Household Survey, referred to in debates on the 1995 Act, put the figure at 6.8 million. (See Hansard, H.C. Vol 258 col 426.) In *Caring about Carers* the Government makes a commitment to providing details of the services or benefits affecting carers on the Internet.

illness, infirmity or disability are unable to provide it for themselves without assistance.'

A **care provider for adults** is defined in Section 80(7) Care Standards Act 2000 as:

'(a) any person who carries on a care home;

(b) any person who carries on a domiciliary care agency;

(c) any person who carries on an independent hospital, an independent clinic or an independent medical agency, which provides prescribed services; and

(d) a National Health Service body which provides prescribed services.'

A **social care worker** is defined in Section 55(2) of the Care Standards Act 2000 which provides that a 'social care worker' is a person who:

'(a) engages in relevant social work (referred to in this Part as a "social worker");

(b) is employed at a children's home, care home or residential family centre or for the purposes of a domiciliary care agency, a fostering agency or a voluntary adoption agency;

(c) manages an establishment, or an agency, of a description mentioned in paragraph (d) or, is supplied by a domiciliary care agency to provide personal care in their own homes for persons who by reason of illness, infirmity or disability are unable to provide it for themselves without assistance.'

Section 55(3) also stipulates that the following people are to be treated as **social care workers**:

'(a) a person engaged in work for the purposes of a local authority's social services functions, or in the provision of services similar to services which may or must be provided by local authorities in the exercise of those functions;

(b) a person engaged in the provision of personal care for any person;

(c) a person who manages, or is employed in, an undertaking (other than an establishment or agency) which consists of or includes supplying, or providing services for the purpose of supplying, persons to provide personal care;

(d) a person employed in connection with the discharge of functions of the appropriate Minister under Section 80 of the 1989 Act (inspection of children's homes etc);

(e) staff of the Commission or the Assembly who –

    (i) inspects premises under Section 87 of the 1989 Act (welfare of children accommodated in independent schools and colleges) or Section 31 or 45 of this Act; or

    (ii) are responsible for persons who do so;

    and staff of the Assembly who inspect premises under Section 79T of that Act (inspection of child minding and day care in Wales) or are responsible for persons who do so;

(f) a person employed in a day centre;

(g) a person participating in a course approved by a Council under Section 63 for persons wishing to become social workers.'

As will be seen the potential liabilities of those who employ 'care workers' and 'social care workers' or those who are 'providers of adult care' and those who rely on the assistance of volunteers with voluntary organisations, and the responsibilities which fall upon such personnel, are much greater than those which can be imposed upon parents, those with parental responsibility, or other unpaid carers.

2.11 The welfare principles

2.11.1 The statutory provisions on the paramountcy principle Under the provisions of s.1(1) CA 1989, Article 3 (1) CNIO 1995, and Section 11(7) CSA 1995, courts are directed that when they are determining any question with respect to the upbringing of a child, the child's welfare shall be the court's paramount consideration. This means that when the court makes decisions, the child's welfare is not just the first consideration but is that which overrides all others. When seeking to provide for the care, control and safety of children with learning disabilities who also present severe challenging behaviour, therefore, parents, carers and professionals must always consider whether their actions are being performed in the paramount interests of the child. This concept is sometimes referred to as the 'paramountcy' of the child's welfare. A diagrammatic interpretation of this approach is set out in Chapter 2 of this Part. The CA 1989, the CSA 1995, and the CNIO 1995 do not, of course, state that the parents must also act in accordance with what might be deemed to be in the paramount interests of their child, but it is submitted that this is the only way in which one can properly interpret the phrase 'parental responsibility' and give it real meaning. If it is to be maintained that not only parents but also other carers and professionals dealing with children are to regard the child's welfare as their paramount consideration then, when looking at any actions which may be taken in respect of the child, one might ask how they will demonstrate that the child's welfare has been given such 'paramount' consideration. Under s.1(3) of the CA 1989, and Article 3(3) CNIO 1995 (but note there is no directly comparable provision for Scotland – see above), a court, considering whether or not to make any orders under the Children Act is directed to what is widely referred to as the 'welfare checklist'. It is suggested that many of the elements on this checklist might be worth considering by any person seeking to provide for the care, control and safety of children, young people and adults with learning disabilities who also present severe challenging behaviour.

2.11.2 The welfare checklist The checklist to which the courts are referred in England, Wales and Northern Ireland, but not in Scotland, are to be found in both the CA 1989 and the C(NI)O 1995.[87] The checklists might be deemed to have more general application including when making decisions about adults with learning disabilities presenting challenging behaviour. Since it was proposed in the 1994 documents that the 'welfare checklist' could be seen as providing guidelines which could apply to anyone where others are making decisions about another person, the list repays close attention. Thus, the list provides for those factors to which the decision maker, in that case the courts, but in challenging behaviour scenarios, the carer, must refer. In particular, the court is directed to have regard to:

- the ascertainable wishes and feelings of the child concerned (considered in the light of his age and understanding);

---

[87] S.1(3) CA 1989 and Article 3(3) C(NI)O 1995.

- his physical, emotional and educational needs;

- the likely effect on him of any change in his circumstances;

- his age, sex, background and any characteristics of his which the court considers as relevant;

- any harm which he has suffered or is at risk of suffering;

- how capable each of his parents and any other person is of meeting his needs;

- the range of powers available to the court in the proceedings in question.

This, then, is the check-list informing the courts as to how they should best interpret whether the proposed action encompasses the child's welfare being seen as the court's paramount consideration. These factors might be equally relevant in informing the views of the wide range of professionals such as carers, support workers and social care workers, as well as parents and carers, who come into contact with adults as well as children with learning disabilities who also present severe challenging behaviour. Only the last provision would really need amendment so that perhaps it would read, 'the range of techniques available to those providing for the care, control and safety of these individuals in any situation involving the manifestation of extremes of severely challenging behaviour'. Again, this leads to the approach set out in the diagrammatic illustration provided at the end of this chapter.

While Scotland does not have a similar welfare checklist, s.11(7) C (S) A 1995 provides that:

> *'In considering whether or not to make an order giving any person parental rights, responsibilities, guardianship or the rights to administer a child's property and is so what order to make the court*
>
> *(a) shall regard the welfare of the child concerned as its paramount consideration and shall not make any such order unless it considers that it would be better for the child than making no order at all; and*
>
> *(b) taking account of the child's age and maturity, shall so far as is practicable –*
>
> > *(i) give him an opportunity to indicate whether he wishes to express his views;*
> >
> > *(ii) if he does so wish, give him an opportunity to express them; and*
> >
> > *(iii) have regard to such views as he may express.'*

It can be seen that the approach taken in the Scottish legislation is not as wide-ranging nor therefore as useful in providing assistance in such situations as the legislation applicable in England, Wales and Northern Ireland.

2.12 Applying functionally and specifically appropriate criteria when assessing care and control

When considering the actions of parents or carers in providing for the safety and welfare of children or adults with learning disabilities, who also present severe challenging behaviour, one must therefore apply functionally and specifically appropriate standards against which it would be reasonable to judge such actions. For example, under normal circumstances any parent or carer would shrink from even considering tying up the hands of a 14-year-old girl or a 24-year-old woman. Let us consider, however, how such action would be viewed in the context of a 14-

year-old girl with learning disabilities, who, as a result of her own actions in tearing at her eyes, has already lost the sight of one eye and is in danger of becoming blind altogether if restraining action is not taken (one of the examples sent in for the work done in 1994. See Appendix 2 of that document *The Real Life Situations sent in by The Council for Disabled Children* MHF 1994). Applying functionally and specifically appropriate criteria, it is more than likely that the parents or carers would find themselves being criticised for failing to take the appropriate action if the girl (or an adult in similar circumstances) were to lose the sight of the other eye because she had not been restrained from engaging in this type of destructive behaviour. Applying such functional and specific criteria in individual cases must inevitably impinge upon the legal system's and the courts' interpretation of lawful *excuse* in relation to any potential liability of parents and other carers under the civil and the criminal law. It must also affect the interpretation of the child being deemed to be *at risk of suffering significant harm,* or not being given a *reasonable standard of parental care* under the public law provisions of the CA 1989, the CNIO 1995 and the CSA 1995 (see the more detailed discussion of the concept of significant harm at para 2.8.1 above) or the 'vulnerable adult' being deemed to be 'at risk of abuse' as defined in *No Secrets*[88] *(see also 2.8.2 above).*

2.13 The influence from the children's legislation of the key concepts of parental responsibility, and the safeguarding of the child's welfare by doing what is reasonable in all the circumstances of the case

It is crucial therefore, that everyone is clear about what is meant by the phrases used in the statutes such as *parental responsibility,* acting *in the paramount interests of the child,* and doing what is *reasonable to safeguard and promote the welfare of children in all the circumstances of the case.* This is because parents and other carers, including professional carers, need to understand not only how to explain their actions in seeking to provide for the care, control and safety of the children in their care, but also how their actions *should* be viewed in the context of these concepts.

When looking after children with learning disabilities presenting severe challenging behaviour, carers know that they may have to employ techniques of care which are not *age appropriate* but which relate more to the *functional age* of the child. For those *children* (and for the purposes of all three jurisdictions, this refers to anyone under the chronological age of 18) who engage in behaviour which is potentially destructive to themselves or others, practices of restraint may be used which are more consistent with the type of care offered to a very vulnerable child unable to protect themselves rather than to a child of average learning ability, or at the other end of the scale with the type of care which psychiatric nurses might have to offer to an adult engaged in behaviour which poses a risk to the patient him or herself or to others.

What is 'reasonable' in all the 'circumstances' of the case?

There needs to be a clear appreciation of the fact that such techniques and practices are generally borne out of a desire on the part of parents and carers to act either as responsible parents or as responsible care-givers seeking to safeguard and promote the child's, young person's or adult's welfare. Indeed, were they to act in any other way the consequences would

---

[88] *No Secrets – Guidance on developing and implementing multi-agency policies and procedures to protect vulnerable adults from abuse* (Department of Health May 2000)

Definitions, Key Concepts and the Interpretation of Terminology **51**

be such that they would be criticised for having *failed to act responsibly,* or otherwise to have *safeguarded and promoted the child's welfare.*

It should be noted, however, that there is a crucial difference where the care is being provided by a parent or other unpaid carer, since such individuals are subject to the duty to take such responsible care of the child, and arguably by extension of any adult, which might be 'reasonable in all the circumstances of the case'.[89] Those circumstances will include the fact that such adults and unpaid carers do not have access usually to the degree of training to which social care employees, or self-employed persons holding themselves out as able to provide such professional care, have access. This is not to say that they do not have any sort of duty of care but that it is of a significantly lower standard than that which would be expected of any paid, and therefore presumptively 'trained', worker. The problem for those who are being cared for by such untrained unpaid carers, who may well be their parents or children or other relatives or indeed even friends, is that they are at greater potential risks where such carers practise some form of physical intervention without the possession of the relevant skills derived from periods of professionally provided relevant training. This is an issue about which all those working in the field should feel concern.

The issues relating to *'parental responsibility', 'reasonable care'* and the *'safeguarding and promotion of children's welfare in all the circumstances of the case'* have been dealt with at great length in this chapter. This is in order to emphasise that, generally speaking, the actions taken by parents and other unpaid carers to seek to provide for the care, control and safety of their children with learning disabilities presenting severe challenging behaviour (and indeed for the care, control and safety of adults with similar problems) are generally motivated by a desire to act *'responsibly'* in the widest sense of that word. Such principles are those which should be adopted, and in the case of professionals further developed and refined as a result of training, by all those who also seek to care for adults with learning disabilities who also present severely challenging behaviour.

Thus, it must be recognised that if children and adults with learning disabilities presenting severe challenging behaviour are to continue to be looked after in their own family environments, and in the best settings for their particular needs, the actions taken by parents, relatives, and other unpaid carers to provide the necessary care and control must be interpreted in the light of what is in the *paramount interests of the child or adult concerned.*

The same principle of the paramountcy of the welfare of the individual applies to those who are being looked after in care or educational settings by professional carers who are under the additional duty of acting in accordance with the best professional practice and guidance currently operative in the field of care for such individuals. Such professionals are subject to the demands of the Codes of Practice for Social Care Workers previously described in Chapter 1 at para 1.2.2.

The important principles to note therefore which must be applied in every situation where a child or adult with learning disabilities is presenting challenging behaviour are: that each person should be considered individually and any steps taken must demonstrably be in the individual's paramount interests; consideration should be given to any other alternative ways of dealing with the challenging behaviour, which do not involve the use of physical interventions; for those who are professionally employed they must be possessed of the relevant skills as a result of specialised training and they would be expected to be fully familiar with points in the individual's care plan for dealing with such situations; that, only if no other options exist for providing for the safety of the individual or others including staff who may be at risk, then a restrictive physical intervention may be used but only for the shortest possible period of time and in the least restrictive way possible. It should be emphasised that professional carers should never be put into the position that they have to resort to the use of such interventions because of shortages of staff. Parents and unpaid carers on the other hand may frequently find themselves in positions where they are the only person available. These principles are set out here in diagrammatic form.

Figure 2.1 Diagram illustrating the principles by reference to which all those caring for those with learning disabilities who also present severely challenging behaviour should work

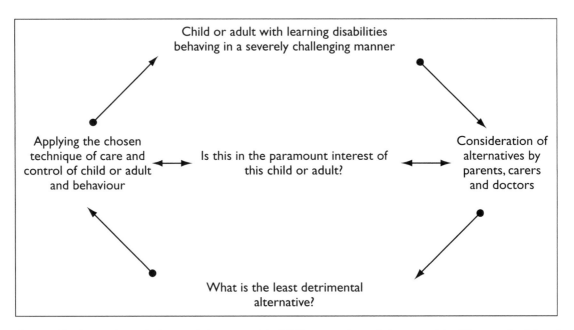

Source: Professor Lyon in her training materials 1981 onwards and then used in Chapter 1 of *Legal issues arising from the care and control of children and young people with learning disabilities who also present severe challenging behaviour* (Mental Health Foundation, 1994). Now adapted to include adults as well as children and young people.

PART II

Challenging behaviours

Chapter 3

Challenging behaviours: causes and prevention strategies

Introduction

This chapter considers briefly the various types of behaviour which may be considered to be challenging and which may therefore give rise to the use of restrictive physical interventions in response to such behaviour. Reference should also be made to the material to be found at paragraph 2.3 where the definitions of challenging behaviour are set out.

3.1 The term 'challenging behaviour'

As Allen has pointed out[90] the term 'challenging behaviour' came to prominence within the UK largely as a result of its use within a series of influential reports from the King's Fund Centre and via the work of the Special Development Team at the University of Kent. The term was originally used by the Association for Persons with Severe Handicaps in North America and was designed to stress the fact that difficult behaviours shown by service users should be viewed most appropriately as the product of an interaction between characteristics of the individual and characteristics of the service settings. Thus as Blunden and Allen have stated '. . . such behaviours represent challenges to services rather than problems which individuals with learning disabilities somehow carry around with them. If services could rise to the "challenge" of dealing with these behaviours they would cease to be problems.'

The definitions of challenging behaviour provided by the work of Emerson have already been set out in Chapter 2 so reference should be made to that part of the report.

3.2 Forms of challenging behaviour

Zarkowska and Clements, however, look to the characteristics or features of the behaviour in order to determine whether those who might seek to provide care, education or training might find such behaviour challenging. Thus, they have suggested that behaviour might be perceived as challenging if consistent with some or all of the following criteria:

- the behaviour itself or its severity is inappropriate given the person's age and level of development;

- the behaviour is dangerous either to the person or others;

---

[90] See Allen, D Behaviour Change and Behaviour Management in *Ethical Approaches to Physical Interventions*, BILD, 2002

- the behaviour constitutes a significant additional handicap for the person by interfering with the learning of new skills or by excluding the person from important learning opportunities;

- the behaviour causes significant stress to the lives of those who live and work with the person and impairs the quality of their lives to an unreasonable degree;

- the behaviour is contrary to accepted social norms.[91]

Both the definitions set out in Chapter 2 and the descriptions of behaviour provided by Zarkowska and Clements generally import a notion of dangerousness which may indeed arise from the reactions of those around the person who displays the behaviour and may not necessarily arise from the actual behaviour itself. Clearly, dangers may also arise from the inherent danger of the behaviour being engaged in, and both self-injury and physical aggression obviously meet these criteria.

The types and categories of challenging behaviours are thus very varied. They depend on the situation, the people involved and their perceptions. However, the forms which such behaviours might take can be grouped into four categories:

- self-injurious behaviour which will result in visual or auditory impairment, such as tearing at one's own eyes and pushing objects into one's ears or engaging in behaviour which unknowingly might put oneself at risk, such as, the Department of Health suggests, running out into a busy road when unaware of the dangers that this may pose;[92]

- aggressive behaviour towards others, which the DoH suggests can include a service user engaging in dangerous or harmful physical contact, or responding to another with physical aggression;[93]

- destructive behaviour damaging property and the immediate environment;

- other 'anti-social' behaviours (including inappropriate sexual behaviour) posing a physical or psychological threat to people and limiting access to community services.

Since 'challenging behaviour' is socially defined it can take very many forms. Harris and Russell[94] described the following challenging behaviours displayed by people with learning difficulties: punching, pushing, slapping or pulling, self-injury, kicking, pinching, scratching, throwing things, pulling hair, biting, unwanted sexual contact, headbutting, using weapons, tearing clothes and choking/throttling. The Additional Needs Net[95] lists a few forms of 'misbehaviours' in a school setting which may not necessarily be associated with children and young people with severe learning disabilities but may well be displayed by those with less severe disabilities: arriving late for lessons, not listening to the teacher, excessive talking, being noisy verbally and non-verbally, not getting on with work, being out of seats without reason, preventing others from being able to work.

---

[91] Zarkowska, E and Clements, J *Problem Behaviour and People with Severe Disabilities – The Star Approach* Chapman Hall (1996)

[92] See Guidance on Restrictive Physical Interventions at para 3.2

[93] ibid, para 3.2

[94] Harris, P and Russell, O *The nature of aggressive behaviour among people with learning difficulties (mental handicap) in a single health district*, Second Report, Norah Fry Research Centre, 1989

[95] supra, n.14

3.3 Causes of challenging behaviour

Relying on previous research,[96] the aim of which was to understand the reasons behind the manifestation of challenging behaviours, the Foundation for People with Learning Disabilities stated, in its *Learning Disability – Fundamental Facts*,[97] that there may be three main explanations for the manifestation of any particular form of challenging behaviour:

- The challenging behaviour is a functional and responsive reaction on the part of the person with a learning disability to a situation that they find challenging. In other words, it enables the individual to exercise some kind of control over the development of a situation (attention-seeking, preventing undesired touching/interaction);

- Some forms of challenging behaviour are a means through which the individual can alter internal levels of arousal;

- Other forms of challenging behaviours can be caused by psychiatric or neurological disorders.

Causes of challenging behaviour are numerous. They can be due to illness/health issues, boredom, lack of stimulation/over-stimulation, attention-seeking, emotional trauma, overcrowding, noise, inappropriate setting, mis-handling/abuse, unsuitable treatment, limited communication skills and under-staffing.

Challenging behaviours may be interpreted as being caused by factors internal or external to the individual presenting the challenging behaviour. Internal factors associated with challenging behaviour include pain, illness, medical conditions such as epilepsy and the side effects of medication. External factors that contribute to challenging behaviours include insufficient stimulation, overcrowding and disruption of routines.

For the purposes of this report, a three-fold division between the possible factors will be attempted in order to regroup the different potential causes of challenging situations.

3.3.1 Biological Challenging behaviours may be caused by biological factors such as chromosomal, genetic and/or neurological deficits in the person with a learning difficulty. The way in which these biological factors are associated with particular kinds of behaviour is sometimes referred to as a behavioural phenotype.

> 'The term "behavioural phenotype" refers to those aspects of an individual's development and behaviour which can be attributed to the presence of a specific genetic or other biological anomaly . . . The emphasis is on a predisposition towards certain behavioural tendencies. Not all individuals with the same genetic anomaly will show a particular behaviour, and not all those who do will show it to the same degree. Such behaviours are important in that they may give a clue to the presence of an underlying genetic cause for the individual's developmental and behavioural difficulties. They may also indicate what combinations of interventions are likely to be most effective.'[98]

---

[96] Emerson, E *Challenging Behaviour: Analysis and Intervention in People with Intellectual Disabilities*, Cambridge University Press, 2nd edn 2001
[97] supra, n.20, refer to pp. 36 and 37
[98] Contact a Family http://www.cafamily.org.uk/behaviou.html downloaded on 7.11.03 – 'UK charity providing support and advice to parents whatever the medical conditions of their child'.

In some instances there is a strongly suggested causal link between the organic factor and the challenging behaviour:

- People with learning disabilities who also suffer from depression and/or dementia (such as Alzheimer's disease) are more likely to present severe challenging behaviour.

- People suffering from epilepsy are prone to violent outburst.

- People with autism or suffering from ADHD[99] are likely to present challenging behaviours, and a high level of adrenaline can contribute to the loss of self-control leading to a potentially challenging situation.[100]

- As regards self-injurious behaviours, lip biting is associated with Lesch-Nyhan and Cornelia de Lange syndromes; knuckle biting with Lesch-Nyhan syndrome and Hypomelanosis of Ito (including wrist biting); finger and toenail picking and head-banging with Smith-Magenis syndrome; and temper tantrums and voracious overeating with Prader-Willi syndrome.[101]

[For further information on behavioural phenotypes, the reader is referred to the following sources of information: Contact a Family http://www.cafamily.org.uk/behaviou.html, O'Brien, G & Yule, W *Behavioural Phenotypes*.[102]]

People with a learning disability and a mental health problem might also present challenging behaviours in certain instances.

3.3.2 Learnt behaviour According to operant learning theory, challenging behaviours may be learned in one of two ways: by positive reinforcement (the presentation of rewards) or negative reinforcement (the removal of aversive stimuli). The process of learning can be described in terms of three sequential elements: the antecedent conditions, or stimuli immediately preceding the behaviour (A); the behaviour itself (B); and the events or consequences which follow the behaviour (C).

$$A \rightarrow B \rightarrow C$$

$$Time \rightarrow$$

Where the consequences of a behaviour are reinforcing, the behaviour in question is strengthened. This means that given the same antecedent conditions, the behaviour is likely to occur again (an increase in frequency), for a longer period of time (an increase in duration) and/or with greater force (an increase in intensity). If the behaviour is not reinforced it will tend to become weaker and will eventually stop occurring altogether. This is referred to as 'extinction'. Reinforcers are, by definition, those events which have the effect of strengthening a behaviour when they consistently occur as consequences. Reinforcing consequences may meet basic human needs, such as food for someone who is hungry or attention for someone who is bored or lonely (these are referred to as 'primary reinforcers') or they may have acquired reinforcing properties by virtue of their long-term association with primary reinforcers. For example, money is a powerful reinforcer for most people because it provides access to a wide range of other reinforcers.

---

[99] Attention Deficit Hyperactive Disorder
[100] Supra, n.90 http://www.bluepsy.com/challenging.html
[101] Supra, n.98 http://www.cafamily.org.uk/behaviou.html
[102] MacKeith Press, 1995

Antecedents are important because they can act as a stimulus or trigger for a behaviour. If the A→B→C sequence has previously led to reinforcing consequences, the presence of the antecedent (A) may act as a stimulus or cue for a person to behave in a particular way.

Challenging behaviour can be seen as learned where the display of a certain behaviour, which is interpreted as challenging, is 'triggered' by an event or a situation (A) that prompts the individual with a learning disability to act in a certain way (B) so as to achieve particular consequences (C), for example, attention from staff or a change in activity. It has been argued that some people with a learning disability have inappropriate learning experiences as children so that challenging behaviours are intentionally reinforced by those around them. The behavioural sequence A→B→C is maintained partly because the reinforcing consequence (giving someone attention or food, for example) results in a temporary reduction in the challenging behaviour which is likely to be reinforcing for carers or staff.

According to Carr[103] behaviour may be encouraged by (1) positive reinforcement, (2) removal of an aversive stimulus, or (3) by the sensory stimulation that it creates, provides or enhances. An example of type (1) is when a person cared for gets more attention from his carer following an incident involving the display of a challenging behaviour. An example of type (2) is when a service user presents a challenging behaviour to express her refusal to do a certain activity organised by the home or her reticence at undergoing a particular treatment. An example of type (3) is when a person with a learning disability displays a self-injurious behaviour, such as repetitive head-banging, as a result of the lack of stimulation over a long period of time.

3.3.3 Ecological Human ecology is the study of the interaction of people and their environments. According to Bronfenbrenner[104] environments include microsystems (activities, roles and interpersonal relations in a setting), mesosystems (the interaction between two or more settings such as school and family) and macrosystems (systems at the subcultural or cultural level).

As stated by Cullen *et al* (1999):[105] 'Challenging behaviour is a function of the interaction between the person (involving their physiological, emotional and cognitive state as well as their public behaviour) and their current environment (which includes the physical setting and other persons)'.

The environmental or ecological cause behind a challenging behaviour includes such factors as lack of stimulation (it has been suggested that self-injury could be said to be a way of stimulating oneself out of boredom), lack of interaction with other people leading to withdrawal (which might be perceived as challenging by the carer), staff shortages and overcrowding (contributing to challenging behaviours as a means to seek attention), inappropriate/unsuitable service settings and/or organisations (some findings suggest that an individual with severe learning disabilities in a crowded room is likely to present a challenging behaviour[106]), and also staff perceptions and attitudes (see paragraph 3.3.5 below).

---

[103] Carr E, *The motivation for self injurious behaviour: a review of some hypotheses*, Psychological Bulletin, 1977, 84, 4, 800–816.

[104] Bronfenbrenner, U *The Ecology of Human Development*, Cambridge MA, Harvard University Press 1979

[105] Cullen C, Brown JF, Combes H & Hendy S, *Working with People who have Intellectual Impairments; What is Clinical Psychology*, Mazillier J & Hall J (eds), 3rd edition 1999

[106] See McGill P, Teer K, Rye L & Hughes D, paper on *The relationship between aspects of the service environment and challenging behaviour in people with learning disabilities*, project completed in September 1996, http://www.doh.gov.uk/research/rd3/nhsrandd/timeltdprogs/pcd/funded/co. . ./a5013htm

'. . . *Within these ecological factors, social and psychological factors are also considered. Challenging behaviour is thus seen as being brought about when the individual is in conflict with relationships or the environment around him/her.*'[107]

For example, the response of carers to a difficult situation can contribute to or exacerbate challenging behaviour. This is illustrated by the following extract of an account of an incident in the lounge of a day care centre which was witnessed by a visitor who wished to remain anonymous.

Case Study: The disturbance began as shouting. Apparently, a woman day centre user was asking for a cup of tea and was being told that the tea break was in another half an hour. The woman didn't seem to be engaged in any kind of activity that she would be disrupted if she stopped for a cup of tea. Indeed, the atmosphere in the lounge was one of informal relaxation – watching TV, chatting. As she was told she couldn't have a cup of tea she became insistent and did start to shout quite loudly. The member of staff (also a woman) raised her voice repeating 'Just ten minutes, wait just ten minutes'. The woman continued to shout and was beginning to sound quite anguished. The staff member moved towards the woman and stood over her saying things like 'Don't be silly, just ten minutes'. The staff member reached out to put her arm on the woman's shoulder and the woman batted her arm away forcefully. The staff member shouted very loudly something like 'Just stop that, you know what happens'. The woman continued to shout back quite aggressively but did not stand up, and this exchange carried on a minute or so until the staff member called for assistance. She was joined by two other members of staff (one of whom was a man) who took the woman from her chair and held her down. I don't know how long the physical intervention lasted as the member of staff I was meeting ushered me out of the room.

I was not concerned that the actual physical intervention was performed incorrectly. However, I felt that it had been used too early as the woman was being aggressive but not violent towards others or herself, and at the time of the physical intervention she was still sitting in a chair and was unlikely to do more than just strike out. My main concern, however, was that this was a situation that was created by the member of staff's inability to diffuse the situation. Even if there was good reason to prevent the woman having a cup of tea, nothing was done to distract her from this or to placate her. The member of staff appeared to argue with the woman as a peer, which I felt was totally unprofessional, and it seemed to me that it was the member of staff's threatening actions that actually escalated the conflict, not the service user.

It is also important to note that the failure of staff members to follow and properly carry out the service user's care plan requirements can contribute to the display of 'challenging' behaviours by the client.

The relationship between the carer and the person cared for has thus come under scrutiny, with carers being advised to first question their own behaviour as well as to try to understand its possible impact on and consequences for the person they care for. Indeed, '. . . challenging behaviour may be shaped and maintained by staff responses'.[108]

---

[107] University of Central England in Birmingham, Faculty of Health and Community Care website: http://www.hcc.uce.ac.uk/cpsu/Packs/LD/challeng.htm

[108] Harbourne A, Challenging Behaviour in Older People: Nurses' Attitudes, Research, *Nursing Standard* 11, 12-39-43 http://www.nursing-standard.co.uk/archives/vol11-12/research.htm

The next two sections consider communication and staff beliefs as two specific aspects of the ecological systems which can influence challenging behaviours.

3.3.4 Means of communication Challenging behaviour can also occur as a result of a breakdown in communication. In this context communicative behaviour is a deliberate or intentional way of letting others know what one is feeling, experiencing or wanting. Challenging behaviours occur when behaviour that is intended as communicative is misunderstood or ignored.

This emphasises the idea that challenging behaviour can be a response to a situation that is confusing or frustrating for the person with a learning disability. Behaviour that is seen as 'challenging' is thus the way in which the person with a learning disability expresses his or her anxiety, fear or frustration.

As stated in *Promoting Well-Being and Preventing Challenging Behaviour*, 'the behaviour is a **communication** that the person needs more or different support from services'.[109]

Thus, certain 'challenging' behaviour may simply be a way of expressing emotions such as distress, anger, frustration, joy, excitement, vivid interest etc. This is especially true for people who experience difficulties in communicating verbally.

In a residential home for adults with learning disabilities and presenting severe challenging behaviour, a resident with cerebral palsy and paralysed from the waist down also suffered from an inability to speak. He would throw soft toys across his room and raise his voice – this was interpreted by his carers as being his way of communicating with them. Depending on his needs, this would mean that he wanted a drink, food, the lights on or off, to be alone in his room, to ask somebody to leave his room, or that he just wanted to throw his toys for his own pleasure.

It is strongly evident that the carer's response to and interpretation of a person's behaviour can be crucial to its understanding and to its qualification as challenging or not.

3.3.5 Care giver's belief, perception and behaviour Given that the identification of challenging behaviour is based upon subjective judgement, it is clear that the perceptions and beliefs of care givers will directly affect what behaviours are regarded as challenging and what responses are considered appropriate. The concept of staff attribution is based on the theory that staff feel a need to explain a situation involving challenging behaviour so that they can feel in control[110] and most likely decide on a subsequent course of action to be taken. The research literature seems to suggest that '. . . variables over which staff could exert some control (eg communication) are viewed as less likely causes of challenging behaviour than those over which they had little or no influence (eg internal factors and general environmental factors)'.[111]

Recent research supports the idea that a caregiver's behaviour and attitude can contribute to 'the long-term maintenance of challenging behaviours through both positive and negative reinforcement processes', the relationship between staff responses and challenging behaviours

---

[109] supra, n.21, Lally, p.2

[110] Fenwick A, On attribution theory: challenging behaviour and staff beliefs, *Clinical Psychology Forum*, 79, pp. 29–31.

[111] Allen D, Mediator analysis: an overview of recent research on carers supporting people with intellectual disability and challenging behaviour, *Learning Disability Bulletin* 117/2, BILD June 2000

thus being described as 'a dynamic behavioural system'.[112] The relationship between the display of challenging behaviours and caregivers' emotional responses and intervention behaviours about the challenging behaviours has led Cullen[113] to describe such a situation as an 'interactional challenge'.

Factors that might influence staff responses to challenging behaviours include staff lack of understanding of the function of challenging behaviours, staff belief that challenging behaviours are to be controlled and not necessarily understood (a belief that can be reinforced by staff training that concentrates on management/intervention techniques), and staff emotional responses to the aversive nature of challenging behaviours.[114]

The behaviour of staff may also be influenced by their understanding of formal and informal rules. Knowledge of rules which apply, for example, to staff working in a learning disability service may be based on contact with other members of staff, information and advice from a professional authority (consultant, occupational therapist, GP) or be inferred by the staff themselves.[115] One consequence of staff behaviour being rule-governed is that if and when an individual with a learning disability behaves in such a way that a rule is broken, this might serve as a trigger and prompt the caregiver to intervene.

Depending on the perception of the challenging behaviour and the causal attribution, staff will experience an emotional response that will influence further action taken in response to the challenging behaviour. The ability of staff to identify accurately the causes behind challenging behaviours is, however, undermined by a lack of knowledge and understanding of the function of a challenging behaviour.[116] It is argued that this precise lack of knowledge and understanding may be a contributing factor to a negative emotional response from the caregiver faced with a challenging situation.

> *'Staff making different attributions are likely to respond in different ways to the same incident of challenging behaviour. For example, a staff member who believes that a service user's self-injury is related to a transient medical condition (eg bad cold) may respond by talking to the service-user to confirm this and subsequently seek some medical relief for the individual concerned. A staff member who attributed the cause of the same behaviour to a permanent medical condition (eg brain damage) may respond by containing the behaviour through physical or medical restraint. A third staff member attributing the cause of the same incident to the difficulty of the task being carried out at the time may simply remove the task and avoid using it in the future.'*[117]

If staff attribute a challenging behaviour to an internal factor – that is, that the behaviour is inherent to the individual displaying it and the assumption is that the individual should be able

---

[112] Mitchell G & Hastings R, Learning disability care staff's emotional reactions to aggressive challenging behaviours: development of a measurement tool, *British Journal of Clinical Psychology* 1998, 37, pp. 441–449.

[113] Cullen, October 1999 n.11 supra

[114] Hastings R, Understanding factors that influence staff responses to challenging behaviours: an exploratory interview study, *Mental Handicap Research*, BILD, 1995, 8, 4, pp. 297–320. http://www.nau.edu/ihd/positive/library/hastings15.pdf

[115] supra Morgan & Hastings

[116] Morgan G & Hastings R, Special educator's understanding of challenging behaviours in children with learning disabilities: sensitivity to information about behavioural function, *Behavioural and Cognitive Psychotherapy*, 1998, 26, pp. 43–52. http://www.nau.edu/ihd/positive/library/morgan1.pdf

[117] Reed T & Watts M, Community staff causal attributions about challenging behaviour in people with intellectual disabilities, *Journal of Applied Research in Intellectual Disabilities* 1997, 10.3, pp. 238–249.

to control the behaviour – they are more likely to experience a negative effect/emotional response.[118] This is the theory of motivation and emotion put forward by Weiner.[119] Staff are more prone to negative emotions (sadness, anger, fear, anxiety[120]) when facing an aggressive or self-injurious behaviour, rather than when facing a stereotyped behaviour.[121] When challenging behaviours are of an aversive nature in the eyes of carers – which would thus make them feel threatened, stressed, anxious, frightened, insecure, etc – research shows that staff are then most likely to engage in 'escape or avoidance behaviour'.[122] In effect, staff will respond by attempting to control the challenging behaviour in order to stop the challenging situation.

Staff reaction to challenging behaviours may also contribute to their re-occurrence (attention sought and given after an incident of challenging behaviour). Research has shown that stereotyped behaviours occur at a lower rate in the presence of staff[123] or when the latter interact with and engage the service users in activities.[124]

'Client behaviours, especially challenging behaviours, have also been shown experimentally to influence staff behaviour.'[125] It is thus argued that, like a spiral effect, challenging behaviours can have an impact on caregivers' attitudes just as staff attitudes can influence the display of challenging behaviours. It has been suggested that, in some instances, 'the belief that people are not responsible for their behaviour (eg as a consequence of a diagnosis of dementia) may serve an important role in helping carers come to terms with this behaviour'.[126] This would be a very important point as research seems to point out that some staff believe the challenging behaviour to be a deliberate and intentional action that can be controlled and therefore changed by the person presenting it.[127]

In contrast, research seems to suggest that most parents who care for young adults with learning disabilities tend to hold the belief that these adults are not responsible for their acts, which then cannot be considered deliberate, as they 'lack the cognitive ability to understand behaviour–contingency relationships'.[128]

Natural carers (as opposed to formal/paid carers) tend to consider the challenging behaviour displayed by the individual they care for as being the result of four possible explanations:[129]

- the behaviour is caused by 'historical and personal factors' relating to the carer;

- the behaviour is the result of the cared-for person's inherent personality make-up;

- the behaviour can be controlled by the person cared for;

- the behaviour is a deliberate attempt to provoke others.

[118] Supra n.108, Harborne
[119] Weiner B, An attribution theory of achievement and motivation, *Psychological Review*. 92.4. pp. 548–573.
[120] supra n.114, Mitchell & Hastings
[121] Hastings R & Remington B, The emotional dimension of working with challenging behaviours, *Clinical Psychology Forum*, 1995, 79, pp. 11–16.
[122] Supra n.114 Mitchell & Hastings
[123] Felce D, Repp A, Thomas M, Ager A & Blunden R, The relationship of staff-client ratios, interactions, and residential placement, *Research in Developmental Disabilities*, 1991, 12, pp. 315–331.
[124] Brusca R, Nieminen G, Carter R & Repp A, The relationships of staff contact and activity to the stereotypy of children with multiple disabilities, *Journal of the Association for Persons with Severe Handicaps*, 1989, 14, pp. 127–136.
[125] Hastings R & Remington B, Staff behaviour and its implications for people with learning disabilities and challenging behaviours, *British Journal of Clinical Psychology* 1994, 33, pp. 423–438.
[126] Supra n.111, Allen D, BILD 2000, citing: Qureshi H, *Parents Caring for Young Adults with Mental Handicap and Behaviour Problems*, Hester Adrian Research Unit, Manchester, 1990.
[127] Supra n.121, Hastings 1995
[128] Supra n.111 Allen, BILD 2000, referring to Qureshi's findings (1990).

As most parents tend to agree on the fact that the challenging behaviour of their relative is not a deliberate act, their general view is that professionals should cease to blame the people cared for and the parent-carers for the challenging behaviours.[130] Moreover, they believe that professionals should avoid resorting to both behavioural intervention and aversive techniques of challenging behaviour management as, due to the lack of cognitive ability, these interventions do not necessarily benefit the people cared for and 'unfairly punish people who are already in a deprived state'.[131]

It is thus argued that the main issue of challenging behaviour management cannot be appropriately addressed unless carers have a clearer understanding of the challenging behaviour, its reasons, as well as its functions. However, research also suggests that 'staff may be more concerned with reducing challenging behaviours than understanding them'.[132]

3.4 Staff training

Recent literature has shown that staff training is an important element in the occurrence, prevention, management and understanding of challenging behaviours. It is argued that appropriate staff training would benefit both staff and the people with learning disabilities and displaying challenging behaviours they care for.

The Health Evidence Bulletin (Wales)[133] provides a list of the literature which considers the role, impact and importance of staff training in the management of challenging behaviours. The findings have been summarised as follows:

- 'Well-trained and skilled staff are identified as essential in the provision of quality community services.' From: *Services for People with Learning Disabilities and Challenging Behaviours or Mental Health Needs.*[134]

- 'A substantial number of staff have not received training, or report that it is inadequate to meet the needs of their job.' From: *Training for staff caring for people with learning disability*[135] and *Residential staff: How they view their training and professional support.*[136]

- 'Some training has been found to be effective in increasing staff knowledge and impacting on practice.' From: *An evaluation of the impact of a one-day challenging behaviour course on the knowledge of health and social care staff working in learning disability services*[137] and *An evaluation of an ongoing consultation model to train teachers to treat challenging behaviour.*[138]

---

[129] Supra n.111, Allen BILD 2000, citing: Orford J, ed. (*Coping with disorder in the family*, Beckemham, Croom Helm, 1997) and Qureshi H (*Impact on families: young adults with learning disability who show challenging behaviour*, in *Research to Practice? Implications of Research on the Challenging Behaviour of People with Learning Disability* (ed. Kiernan C) British Institute of Learning Disabilities, 1993, pp. 89–115).

[130] Supra n.111 Allen, BILD 2000, referring to Turnbull AP & Ruef M's findings: Family perspectives on problem behaviour, *Mental Retardation* 34, pp. 28–93.

[131] Supra n.111, Allen, BILD 2000, referring to Qureshi's findings (1990).

[132] Supra n.121, Hastings, 1995

[133] 31 December 1999 http://hebw.uwcm.ac.uk/learningdisabilities/chapter9.htm

[134] Department of Health, *Report of the Project Group*, London: HMSO 1993.

[135] Smith B, Wun W-L & Cumella S, *British Journal of Learning Disabilities* 1996, 24: 20–5.

[136] McVilly KR, *British Journal of Learning Disabilities* 1997, 25: 18–25.

[137] McKenzie K, Matheson E, Patrick S *et al*, *Journal of Learning Disabilities* 2000, 4(2): 153–165

- 'Training has not always been found to be cost-effective or to have long-term benefits.' From: *A Review of Some Important Issues in Research and Services for People with Learning Disabilities and Challenging Behaviour.*[139]

- 'Evaluating the effectiveness of staff training is difficult.' From: *Evaluating a training package for staff working with people with learning disabilities prior to hospital closure.*[140]

- 'It is important to establish clearly the type and nature of the training needs of the service in question and to establish which goals the training is designed to meet and which outcome measures will be used to evaluate effectiveness.' From: *A Review of Some Important Issues in Research and Services for People with Learning Disabilities and Challenging Behaviour.*[141]

The bulletin concluded that 'there is currently insufficient evidence to unequivocally establish the effectiveness of staff training alone in improving staff practice in managing challenging behaviour'.

Nonetheless, staff training is an important element in preparing staff when facing a challenging situation and giving them the means to understand both themselves and the people they care for.

> '... *Professionals involved in the design of behavioural programmes need to be aware of the nature of staff's own beliefs about challenging behaviours, and the reality of working with such actions on a regular basis. In particular, programme designers should incorporate methods of dealing with staff's emotional reactions to challenging behaviours, especially when the interventions are likely to lead to increases in the behaviours in the short term.*'[142]

For further details on the issue of assessing staff's reaction to challenging behaviour, the reader is referred to the research article written by Mitchell & Hastings, *Learning disability care staff's emotional reactions to aggressive challenging behaviours: Development of a measurement tool.*[143] As for information on training outcomes, *Training Carers in Physical Interventions – Research towards Evidence-based Practice*[144] provides a summary of research literature which contains some evaluation of various training programmes.

In conclusion, there is indeed a shift from a first impulse to control a situation and impose a set of socially accepted behavioural rules towards a desire to understand and adapt to the needs of the person for whom care is being provided. The aim is then to design ways of improving the environment of an individual labelled as having a learning difficulty and presenting challenging behaviour, and to provide coping mechanisms for the individual with a learning disability when faced with particular situations, which in the past might have triggered a particular challenging behaviour.

---

[138] Taylor I, O'Reilly M & Lancioni G, *International Journal of Disability*, Development and Education 1996, 43(3): 203–18
[139] Cullen C, Scottish Executive review of services for people with a learning disability, 2000
[140] Harper DJ, *The British Journal of Developmental Disabilities* 1994, XL(1): 45–53
[141] supra n.11, Cullen, 2000
[142] supra n.125, Hastings, 1995
[143] Supra n.114, Mitchell & Hastings, 1998
[144] Allen D, BILD, 2001

3.5 Prevention strategies

This section aims to give a non-exhaustive overview of possible prevention strategies in dealing with challenging situations. However, depending on the challenging behaviour, the situation and the people involved, certain techniques will be more appropriate than others. It is therefore up to the carers, professionals and parents involved to use their discretion in deciding what course of action is appropriate and necessary in the circumstances, whether it is a situation of inappropriate sexual behaviour, self-injurious behaviour, violence against staff or another third party, behaviour inappropriate to social norms or disturbing behaviour in school/residential home/health settings.

The report does not claim any authority on this matter and merely attempts to set the relationship between challenging behaviours and the law into context. Thus, a court of law would consider, before any physical intervention was resorted to, whether the intervention was a TINA situation and whether all preventative measures had been taken but failed to provide a safer outcome to the challenging situation.

Whatever action is taken, carers should always keep in mind the essential need to assess, balance and protect both the person cared for and the carer's best interest and safety.

3.5.1 Feeling-based model of prevention One approach to be found in the workbook *Promoting Well-Being and Preventing Challenging Behaviour*[145] suggests that to avoid challenging situations, a carer must know about the person for whom they care. This means knowing about an individual's fact of life, how this individual expresses distress/stress, joy/happiness, pain or boredom. This knowledge will enhance a carer's understanding of the person and of the possible circumstances that could trigger a challenging situation. This understanding will enable the carer to either prevent a challenging situation/behaviour from occurring or to respond in a manner which is considerate, appropriate and beneficial to both the person cared for and the services.

This workbook proposes three steps to follow to get to know the needs of a person with a learning difficulty and to minimise the risk of a challenging situation arising:

- consideration of the feelings of the person cared for;

- focus on 'moment-to-moment sensitivity' to verbal or non-verbal signs of a person's feelings;

- attention to 'forward planning', which looks at ways a person's enjoyment of life can be enhanced.

In her conclusion, Lally states that:

> *'traditional models of prevention are mainly focused on the person "showing challenging behaviour" before consideration is given to how to prevent the behaviour recurring. The flaw in these models is related to the vicious circle of challenging behaviour: if someone acts in ways that staff find stressful, the level of stress may affect the ability and motivation of staff to change the behaviour. This workbook has*

---

[145] supra, n.21, Lally

described a feeling-based model of prevention, based on a person's level of happiness.'[146]

3.5.2 Management strategies for challenging behaviours Slevin reviews the literature supporting the use of various management strategies for challenging behaviours that can be considered by caregivers and professional carers outside the institutional environment and provides a summarised list of therapy approaches which might be of help in reducing the occurrence of challenging behaviours in people with learning disabilities:[147] gentle teaching, Phenothiazine drugs, cognitive therapy, counselling, community support team, special treatment units, music therapy, multi-sensory therapy (Snoezelen), massage, aromatherapy and complementary therapies.[148]

The strategies which are more often used in the context of challenging behaviour management, and which are, for the most part, strongly supported by evidence as to their efficacy and benefits, are listed below:

- *Behavioural therapy* focuses on modifying the challenging behaviour displayed by the person with learning disabilities. The behaviour modification strategy aims to help the individual unlearn or reduce the occurrence of challenging behaviours.[149]

- *Multi-element behavioural support* aims to teach the individual with learning disabilities and displaying challenging behaviours new skills and approaches that can be used instead of the challenging behaviour displayed. An important element of this strategy is that the individual's self-worth and sense of accomplishment are encouraged.[150]

- Philosophical approaches, as explained by Slevin, aim to 'break down the whole concept of the "social norm", and replace it with respect for people as individuals' by focusing on valuing the 'under-valued'. The crucial principles that are attached to the philosophical approaches are 'chiefly individual empowerment; community participation; human rights; equality of opportunities and access to education, employment, recreation, services, and fairness'.[151]

- Shared care strategies combine the expertise and qualities of both professionals and carers in attempting to manage challenging behaviours. This strategy implies 'the shift of power from the professional to those directly responsible for supporting and caring for the individual with a learning disability through the transfer of skills and information.'[152] This is especially relevant for caregivers who operate in the community and carers of family members with learning disabilities and displaying challenging behaviours.

3.5.3 The best strategies – applied behaviour analysis It has been suggested by Allen that the most effective strategies for managing challenging behaviour known at the present time are derived from applied behaviour analysis. He points out that there are a number of thorough meta-analytical studies that have reviewed the strengths and weaknesses of these approaches

---

[146] supra, n.21, Lally, p.68
[147] Supra n.111, Slevin BILD 2000
[148] For detailed reference, see Slevin supra.
[149] Martin G & Pear J, *Behaviour modification: what it is and how to do it*, Prentice-Hall, 1992.
[150] Donnellan AM, LaVigna GW, Negri-Shoultz N & Fassbender LL, *Progress without punishment: effective approaches for learning with behavioural problems*, Columbia University, 1988.
[151] Supra, n.111 Slevin, BILD 2000
[152] Supra, n.111 Slevin, BILD 2000

and suggests that the most recent by Carr and others[153] focused on the use of positive behavioural strategies which avoided the use of aversive procedures. Carr's review found that, using a criterion of a 90% reduction in challenging behaviour from baseline levels, these strategies were successful approximately 52% of the time. If a criterion of an 80% reduction was applied, the rate increased to around 68%. Yet, as Allen notes,[154] given their effectiveness it is alarming to find that current research suggests that such non-aversive procedures appear to be used in only between 2% and 20% of people with severe challenging behaviours.

Allen states that this may be one of the reasons why challenging behaviours often appear to endure over a long period of time but questions why, given the lack of evidence to support the efficacy of the use either of psychotropic medication or the use of restrictive physical interventions, services still routinely engage in the use of such reactive procedures instead of in the more effective appropriate behavioural change strategies.

Allen therefore, in common with others with considerable experience in the field, comments[155] that a major challenge for both commissioners and providers is to ensure that these positive behaviour change strategies are more routinely implemented within mainstream services. He notes that without this investment, rates of use of reactive procedures will inevitably rise and is clearly in agreement with Carr when he observes that '. . . if you focus on crisis management alone, what you typically find is that problem behaviours occur again at some future time, thereby making more crisis interventions and management necessary. You can become trapped in a scenario that has no end, except frustration and despair.'[156] The research does, however, suggest that physically aggressive behaviours, in other words those which service providers are most likely to meet with restrictive physical interventions, are the least responsive to behavioural intervention.

It is clear that despite the best therapeutic efforts, carers supporting people displaying extreme physically aggressive behaviour are likely, in an effort to protect themselves or others, to have to resort to the use of restrictive physical interventions on occasion, and this report seeks to provide advice on the relevant applicable law in such circumstances.

[153] Carr, EG; Horner, RH; Turnbull, AP; Marquis J.G; McLaughlin DM;, McAtee, ML; Smith CE: Ryan KA; Rueff, MB & Doolabh, *Positive Behaviour Support for people with Developmental Disabilities: A research Synthesis.* American Association on Mental Retardation, Washington (1999)

[154] Cited at note 90 above

[155] Cited above at note 90

[156] Carr EG, Levin L, McConnnachie G, Carlson JI, Kemp DC & Smith CE, *Communication-Based Intervention for Problem Behaviour. A User's Guide for Producing Positive Change*, Baltimore (1994)

Chapter 4

Responses to challenging behaviour focusing on physical interventions

Introduction

This work is concerned principally with legal issues arising from the use of restrictive physical interventions, including the administration of medicines and the use of detention. This chapter deals with the legal implications of different responses, including issues of capacity and consent under the law. It further seeks to analyse the various different pieces of legislation which may be relevant and to reflect on the various documents of 'Guidance' which have been issued by various government departments over the years and which are still applicable. These include: Circular 93/13 issued by the Department of Health on The Permissible Forms of Control in Children's Residential Care; Circular 10/98 issued by the Department for Education and Science (as it was then) on The Use of Force to Control or Restrain Pupils. In particular, this chapter also seeks to deal in detail with the latest Guidance LEA 0242/2002 issued by the Department for Education and Skills and the Department for Health on *The Use of Restrictive Physical Interventions for Staff Working with Children and Adults who Display Extreme Behaviour in Association with Learning Disability and/or Autistic Spectrum Disorder*. Guidance issued by the relevant government departments with responsibilities for the education and care of children, young people and adults with learning disabilities, who also present severely challenging behaviour, does not have the binding force of statute law but must be followed unless there are exceptional circumstances justifying its not being followed. (See Chapter 1 paragraph 1.1.3) Thus far there have been no cases where such exceptional circumstances have been admitted. However, in any cases taken before the courts, any person employed or who employs individuals in any caring or educational capacity in relation to such children, young people and adults, would have to show that they had complied closely with the demands of such Guidance if they were not to be found at fault or liable in some way. It should be emphasised that such Guidance does not legally bind those who are acting as 'unpaid carers' as defined by the Carers (Recognition of Services) Act 1995 which might include a person's parents, children, other relatives or friends. Such carers would, however, benefit from reading and trying to understand the Guidance which is binding upon those performing similar tasks in an 'employed' or 'volunteer working for a voluntary organisation' capacity, as explained in Chapter 1 and defined and expanded upon in the Glossary of Terms. As a result of considering the various legal provisions, the accompanying interpretative Departmental Guidance and the possible interpretations to be given to such Guidance by the courts, this again has to be a long chapter. It is, nevertheless, one which should be very carefully considered by all who work in this field. Separate Guidance has been issued for Scotland and this is therefore considered in Chapter 11 at paragraph 11.6.

4.1 Challenging behaviour and best practice

It is outside the scope of this report to detail the current best practice in this area. If a case were to go to court it would be expected that the parties to an action would call experts to advise the court on what is at that stage the best practice observed by professionals in the field. The court will then make its own decision informed by the experts' advice and opinions laid before the courts. Given the rapidly changing state of knowledge and practice in this area it would not be advisable for a report dealing with legal issues to suggest what is currently the best practice since this would very rapidly become out of date.

It is, however, worth noting that parents, carers and professionals should always assess behaviour before deciding on a course of action. An assessment should:

- identify the behaviour;

- decide who the behaviour is a problem for – in some cases the behaviour is a problem for the carer but not for anyone else;

- decide what function the behaviour serves (in other words, what the motivation is for that person's behaviour);

- decide what the consequences of that behaviour are.

The assessment process will enable the parent, carer or professional to decide whether to intervene to change that behaviour.

Assuming that an intervention is needed, research shows that the most effective strategies for challenging behaviour are derived from Applied Behaviour Analysis.[157] This provides a long-term strategy for supporting a person with challenging behaviour to ameliorate the behaviours over time. Such services will also need to have strategies in place for responding to challenging behaviours when they occur. These are known as reactive management strategies.

4.1.2 The legal implications of reactive management strategies   Reactive management strategies may include medication, environmental changes and physical interventions. Any of these approaches may be lawful or unlawful in a particular context. For example, the use of medication should generally only be engaged in as part of a proper medically agreed programme of treatment and also with the consent of the person being treated. This may cause problems when working with those with severe learning disabilities and may give rise to the possibility of an assault or battery being perpetrated. Environmental changes, which may include the use of numbered locks on doors, may amount to false imprisonment. The use of physical interventions may again give rise to the possibility of assault or battery being perpetrated upon an individual, particularly when staff have had no training and the physical intervention has been used without an appropriate assessment or behaviour management strategy being in place.

4.2 Physical intervention

4.2.1   Physical intervention can be described as 'any method of responding to challenging behaviour which involves some degree of direct physical force to limit or restrict movement of

---

[157] *Ethical Approaches to Physical Interventions*, BILD, 2003.

mobility.'[158] The idea is that there is some kind of resistance exercised by the person to whom the force is applied.

There are various forms of physical intervention, for instance: blocking someone's path by restraining them by the arm or by using a barrier; preventing someone from leaving an area against their will; using devices, materials or equipment to limit a person's mobility; pressing an individual against a wall or down on the floor to prevent any movement; preventing a child or adult from running across a road with heavy traffic or preventing a person from jumping out of a window. All such interventions may constitute the offences of assault or assault and battery or of false imprisonment.

4.2.2 Guidance on the Use of Restrictive Physical Interventions for Staff Working with Children and Adults who Display Extreme Behaviour in Association with Learning Disability and/or Autistic Spectrum Disorders 2002[159]

Published jointly by the Departments of Health and for Education and Skills, this government Guidance aims to provide some advice on how, when and why to use physical intervention and seeks to take into account the provisions of the Human Rights Act 1998 as regards the child's/adult's right to respect for his/her life, the right to liberty and security, and the right not to be subjected both to inhuman treatment and discrimination.[160] The underpinning principles of this Guidance are that:

- the use of force should, wherever possible, be avoided;

- there are occasions when the use of force is appropriate;

- when force is necessary, it must be used in ways that maintain the safety and dignity of all concerned.[161]

Restrictive physical interventions aim to control an individual's behaviour in order to prevent movement or mobility or to disengage from dangerous or harmful physical contact, and can be employed using bodily contact, mechanical devices or changes to the person's environment.[162] On the other hand, non-restrictive physical interventions aim to help a person's mobility and uses devices not to restrict but to support or protect a person from the risk of injury.

The Guidance covers situations where physical intervention is used as an emergency response mechanism to an unforeseen circumstance, or as a method of challenging behaviour management which is incorporated within a care plan.

The Guidance suggests that the use of physical intervention can be justified when employed in the following cases:

- to prevent movement or mobility;

- to break away or disengage from a dangerous situation;

[158] Harris J, Allen D, Cornick M, Jefferson A & Mills R, *Physical Interventions: A Policy Framework*, BILD, 2000, page 2 (BILD P.I. – policy framework)

[159] Departments of Health and Department for Education and Skills, *Guidance on the Use of Restrictive Physical Interventions for Staff Working with Children and Adults who Display Extreme Behaviour in Association with Learning Disability and/or Autistic Spectrum Disorders*, July 2002, ref: LEA/0242/2002 (DoH guidance on P.I.)

[160] supra, n.159, DoH Guidance on PI, para.1.11

[161] supra, n.159, DoH Guidance on PI, refer to p. 4

[162] supra, n.159, DoH Guidance on PI, para.3.1

- to separate the person from a 'trigger';[163]

- to protect an individual (service user, carer, third party) from a dangerous situation;

- to remove a weapon or implement for inflicting self-injury from an individual.[164]

The Guidance stresses that physical intervention should only be used as a last resort, that is when all other modes of coping with a challenging behaviour have failed or when primary and secondary prevention methods proved to be inadequate to respond to certain circumstances or inefficient in ensuring containment of the challenging behaviour.

BILD defines primary intervention as being a course of action which 'involves changing aspects of the person's living and working environment to reduce likelihood that challenging behaviour will occur', whereas secondary intervention 'concerns the actions taken once a combination of setting conditions and a trigger has precipitated a sequence of behaviours which could escalate into violence and aggression. The aim of secondary intervention is to stop the behaviour building up into a full-blown "incident"'.[165]

Primary prevention is of the utmost importance in ensuring quality of care and service to the person with a learning disability presenting a challenging behaviour. This provides the individual with a safe environment that takes into consideration the needs and wishes of both the person with a learning disability and the carers.

Secondary prevention comes into play as a second-degree intervention where it is felt that a situation could get out of hand. The techniques used here are predominantly 'defusion' ones. the aim of which is to calm a situation or person down, trying to avoid a critical point while keeping in mind the best interests of both the person cared for and the carer.

As mentioned previously, physical intervention can be used in either situation where it is part of a care plan or in response to an emergency situation.

The Guidance provides that when the use of physical intervention is part of a planned strategy, it is thus part of a broader treatment and as such is discussed in advance by a multidisciplinary or school team which includes the individual presenting the challenging behaviour so as to encourage development and self-management. It is also described and recorded in a care plan, and is then 'implemented under the supervision of an identified member of staff who has relevant qualifications and experience'.[166]

Unplanned use of force can be justified if deployed to prevent a risk of injury or serious damage to property; or in schools, to prevent a pupil's prejudicial behaviour interfering with the maintenance of good order and discipline in the school and among fellow pupils.

Whenever the use of physical intervention is necessary in a particular circumstance, it must adhere to the following requirements:

---

[163] A trigger is a circumstance or event that triggers a person with a learning disability into acting out a pattern of behaviour that proves challenging to parents, carers and services.

[164] supra, n.159, DoH guidance on P.I., para 3.1 and 3.2

[165] supra, n.158, BILD P.I. – policy framework, p.21 and 22.

[166] supra, n.159, DoH Guidance on P.I., para 3.8 and 3.9

- The scale and nature of any physical intervention must be proportionate to both the behaviour of the individual to be controlled and the nature of the harm they might cause;

- These judgements have to be made at the time the incident occurs, taking due account of all the circumstances, including any known history of other events involving the individual to be controlled;

- The minimum necessary force should be used, and the techniques deployed should be familiar to the staff involved, safe to use and described in the service user's support plan.[167]

In any event, according to paragraph 10.7 of the Guidance the use of physical intervention must be regulated by a specific policy. This policy should set out the rules and procedures on how to deal and cope with challenging situations as well as how and when to use physical intervention. Such a policy should include information on prevention procedures that should be followed before resorting to physical intervention as such intervention should only be employed as a last resort when there is no other alternative.

Paragraph 10.8 of the Guidance sets out that a policy should include:

- strategies for preventing the occurrence of behaviours which precipitate the use of a physical intervention;

- strategies for 'de-escalation' or 'defusion' which can avert the need for a physical intervention;

- procedures for post-incident support and debriefing for staff, children, service users and their families;

- the concept of reasonable force where 'reasonableness' is determined with reference to all the circumstances, including:

  ○ the seriousness of the incident;

  ○ the relative risks arising from using a physical intervention compared with other strategies;

  ○ the age, cultural background, gender, stature and medical history of the child or service user concerned;

  ○ *the application of gradually increasing or decreasing levels of force in response to the person's behaviour.*

The Guidance also brings up the issue of the duty of care owed by the carers and services towards service users, as well as the one owed by schools towards their pupils. This has major implications with regards to tort law, where a duty of care is a first requirement in proving that an offence of negligence has occurred.[168] The Guidance also refers to the elevated risks associated with different techniques of physical interventions.

4.2.3 The risk of abuse As is suggested in the Department of Health Guidance issued with regard to the protection of vulnerable adults from abuse, the use of physical intervention is

---

[167] supra, n.159, DoH Guidance on P.I., para.3.4
[168] see section on civil offences

always accompanied by the risk of physical or psychological injury, financial damage or emotional trauma due to the potential abuse which may result from the use of such techniques. The notion of abuse is defined in the Department of Health Guidance *No Secrets*[169] as 'a violation of an individual's human and civil rights by any other person or persons',[170] and, in particular, that physical abuse could include 'hitting, slapping, pushing, kicking, misuse of medication, restraint, or inappropriate sanctions'.[171]

Physical intervention implies the presence of a potential risk of harm. Therefore any use of force for restraint, restriction and control purposes that is unnecessary and disproportionate is a form of abuse, and thus entails a potential breach of the law and a breach of an individual's human rights.

Physical intervention can become abuse when it is used in order to force an individual to comply with rules or somebody else's wishes; when it is deployed because there is a staff shortage, or because it is the easiest option for the person employing the force; when the force used is not commensurate to the situation at hand; and when the force will cause injury.

According to the Foundation for People with Learning Disabilities, there are an estimated two million people in the UK with either a mild or a severe learning disability. A survey conducted by Mencap suggests that 23% of adults with learning disabilities are subjected to physical abuse.[172]

4.2.4 Use of physical intervention There are various methods of physical intervention which are practised in settings all over the country. Whichever method is used, it must be adequate to the situation and must also be legal. This now imports not only notions of compliance with the particular provisions of the domestic law of tort or criminal law but it must also not offend against the individual's human rights. That is, the carer must identify the nature of the individual's behaviour before deciding on the best course of action – this will enable the carer to decide what method of physical intervention is best employed, whether force is needed and what degree of force is required and acceptable by law, and will not represent a disproportionate interference with the individual's human rights.

The *Positive Behavioural Management* trainer's manual produced by Positive Response Training[173] suggests that there are two possible practical responses to a challenging situation which are either a self-protective technique or a restrictive strategy, the latter being brought about by a crisis situation.

Examples of situations

- Aggressive behaviour towards a carer eg when an occupational therapist is faced with a child firmly and painfully squeezing the therapist's face during 1:1 treatment;

- Aggressive behaviour towards a third party eg when a service user attacks another service user by pulling his/her hair or biting;

---

[169] Department of Health, *No Secrets: Guidance on developing and implementing multi-agency policies and procedures to protect vulnerable adults from abuse*, 2000
[170] supra n.169, *No Secrets*, para.2.5
[171] supra n.169, *No Secrets*, para.2.7
[172] *Living in Fear*, London: Mencap, 1999
[173] Positive Response Training Ltd, *Positive Behavioural Management: Preventing & Responding to Aggressive Behaviour in Persons with Intellectual Disabilities, Trainer's Manual*, PRT 1999

- Self-injurious behaviour eg when a person keeps on banging his/her head against the wall or any other hard surfaces, which can lead to serious injury and damage;

- Damaging property or the environment eg when an individual expresses his/her anger or frustration by throwing chairs across the room;

- Anti-social behaviour eg when a carer who takes a male service user out to socialise is faced with him persistently touching his private parts out of habit and finally displaying them in public places;

- Use of physical intervention in emergency situations eg when a carer has to prevent a child with ADHD[174] from jumping out of a window 40 feet high;

- Use of physical intervention as part of a care plan eg either as an agreed response between the person with a learning disability and his care team to a challenging behaviour or for therapeutic purposes (eg when using such equipment as a soft spinal jacket employed to help a child with no spine posture gain a good base for their trunk and head control);

- Unacceptable use of physical intervention eg when a carer uses physical intervention too freely in any given situation to gain control over the person they care for.

Methods

This section aims to describe the kind of methods used to deal with challenging behaviour. However, it is important to point out that there is no universal definition or consensus on what these methods actually are. In other words, there may be differences between the theory of a method and how it is deployed in practice.

Seclusion

Seclusion is the act of isolating an individual from other people. For example, a person living in a residential home demonstrates 'challenging behaviour' that can be harmful to both the rest of the residents and the carers. She is removed from the common room or public setting and placed alone in a room against her will and remains there under supervision for the shortest time possible.

In the case of *S v Airedale NHS Trust* 2002, the Court defined seclusion as being '. . . the supervised confinement of a patient in a room, which may be locked to protect others from significant harm. Its sole aim is to contain severely disturbed behaviour which is likely to cause harm to others.' The judgement stated that 'Seclusion should be used as a last resort, for the shortest possible time. Seclusion should not be used as a punishment or threat; as part of a treatment programme; because of shortage of staff; where there is any risk of suicide or self-harm.'[175]

Seclusion is resorted to in extreme cases, as an emergency procedure, that is when there is a significant risk that the person presenting the challenging behaviour poses a physical threat to other people and no other method of management has proved effective in preventing the possibility of harm being caused. Seclusion cannot be used where the threat is only of a destructive nature, that is, directed at objects in the environment.

---

[174] Attention Deficit Hyperactivity Disorder
[175] [2002] 2 WLR 1876

Seclusion is a difficult experience for people who are subjected to it. Being denied their freedom of movement, confined within a place and set apart from others, all under the watchful eyes of a carer can be interpreted as a form of imprisonment, which implies the elements of fault, responsibility and punishment. Other people, for example some people with autism, may actually prefer seclusion to being held by another person.

The Joint Review by the Royal College of Psychiatrists and Royal College of Nursing entitled *Strategies for the management of disturbed and violent patients in psychiatric units* provides some more guidance on the use of seclusion.[176]

Time-out

In contrast to seclusion, time-out is a method which can be part of a therapeutic programme to manage a challenging behaviour. The individual with challenging behaviour is taken away from a place or an activity that is considered rewarding to them when their behaviour becomes unmanageable. The person is not necessarily confined, but can merely be taken out of a room or a few paces away from where an activity is being held.

Time-out is defined in paragraph 19.9 of the Mental Health Act 1983 Code of Practice as 'a behaviour modification technique which denies a patient for a period of time (lasting from a few seconds to no more than fifteen minutes) opportunities to participate in an activity or to obtain positive reinforcers following (normally immediately) an incident of unacceptable or unwanted behaviour, and which then returns the patient to his/her original environment. Time out should never include the use of a locked room.'

The concept is similar to that of seclusion. Where, however, the latter's aim is to contain an individual's behaviour, time-out is concerned with teaching the person to replace or alter a challenging behaviour with a more acceptable or manageable one. The use of time-out, as a psychological strategy 'should be based on a proper functional analysis rather than a spontaneous reaction to unwanted behaviour'.[177] Failure to understand this distinction can lead to cases of abuse, that is when time-out is, in practice, just another word for seclusion.

4.3 The use of medication as an intervention

4.3.1 Medical treatment and issues of consent and capacity

Certain 'psychoactive' and 'anti-psychotic' medications are used in the treatment of challenging behaviours. How effective they are is arguable. Some studies seem to show that anti-psychotic medications are not very effective.[178] Despite this, there are also findings to show that people with a learning disability and challenging behaviour will face medicated treatment more often than any other people in society[179] and instead of environmental changes or 'positive behavioural support'.[180]

---

[176] Council Report 41, approved by Council March 1996, http://www.rcpsych.ac.uk/publications/cr/cr41.htm (CR 41)

[177] supra n.82, CR 41, refer to p.14

[178] Brylewski J & Duggan L, Anti-psychotic medication for challenging behaviour in people with intellectual disability: a systematic review of randomised controlled trials, *Journal of Intellectual Disability Research*, 43, 1999, pages 360–371

[179] Kiernan C, Reeves D & Alborz A, The Use of Anti-psychotic Drugs with Adults with Learning Disability and Challenging Behaviour, *Journal of Intellectual Disability Research*, 39, 1995, pages 263–274

[180] Emerson E, Robertson J, Gregory N, Hatton C, Kessissoglou S, Hallam A & Hillery J, the Treatment and Management of Challenging Behaviours, supra n.96

It is argued that the reason behind the continued use of psychotropic medication in the management of challenging behaviour is due to a need to reduce the prevalence of such behaviour rather than working with the individual with the challenging behaviour.

There are various forms of psychotropic drugs, such as antipsychotics, anxiolytics, antimanics, antidepressants, antiepileptics, stimulants and opiate antagonists, which were originally used in cases of mental illness such as schizophrenia.[181] Yet despite the lack of relation (ie formal diagnosis) between challenging behaviour and mental illness, these drugs have in the past been widely used to manage challenging behaviours. Cullen goes on to say that there is a general concern about the issue of using psychotropic medication in dealing with challenging behaviours. 'The concerns include:

- the relatively high rates of prescribing;

- the common incidence of poly-pharmacy;

- detrimental side-effects from some drugs that are often not closely monitored;

- lack of an evidence base;

- absence of data to determine whether or not drugs are having an effect.'[182]

Nevertheless, psychotropic drugs are still used, either as part of a therapeutic treatment or in an emergency situation. In the case of a therapeutic treatment the issue of consent is raised and, with it, the question of capacity. In the case of an emergency use of the medication the possible offence of battery becomes an issue.

These concerns have been voiced more recently by Brylewski and Duggan:[183] 'Evaluation of these treatments requires urgent attention. Until then, clinical practice in relation to this vulnerable group will be based on opinion, judgement and fashion, rather than evidence.'

4.3.2 Consent and capacity to give such consent

'"Consent" is the voluntary and continuing permission of the patient to receive a particular treatment, based on an adequate knowledge of the purpose, nature, likely effects and risks of that treatment including the likelihood of its success and any alternatives to it.'[184]

Consent should usually be sought and given before any medical care, treatment or examination is undergone on a patient. 'Treating [a patient] without their [consent] or despite a refusal of consent will constitute the civil wrong of trespass to the person and may constitute a crime.'[185]

The rules for valid consent will vary according to the nature of the condition that needs treating, that is whether it is a physical or mental disorder (the latter being covered by the Mental Health Act 1983). However, in general, for consent to be valid three elements are required:

---

[181] Kennedy CH & Meyer KA, The Use of Psychotropic Medication for People with Severe Disabilities and Challenging Behaviour: current status and future directions, *Journal of the Association for Persons with Severe Handicaps*, 23, 1998, pp. 83–97

[182] supra, n.11, Cullen 1999, refer to p. 7

[183] Brylewski and Duggan, 2003, cited by Allen D at BILD Physical Interventions conference 2003

[184] Department of Health and Welsh Office, *Code of Practice, Mental Health Act 1983* (MHA'83), published August 1993, para 15.12

[185] *Re T* [1993] Fam 95

1. The person giving the consent must have the capacity to do so.[186]

Capacity is the right to express one's mind by determining what is the best or chosen course of action to be taken in a given situation. The concept of capacity implies that a person has the ability to comprehend the nature of his or her condition and the proposed treatment. The person must understand the information and the possible consequences of consenting or not to such a treatment, and be able to make a decision based on the understanding of the information provided. The level of capacity required depends on the seriousness or gravity of the decision that needs to be taken, and so capacity is reviewed on a case-by-case basis.

The basic principles of capacity are laid out both in the Department of Health's *Reference Guide to Consent for Examination and Treatment* (henceforward referred to as the Reference Guide) and in the Mental Health Act 1983 *Code of Practice* (henceforward referred to as the Code of Practice). According to the Code of Practice a patient has capacity if he or she shows the ability to:

- understand what medical treatment is, that somebody has said that he or she needs it and why the treatment is being proposed;

- understand in broad terms the nature of the proposed treatment;

- understand its principal benefits and risks;

- understand what will be the consequences of not receiving the proposed treatment;

- possess the capacity to make a choice.[187]

Any consent provided must be given voluntarily and on the basis that the patient has received sufficient information to enable him or her to reach an informed decision.[188]

Once it is established that the patient understands the particular situation, that is, has capacity, his or her decision to consent or not is valid whether the reasons behind the decision are (un)reasonable, (ir)rational, (un)known or (non)existent.

A patient's choice to withhold consent to a life-saving treatment must be respected, even if they later die, once they have been recognised as having mental capacity.[189]

It is assumed that adults automatically have legal capacity. However, if there are any doubts about a person's capacity, the medical staff are required to proceed to an assessment of the patient's capacity. Where an assessment is made that the individual is unable to give consent no one, under the current law in England, Wales and Northern Ireland, is able to give consent to the examination and treatment of an adult. Therefore, as the Reference Guide states 'parents, relatives or members of the healthcare team can *not* consent on behalf of such an adult'.[190] As the Guide goes on to state, however, 'in certain circumstances it will be lawful to carry out such examinations or treatment'. The Guide emphasises that a key principle concerning treatment of the incapable adult is that of a person's best interests. 'Best interests', it states, 'are not confined

---

[186] For detailed guidance on what this may include see the *Reference Guide to Consent for Examination and Treatment* produced by the Department of Health, 2001.
[187] supra, n.43, Code of Practice MHA'83, para 15.10
[188] See *Reference Guide* at pp. 5 and 6
[189] *B v An NHS Trust* [2002] All ER (D) 362
[190] See Chapter 2 para 1 *Reference Guide* at n.186 above

to best *medical* interests' and the Guide states that 'case-law has established that other factors which may need to be taken into account include the patients' values and preferences at any stage when they may have been competent, their psychological health, well-being, quality of life, relationships with family or other carers, spiritual and religious welfare and their own financial interests.'[191] The Guide goes on to state that 'it is good practice for the healthcare team to involve those close to the patient in order to find out about the patient's values and preferences before loss of capacity, unless the patient has previously made clear that particular individuals should not be involved.' The Guide also suggests, as is borne out by the following consideration of case-law, that the High Court can give a ruling on these matters and on the lawfulness or unlawfulness of a proposed procedure. The Guide stresses however that certain procedures must be referred to the court for determination before they can be undertaken in relation to adults with incapacity, and these include:

- sterilisation for contraceptive purposes;

- donation of regenerative tissue such as bone marrow;

- withdrawal of nutrition and hydration from a patient in a persistent vegetative state;

- where there is doubt as to the patient's capacity or best interests.[192]

In *St George's Healthcare NHS Trust v S (Guidelines)* 1999[193] a pregnant woman was advised by her social worker and the doctors that she should have a Caesarean operation due to her suffering from preeclampsia. She refused to follow the advice as she wanted a natural birth. However, the social worker first had her admitted into a mental hospital under Section 2 of the Mental Health Act 1983, then was granted a declaration that it was legal to operate on the woman despite her lack of consent. Once she gave birth to her baby, she released herself from the hospital where, apart from the operation, she had had no other treatment imposed on her to deal with any mental illness. On appeal, the court decided that an individual could refuse treatment even though his or her life depends on it.

As regards capacity, the court gave the following guidelines:

> 'If the capacity of the patient is seriously in doubt it should be assessed as a matter of priority. In many such cases the patient's general practitioner or other responsible doctor may be sufficiently qualified to make the necessary assessment, but in serious or complex cases involving difficult issues about the future health and well-being or even the life of the patient, the issue of capacity should be examined by an independent psychiatrist.'

It should be noted, however, that the assessment is only concerned with the patient's ability to comprehend the information given to him or her in order to make his or her decision; it is not concerned with the soundness or reasonableness of the decision.[194]

In *Re C (Adult: Refusal of Medical Treatment)* 1994[195] a mentally disordered patient had a gangrenous foot but refused an amputation which according to medical advice would save his life. The court decided that the patient's mental state was not so impaired as to negate his

---

[191] See *Reference Guide* n.186 Chapter 2 p.12
[192] *Reference Guide* n.186 at p.13
[193] [1999] Fam 26
[194] *Re T* [1993] Fam 95
[195] [1994] 1 WLR 290

capacity to understand his situation and the consequences of such a decision. Therefore his capacity in this regard was accepted. It also turns out that the patient did survive his gangrene without any amputation.

Therefore, a person can make a decision based on his spiritual, religious and philosophical beliefs, and need not justify his reasons; but if the decision is based upon a misconception or denial of his condition and possible treatments, it may be argued that the person lacks capacity. In such a case, medical doctors can go against a patient's wishes if they feel that it is in the best interest of the patient.

In _Re F (Mental Patient: Sterilisation)_ 1990,[196] a sexually active woman with learning disabilities was deemed incapable of giving or withholding her consent to an operation that would sterilise her. A court order was issued at the request of her mother and carers rendering legal such an operation despite her lack of consent as it was considered in her best interest – from a mental health point of view – that she should not be subjected to any risk of future pregnancy.

The 'best interest' principle is said to mean that the treatment is:

- necessary to save life or prevent a deterioration or ensure an improvement in the patient's physical or mental health; and

- in accordance with a practice accepted at the time by a responsible body of medical opinion skilled in the particular form of treatment in question.[197]

The best interests, however, are not exclusively concerned with medical issues. It also implies looking at the patient's wishes, overall well-being (psychological, financial, spiritual) and their concerns about family life.

The Law Commission Report 231 on Mental Capacity adds the following factors to be considered when making a decision on behalf of a person who has not the capacity to do so:

(1) the ascertainable past and present wishes and feelings of the person concerned and the factors which he or she would consider if able to do so;

(2) the need to permit and encourage the person concerned to participate, or to improve his or her ability to participate, in anything done for and any decision affecting him or her;

(3) if it is practicable and appropriate to consult them, the views as to that person's wishes and feelings and as to what would be in the best interests of that person of:

(i) any person named by him or her as someone to be consulted;

(ii) any person (such as a spouse, relative or friend or other person) engaged in caring for or interested in the person's welfare;

(iii) the donee of a continuing power of attorney granted by him or her;

(iv) any manager appointed by the court; and

(4) whether the purpose for which any action or decision is required can be as effectively achieved in a manner less restrictive of the person's freedom of action.[198]

---

[196] [1990] 2 AC 1
[197] Code of Practice Mental Health Act 1983, para.15.19
[198] _Mental Incapacity_ – Law Commission Report 231, A Summary of the Law Commission's Recommendations, http://www.lawcom.gov.uk/library/lc231/summary.htm

The case of _Re MB_ 1997[199] defines incapacity as:

> '_some impairment or disturbance of mental functioning, which renders the person unable to make a decision whether to consent to or to refuse treatment. That inability to make a decision will occur when:_
>
> - _the person is unable to comprehend and retain the information which is material to the decision, especially as to the likely consequences of having or not having the treatment in question;_
>
> - _the patient is unable to use the information and weigh it in the balance as part of the process of arriving at a decision.'_

As regards children, their capacity will vary according to their age. Any young person between the ages of 16 and 18 is recognised as having the capacity to give consent (unless proven otherwise). The matter is different for children under 16. (see Chapter 2.)

Young people who are under the age of 16 can sometimes give consent as long as they are fully aware of their condition and the suggested treatments, and understand the information to make a decision. It is acknowledged that children can attain a certain degree of maturity that enables them to comprehend certain situations. Therefore, a child under 16 can consent to certain interventions, and not to others, depending on the gravity and the complexity of the decision. This concept is known as the 'Gillick competence' and is summarised in the case of _Gillick v West Norfolk and Wisbech AHA_ 1986,[200] in which a mother sought to challenge the legality of a fourteen-year-old girl consenting to receive contraceptive advice and/or treatment from her doctor without her parent's knowledge.

The Court of Appeal decided that 'as a matter of law the parental right to determine whether or not their minor child below the age of 16 will have medical treatment terminates if and when the child achieves sufficient understanding and intelligence to enable him to understand fully what is proposed'. In other words, it is recognised that a child under 16 can be legally capable of giving or refusing consent to a treatment if they show enough maturity, intelligence and comprehension as to the nature and implications of such a treatment. Although it is also acknowledged that parents are often the best judges as to what is in the best interest of their child, in some rare cases, the doctor might be the one best qualified to make that judgement. What happens in a dispute between the parents and the doctors is discussed briefly in Part I Chapter 2 at para 2.9.3(b).

2. The person giving the consent must be sufficiently informed as to the nature, purpose, potential risks and consequences of the proposed treatments, as well as to any alternative therapeutic methods available.

S.14.13(a) of the Mental Health Act 1983 provides that 'the patient must be informed, in terms which he is likely to understand, of the nature, purpose and likely effects of the treatment proposed'.

As was stated by Lord Bridge in _Sidaway_ 1985,[201] doctors' professional functions involve three phases: diagnosis, advice and treatment. As regards diagnosis and treatment, the test for the

---

[199] [1997] 2 FLR
[200] [1986] AC 112
[201] _Sidaway v Board of Governors of the Bethlem Royal Hospital_ [1985] AC 871

duty of care owed by the doctors to their patient is known as the Bolam test,[202] that is 'the standard of the ordinary skilled man exercising and professing to have special skill'.

Mrs Sidaway sued her neuro-surgeon for negligence as, she argued, he did not disclose sufficient information about the risk of an operation that could affect her spinal cord and leave her disabled (which is what actually happened). Her claim was dismissed at first instance, on appeal and finally by the House of Lords. Their lordships decided that the Bolam test would also apply to doctors' duty to inform their patients. In other words, a doctor will not be negligently liable if he acted in a manner that is considered to be current good practice by a responsible body of medical experts as regards a particular form of treatment and the information to be provided.

Lord Bridge thus stated that the decision as to how much information should be disclosed to enable the patient to make a decision about treatment is primarily a question of clinical judgement. He also added that 'the judge might in certain circumstances come to the conclusion that disclosure of a particular risk was so obviously necessary to an informed choice on the part of the patient that no reasonably prudent medical man would fail to make it'. The cases Lord Bridge was referring to are operations that involve a substantial risk of grave adverse consequences.

There is also the suggestion that if there is a 10% chance that the risk is likely to happen following the recommended treatment, this corresponds to a 'significant risk' and doctors should give the appropriate warning to their patients. This view was confirmed in _Pearce v United Bristol Healthcare NHS Trust_ 1999,[203] in which failure to inform a pregnant woman who was 14 days beyond term that delaying the birth could result in the baby being stillborn was not deemed negligent. Indeed, it was argued that the risk was only estimated at 0.2%. In practice, as doctors come under greater pressure from the threat of litigation, they explain the degree of risk more fully.

3. The consent must be given freely and voluntarily.

The Mental Health Act 1983 provides that 'permission given under any unfair or undue pressure is not "consent"' (para 15.12). Moreover, patients must be advised of their right to withdraw their consent to a treatment at any time before it is undergone.[204] The General Medical Council[205] advises doctors to review the patient's decision to consent to treatment, especially in the following circumstances:

- significant time has elapsed between obtaining consent and the start of treatment;

- there have been material changes in the patient's condition, or in any aspects of the proposed treatment plan, which might invalidate the patient's existing consent;

- new, potentially relevant information has become available, for example about the risks of the treatment, or about other treatment options.[206]

---

[202] From the case _Bolam v Friern Hospital Management Committee_ [1957] 1 WLR 582, which will be referred to more extensively in the section concerning the civil offence of negligence.

[203] (1999) 48 BMLR 118

[204] s.14.13(a) Mental Health Act 1983

[205] http://www.gmc-uk.org/standards/default.htm, _Seeking patients' consent: the ethical considerations_ (Nov 1998), GMC

[206] supra. n.205, GMC, para 32

4.3.3 Forms of consent The GMC states in its ethical guidance section that doctors must consider both the extent of their patients' understanding of the nature and implications of the proposed treatment as well as the form in which consent is given.

'Patients can indicate their informed consent either orally or in writing. In some cases, the nature of the risks to which the patient might be exposed make it important that a written record is available of the patient's consent and other wishes in relation to the proposed investigation and treatment. (...)

Except in an emergency, where the patient has capacity to give consent you should obtain written consent in cases where:

- *the treatment or procedure is complex, or involves significant risks and/or side effects;*

- *providing clinical care is not the primary purpose of the investigation or examination;*

- *there may be significant consequences for the patient's employment, social or personal life;*

- *the treatment is part of a research programme.'*[207]

Implied consent is when a patient's conduct can be interpreted as complying with the doctor's directions, such as: lying on an examination table, or offering one's arm for blood test. However, the GMC warns that medical professionals should be careful not to imply consent too readily and argues that 'a patient's apparent compliance with a procedure (...) does not in itself indicate that the patient has understood what [the medical professionals] propose to do and why'.[208]

4.3.4 Consent to medical treatment and the Human Rights Act 1998 In the case of _R (on the application of John Wilkinson) v Broadmoor Hospital_ 2001,[209] the doctors at Broadmoor Hospital were responsible for the care of a psychiatric patient who suffered from a personality disorder. They recommended that the patient should undergo a medicated treatment which would involve the use of anti-psychotic drugs. However, the patient refused the treatment. Despite his refusal to consent to treatment, and the fact that there were contradictory opinions as to his incapacity to consent, one of the doctors obtained a certificate of authorisation under the terms of the Mental Health Act 1983 to allow him to proceed with the treatment. The doctor felt that it would be appropriate to resort to physical restraint in order to apply the treatment as the patient's reaction to compulsory medication would be one of great anxiety and agitation and might involve an aggressive behaviour on his part.

The patient started judicial proceedings challenging the decision to impose the treatment on him arguing that this was a violation of the European Convention on Human Rights, namely Article 2 (right to life), 3 (prohibition of torture), 6 (fair trial), 8 (respect for private and family life) and 14 (prohibition of discrimination). In the first instance he was refused the right to have the medical witnesses cross-examined. He therefore appealed to the Court of Appeal.

[207] supra. n.205, GMC, para.27
[208] supra. n.205, GMC, para.31
[209] [2001] EWCA Civ 1545

The Court of Appeal held: that national courts have to consider issues of convention rights since the introduction of the Human Rights Act 1998; that they have competence to reach their own views on the merits of a medical decision; and that they must observe whether a patient's European Convention rights would be infringed.

Lord Justice Brown stated: 'the court must inevitably now reach its own view both as to whether this appellant is indeed incapable of consenting (or refusing consent) to the treatment programme planned for him by [the doctor] and, depending upon the court's conclusion on that issue, as to whether the proposed forcible administration of such treatment (a) would threaten the appellant's life and so be impermissible under Article 2, (b) would be degrading and so impermissible under Article 3, and (c) would not be justifiable as both necessary and proportionate under Article 8.2 given the extent to which it would invade the appellant's right to privacy'. He stated, however, that Article 14 did not seem to add anything to the debate.

Lord Justice Brown finally concluded that 'it is the appellant's case in this regard that a number of his civil rights are affected by the [doctor's] decisions to subject him to forcible treatment and that he is accordingly entitled to a determination by an independent and impartial tribunal of the lawfulness of the interference with those rights'. Article 6 of the Convention would thus be respected, although this Article does not necessarily imply that a mental patient can always challenge a treatment plan before its implementation. The patient in this case was entitled to challenge the doctor's decision to impose forcibly a treatment on him.

[See Section 4.1 above on Best Practice in Dealing with Challenging Behaviour, and the discussion above with regard to The Use of Medication.]

4.4 Control and restraint

Control and restraint approaches emerged from the Prison service and were also commonly employed in Special Hospitals. Eventually, control and restraint techniques were taught in learning disability services and with training which may include breakaway techniques, control techniques and protective equipment (eg protective shields) and infliction of calculated pain as a means of control over an individual.

Today 'control and restraint' refers to a wide range of models and techniques, which may include any of the techniques described above. However, pain compliance is less common as the calculated use of pain to control an individual with learning disabilities is considered inappropriate.

Control and restraint techniques eventually came under scrutiny and heavy criticism after official enquiries were conducted at Ashworth Hospital (1992) and Broadmoor Hospital (1992), and in a Report from the Royal College of Psychiatrists (1995).[210]

---

[210] For an account of these reports and criticisms, see http://fp.prtraining.f9.co.uk/history.htm Positive response – History

4.5 Restraining garments

These include such equipment as the straight-jacket, 'a harness to prevent a child wandering in the nights, splints or gloves to prevent self-injury or occlusive devices to prevent tooth-grinding',[211] use of straps and wedges.

4.6 A consideration of Guidance issued by the Department of Health in respect of the Permissible Forms of Control in Children's Residential Care – Circular 93/13

4.6.1 Introduction and Background   Although it is now some ten years old, the Guidance issued by the Department of Health in respect of the *Permissible Forms of Control in Children's Residential Care* is described as still being the current applicable Guidance in the Guidance on Physical Interventions issued in July 2002 and is now considered in some detail. Although this Guidance does not refer specifically to the care and control of children with learning disabilities who also present severe challenging behaviour, the Guidance the DoH gives, in relation to children of normal capacities, may be of varying relevance to children with learning disabilities who also present severe challenging behaviour.

Certain parts of the document are more pertinent to this report than others, thus the focus is on those relevant sections and the information given herein draws very heavily on that document.

This report considers *The Department of Health Guidance on Permissible Forms of Control in Children's Residential Homes* for very specific reasons. It is probable that children with learning disabilities who also present severe challenging behaviour will spend some time in a residential setting either as part of a weekend respite programme, or as short term respite care or perhaps when a carer is incapacitated. This group of children is likely to need more frequent controlling which is lengthier in duration and more intense in nature than for children of more normal capacities. As a result, such children may be more susceptible to abuse. The Guidance given by the Department of Health states which sanctions may be used and the procedures to be followed when such sanctions are in operation. Such Guidance is important and essential in the care and control of normal children, not just the children who are the subject of the report.

In addition as has been noted elsewhere, (see Part 1 Chapter 1) the DfES has issued a number of Circulars dealing with issues relating to pupil behaviour, (see for example the Guidance on Physical Interventions discussed at 4.2 above) and yet more are under discussion currently. Thus the Department has recently issued *Guidance on the use of restrictive physical interventions for pupils with severe behavioural difficulties* (LEA/0264/2003). (See the detailed discussion on these developments at para 1.2.3.1 above).

Again, as is stated in Part 1 Chapter 1, *The Mental Health Act 1993 Code of Practice* (the Department of Health and Welsh Office, 1993) also contains invaluable guidance but constant reference is made to this document throughout this report and considering it in this chapter would have led to needless duplication. The Code of Practice has also been published by HMSO and is a document which is perhaps more generally accessible (than the Circulars) to members of the public who might consider it relevant to their situations.

---

[211] supra n.210, CR 41

The Department of Health *(Guidance on Permissible Forms of Control in Children's Residential Care,* Department of Health LAC (93) 13) issued in April 1993 thus provides guidelines concerning forms of control in children's residential care but not in any other setting. The Guidance does not relate to the specific problems of children with learning disabilities who also present severe challenging behaviour. Clearly, such children represent unique problems in terms of permissible forms of control, which need to be specifically addressed. Furthermore, the guidelines relate solely to children in children's residential homes. This leaves those professionals in hospitals, schools and day centres technically outside the scope of the recommendations, but many local authorities, as has been noted, have decided to apply the guidelines to all their local establishments even though they are not required by law to do so.

It might, however, be useful to set out here for the information of parents and carers those provisions of the Guidance which might be deemed to be of some relevance or have some bearing on the issues arising from the care and control of children with learning disabilities who also present severe challenging behaviour. There are, of course, dangers in summarising or extracting sections from such Guidance and parents, carers and other professionals would obviously be well advised to read the whole of the Guidance issued by the Department of Health which for space reasons it is impossible to reproduce here. The Guidance is divided into some twelve sections.

Section 1: Introduction

In the introductory section the Department acknowledges that children placed in children's residential homes have tended to be older and more severely disturbed than their predecessors. The need for the proper care and control of these young people has been highlighted by two major factors:

(a) a recognition that existing Guidance issued pursuant to The Children Act 1989 did not offer enough positive advice about the control of often volatile young people; and

(b) increasing concern by the Government and the wider public that the current framework might be perceived as having gone too far in stressing the rights of children at the expense of upholding the rights and responsibilities of parents and professionals in supervising them. The Guidance on permissible forms of control is therefore to be seen, says the Department of Health, as part of the Government's efforts to adopt a concerted approach to these issues, an approach now consolidated with the issuing by the DfEE of Circular 10/98 on *Section 550A Education Act 1996 and the Use of Force to Control or Restrain Pupils* and the issuing by the DfES and the DoH of the *Guidance on Physical Interventions* in 2002. This Introduction goes on to stress that the aim must be to create an environment which gives a definite structure and sense of order to the lives of these children, in which they can develop and be educated. If that, and the associated control and discipline are lacking, they are likely to experience further difficulties when they leave residential care.

It is emphasised that this Guidance applies to children's residential homes run by local authorities, voluntary organisations and private bodies. It does not extend to psychiatric wards and schools (except those schools which are registered children's homes), but these are now covered by the Physical Interventions Guidance.

Even based on what is said in the Introduction, it is clear that the Guidance does not address practically the problems encountered by those caring for children with learning disabilities coupled with severe challenging behaviour.

Section II: The law relating to interventions to restrain or restrict the liberty of children in care

Section II refers to the fact that the legal constraints on physical intervention to restrain or restrict liberty in the childcare field derive principally from The Children Act 1989. It should be noted, however, that the provisions which are referred to are exclusively those relating to the use of secure accommodation as provided in section 25 Children Act 1989 (hereinafter referred to as CA 1989). It should be noted that those provisions in Parts VI to VIII of the Act and Regulations issued pursuant thereto, which deal with the regulation of children's homes, provided by local authorities, voluntary organisations and private bodies, and all other provisions were drawn up with reference to children of normal capacities and understanding. Both the provisions of the CA 1989 and the consequent regulations have then had to be interpreted and expanded upon in the advice issued by the Department of Health. Aside, therefore, from the conditions which are laid down in section 25 with regard to the use of secure accommodation, there are no other provisions contained in the Children Act 1989 itself relating to the use of any restraint or the imposition of any restriction of liberty with regard to children who are not being looked after by local authorities either in their own children's homes or in homes provided by voluntary organisations or private bodies. While the Guidance refers readers on to the Children's Homes Regulations 1991, the Children (Secure Accommodation) Regulations 1991 and the Children (Secure (Accommodation) (No. 2) Regulations 1991, it should again be noted that these regulations have now been updated and replaced by the Children's Homes Regulations 2002 (DoH 2002) and the National Minimum Standards for Children in Residential Care (DoH 2002). It should also be noted that these regulations apply only in the context of children in residential care, while there are separate regulations and Minimum Standards governing the position of children in foster placements. These are to be found in the new Fostering Services Regulations 2002 (DoH 2002) and the new National Minimum Standards for Fostering. (see DoH 2002) Nevertheless, the Guidance does go on to point out that, even in relation to the care of these children, the common law position on unlawful restriction of liberty and the criminal law relating to assault will also be relevant and it suggested that guidance on these areas would have to be sought from local authority lawyers. This is even more so the case when considering generally the position of children with learning disabilities who also present severe challenging behaviour in other than residential child care settings.

Section III: Children remanded or detained within local authority accommodation

Section III deals with children remanded to or detained within local authority accommodation under Criminal Justice Provisions and will not be further considered here.

Section IV: The restriction of liberty

Section IV deals with the restriction of liberty and the use of accommodation for such purpose. Generally speaking, the Guidance advises that this is only to be done in accordance with the provisions of Section 25, ie by using accommodation specifically provided for the purpose of restricting liberty ('secure accommodation'). As to what constitutes such accommodation is ultimately a matter, says the Department, which must be determined by the court but nevertheless the Guidance recognises that action may need to be taken to restrict the liberty of children which falls short of locking them up. The Department advises that such action should be restricted to circumstances where immediate action is necessary to prevent injury to any person or damage to property and that local authorities should seek legal advice when formulating their guidance to staff. The Guidance continues by saying that, 'in the ordinary course of maintaining control over a child or children, an adult may tell them to do things which they do not want to accept, including refusal of permission to leave the building'. If a child complies with reasonable instructions, the question of restricting liberty by the use of accommodation does not normally arise. In the case of children with learning disabilities who also present severe challenging behaviour it is likely that some of the children will not comprehend either the concept of refusal of permission to leave the building or compliance with reasonable instructions. The DoH Guidance does not deal in this section with that problem. The Guidance states that 'for a young child, the potential danger in leaving a home is real and obvious, and the case for action to prevent this is clear. In addition to physically restraining such a child, it may be necessary to hold or closely supervise him for a matter of hours to ensure he does not run off. However, for an adolescent whose absence from the home is judged unlikely to lead to injury or serious damage, physical restraint would be inappropriate.' Again, in relation to children with learning disabilities who also present severe challenging behaviour, it would appear that as a result of this advice carers might be engaged in prolonged periods of holding or close supervision of young children and of physical restraint of adolescents, since their absence from the home is almost certainly likely to lead to injury to themselves or others, or to serious damage and thus physical restraint is implicitly appropriate.

The DoH Guidance explicitly recognises that there are practical limitations on the ability of staff to prevent young people of normal understanding running away from an open children's home and the Guidance states that 'where there is concern for a child likely to run away and suffer significant harm or inflict injury, then consideration should be given to whether the criteria for placement in secure accommodation can be satisfied'. In most cases of children with learning disabilities who also present severe challenging behaviour this would not be an appropriate response.

The last paragraph of this section provides that 'if staff require a child to remain in a building or part of a building for an unreasonable length of time without relief, then this may constitute the use of accommodation to restrict liberty, even though no actual locking up is involved. This will depend upon circumstances **including the space available to the child within which he is restricted, his age, competence and physical and emotional well-being**' (authors' emphasis added). It is strongly suggested that this direction to have regard to both the nature of the child's restriction and to the child's competence, would allow those caring for children with learning disabilities who also present severe challenging behaviour to take functionally and specifically appropriate action to provide for their care, control and safety. Such action will in many cases have to go beyond that which would be taken in relation to children without learning disabilities and challenging behaviour. Staff on CSCI Inspection teams must receive the appropriate training and guidance in order to be able to recognise when such action is both appropriate and necessary to preserve the best interests of the child.

Section V: Physical restraint

Section V of the Guidance deals with those situations in which the Children's Homes Regulations 1991 might be applicable, although these have now been replaced by the 2002 regulations. Both the 1991 and the 2002 Regulations detail the disciplinary measures which are prohibited in children's homes and included within these is corporal punishment. The Guidance on Permissible Forms of Control in Children's Residential Care points out that 'the Regulations do allow for action to be taken in an emergency'. Thus, Section 8(3)(b) of the Children's Homes Regulations 1991 provided that the taking of any action immediately necessary to prevent injury to any person, or serious damage to property, is not prohibited. Injury, in this context, means 'significant injury and could include for example actual or grievous bodily harm, physical or sexual abuse, risking the lives of or injury to, the self or others by wilful or reckless behaviour and self-poisoning. It must be possible to show that, unless immediate action had been taken, there were strong indicators that injury would follow.' The Guidance on permissible forms of control in children's residential care defines physical restraint as being 'the positive application of force with the intention of overpowering the child in order to protect the child from harming himself or others or seriously damaging property'. This is what was referred to earlier in the introduction as *lawful excuse*.

The Guidance further goes on to advise that 'a staff member who has reason to be concerned about a young person who indicates his intention to leave without permission, or run away, should take vigorous action which includes issuing clear instructions and warnings about the consequences of non-compliance; the use of the staff member's physical presence to obstruct an exit and thereby create an opportunity to express concern and remonstrate with the child; and also holding the child by the arm to reinforce a point or secure the child's attention'. It is clear from this portion of the Guidance that an excuse or a justification is being provided for action which would otherwise technically amount to the crime, and or tort, of assault. The Guidance continues that 'where it is clear that if the young person were to leave the unit and there was a strong likelihood of injury to himself or others, *it would be reasonable to use physical restraint* [as defined above] to prevent him from leaving'.

It should be noted, however, that in the context of dealing with children with learning disabilities who also present severe challenging behaviour, the use of physical restraint rather than other approaches such as withdrawal or even locking in a room may exacerbate the situation. Further advice provided in Section V(5) states that 'physical restraint should avert danger by preventing or deflecting a child's action, or perhaps by removing a physical object which could be used to harm himself or others. Physical restraint skilfully applied may be eased by degrees as the child calms down in response to the physical contact.' The Guidance then sets out in summary form the basic principles already described relating to the use of physical restraint, which also emphasise that restraint should be an act of care and control and not punishment, and that physical restraint should not be used to force compliance with staff instructions when there is no immediate risk to people or property.

The recognition in this portion of the Guidance of the extremes to which it might be necessary to resort in the course of dealing with children without learning disabilities, serves to emphasise that the actions of parents or carers seeking to care for children with learning disabilities who also present severe challenging behaviour, may be viewed in a rather different light. As has been stated repeatedly already in this report, actions need to be viewed by practitioners according to functionally and specifically appropriate criteria.

Section VI: The care and control of children outside the home

The next section (Section VI) deals with the care and control of children who make trips outside the residential care setting and provides no guidance of direct relevance to children with learning disabilities who also present severe challenging behaviour other than the single sentence which says that 'there may be children for whom going out presents risks of harm to themselves or getting into trouble' (para 6.1).

Section VII: Positive care practices aimed at creating an environment conducive to good care and control

Section VII deals with positive care practices aimed at creating an environment conducive to good care and control. This section again envisages dealing with children with whom one might be able to establish a dialogue but it does not seem to encompass situations where one might be dealing with children with learning disabilities who also present severe challenging behaviour with whom dialogue may not be possible. One point, however, is worth mentioning in that it could be said to be of general application to all those looking after children who are not parents or permanent substitute carers. This is contained in para 7.4 and provides that 'managers *[for this substitute any person looking after the child]* must ensure that their staff are familiar with the relevant histories of children for whom they have responsibilities. Staff should take this into account in deciding how they respond to a child, and in making judgements about making appropriate interventions. This history should be noted in care plans which may include agreed approaches to the control of individual children who present particular behavioural difficulties.'

Section VIII: How the age, understanding and competence of a child can bear on appropriate methods of control

This is the most useful section of the Guidance for the purposes of those dealing with children with learning disabilities who also present severe challenging behaviour. This remains the case even after the issuing of the Guidance on Physical interventions in 2002. Paragraph 8.3 provides that 'children of any age may have an impaired ability to recognise and understand danger. This may, for example, be because of serious learning disabilities, autism or severe emotional disorder. For such children there may be a need to take action including the use of physical restraint, and the need for physical intervention may be more frequent.' The Guidance further states that brief periods of withdrawal away from the group into a calming environment may be more effective for the severely agitated child than holding or physical restraint. Indeed parent representatives on the Learning Disabilities Sub-Committee Working Party at the Mental Health Foundation back in 1993 pointed out that in relation to autistic children in particular, the use of holding or the application of physical restraint would result in an exacerbation of their challenging behaviour. Paragraph 8.4 advises that in homes which look after such children there will be a particular need to ensure that children do not have unsupervised access to unsafe areas including outside of the house or grounds. The safety of the child is said to be 'important'. It is suggested that homes should adopt normal domestic approaches to security, including for example, the locking of all external doors at night. The Guidance advises that the reasonable application of these practices would not constitute restriction of liberty.

Paragraph 8.5 states that the use of locked doors should not be an easy means of saving staff time or to keep their numbers inappropriately low. Nevertheless, this very statement envisages that there may be times and circumstances in which the use of locked doors may be deemed to be appropriate and this issue is explored further in this report. Paragraph 8.5 goes on to state that staff should be energetic in their efforts to find ways of keeping each child safe which minimise the need for physical control and restriction of liberty. The final paragraph of Section VIII may give some cause for concern in that it advises that 'on no account should children be locked into their bedrooms at night whatever their age and competence. However, in some circumstances, close night-time supervision may be required.'

The advice that children should never be locked into their bedrooms at night can of course raise questions of interpretation with regard to the meaning of the phrase 'locked into' but can also invite total disagreement. Bearing in mind the consideration which has been given earlier at para 2.9 of Part 1 Chapter 2 to the concept of 'responsible' parenthood, there may well be situations in which parents or other carers might be deemed to be acting irresponsibly in relation to the child with learning disabilities, who also presents severe challenging behaviour, if they were not to take action to prevent the child exposing him or herself to danger. No-one could reasonably suggest that a young child without learning disabilities be left alone in a house with unlocked doors leading to a main road, during the daytime. Yet at night time leaving a child of no or very little understanding of what may constitute a serious risk to himself or others in an unlocked bedroom with access to all manner of dangerous and hazardous household appliances could be described as an act of gross parental irresponsibility if serious injury to that child or another child or young person in the family occurred.

Section IX: General principles governing interventions to maintain control

Section IX deals with the general principles governing interventions to maintain control. For these purposes, Principle (vi) which can be found at para 9.1 is the most relevant, ie 'the age and competence of the child should be taken into account in deciding what degree of intervention is necessary'.

Section X: Methods of care and control of children which fall short of physical restraint or the restriction of liberty

Section X deals with methods of care and control of children which are described as falling short of physical restraint or the restriction of liberty and include placing a hand on the child's arm, holding the child if he is highly distressed, using the care worker's physical presence, (eg to obstruct a doorway) and entering into a dialogue with the child or young person. Guidance is also given in this section with regard to those situations in which physical contact with a child may be deemed to be appropriate. Again, with regard to children with learning disabilities who also present severe challenging behaviour, it should be pointed out that any sort of physical contact may well exacerbate behavioural problems.

Section XI: Training

Section XI deals with training issues and provides that managers of children's homes (which could be extended to include those running schools, day centres and health care establishments), may wish to consult with professionals in the psychiatric centre who may be able to advise them on a source of training in safe methods of restraint. The Guidance states that managers should satisfy themselves that training is relevant and appropriate and that it is part of a programme which puts its use within the full context of care and control in residential child care.

Section XII: The responsibilities of management

Finally, Section XII emphasises the responsibilities of management in putting the Guidance into operation but makes it clear that no matter how much advice is given, good practice will depend on how the Guidance is interpreted by different staff faced with a range of situations, not all of which can be anticipated. 'In devising means of monitoring the use of physical methods of control, managers are lastly directed to have regard to the provisions of The Children's Homes Regulations 1991, now which require that full records are kept of the particulars of instances in which restraint and control are exercised.' As was pointed out earlier, these Regulations have now been replaced by the Children's Homes Regulations 2002 but the same emphasis is placed on the importance of keeping full records. It should be pointed out that the value of such a direction in relation to those looking after children with learning disabilities who also present severe challenging behaviour is limited to those caring for children in an institutional setting rather than to parents or perhaps foster carers. However, many specialist foster care schemes catering for children with learning disabilities presenting severe challenging behaviour do require that carers keep records of all those occasions when it is necessary to use physical interventions, and that these recorded incidents are then discussed at reviews of the child's case.

4.7 The provisions of s.550A Education Act 1996 and DfES Circular 10/98 – The Use of Force to Control or Restrain Pupils

4.7.1   As was noted in Chapter 1, the Education Act 1997 provided for a new s.550A to be inserted into the Education Act 1996 in order to confer a statutory power on a member of staff in a school to use such force as is <u>reasonable in the circumstances</u> for the purpose of preventing the pupil from committing an offence (which interestingly in the section is not defined as meaning a criminal offence); causing personal injury to or damage to the property of any person including the pupil himself or engaging in behaviour which is prejudicial to the maintenance of good order and discipline in the school whether it occurs during a lesson or otherwise.

Section 550A provides for the power of members of staff to restrain pupils, thus:

> *(1) A member of the staff of a school may use, in relation to any pupil at a school, such force as is reasonable in the circumstances for the purpose of preventing the pupil from doing (or continuing to do) any of the following, namely –*
>
> > *(a) committing any offence,*
> >
> > *(b) causing personal injury to, or damage to the property of, any person (including the pupil himself), or*
> >
> > *(c) engaging in any behaviour prejudicial to the maintenance of good order and discipline at the school or among any of its pupils, whether that behaviour occurs during a teaching session or otherwise.*
>
> *(2) Subsection (1) applies where a member of the staff of a school is –*
>
> > *(a) on the premises of the school, or*
> >
> > *(b) elsewhere at a time when, as a member of its staff, he has lawful control or charge of the pupil concerned;*
> >
> > *but it does not authorise anything to be done in relation to a pupil which constitutes the giving of corporal punishment within the meaning of section 548.*

3) Subsection (1) shall not be taken to prevent any person from relying on any defence available to him otherwise than by virtue of this section.

(4) In this section –

"member of staff", in relation to a school, means any teacher who works at the school and any other person who, with the authority of the headteacher, has lawful control or charge of pupils at the school;

"offence" includes anything that would be an offence but for the operation of any presumption that a person under a particular age is incapable of committing an offence.'

4.7.2 It should be noted that this section does not authorise the use of corporal punishment, which as explained in Chapter 1 has been outlawed in all educational settings since the implementation of s.131 School Standards and Framework Act 1998 and the Standards in Scotland's Schools Act 1998 on 1 September 1999 (see subsection 2). This point was emphasised by E Forth MP, Under-secretary of State for Education, Hansard, House of Commons Volume 289, columns 80-81, 27 January 1997) but he emphasised the provision in s.550A aims in particular to give teachers:

> *'the power to restrain pupils who are harming one another – or even, as might occasionally happen, harming themselves – or causing disruption in the classroom ... There have been cases of teachers being investigated by Social Services Departments or the Police for trivial instances of restraint of pupils. That is absurd and it is one of the reason why we tabled the new clause ... Teachers and appropriate other staff in schools, such as lunchtime supervisors, should be allowed, without fear of prosecution to use moderate physical restraint where it is necessary to stop pupils fighting. Occasionally, where a pupil is damaging school property or indulging in persistent, defiant disruption which is causing a complete breakdown in good order and discipline in the classroom, there may be nothing for it for the teacher to lead that pupil away by the arm, even though the pupil is not necessarily causing injury to himself or others, or would not be guilty of an offence because he is under the age of criminal responsibility.' (authors' emphasis added).*

4.7.3 Under S550A ss.(1), the test as regards the degree of force which may legitimately be used is one of 'reasonableness', a concept with which those reading this report will have become very familiar by now. The Minister explained: 'Ultimately, of course, it would be for the courts to determine what constitutes reasonable force, but I would expect that a court would decide that the new clause would not authorise the use of force to restrain a pupil from committing trivial misdemeanours. Force should be used only as a last resort to prevent seriously bad behaviour and, in any event, any force used should be proportionate to the misbehaviour.'

According to subs.(3) Section 550A does not remove from a teacher the right to use force in certain other circumstances. These are not specified but might be taken to include self-defence or the use of 'such force as is reasonable in the circumstances in the prevention of a crime' (see s.3 Criminal Law Act 1967).

4.7.4 It should be noted that the effect of the definition of 'offence' in subsection 4 is that where a pupil is presumed incapable of committing a crime due to lack of *mens rea* (ie the mental element) (or lack of criminal responsibility, applicable to a child under the age of ten or a child of any age lacking the necessary mental capacity, which would be the case for most children with learning disabilities who also present with severe challenging behaviour) this does not mean that the lawful exercise of the s.550A power of restraint, if the pupil has committed the conduct which forms the *actus reus* (ie the actual deed) for the offence, is precluded.

4.7.5 DfES Circular 10/98 – Section 550A of the Education Act 1996: The Use of Force to Control or Restrain Pupils Circular 10/98 provides guidance on how s.550A Education Act 1998 might be interpreted and this will now be considered.

Introduction

The Circular is divided up into some 14 parts beginning with the Introduction which focuses on the common misconception, first identified in the 1994 edition of this work, that since the Children Act 1989, any physical contact with a child is in some way unlawful. As the lead author pointed out in 1994, and as the circular repeats 'This is not true'. Where necessary, it has always been lawful to use reasonable force to control or restrain pupils but this power to use physical force has now been specifically given to teachers and others authorised by a headteacher of a school, to control or restrain pupils by virtue of s.550A.

Corporal punishment

4.7.6 Paragraph 2 of the Circular emphasises that nothing in this circular should be taken to suggest that it is sanctioning the use of corporal punishment which, it states, has been banned in all schools and nurseries whether state or independent since 1 September 1999.

Further guidance

4.7.7 Paragraphs 3 and 4 make reference to the intention to issue new Guidance on the use of Physical Interventions in due course which has now of course been done. (see the discussion at para 4.2 above.)

The necessity to have a school policy

4.7.8 Paragraphs 5 to 7 stress the importance of schools having clear policies in place governing the use of restraint and it is clearly stated that all staff, governors, pupils and parents need to know what options are open to the members of staff, what is acceptable and what is not. It is stated that the headteacher should draw up a policy setting out the guidelines about the use of restraint and that these should be discussed with staff and with governors. It is suggested that heads should refer to any model policies about touching, holding or restraining pupils that the LEA has developed and that they should also refer to the Guidance on Physical Interventions. Finally, it states that a statement of the school's policy should be included with the information the school gives parents about the school's policy on discipline.

Planning for incidents

4.7.9 Paragraph 8 deals with the important issue of planning for incidents, stating that if a school is aware that a pupil is likely to behave in such a way that may require physical control or restraint it will be sensible to plan how to respond if the situation arises. Such planning, it states, needs to address:

- managing the pupil (eg reactive strategies to de-escalate a conflict, holds to be used);

- involving the parents to ensure that they are clear about what specific action the school might need to take;

- briefing staff to ensure they know exactly what action they should be taking (this may identify a need for training or guidance);

- ensuring that additional support can be summoned if appropriate;

- in some cases, particularly in SEN settings, the school may also need to take medical advice about the safest way to hold pupils with specific health needs.

Paragraphs 9 and 10: The provisions of section 550A

4.7.10   Paragraph 9 then sets out the details of s.550A which has been set out above at para 4.5.1 and paragraph 10 emphasises that the section applies when a teacher, or other authorised person, is on the school premises, and when he or she has lawful control or charge of the pupil concerned elsewhere eg on a field trip or other authorised out-of-school activity.

Paragraphs 11 to 12: Who may be termed authorised staff?

4.7.11   Paragraphs 11 and 12 deal with the issue of who may be deemed to be authorised staff for the purposes of being allowed to use reasonable force to control or restrain pupils. It stresses that the section allows other people to do so, in the same way as teachers, provided they have been authorised by the headteacher to have control or charge of pupils. Such staff, the Circular states, might include classroom assistants, care workers, midday supervisors, specialist support assistants, education welfare officers, escorts, caretakers, or voluntary helpers including people accompanying pupils on visits, exchanges or holidays organised by the school.

Paragraph 12 states that headteachers should identify people, other than teachers, whom they wish to authorise to have control or charge of pupils and therefore be able to use force if necessary. Authorisation may be on a permanent or long-term basis because of the nature of the person's job, or short-term for a specific event such as a school trip. The headteacher should explicitly inform the people concerned, and ensure that they are aware of and properly understand what the authorisation entails. To ensure that, the Circular states that headteachers may find it helpful to arrange for a senior member of the teaching staff to provide training or guidance. They should keep an up-to-date list of authorised people and ensure the teachers know who they are.

Paragraph 13: Action in self-defence or in an emergency

4.7.12   Paragraph 13 states that section 550A does not cover all the situations in which it might be reasonable for someone to use a degree of force. For example, everyone has the right to defend themselves against an attack provided they do not use a disproportionate degree of force to do so. Similarly, in an emergency, for example if a pupil was at immediate risk of injury or on the point of inflicting injury on someone else, any member of staff would be entitled to intervene. The purpose of section 550A is to make it clear that teachers, and other authorised staff, are also entitled to intervene in other, less extreme, situations.

Paragraphs 14 to 15: Types of incidents

4.7.13 Paragraph 14 discusses the types of incident which might arise in which the use of reasonable force might be appropriate and that such incidents might fall into three broad categories:

(a) where action is necessary in self-defence or because there is an imminent risk of injury;

(b) where there is a developing risk of injury, or significant damage to property;

(c) where a pupil is behaving in a way that is compromising good order and discipline.

Paragraph 15 provides examples of situations that fall within one of the first two categories including where:

(i) a pupil attacks a member of staff, or another pupil;

(ii) pupils are fighting;

(iii) a pupil is engaged in, or is on the verge of committing, deliberate damage or vandalism to property;

(iv) a pupil is causing, or at risk of causing, injury or damage by accident, by rough play, or by misuse of dangerous materials or objects;

(v) a pupil is running in a corridor or on a stairway in a way in which he or she might have or cause an accident likely to injure him or herself or others;

(vi) a pupil absconds from a class or tries to leave school (NB this will only apply if a pupil could be at risk if not kept in the classroom or at school).

Examples of situations that fall into the third category, the Circular suggests, are:

(i) a pupil persistently refuses to obey an order to leave a classroom;

(ii) a pupil is behaving in a way that is seriously disrupting a lesson.

Paragraphs 16 to 18: What is meant by 'reasonable force'?

4.7.14 Paragraphs 16 to 18 make it clear that since there is no legal definition of what is reasonable force it is not possible to set out comprehensively when it is reasonable to use force, or the degree of force that may reasonably be used. It will always depend on all the circumstances of the case. But paragraph 17 states that there are two relevant considerations:

(i) The use of force can be regarded as reasonable only if the circumstances of the particular incident warrant it. The use of any degree of force is unlawful if the particular circumstances do not warrant the use of physical force. Therefore physical force could not be justified to prevent a pupil from committing a trivial misdemeanour, or in a situation that clearly could be resolved without force.

(ii) The degree of force employed must be in proportion to the circumstances of the incident and the seriousness of the behaviour or the consequences it is intended to prevent. Any force used should always be the minimum needed to achieve the desired result.

Paragraph 18 stresses that whether it is reasonable to use force, and the degree of force that could reasonably be employed, might also depend on the age, understanding, and sex of the pupil.

Paragraphs 19 and 20: Practical considerations

4.7.15   The Circular emphasises that before intervening physically a teacher should, wherever practicable, tell the pupil who is misbehaving to stop, and what will happen if he or she does not. It states that the teacher should continue attempting to communicate with the pupil throughout the incident, and should make it clear that physical contact or restraint will stop as soon as it ceases to be necessary. The Circular advises that a calm and measured approach to a situation is needed and teachers should never give the impression that they have lost their temper, or are acting out of anger or frustration, or to punish the pupil.

It goes on to state in paragraph 20 that sometimes a teacher should not intervene in an incident without help (unless it is an emergency). For example, when dealing with an older pupil, or a physically large pupil, or more than one pupil, or if the teacher believes he or she may be at risk of injury. In those circumstances the teacher should remove other pupils who might be at risk, and summon assistance from a colleague or colleagues, or where necessary phone the police. The teacher should inform the pupil(s) that he or she has sent for help. Until assistance arrives the teacher should continue to attempt to defuse the situation orally, and try to prevent the incident from escalating.

Paragraphs 21 to 27: The application of force

4.7.16   These paragraphs give detailed advice on the actual use of force. Paragraph 21 advises that physical intervention can take several forms. It might involve staff:

(i)   physically interposing between pupils;

(ii)   blocking a pupil's path;

(iii)   holding;

(iv)   pushing;

(v)   pulling;

(vi)   leading a pupil by the hand or arm;

(vii) shepherding a pupil away by placing a hand in the centre of the back; or

(viii) (in extreme circumstances) using more restrictive holds.

Paragraph 22 states that in exceptional circumstances, where there is an immediate risk of injury, a member of staff may need to take any necessary action that is consistent with the concept of 'reasonable force': for example to prevent a young pupil running off a pavement onto a busy road, or to prevent a pupil hitting someone, or throwing something.

Paragraph 23 advises that in other circumstances, staff should not act in a way that might reasonably be expected to cause injury, for example by:

(i)   holding a pupil around the neck, or by the collar, or in any other way that might restrict the pupil's ability to breathe;

(ii)   slapping, punching or kicking a pupil;

(iii) twisting or forcing limbs against a joint;

(iv)   tripping up a pupil;

(v)   holding or pulling a pupil by the hair or ear;

(vi)   holding a pupil face down on the ground.

Paragraph 24 states that staff should always avoid touching or holding a pupil in a way that might be considered indecent.

Paragraph 25 of the Circular stresses that where the risk is not so urgent the teacher should consider carefully whether, and if so when, physical intervention is right. Teachers, it advises, should always try to deal with a situation through other strategies before using force. All teachers need developed strategies and techniques for dealing with difficult pupils and situations which they should use to defuse and calm a situation. Advice about this, the Circular stated, would be included in the draft guidance on pupil behaviour and discipline policies referred to in paragraph 3, but this has yet to be issued. In a non-urgent situation, the Circular advises that force should only be used when other methods have failed.

The Circular goes on to state in para 26 that that consideration is particularly appropriate in situations where the aim is to maintain good order and discipline, and there is no direct risk to people or property. As the key issue is establishing good order, any action which could exacerbate the situation needs to be avoided. The possible consequences of intervening physically, including the risk of increasing the disruption or actually provoking an attack, need to be carefully evaluated.

Paragraph 27 stresses that the age and level of understanding of the pupil is also very relevant in those circumstances. Physical intervention to enforce compliance with staff instructions is likely to be increasingly inappropriate with older pupils. It should never be used as a substitute for good behavioural management.

Paragraphs 28 to 30: The recording of incidents

4.7.17   These paragraphs provide detailed advice on the recording of incidents. Paragraph 28 emphasises that it is important that there is a detailed, contemporaneous, written report of any occasion (except minor or trivial incidents) where force is used. It may help prevent any misunderstanding or misrepresentation of the incident, and it will be helpful should there be a complaint.

Paragraph 29 stresses that schools should keep an up-to-date record of all such incidents, preferably in an incident book. Immediately following any such incident the member of staff concerned should tell the headteacher or a senior member of staff and provide a written report as soon as possible afterwards. That should include:

(i)   the name(s) of the pupil(s) involved, and when and where the incident took place;

(ii)   the names of any other staff or pupils who witnessed the incident;

(iii)   the reason that force was necessary (eg to prevent injury to the pupil, another pupil or member of staff);

(iv)   how the incident began and progressed, including details of the pupil's behaviour, what was said by each of the parties, the steps taken to defuse or calm the situation, the degree of force used, how that was applied, and for how long;

(v)   the pupil's response, and the outcome of the incident;

(vi)   details of any injury suffered by the pupil, another pupil, or a member of staff and of any damage to property.

The Circular advises that staff may find it helpful to seek advice from a senior colleague or a representative of their professional association when compiling a report, and states that they should also keep a copy of the report.

Paragraph 30 points out that incidents involving the use of force can cause the parents of the pupil involved great concern, and thus that it is always advisable to inform parents of an incident involving their child, and give them an opportunity to discuss it. The Circular states that the headteacher, or member of staff to whom the incident is reported, will need to consider whether that should be done straight away or at the end of the school day, and whether parents should be told orally or in writing.

Paragraphs 31 to 32: Complaints

4.7.18   Paragraphs 31 to 32 gives advice about dealing with complaints. Thus it states that involving parents when an incident occurs with their child, plus a clear policy about physical contact with pupils that staff adhere to, should help to avoid complaints from parents. It will not prevent all complaints, however, and a dispute about the use of force by a member of staff might lead to an investigation, either under disciplinary procedures or by the police and social services department under child protection procedures. DfEE Circular 10/95: Protecting Children from Abuse gives guidance about the latter, and about procedures for dealing with allegations against teachers. (This is to be replaced by a new Circular from 1 June 2004 issued by the DfES which is currently out for consultation under the title *Safeguarding Children*.) (see 4.8 post)

Paragraph 32 advises that there is a possibility that a complaint might result in a disciplinary hearing, or a criminal prosecution, or in a civil action brought by a pupil or parent. In those circumstances it would be for the disciplinary panel or the court to decide whether the use and degree of force was reasonable in all the circumstances. In that event, however, the panel, or court, would have regard to the provisions of section 550A. It would also be likely to take account of the school's policy on restraint, whether that had been followed, and the need to prevent injury, damage, or disruption, in considering all the circumstances of the case.

Paragraphs 33 to 34: Physical contact with pupils in other circumstances

4.7.19   Paragraphs 33 to 34 give advice about those circumstances in which it might be deemed appropriate to have physical contact with a child or young person. Thus the Circular states that there are occasions when physical contact with a pupil may be proper or necessary other than those covered by section 550A of the 1996 Act. It acknowledges that some physical contact may be necessary to demonstrate exercises or techniques during PE lessons, sports coaching, or CDT, or if a member of staff has to give first aid, and that young children and children with special educational needs may need staff to provide physical prompts or help. The Circular advises that touching may also be appropriate where a pupil is in distress and needs comforting, and that teachers should use their own professional judgement when they feel a pupil needs this kind of support.

Paragraph 34 points out that there may be some children for whom touching is particularly unwelcome. For example, it states that some pupils may be particularly sensitive to physical contact because of their cultural background, or because they have been abused. The Circular points out that it is important that all staff receive information on these children, and that the school will need to develop clear common practice towards particular groups of children and events. The Circular advises that there should be a common approach where staff and pupils are of different sexes. Physical contact with pupils becomes increasingly open to question as pupils reach and go through adolescence, and staff should also bear in mind that even innocent and well-intentioned physical contact can sometimes be misconstrued.

4.8 Good practice

While two further documents, *Clear Expectations, Consistent Limits – Good practice in the care and control of children and young people in residential care*[212] (mainly relevant to Scotland), and *Taking Care, Taking Control*[213] (relevant to the whole of the UK), are principally addressed to residential staff caring for children and young people with learning disabilities, they may be seen as providing further guidance on the use of physical intervention which may be useful when considering the support and care of adults with learning disabilities and presenting challenging behaviours.

Certain situations may require that an individual be restrained: if that individual presents a danger to himself or herself and/or to others, if the behaviour represents an act of criminal damage to property; and in the case of children and young people, if that individual wants to leave the residential home without authorisation and this would represent a danger to himself or herself, others or to property.

However, physical intervention must only be employed as a last resort. If, and when all other actions on the part of the staff fail, to prevent a challenging situation from arising, and if, given the circumstances, staff feel that it is necessary to physically intervene staff should follow the guidelines laid out in their institution's policy documents which should include some or all of the principles considered in each of these two documents.

4.8.1 Taking Care, Taking Control Module 6 of the training pack sets out the following requirements when engaging in physical intervention for the management of a challenging situation:

- The techniques should only be used in children's homes where there is an ethos of anticipating and defusing trouble whenever possible;

- Consideration must be given to the young person's stage of development (including age and gender);

---

[212] Prepared for the Social Work Services Inspectorate by the Centre for Residential Child Care, 1997.
[213] 'Designed to help develop positive care and control practices for children and young people in residential care', DoH, Crown copyright, 1996

- There should be no reliance on threatening or inflicting pain, as this would constitute child abuse (eg corporal punishment[214]);

- Holds do not apply pressure that works against the joints as the young person may not be able to feel the pain straightaway due to the adrenaline rush acting as an anaesthetic;

- The technique should favour taking the young person in a seated position, rather than routinely resorting to the supine position – it is argued that this would particularly be traumatic to victims of previous sexual abuse. Furthermore, the supine position is not considered safe as it has contributed to fatal consequences in some cases[215];

- There should be a minimum of movement so as to avoid the risk of toppling over which is consequent with a risk of injury – the aim is keep everyone involved static;

- Carers can keep talking to the young person as they restrain him/her – this is especially made easier when the young person is in a seated position as this has a sense of 'normality' and will encourage a return to reason;

- Approach the young person from the side, not face to face, as this could be interpreted as confrontational and encourage the challenging behaviour;

- Techniques allow carers to phase up or phase down the hold or restraint as the young person regains control – again, this is especially true when the young person is in a seated position – 'if a young person who has been physically abusing staff switches to verbal abuse during restraint, this is a signal that they are starting to regain control and that the peak of physical danger has passed'[216];

- Carers can break away at any time – so that staff are not tempted to escalate the restraint using desperate and inappropriate techniques. The breakaway technique is seen as a safe option towards avoiding an escalation of the challenging behaviour. Carers are reminded that letting the person go does mean that they lose any ground – 'breaking away gives the opportunity for a few moments to think what to do next, and avoids the situation where what starts as restraint ends up as a fight'.[217]

Carers are then advised to re-instate a sense of comfort and safety in the young person, so as to let them know that it is not a case of staff against clients. Furthermore, staff should always keep a record of the incident in an incident recording book.

4.8.2 Clear Expectations, Consistent Limits This document provides the following guidelines on physical intervention techniques:

Breakaway techniques: staff are advised to assess and stay clear of a challenging situation if and when it is in their best interest to do so (safety reasons) and the young person's behaviour does not represent a danger to himself or herself, others and/or property. The paper insists that all staff should be trained in breakaway techniques following induction.

---

[214] See chapter on criminal liabilities for further details.
[215] Patterson B, Bradley P, Stark C, Saddler D, Leadbetter D and Allen D, Deaths Associated with Restraint Use in Health and Social Care in the United Kingdom – The Results of a Preliminary Survey, *Journal of Psychiatric and Mental Health Nursing*, 10.1 Feb 2003
[216] Module 6, p.3.
[217] Module 6, p.3.

Physical restraint: policies must be established in order to provide staff with clear guidance as to what they are to do in a challenging situation and as to the circumstances when they are allowed to resort to physical intervention.

The policy should include the choice of a method or techniques of restraint which are employed in the particular residential home/care setting/agency. Carers must only use methods that are allowed and approved by the care setting they work in.

The document stresses the point that 'all training should major on the philosophy of care, on de-escalation techniques . . . and only in the context of these should self protection and restraint techniques be taught'.[218]

Choosing the 'right' or rather the more appropriate method of intervention when facing a challenging situation is a difficult task as it can, and will most certainly, have repercussions and consequences, at a professional, personal and legal level.

The document lists a series of questions which raise issues that should be kept in mind when deciding on a choice of method of physical intervention[219]:

- Is there a hierarchy of responses?
- Is the method age-appropriate?
- Is the risk to staff considered and minimised?
- Will the average member of staff be able to master the techniques?
- Does it require excessive staff numbers?
- Are 'Breakaway' techniques included?
- Is dignity compromised unnecessarily?
- Will it work in confined spaces?
- Are there any contra indications? (eg Will it work in your setting?)
- Are grips secure?
- Is unnecessary pain avoided?
- In methods that involve descents to the floor, is the subject's head protected?
- Are the descents controlled?
- Is unnecessary pressure on the subject's back avoided?
- Does it contain techniques which would enable staff to move the subject safely whilst under restraint?
- Does the system have a formal mechanism through which the approved techniques can be evaluated and adapted on the basis of operational experience?
- Does the system have a formal quality assurance mechanism to accredit and regulate instruction and practice?

---

[218] *Clear Expectations...* p.35
[219] Adapted from Lindsay M (ed.), Leadbetter D: *Physical restraint: practice, legal, medical, and technical considerations*, Centre for residential child care, Practice paper No.1, Glasgow 1995

The residential home policy document should also include a clear reference to the methods of physical interventions which are not allowed and should therefore not be used as they are not appropriate and might prove to be very dangerous (ie fatal, even). *Clear expectations . . .* states that some physical intervention techniques are unacceptable if and when they involve: 1) locking in, 2) the intentional use of pain, 3) the humiliation of the person presenting the challenging behaviour and 4) an unnecessarily and inappropriate high degree of force which is disproportionate to the challenging behaviour displayed and the dangers it presents to carers, the client, third parties and/or property.

Policy documents, which are drawn up by residential homes, agencies and other care settings, are a necessary means of informing staff on good practice and warning them against situations that can give rise to criminal and civil liabilities. The next chapter of the report will thus look into the responsibility held by employers in conforming to health and safety regulations and in providing care employees with appropriate work settings and guidance.

4.9 Detention of pupils outside school hours

A new section 550B was inserted into the Education Act 1996 by the provisions of s.5 Education Act 1997, which placed the imposition of detentions on school pupils on a statutory footing for the first time. The mere fact that pupils have learning disabilities and present severe challenging behaviour would not make the imposition of such a detention unlawful provided it is one of the range of disciplinary measures publicised within the school and to parents of pupils at the school. Caution should be exercised, however, in relation to the use of detentions on such pupils who will not necessarily react at all well to having to spend extra time in school or miss out on the trip home with their friends.

Section 550B thus provides that:

> (1) *Where a pupil to whom this section applies is required on disciplinary grounds to spend a period of time in detention at his school after the end of any school session, his detention shall not be rendered unlawful by virtue of the absence of his parent's consent to it* **if the conditions set out in subsection (3) are satisfied.**

> (2) *This section applies to any pupil who has not attained the age of 18 and is attending –*

>> (a) *a school maintained by a local education authority;*

>> (b) *a grant-maintained or grant-maintained special school; or*

>> (c) *a city technology college or city college for the technology of the arts.*

> (3) **The conditions referred to in subsection (1) are as follows –**

>> (a) *the head teacher of the school must have previously determined, and have –*

>>> (i) *made generally known within the school, and*

>>> (ii) *taken steps to bring to the attention of the parent of every person who is for the time being a registered pupil there, that the detention of pupils after the end of a school session is one of the measures that may be taken with a view to regulating the conduct of pupils;*

> *(b) the detention must be imposed by the head teacher or by another teacher at the school specifically or generally authorised by him for the purpose;*
>
> *(c) the detention must be reasonable in all the circumstances; and*
>
> *(d) the pupil's parents must have been given at least 24 hours' notice in writing that the detention was due to take place.*
>
> *(4) In determining for the purposes of subsection (3)(c) whether a pupil's detention is reasonable, the following matters in particular shall be taken into account.*
>
> > *(a) whether the detention constitutes a proportionate punishment in the circumstances of the case; and*
> >
> > *(b) any special circumstances relevant to its imposition on the pupil which are known to the person imposing it (or of which he ought reasonably to be aware) including in particular –*
> >
> > > *(i) the pupil's age;*
> > >
> > > *(ii) any special educational needs he may have;*
> > >
> > > *(iii) any religious requirements affecting him; and*
> > >
> > > *(iv) where arrangements have to be made for him to travel from the school to his home, whether suitable alternative arrangements can reasonably be made by his parent.*
>
> *(5) Section 572, which provides for the methods by which notices may be served under this Act, does not preclude a notice from being given to a pupil's parent under this section by any other effective method.'*

(authors' emphasis added)

The purpose of s.550(b) which this section introduced, was explained by Eric Forth, the Minister of State, thus:

> *'Schools will for the first time be given explicit statutory authority to detain badly behaved pupils after school without their parent's consent. That will ensure that detention as a sanction is more readily available, free of the potential risk of a legal action against the school for false imprisonment.'*

The position at common law appears to be that detention is a lawful form of punishment provided it is used reasonably and not for improper reason. There has, however, been some doubt as to whether it is lawful to detain a whole class where there is known to be only one culprit (see *Terrington v Lancashire County Council* (1986)).

This section thus confirms and regulates the power of schools to provide for the detention of pupils aged under 18 in prescribed categories of schools after the end of a school session either morning or afternoon. It also guides teachers by defining the factors to be considered in judging the reasonableness of a detention in particular circumstances. The section also states that detention can only be given where the fact that it is one of the measures to be used to regulate the conduct of pupils has been made generally known within the school, steps have been taken to bring it to the attention of parents, and, for any particular detention, the requisite 24 hours' notice has been given.

4.10 Duties on local education authorities and schools to safeguard and promote the welfare of children

In response to the circumstances surrounding the death of Lauren Wright, where teachers and others at the school Lauren attended failed to report concerns about her health and physical condition, the Government introduced late amendments to the Education Act 2002, which are to be brought into force on June 1, 2004. Section 175 places specific new duties upon local education authorities and the governors of all state schools to make arrangements for ensuring that that their functions are carried out in such a way as to safeguard and promote the welfare of all children in their schools. Similar provision to that made in section 175 is made for all independent schools and educational establishments by section 157 of the Education Act 2002, which will be expanded upon in Regulations to be issued by the Secretary of State for Education. New Guidance on these provisions entitled *'Safeguarding the Children* – Child protection: Guidance about child protection arrangements for the education service', is currently out for consultation and subject to any changes made as a result of the consultation will be introduced on June 1 2004, the same date set for implementation of the new statutory provisions.

Section 175 Education Act 2002

In recognition of the problem of responsibility for all child protection concerns relating to children and young people within the school including those arising out of bullying, the Government has now enacted s.175 EA 2002 which provides:

(1) A local education authority shall make arrangements for ensuring that the functions conferred on them in their capacity as a local education authority are exercised with a view to safeguarding and promoting the welfare of children.

(2) The governing body of a maintained school shall make arrangements for ensuring that their functions relating to the conduct of a school are exercised with a view to safeguarding and promoting the welfare of children who are at the school.

(3) The governing body of an institution within the further education sector shall make arrangements for ensuring that their functions relating to the conduct of the institution are exercised with a view to safeguarding and promoting the welfare of the children receiving education or training at the institution.

(4) An authority or body mentioned in ss 1-3 shall in considering what arrangements are required to be made by them under that subsection have regard to any guidance given from time to time by the Secretary of State.

(5) In this section 'child' means a person under the age of 18; 'governing body' in relation to the FE sector has the meaning given to it by s. 90 Further and Higher Education Act 1992; 'maintained school' means a community, foundation or voluntary school, special school or nursery school.

This section imposes an even heavier duty on schools to safeguard and protect all children in all school environments than that previously envisaged. It must be read with special care by those seeking to provide for the education of children and young people with learning disabilities and severe challenging behaviour.

PART III

Employer's Responsibility

Chapter 5

Employer's responsibility in England and Wales

Introduction

This chapter looks at the employer's responsibility and possible liabilities as regards his relationship with his employees and third parties. This is an important area of the law for any employee as well as for all employers. Those working with children and adults with learning disabilities and severe challenging behaviour should have a basic knowledge of the concepts of employer's responsibility in order to understand the arena of duties and responsibilities within which they work. What follows therefore is a brief indication of the relevant provisions.

In tort law, an employer can be found liable for the act of his employees even though he is not the tortfeasor, ie the person actually committing the wrong. In contrast, as a general rule in criminal law the employer cannot be held liable for the acts of his employees, for he is only accountable for his own action, or as an accessory to the crime committed by the employee.

5.1 Criminal vicarious liability

In _Huggins_ 1730,[220] the court stated that any person involved in a crime should 'each answer for their own acts and stand or fall by their own behaviour' and that for an employer to be affected by the act of his employee, there must be a command of the employer.

The exceptions to this rule are when an employer will, very rarely, be found vicariously liable for common law offences such as public nuisance or criminal libel. Statutes can also occasionally impose a strict liability on the part of the employer. More often the commission of a statutory offence will be found through the court's interpretation of the statute's wording or under the principle of delegation (ie that in specifically delegating tasks to the employee, the employer can then be found responsible for his employee's acts).

However, for this report, the focus will be on the employer's responsibility under the law of torts.

5.2 Employer's civil liabilities

Whereas vicarious liability is about imposing liability on the employer for the act of his employees, without any fault of his own, the notion of employer's liability is concerned with rendering the employer accountable for any breach of his duty of care towards his employees.

---

[220] (1730) 2 Strange 883

5.2.1 Civil vicarious liability   An employer can be found liable for the wrongful acts of his employees when the acts were committed in the course of their employment and authorised by the employer.

Despite the many criticisms of this principle, based mainly on the fact that the offence is not fault-based as the employer did not actually commit the tort, the reasons justifying such a liability are substantial enough. Thus, the employer exercises some degree of control over his employees; it can prove difficult for a claimant to trace the person who actually committed the tort, and even if that person is identified, they might not be worth suing or insured. Therefore, the employer is often more able to bear the weight of paying compensation, as he is also under an obligation to take out an insurance policy for public liability.

There are three components to the principle of vicarious liability: the wrongful act must be a tort, committed by an employee, in the course of his employment.

1. The act is a tort

If the employee did not commit a tortious act the general rule is that the employer cannot be vicariously liable. This means that if there is no breach of duty on the employee's part, then it follows that there is no breach of duty on the employer's part. Vicarious liability is based on the concept that the employer is held liable for a wrongful act committed by his employees, despite it being no fault of his own. Therefore, if no breach has occurred, then there is no tort and no liability.

2. Committed by an employee

An employer can only be liable for the acts of his employees. The courts have devised three possible tests that can determine the 'employee' as opposed to an 'independent contractor' status.

The original test is known as the control test, which measures the nature and degree of control exercised by the employer over his employees,[221] taking into account such elements as the ability to select staff and pay their wages, to control them as to their duties and how they are to be performed, and also the power to dismiss.[222]

The main issue is whether the relationship between an employer and an employee is based on either a contract for services or a contract of service.

If the contract is one for services, then the person paying for the services can only require what is to be done. The relationship is thus concerned with the end result, the outcome of a particular service rendered by an independent contractor. There can be no question of vicarious liability. On the other hand, if the contract is one of service, then the employer exercises a more substantial degree of control over the employee as he can order both what and how a task is to be carried out.[223] The employer can be vicariously liable.

The second test established in _Stevenson, Jordan and Harrison Ltd v McDonald and Evans_ 1952[224] is called the 'organisation' or 'integral part of the business' test and this suggests that

---

[221] _Performing Rights Society v Mitchell_ (1927)
[222] _Lord Thankerton in Short v Henderson_ (1946)
[223] _Collins v Hertfordshire CC_ [1947] 1 All ER 633
[224] [1954] 1 TLR 101

a person could be said to be an employee depending on the degree, and the extent to which that person is involved and integrated into the company. The more a person is a part of the company, the stronger the assumption that he is an employee. Lord Denning thus stated '(. . .) under a contract of service, a man is employed as part of the business; whereas, under a contract for services, his work, although done for the business, is not integrated into it but is only accessory to it'. This position was confirmed in *Whittaker v Minister of Pensions and National Assistance*.[225]

The third and most recent test, which is also the most commonly used, is known as the 'economic reality', 'multiple' or 'financial risk' test.

The case of *Montreal v Montreal Locomotive Works*[226] details the elements to be taken into consideration including the notion of control, ownership of the tools, chances of profit and the potential risk of loss. The idea is that the test will look at the economic reality of the relationship between the employer and the employees. An employee is paid for the work he performs, he is not in a position to contribute to either the profits of the company or to take responsibility for the losses.

In *Market Investigations Ltd v Minister of Social Security*[227] the Court stated that the test to determine whether a person is an employee or a contractor came down to one question: 'is the person who has engaged himself to perform these services performing them as person in business on his own account?' if the answer is yes, then it is to be assumed that the person is a contractor under a contract for services; if no, then it is an employee under a contract of service. In this case, the court added two more factors to the list in *Montreal*,[228] namely whether the person hires his own helpers, and the extent of responsibility that he exercises as regards investment and management.

In *Ready Mixed Concrete v Minister of Pensions and NI*[229] in 1968 the court looked at the last two factors in particular. It found that a situation where 'owner-drivers' who were part of a company that organised delivery of concrete and who owned the vehicles and shared profits and risks of economic loss, did not accord with a master-servant relationship. This was despite the fact that the vehicles were actually only used for professional purposes and being painted in the company's colours and that they could not be disposed of without consent/permission from the company. This did not amount to a contract of service, but rather to a contract of carriage ie a contract for services.

3. 'In the course of his employment'

The basic rule is that an employer can only be held liable for the act of his employees when the tort was committed during the course of employment, as opposed to if they were committed by an employee who had been engaged, not on his employer's business, but on 'a frolic of his own'.[230]

---

[225] [1967] 2 QB 148
[226] [1947] 1 DLR 161
[227] [1969] 2 QB 173
[228] [1947] 1 DLR 161
[229] [1968] 2 QB 497
[230] *Joel v Morison* (1834) 6 C&P 501

'*A master is not responsible for a wrongful act done by his servant unless it is done in the course of his employment. It is deemed to be so done if it is either (1) a wrongful act authorised by the master, or (2) a wrongful and unauthorised mode of doing some act authorised by the master. But a master, as opposed to the employer of an independent contractor, is liable even for acts which he has not authorised, provided they are so connected with acts which he has authorised that they may rightly be regarded as modes, although improper modes, of doing them.*'[231]

There are two kinds of act for which the employer might be found vicariously liable. An employer will be held liable for the wrongful acts of his employee that were authorised by him, and for the acts that were wrongfully performed by the employee, even when the act itself was forbidden by the employer.

The authority most often referred to in cases of intentional wrongdoing and vicarious liability is *Morris v C W Martin & Sons Ltd*.[232] In this case, a woman had entrusted her mink coat to a dry cleaning shop where an employee eventually stole the item. The court found that the defendants were liable for what amounted to negligence and conversion by their servant in the course of his employment.

There is no definite test to define whether an act was committed during the course of employment or not. However, in a recent case, *Lister and others v Hesley Hall Ltd*[233] the House of Lords looked at the responsibility of the employer as regards offences of a sexual nature against children in foster homes.

Prior to *Lister*, the case of *Trotman v North Yorkshire County Council*[234] had established that employers such as local authorities and schools could not be held liable for assaults committed by their staff on children in their care, the rationale being that the assault was committed independently of the duties required by the carer's position.

In *Lister*, children had been sexually abused by their carer. Lord Steyn, reflecting on the case of *Lloyd v Grace, Smith & Co*,[235] stated that: 'it finally established that vicarious liability is not necessarily defeated if the employee acted for his own benefit. On the other hand, an intense focus on the connection between the nature of the employment and the tort of the employee became necessary.' He later added that 'the question is whether the warden's torts were so closely connected with his employment that it would be fair and just to hold the employers vicariously liable. On the facts of the case the answer is yes. After all, the sexual abuse was inextricably interwoven with the carrying out by the warden of his duties in Axeholme House. Matters of degree arise. But the present cases clearly fall on the side of vicarious liability.'

In *Lister*, Lord Hobhouse of Woodborough also stated that:

[231] *Ibid*
[232] [1966] 1 QB 716
[233] [2002] 1 AC 215
[234] The Times, 10 September 1998
[235] [1912] AC 716

'what these cases and <u>Trotman</u>'s case in truth illustrate is a situation where the employer has assumed a relationship to the plaintiff which imposes specific duties in tort upon the employer and the role of the employee (or servant) in that he is the person to whom the employer has entrusted the performance of that duty (...). These cases are examples of that class where the employer, by reason of assuming a relationship to the plaintiff, owes to the plaintiff duties which are more extensive than those owed by the public at large and, accordingly, are to be contrasted with the situation where a defendant is simply in proximity to the plaintiff so that it is foreseeable that his acts may injure the plaintiff or his property and a reasonable person would have taken care to avoid causing such injury.'

Lord Hobhouse continued, making the point that:

'the defendant admits it had a duty of care towards the plaintiffs. That duty of care was to take all reasonable steps to safeguard the plaintiffs (and other pupils) in their physical, moral and educational development whilst at the school. In carrying out that duty of care the defendant, a limited company, necessarily had to appoint a hierarchy of responsible agents ... each of whom had either general or particular responsibilities which bore upon this duty of care.'

Finally, Lord Hobhouse concluded that:

'the classes of persons or institutions that are in this type of special relationship to another human being include schools, prisons, hospitals and even, in relation to their visitors, occupiers of land. They are liable if they themselves fail to perform the duty which they consequently owe. If they entrust the performance of that duty to an employee and that employee fails to perform the duty, they are still liable. The employee, because he has, through his obligations to his employers, adopted the same relationship towards and come under the same duties to the plaintiff, is also liable to the plaintiff for his own breach of duty.'

Lord Hobhouse summarised the issue of deciding whether a wrongful act was committed within the course of employment by asking the following question: 'what was the duty of the servant towards the plaintiff which was broken by the servant and what was the contractual duty of the servant towards his employer?'. The issue of negligence does not appear to be necessary to bring a claim for vicarious liability as regards cases of abuse in a care setting.

The impact of the *Lister* case on vicarious liability for assaults of a non-sexual nature was brought up in *Mattis v Pollock*,[236] where a bouncer who had been chased home from the nightclub where he worked following an altercation with the claimant, came back towards the club and stabbed the claimant about 100 yards away from the entrance to the club. The claimant brought a claim against the owner of the nightclub, Mr Pollock.

It was argued by the defendants that there were two limbs (elements or parts) to the test in *Lister*. The first one was concerned with whether there was a sufficient close connection between the wrongful act and the nature of the employment. The second limb looked at whether there was a duty of care owed by Mr Pollock to the claimant which he had 'delegated'

---

[236] [2002] EWHC 2177

to the bouncer. The court decided that none of the limbs were met in this case, stating that the stabbing incident occurred 15 minutes after the initial incident and the bouncer had left the premises and then returned. Besides, said the court, the duty of care ended when the bouncer left the nightclub, it did not extend to the fact that the bouncer would seek revenge against the claimant later on.

5.2.2 Employer's liability This section looks at the employer's liability vis-à-vis his employees as regards injuries and violence at the workplace. The issues considered here are the employer's duties under the common law and his statutory obligations. In particular, this section will attempt to identify the employer's position as regards his providing adequate training in physical intervention.

5.2.2.1 Common law duties The employer's common law duty towards his employees is personal, 'whether he performs or can perform it himself, or whether he does not perform it or cannot perform it save by [employees] or agents'.[237] Consequently, this personal duty is non-delegable, whether it is imposed at common law or by statute.

This means that the employer can delegate the performance of a duty to either an employee or an independent contractor. He cannot, however, delegate the responsibility that is attached to the performance of that duty. In other words, the employer remains responsible for the negligent way a duty might be performed, and this, despite the fact that the employer may be under an obligation to delegate a certain duty to a specialised person.

There are four common law duties that the employer has to abide by in order to anticipate issues of safety and the risk of injuries. 'It is the duty of employers, for the safety of their employees, to have reasonably safe plant and machinery. It is their duty to have premises which are similarly reasonably safe. It is their duty to have a reasonably safe system of work. It is their duty to employ reasonably competent fellow workmen.'[238]

a) Competent staff

An employer is under an obligation to select competent staff and to provide them with proper instruction as to the use of any work equipment.

In *Hudson v Ridge Manufacturing Co Ltd*[239] the plaintiff was seriously injured in the course of work after being tripped by a fellow worker as a prank. The latter worker had been a nuisance to other fellow workers for some time and was known as a practical joker. Although he had been reprimanded in the past and warned to stop his pranks, as someone would get hurt some day, no other action had been taken by the employer.

In this case, Streatfeild J stated that 'if (. . .) a fellow workman is not merely incompetent but, by his habitual conduct, is likely to prove a source of danger to his fellow employees, a duty lies fairly and squarely on the employers to remove that source of danger'.

In *General Cleaning Contractors v Christmas*[240] a window cleaner, who had been working for the cleaning contractor company for 20 years, injured himself when he was cleaning the outside

---

[237] *per* Lord Wright, *Wilsons & Clyde Coal Co Ltd v English* [1937] AC 57
[238] *per* Streatfeild J in *Hudson v Ridge Manufacturing Co Ltd* [1957] 2 QB 348
[239] [1957] 2 QB 348
[240] [1953] AC 180

of a window 27 feet high and fell off the window sill when the window slammed shut. It is apparent that the employers failed to provide instructions to their workers to test the windows before cleaning them, and did not provide their employees with wedges or blocks to prevent the window shutting.

The House of Lords was of the opinion that the employers 'were to blame in not taking all reasonable steps to see that the system of work which they required their men to adopt was made as safe as possible'. Lord Oaksey further stated that 'it is the duty of an employer to give such general safety instructions as a reasonably careful employer who has considered the problem presented by the work would give to his workmen (. . .) [and they should take reasonable care to lay down a reasonably safe system of work', whether the workers are experienced or not'.

This duty to employ competent staff implies that an employer might be led to dismiss any incompetent staff. An employer will still be liable, however, for the negligent act of an incompetent employee.

b) Safe place of work

In the case of _Latimer v AEC Ltd_,[241] the claimant was a worker in a factory who was injured after he slipped on a film of oil that had been deposited by flood water on the factory floor. The court stated that an employer is under a common law duty to take all reasonable steps as would be expected from a reasonable prudent man in order to secure a safe place of work. The employer must consider the degree of the potential risk and the probability for its occurring when deciding on a specific course of action to ensure safety.

The fact that an employee has been warned by his employer or is aware of a potential danger in carrying out his tasks is not enough for an employer to avoid his duty of care.

In _London Graving Dock Co Ltd v Horton_[242] it was found that even though an employee has a knowledge and/or understanding of the danger in his line of work and carries on performing his job, this does not imply that the employee has freely and voluntarily accepted that risk. This principle also applies in cases where the employee is both experienced and familiar with the potential risks incurred by his job.

In _McCafferty v Receiver for the Metropolitan Police District_[243] the employee was a ballistics expert police officer who suffered from ringing in his ears after he fired guns in a enclosed space with only cotton wool as an ear protective device. The court held that the employer was liable for injury as they could not discharge their duty by merely delegating to the employee the responsibility to take safety measures.

c) Proper plant and equipment

In _Smith v Charles Baker & Sons_,[244] the employee 'undertook a dangerous work of drilling holes, while over his head (unless he moved away) stones were being hauled by a crane. That

[241] [1953] AC 643
[242] [1951] AC 737
[243] [1977] 1 W.L.R. 1073
[244] [1891] AC 325

work he entered upon knowing it was dangerous to that extent.'[245] However, this consent to undertake such a risk did not include a consent to a danger 'arising from unfit machinery'. Lord Herschell stated that the employer is under a duty to take 'reasonable care to provide proper appliances, and to maintain them in a proper condition, and so to carry on his operations as not to subject those employed by him to unnecessary risk'.

In the absence of proper and necessary equipment to perform a task, which results in an accident injuring an employee, the employer will be liable for that injury. On the other hand, an employer is not under an obligation to provide the most up-to-date equipment available to their employee.

In _Toronto Power Co Ltd v Paskwan_,[246] Sir Arthur Channell stated that an employer 'does not warrant the plant, and if there is a latent defect which could not be detected by reasonable examination, or if in the course of working plant becomes defective and the defect is not brought to the master's knowledge and could not by reasonable diligence have been discovered by him, the master is not liable, and, further, a master is not bound at once to adopt all the latest improvements and appliances'.

Although employers are under a duty to provide proper equipment, they are not required to impose the use of such equipment on their employees. In _Qualcast (Wolverhampton) Ltd v Haynes_[247] an experienced moulder handling a ladle of molten metal suffered injury when some of the metal accidentally slipped onto his foot. He was not wearing protective spats, although these were available from the employer on demand.

The House of Lords stated that 'though indeed there may be cases in which an employer does not discharge his duty of care towards his workmen merely by providing an article of safety equipment, the Courts should be circumspect in filling out that duty with the much vaguer obligation of encouraging, exhorting or instructing workmen or a particular workman to make regular use of what is provided'.

This view was confirmed in _McWilliams v Sir William Arrol & Co Ltd_[248] in which the House of Lords was of the opinion that an employer in the steel erectors business could not be held liable for failing to instruct, order, direct or exhort a workman to wear a safety belt. Indeed, it was a generally recognised view amongst the workmen on the site that such a belt was more of a hindrance and a hazard and thus would not be worn.

When an employee makes improper use of work equipment and suffers injury as a result, the employer will be discharged. In _Parkinson v Lyle Shipping Co Ltd_[249] a donkeyman greaser who was injured after lighting a Scotch boiler in the employer's motor vessel argued that the machinery was faulty because the employer had not kept it in good working condition. The court found that the machinery was not faulty and that the donkeyman greaser had been negligent in not checking the air controls and by standing in front of the furnace while lighting the boiler.

---

[245]   _per_ Lord Morris
[246]   [1915] AC 734
[247]   [1959] A.C. 743
[248]   1962 SLT 121
[249]   [1964] 2 Lloyd's Rep 79

d) Safe system of work

Whether an employer should provide a safe system of work as a precautionary measure is to be assessed on a case-by-case basis. Indeed, depending on the circumstances, it is possible to leave the question of work safety to the employee himself. Nonetheless, even though the employer might delegate his duty, he retains responsibility for any default in the system of work.

In *Speed v Thomas Swift & Co Ltd*[250] a dock labourer was injured when attempting to load a ship with drums of caustic soda by means of 'married gear'. An accident occurred which was caused by a failure to remove the material section of the ship.

In this case, Lord Green MR stated that:

> '*the duty of providing a safe system must be considered, not generally, but in relation to the particular circumstances of each job. (...) The provision of such a system falls within the master's province of duty. If he delegates it, he remains responsible for any inadequacy in the system just as much as if he had personally provided it, and he cannot excuse himself by saying that he had good grounds for relying on the competence of the person to whom he delegated the duty.*'

There is no clear definition of 'system of work'. However, Lord Green attempts to give some guidance on its meaning. He ventured that 'a system of working may consist of a number of elements and what exactly it must include will (. . .) depend entirely on the facts of the particular case. (. . .) [A system of work includes], or may include according to circumstances, such matters as:

- The physical lay-out of the job;
- The setting of the stage; (. . .)
- The sequence in which the work is to be carried out;
- The provision in proper cases of warnings and notices; and
- The issue of special instructions.

A system may be adequate for the whole course of the job or it may have to be modified or improved to meet circumstances which arise. Such modifications or improvements appear (. . .) equally to fall under the head of system.' He also added that this list is not an exhaustive one.

This head (part) of the employer's duty of care extends to the idea of a safe system of work devised to protect employees' mental as well as physical health. In *Petch v Customs and Excise Commissioners*[251] a former civil service employee claimed that his mental breakdown during the period of his employment was caused because of a heavy workload and that his employer had been negligent. The Court of Appeal held that since the mental breakdown had not been foreseeable, the employer could not be held liable. However, it was recognised that an employer ought to take reasonable steps in devising a safe system of work that would reduce the risk of psychiatric injury for employees, such as depression and mental breakdown.

This was confirmed in *Walker v Northumberland County Council*[252] where a social services manager suffered psychiatric injury as a result of an increased workload and a lack of action

---

[250] [1943] KB 557
[251] [1993] I.C.R. 789
[252] [1995] PIQRP 521

on the part of the council to provide him with sufficient field workers and work guidance to cope with this workload. The plaintiff suffered a first and then second nervous breakdown two years later. Although the first breakdown had not been foreseeable, it was argued that a second breakdown was, if not inevitable, at least likely to occur. The duty of an employer to provide a safe system of work thus extends to cases of psychiatric illness.

As regards the duty of care of public body employers towards their employees, Coleman J added that:

> 'the duty of an employer public body, whether in contract or tort, to provide a safe system of work is (. . .) a duty only to do what is reasonable, and in many cases it may be necessary to take into account decisions which are within the policy-making area and the reasons for those decisions in order to test whether the body's conduct has been reasonable. In that exercise there can be no basis for treating the public body differently in principle from any other commercial employer, although there would have to be taken into account considerations such as budgetary constraints and perhaps lack of flexibility of decision-taking which might not arise with a commercial employer.'

An employee who suffers from a psychiatric injury after witnessing a shocking event resulting from the employer's negligence could bring a claim for compensation. However, that employee will have to prove that he is either a 'primary victim' or a 'secondary victim'. This is not an easy matter as Lord Steyn stated in _White v Chief Constable of South Yorkshire_:[253] 'the law on the recovery of compensation for pure psychiatric harm is a patchwork quilt of distinctions which are difficult to justify'.

In this case, police officers who were on patrol at a football match at the Hillsborough Football Stadium suffered from post-traumatic disorder after helping with the human consequences in the aftermath of the disaster.

Lord Steyn considered the issue from the perspective of the law of tort. He stated that 'the duty of an employer to care for the safety of his employees and to take reasonable steps to safeguard them from [physical] harm [does not imply that an employer has] a duty not to cause the employee psychiatric injury'.

Therefore, if an employee does fall within the meaning of primary or secondary victim, the employer might be held liable for psychiatric injuries. Moreover, it was stated that a psychiatric injury must be a recognised psychiatric illness (not emotions such as grief or distress), and that the injury must have been reasonably foreseeable by the employer.

A primary victim is someone who is directly involved in the incident and is within the range of foreseeable personal injury.

In _Page v Smith_,[254] a man was involved in a car accident. Although he did not incur any physical injury, he had been suffering from a condition called myalgic encephalomyelitis, more commonly known as chronic fatigue syndrome. The condition had manifested itself on and off for the 20 years prior to the car accident. The accident, however, triggered a more permanent

---

[253] [1999] 2 AC 455
[254] [1996] AC 155

occurrence of the fatigue syndrome which made it unlikely for the victim of the accident to ever go back to full-time employment.

It was held that the plaintiff suffered from a recognised psychiatric illness (ie post-viral fatigue syndrome, not just mere emotions such as distress and/or grief) and that the injury was considered reasonably foreseeable. 'Foreseeability of nervous shock is to be judged in the light of what would be suffered by a person of normal fortitude.'[255] The victim had been a direct participant in the car accident and had not been just a mere bystander.

In _White v Chief Constable of South Yorkshire_ 1999, Lord Hoffman stressed the requirements that are necessary for a claimant to qualify as a secondary victim, ie someone in the position of spectator or bystander:

'• The plaintiff must have close ties of love and affection with the victim. Such ties may be presumed in some cases (eg spouses, parent and child) but must otherwise be established by evidence.

• The plaintiff must have been present at the accident or its immediate aftermath.

• The psychiatric injury must have been caused by direct perception of the accident or its immediate aftermath and not upon hearing about it from someone else.'

If an employee qualifies in this category, he will have a chance of suing for damages.

However, if an employee suffers harm or injury due to the application of a widely accepted and established practice in the employer's particular field, there might be some difficulty in proving that the employer was negligent in following that general practice.

In _Thompson v Smiths Ship Repairers (North Shields) Ltd_,[256] the plaintiff was a labourer employed in a ship-repair yard and claimed damages against his employers for hearing impairment resulting from excessive noise in the course of his employment period.

Mustill J stated that:

> 'not one employer is exonerated simply by proving that other employers are just as
> negligent, but that the standard of what is negligent is influenced, although not
> decisively, by the practice in the industry as a whole. (. . .) This principle applies not
> only where the breach of duty is said to consist of a failure to take precautions
> known to be available as a means of combating a known danger, but also where the
> omission involves an absence of initiative in seeking out knowledge of facts which are
> not in themselves obvious. The employer must keep up to date, but the court must be
> slow to blame him for not ploughing a lone furrow.'

In other words, an employer can only rely on the standard practice as long as there are no other more available practices accepted and encouraged by the industry and as a result of social changes. If it is proven that the employer could have accessed more advanced and modern information on accepted safe practices or on precautions that could/should be taken, he might be found negligent. The court reserves the right to use discretion when considering whether a

---

[255] _per_ Lord Keith of Kinkel
[256] [1984] QB 405

practice poses an actual danger and therefore cannot be held to be reasonable and/or acceptable, despite a general agreement in the industry that it is common practice.

The duty to provide a safe system of work implies two elements that are both inter-dependant and vital to an employer's potential liability. A system of work requires a devising of the system and its appropriate operation. In the context of this report, this means that a policy or instructions as to the use of physical interventions in challenging situations is not to be seen as the be-all and end-all of a safe system of work but its application is of equal importance. In other words, this means that a system of work can be well designed, but if its application is faulty, the employer could face liability.

In *McDermid v Nash Dredging and Reclamation Co Ltd*[257] a man was employed as a deckhand for dredging work on a fjord in Sweden. McDermid's duty was to untie a rope from the dredger and then give the captain a signal telling him that it was safe to start the engine. However, the captain failed to wait for the signal and McDermid's leg was seriously injured as a result.

If the system is not being operated it means that the system is not being provided at all.[258] Lord Brandon of Oakbrook further stated that as the duty is personal it cannot be delegated, 'if it is not performed, it is no defence for the employer to show that he delegated its performance to a person, whether his servant or not his servant, whom he reasonably believed to be competent to perform it. Despite such delegation the employer is liable for the non-performance of the duty.'

5.2.3 Statutory duties   Negligence and breach of statutory duty are two distinct and different torts. Whereas negligence is concerned with a person's duty of care not to cause harm/damage/injury to another, a statutory duty is an explicit obligation or prohibition to perform a duty in a specified manner enacted by Parliament. The Act often provides guidance on adequate remedies available for a breach of such duty; alternatively, there may be other means of enforcement, such as common law remedies.

In *London Passenger Transport Board v Upson*,[259] a woman who attempted to cross a pedestrian street with the lights against her was injured by a bus, whose driver had failed to stop his vehicle in time to avoid the collision. It was argued that the driver could not have seen the woman as a taxi-cab stopped at the crossing was obstructing his view. It was held that the bus driver owed the pedestrian a statutory duty to slow down his speed, when in a situation where the view is unclear, so as to be able to stop the vehicle in time and avoid any harm.

In the House of Lords' judgement, Lord Wright stated that 'the statutory right has its origin in the statute, but the particular remedy of an action for damages is given by the common law in order to make effective, for the benefit of the injured plaintiff, his right to the performance by the defendant of the defendant's statutory duty. It is an effective sanction. It is not a claim in negligence in the strict or ordinary sense.'

---

[257]   [1987] AC 906
[258]   *per* Lord Hailsham of St.Marylebone
[259]   [1949] AC 155

5.2.3.1 Health and safety related matters Note: this section is applicable to all jurisdictions, ie England, Wales, Northern Ireland and Scotland. Should the need for differentiation arise, express mention to the relevant jurisdiction will be made in this report.

The **Health and Safety at Work Act 1974**[260] is an important piece of legislation that applies to the whole of the United Kingdom and is the basic legal source on health and safety matters in any work activity. This Act sets out the general principles of law in this field and specifies the duties and obligations imposed on all employers towards their employees and third parties, such as members of the public or more specific classes/categories of people depending on the situation. The main obligation is that efforts must be made 'so far as is reasonably practicable' to ensure that every measure is taken to avoid employees and third parties coming to harm due to work-related risks.

The Act also extends to the Health and Safety Commission (HSC) the power to advise the government on drawing health and safety regulations, and grants the Health and Safety Executive (HSE) authority to issue guidance and codes of practice to which employers can refer to in order to better understand and comply with the legal requirements regulating health and safety issues.

The Act is supported by two sets of regulations in particular, which are relevant to the present report: the **Manual Handling Operations Regulations 1992**[261] and the **Management of Health & Safety at Work Regulation 1999.**[262]

Overall, these legislative requirements lay a responsibility on employers to ensure that the health and safety of their employees and third parties are protected. The regulations set out guidelines for both employers and employees that are to be followed in order to help guarantee that a structure is in place for that purpose. One of the main points is that a risk assessment must be carried out so as to establish what the risks are and how they can be tackled. Furthermore, the evaluation of work-related risks must be supported by and laid out in policies and made available to all relevant parties.

The HSE explains the roles fulfilled by the various documents that are made available to employers.[263]

Guidance

Guidance deals with issues which are industry-specific or focus on particular processes, procedures and/or problems. Such Guidance is not law; however, it is usually helpful to follow such Guidance in attempting to meet most of the legal requirements. The Health and Safety Executive explains that the main purposes of the Guidance which it issues are:

'• to interpret – helping people to understand what the law says – including for example how requirements based on European Community Directives fit with those under the Health and Safety at Work Act;

• to help people comply with the law;

• to give technical advice'.[264]

---

[260] Also referred to as Health and Safety Act
[261] Also referred to as MHOR
[262] Also referred to as the Management Regulations
[263] HSE, Health & Safety Regulation, *A Short Guide*, weblink: http://www.hse.gov.uk/pubns/hsc13.htm#4
[264] supra n.263, HSE, A *Short Guide*

Codes of Practice

Codes of Practice, as the expression suggests, are less about theory and more about pragmatic issues arising from applying the legal requirements in practice. They offer employers guidance on 'good practice' and give advice on what is 'reasonably practicable' in their work activity/industry.

> *'Approved Codes of Practice have a special legal status. If employers are prosecuted for a breach of health and safety law, and it is proved that they have not followed the relevant provisions of the Approved Code of Practice, a court can find them at fault unless they can show that they have complied with the law in some other way.'*[265]

Regulations

Regulations are secondary legislation enacted by Parliament, and are therefore legal obligations and duties from which employers cannot derogate. They are written in a 'goal-setting' fashion in that they stipulate *what* is to be achieved, which allows employers the freedom to choose on a course of action in order to eliminate risks in their work place.

Employers can refer to Guidance and Codes of Practice although they are under no obligation to follow their guidelines. On the other hand, they still have a duty to do what is 'reasonably practicable' to safeguard and promote their employees and third parties' safety.

> *'. . . But some risks are so great, or the proper control measures so costly, that it would not be appropriate to leave employers discretion in deciding what to do about them. Regulations identify these risks and set out specific action that must be taken. Often these requirements are absolute – to do something without qualification by whether it is reasonably practicable.'*[266]

5.2.3.2 Health and Safety at Work Act 1974 Section 2 of the Act provides that an employer is under a duty to ensure the health, safety and welfare of his employees when they are performing work duties in the course of their employment, so far as is reasonably practicable. The Act also imposes on employers an obligation to develop and draft a health and safety policy statement, which should include mention as to the arrangements and organisation of foreseeable risk management. Employers must also provide employees with a safe work place and safe systems of work, as well as with relevant information, instruction, training and supervision.

Section 3 of the Health and Safety Act extends the duty to ensure the health and safety of people who are not employees, but who might nonetheless be affected by the employers' work activities. In a care setting, this would include people such as visitors, external professionals, contractors, etc.

Section 7 of the Act imposes a responsibility on employees to take reasonable care for their own health and safety, as well as for their fellow workers and whoever else might be affected by their act or omissions. Moreover, an employee must co-operate with his employer in so far as is necessary in order to abide by the legal obligations and duties laid down in the Health and Safety Act.

---

[265] supra n.263, HSE, A *Short Guide*
[266] supra n.263, HSE, A *Short Guide*

5.2.3.3 Management of Health and Safety at Work Regulations 1999   The Regulations are more specific than the Health and Safety Act in that they clearly identify measures that need to be taken in order to observe the legal duties laid down in the Health and Safety Act.

Employers are under a duty to design, develop and install a system of risk management, which will ensure the health and safety of all employees and members of the public who might be affected by their work activities.

Employers are to take the following actions:

- Under Regulation 3(1), employers must conduct a **'suitable and sufficient' assessment of risks to the health and safety** of employees when they are at work, and of people who are not in employment and who might be affected by the employers'/employees' actions or work activity.

- Under Regulation 3(3), employers must **review their risk assessment** if the latter is no longer valid or if there has been a significant change that commands such an action.

- Any **preventative and protective measures** must be conducted in accordance with the principles laid down in schedule 1 of the Management Regulations (see below).

- Under Regulation 5(1), 'every employer shall make and give effect to such arrangements as are appropriate, having regard to the nature of his activities and the size of his undertaking, for the **effective planning, organisation, control, monitoring and review of the preventive and protective measures**'.

- Under Regulation 7(1), employers must ensure that they **employ competent staff**. The latter are regarded as 'competent' when they have sufficient training, experience, knowledge and/or any other qualities relevant to the proper fulfilment of the Management Regulations' legal requirements.[267]

- Under Regulation 8, employers must ensure that **emergency procedures are in place** in case of 'serious or imminent danger and for danger areas'. Employees must be made aware of these procedures, 'so far as is practicable'.

- Under Regulation 10, employers must **provide employees with 'comprehensible and relevant information'** on risk assessment findings and protective and preventative measures.

- Under Regulation 11, employers must help facilitate co-operation and co-ordination between employees and amongst people who share a same work place.

- Under Regulation 13, employers are under an obligation to provide employees with **adequate training in health and safety.**

Schedule 1 sets out the general principles of the Management Regulations stipulated in regulation 4:

(a) avoiding risks;

(b) evaluating the risks which cannot be avoided;

(c) combating the risks at source;

---

[267] Regulation 7(5) Management of Health and Safety at Work Regulations 1999

(d) adapting the work to the individual, especially as regards the design of workplaces, the choice of work equipment and the choice of working and production methods, with a view, in particular, to alleviating monotonous work and work at a predetermined work-rate and to reducing their effect on health;

(e) adapting to technical progress;

(f) replacing the dangerous by the non-dangerous or the less dangerous;

(g) developing a coherent overall prevention policy which covers technology, organisation of work, working conditions, social relationships and the influence of factors relating to the working environment;

(h) giving collective protective measures priority over individual protective measures; and

(i) giving appropriate instructions to employees.

It is not uncommon for more than one regulation to apply to a work activity or industry, and employers have to keep informed and clear as to their obligations and duties. In a *Guide to Risk Assessment Requirements*,[268] the HSE states that the Management Regulations always apply, regardless of the work activity. Indeed,

> '... *the assessment provisions of the Management Regulations are superimposed over all other workplace health and safety legislation including the general duties in the Health and Safety at Work Act. This makes the Management Regulations risk assessment provisions very wide-ranging and all-embracing. They are comprehensive in coverage of places, activities and other sources of hazard. They require [the employer] to assess all the risks in [the] workplace.*'[269]

The employer is responsible for the assessment of risks in the workplace and must ensure that this is done properly and adequately. However, the obligation does not imply that the risk assessment must be conducted by the employer himself or herself, as this can be done by a qualified and/or competent other.

5.2.3.4 The Manual Handling Operations Regulations 1992 The MHOR impose a duty on employers to avoid, 'so far as is reasonably practicable', situations where employees are at risk of injuring themselves lifting and carrying loads manually.[270]

If the employer is in a position where he is unable to comply with this provision, ie he cannot avoid or eliminate the need for his employees to engage in manual handling operations, the MHOR provides that the employer must:

- Conduct a 'suitable and sufficient' assessment of all manual handling operations that might be undertaken by his employees. The assessment shall undergo a review if and when it is no longer valid or there is a significant change;

- Take appropriate measures aimed at reducing the risks of injury that might be caused by the manual handling operations 'to the lowest level reasonably practicable';

- Provide employees who undertake manual handling operations with general indications on the specifics of the load (eg weight), in so far as it is reasonably practicable.

---

[268] Health & Safety Executive, weblink: http://www.hse.gov.uk/pubns/indg218.pdf
[269] supra n.263, HSE, weblink: http://www.hse.gov.uk/pubns/indg218.pdf
[270] Regulation 4 MHOR

The employer's duty to avoid risk of injury within the context of this regulation does not extend to other people who are not employed, and it does not include members of the public. However, as mentioned in the previous section, employers do have a duty of care towards members of the public under the Management Regulations.

The HSE has issued guidance on the MHOR to provide employers with a clearer understanding of what is expected of them. In brief, an employer's duty under this regulation is to: '

- **Avoid** the need for hazardous manual handling, as far as reasonably practicable;

- **Assess** the risk of injury from any hazardous manual handling that can't be avoided; and

- **Reduce** the risk of injury from hazardous manual handling, as far as is reasonably practicable'.[271]

As well as imposing duties on employers, the MHOR also renders employees responsible for the appropriate use of 'any machinery, equipment, dangerous substance, transport equipment, means of production or safety device' provided by the employer, following instructions and/or training provided for that purpose.[272] Furthermore, employees must 'follow appropriate systems of work laid down for their safety . . . co-operate with their employer on health and safety matters, inform the employer if they identify hazardous handling activities, take care to ensure that their activities do not put others at risks.'[273]

For further details on manual handling, the reader might refer to the HSE website.[274]

5.2.3.5 Risk assessment   Risk assessment plays a vital part in any discussion around the possibility of introducing the use of physical intervention as part of an individual's care plan in response to a challenging behaviour. It must also be incorporated in a policy statement on physical restraint in order to give staff guidelines on recognising and preventing risks in certain given situations.

Five steps to risk assessment

The HSE has provided a leaflet that spells out the five steps which employers are advised to follow when conducting a risk assessment.[275] The guidelines are not compulsory; however they are a good indication of what would constitute good practice.

The following gives a brief summary of the five steps to risk assessment. For further details, refer to the HSE website[276] and other publications.

Step 1: Look for hazards

This means looking at foreseeable risks, ie observing possible causes of harm that can reasonably be expected to occur and/or affect people in the work place.

---

[271] Health & Safety Executive, *Getting to Grips with Manual Handling – A Short Guide for Employers*. Web link: http://www.hse.gov.uk/pubns/indg143.pdf
[272] Regulation 14 MHOR
[273] supra n.271, *Getting to Grips with Manual Handling*, HSE, p.4
[274] www.hse.gov.uk
[275] *Five Steps to Risk Assessment*, HSE Books, weblink: http://www.hse.gov.uk/pubns/indg163.pdf
[276] www.hsebooks.co.uk

Step 2: Decide who might be harmed and how

One must consider a wide range of people who might be expected to be affected or incur injury when present in the work place, including staff, patient/clients/residents, visitors and any other relevant third parties.

Step 3: Evaluate the risks and decide whether the existing precautions are adequate or whether more should be done

'Even after all precautions have been taken, some risk usually remains. What you have to decide for each significant hazard is whether this **remaining risk is high, medium or low**.'[277]

The person conducting the risk assessment must aim to reduce the hazard to a minimum risk level. Extra measures might be needed and, arguably, must be taken if reasonably practicable.

Step 4: Record your findings

If more than five employees are employed, either to support people with learning disabilities or as maintenance staff, then the findings of the risk assessment must be recorded, stating what the hazard is, the potential risk and any relevant conclusions. The findings must also be made available to employees and be kept as a written record for future reference (ie as evidence of compliance with the law, as a reminder, for inspections or potential civil liabilities, etc).

It is argued that a risk assessment need not go beyond what is necessary, as it only needs to 'be suitable and sufficient'.[278]

Step 5: Review your assessment and revise it if necessary

Risk assessment must be reviewed as a means of checking whether the precautions and measures taken to remedy or isolate certain hazards are still working. Furthermore, if there is a significant change in the work activity and/or work place, the risk assessment must be updated and amended to include new potential risks that can be reasonably expected to occur.

Definition of risk

The HSE describes a hazard as 'anything that can cause harm' and defines a risk as 'the chance, high or low, that somebody will be harmed by the hazard'.[279]

In the context of people with learning disabilities and challenging behaviours, the notion of risk varies depending on individuals' perspectives.

A publication from the Foundation for People with Learning Disabilities[280] investigated this issue and concluded that 'the people with learning disabilities, relatives and specialist professional carers who [were] interviewed all had different ideas about the nature of risk'.[281]

---

[277] supra n.275, *5 Steps to Risk Assessment*, HSE leaflet, p. 5
[278] supra n.275, *5 Steps to Risk Assessment*, HSE, leaflet, p. 6
[279] supra n.275, *5 Steps to Risk Assessment*, HSE leaflet, p. 3
[280] hereinafter, the Foundation
[281] Alaszewski H, Parker A & Alaszewski A, *Empowerment and Protection – The Development of Policies and Practices in Risk Assessment and Risk Management in Services for Adults with Learning Disabilities*. Mental Health Foundation, 1999, p. 13

The authors of the Foundation document worked with focus groups and collected their views on the issue of risk. Their findings are as follows:

> 'The **adults with learning disabilities**[282] *did not appear to have a sophisticated understanding of risk and often appeared willing to accept that others made judgements and decisions on their behalf.*
>
> *. . . **Specialist professionals**,*[283] *both in community and residential settings, were very supportive of the idea of risk as an opportunity for personal development, but were also conscious of the potential for their clients to be harmed . . . For a minority of professional carers, risk was created by a lack of information but this could be overcome.*
>
> *The majority of **families**[284] saw risk in terms of the potential for physical danger and there was a tendency to think of their relatives with learning disabilities as perpetual children requiring protection...*'[285]

In any case, risk is acknowledged as being an integral part of everyone's life, including individuals with learning disabilities. The issue faced by families and professionals caring for the latter is to achieve a healthy balance between the promotion of the individual's freedom and the safeguard of her physical and mental safety.[286]

Risk assessment in relation to challenging behaviours

David Allen[287] has adapted the five steps in risk assessment to the specific issue of physical interventions in dealing with challenging behaviours.[288] The example below is a model that '[takes] into account particular aspects of risk planning that are relevant to consider when supporting people with intellectual disability and challenging behaviour'.[289] The present will give a brief outline of this model. (For further details, the reader should refer to the original document by David Allen.)

The risk assessment should:

1. **Specify the behaviours of concern**

   This should give details of the frequency, rate and duration of the challenging behaviour.

2. **Specify who might be at risk and how**

   This includes the person with learning disabilities, his fellow residents/clients/service users/patients, carers, members of the public, and any other relevant third parties ie people who might be affected by the challenging behaviour.

---

[282] added emphasis
[283] added emphasis
[284] added emphasis
[285] supra, n.281, Alaszewski *et al*, p. 13
[286] for further details on the issue of risk and freedom, see section on the Adults with Incapacity (Scotland) Act 2000
[287] Allen D, *Ethical Approaches to Physical Interventions – Responding to Challenging Behaviour in People with Intellectual Disabilities*, BILD, Kidderminster, 2002
[288] supra n.287, Allen D, Chapter 5 – *Devising Individualised Risk Management Plans*, pp. 71–88
[289] supra n.287, Allen D, p. 77

3. **Identify the conditions under which the probability of the behaviour occurring is increased**

This means looking at the possible causes for the displaying of a challenging behaviour, including situations, events, health issues, environment and/or any other element that triggers a challenging response on the part of the person with learning disabilities.

4. **Specify what primary preventative strategies should be employed**

Since physical intervention is a means of dealing with challenging behaviour as a last resort, carers are encouraged and strongly advised to develop primary intervention plans. This involves 'changing aspects of a service user's living, working and recreational environments so that the probability of challenging behaviour occurring is reduced in the first instance. It also involves the use of interventions designed specifically to modify user behaviour.'[290]

5. **Clearly describe the early behavioural indicators that the person may be losing self-control**

It is important that carers can read the signs presented by the person they support, which suggest that the latter is being affected by a situation and is therefore likely to display a challenging behaviour. Allen uses the analogy of a traffic signal, which goes from green (normal level of activity and behaviour), through to amber (stage at which the individual is showing signs of agitation or distress), to red (which is the display of the challenging behaviour). 'By producing clear operational definitions of behaviours seen at the amber stage, carers can be cued in to the need to take immediate action and thereby avoid passing onto "red". Many episodes of aggressive behaviour occur because carers fail to recognise these signs or, more commonly, fail to alter their own behaviour once the signs become evident.'[291]

6. **Specify what secondary preventative strategies should be employed**

'Secondary prevention involves the identification of initial signs of agitation followed by early intervention to defuse agitation and later the course of behaviour, thus avoiding a full-blown incident.[292] These strategies may include plans for terminating aversive events, distracting the person, defusion, and diversion to a reinforcing activity.'[293]

For further information on secondary preventative measures, the reader might refer to LaVigna and Willis, in *The role of positive programming in behavioral treatment*.[294]

7. **Specify what physical interventions may need to be employed**

Allen refers to the expression 'reactive behaviour management strategies' and describes it as a set of physical responses that a carer has to envisage and follow when primary and secondary measures have failed to diffuse a situation. The strategies recommended, which have to be used in accordance with the service user's specific needs and characteristics in mind, are:

- Increasing personal space;

- Self-protective breakaway procedures;

- Minimal restraint.

---

[290] supra n.287, Allen D, p. 77, quoting Doyle *et al*, *Preventing and Responding to Aggressive Behaviour. A Training Manual*, Cardiff 1996; and Harris *et al*, *Physical Interventions. A Policy Framework*, BILD and NAS 1996.
[291] Supra n.287, Allen D, p. 79
[292] reference made to Doyle *et al*, 1996; and Harris *et al* see supra n.14
[293] supra n.287, Allen D, p. 79
[294] LaVigna GW, Willis TJ & Donellan AM, The role of positive programming in behavioral treatment. In Cipani E (ed), *The Treatment of Severe Behaviour Disorders*, Washington: AAMR, (1989), p. 59–83

8. **Record any residual unmanaged risks**

Risks can be reduced to a minimum. However, it is unlikely that they will be definitely and permanently erased. Therefore, 'ensuring that risk assessment and management plans are firmly anchored by a knowledge of what the person has done in the past . . . represents one means of trying to ensure that plans are both comprehensive and realistic. . .'.

9. **Specify the procedures to be followed after an incident for both the service user and carers**

Both the service user's and the carer's needs must be attended to after an incident. For the service user, this includes looking into activity or environmental changes, for example. As for the carer, he or she could be presented with options such as de-briefing sessions or adequate physical interventions training programmes.

10. **Specify how the risk management plan will be used to support access to community living**

Over-protective attitudes towards the service user are targeted here. Providing care and ensuring the safety of an individual with learning disabilities can prove difficult and be open to criticism. As stated by Morgan,[295] 'the fear of criticism and blame leads to an all too frequent, but understandable, retreat into a defensive practice'.

Behaviour management plans must therefore be designed with the individual's needs in mind and must 'form part of a package of interventions that will lead to an enhanced lifestyle for the person concerned'.[296]

11. **Specify how plans should be recorded and reviewed**

The recording of risk management plans is necessary if such plans are to be effective. It serves both as a reminder and a source of information. 'Having identified risks and agreed strategies for minimising those risks, it is vital that feedback is sought on the effectiveness of the procedures advocated and their impact upon both the service user and their carers'.[297]

12. **Record agreement with the plan**

Discussions on the design of risk management plans should be conducted by a multi-disciplinary panel, including the service user, carers, and any other relevant representatives. The plan should record the presence of the persons involved in agreeing on a behavioural management strategy.

13. **Specify a review date**

'Risk management plans should be living documents'.[298] People evolve and change, so do their needs and behaviour patterns, therefore it is argued that plans should be reviewed on a regular basis and should determine a procedure which covers urgent situations where a plan might need to be reviewed promptly.

---

[295] Morgan S, *Assessing and Managing Risk. Practitioner's Handbook*, Pavilion, Brighton, 1998, p.18
[296] supra n.287, Allen D, p. 81
[297] supra n.287, Allen D, p. 81
[298] supra n.287, Allen D, p. 81

It is argued that risk assessment should provide a safe environment for both carer and service user. One way this can be achieved is by providing carers with adequate training in health and safety, as well as in physical intervention techniques if when appropriate, reasonable and necessary. As suggested by Allen, 'risk assessment can also be used as a means of identifying reasonable responses in situations where such interventions may be required. Thus, the level of response required by carers can be matched to the level of challenging behaviour shown by a service user on the basis of a prediction of their future behaviour pattern.'[299]

Risk assessment in relation to violence towards staff

The five steps to risk assessment also apply in situations where staff are at risk of incurring injury due to voluntary or involuntary aggressive behaviours aimed at their physical integrity.

Employers are under an obligation, under the Reporting of Injuries, Diseases and Dangerous Occurrences Regulations 1995, to report instances of aggressive incidents towards staff if the employee has been off work for more than three days due to the assault on their person.

Furthermore, under the Safety Representatives and Safety Committees Regulations 1977 and the Health and Safety (Consultation with Employees) Regulations 1996, employees have a right to be consulted on issues of health and safety, and employers should also consult with safety representatives when the work organisation employs a substantial number of employees.

The HSC provides further information on the matter, and the reader may refer to the guidance on assessment and management of *Violence and Aggression to Staff in Health Services*[300] for a fuller outline of how the five steps to risk assessment apply within the health services.

5.2.4 Employer's responsibility to provide P.I. training As regards the provision of adequate P.I. training provided by employers, the Scottish courts appear to be of the opinion that it is an employer's duty to provide the means for their staff to protect themselves against physical violence.

In _McLeod v Aberdeen City Council_,[301] an auxiliary employed to work in a school for children with special needs suffered physical injuries after being repeatedly kicked and head-butted while attempting to remove a disruptive pupil from a room in which he was allowed to be. As a consequence, she sued the council for these injuries and ultimately the court ruled that the case should proceed to trial.

The council attempted to refute the auxiliary's claim by arguing that the pupil's previous behaviour was both irrelevant and inconclusive to support the notion of foreseeability of injury; the auxiliary had also failed to provide any evidence of such previous incidents involving physical assault.

The council also argued that there is no recognised body of training and that the techniques employed by the auxiliary to deal with the pupil are recognised practices that any reasonable employer should endeavour to teach his staff. Moreover, the council argued that there is no

---

[299] supra n.287, Allen D, p. 81
[300] Health & Safety Commission, Health Services Advisory Committee, HSE Books, 1997
[301] (1999) GWD 23–1115

evidence that it is general practice to provide such training or that failure to do so would amount to unreasonable and unnecessary danger for both staff and pupils. Finally, the council added that the auxiliary could not prove that even if she had received training the techniques taught would have prevented her injuries from happening.

The court decided that the case should proceed and Lord Dawson was of the opinion that the council could have a duty to provide their employees with training allowing staff to protect themselves from violence from pupils and other third parties. Such a duty would be subject to foreseeability of such violence occurring in the course of the auxiliary's employment duties.

The judge further added that the council, as an education authority, is presumed to have had adequate knowledge of the pupil's tendency to respond to physical restraint with violence, which could thus mean that it was reasonably foreseeable. Lord Dawson reminded the court that P.I. techniques are made available to employers in the care industry so it would be 'folly' not to provide staff with training in techniques that would help reduce or prevent violence and which would also contribute to minimise any risk of injury as a result.

In contrast to the Scottish court's position, the English courts seem reluctant to impose such a duty upon employers.

In _Purvis v Buckinghamshire County Council_[302] a welfare assistant employed by the council in the moderate learning difficulties department of a school suffered a back injury after attempting to restrain a pupil from running away and sued the council for negligence and breach of statutory duty.

The court in this case held that the assistant's two years' experience in the department was sufficient evidence that she was adequately qualified to deal with such a situation. Although it was conceded that there are programmes available to teach staff how to safely restrain a child, it was held to be doubtful that such training would have prevented the back injury from occurring. The council had thus not been judged negligent.

It was conceded that there was a breach of the statutory duty specified in Reg.4(1)(b)[303] of the Manual Handling Operations Regulations 1992 as regards the duty to provide a risk assessment[304] and thus minimise the risk of injury.[305] However, such a breach was held to be only minor, as of a technical nature, and irrelevant as to the causation of the back injury.

In _Daws v Croydon London Borough Council_,[306] (a county court decision) a teacher working in a school for emotionally and behaviourally disturbed children suffered a back injury following an attempt to restrain a pupil who was hanging on a bar up in the classroom's ceiling. The court in this case actually held that the employer had not been negligent in not providing the teacher with training in physical restraint techniques. The rationale for this judgement is that there is no extensive evidence as to the specialist training available in physical restraint and

---

[302] [1999] Ed. C.R 542, ELR 231
[303] 4(1) Each employer shall (...) (b) where it is not reasonably practicable to avoid the need for his employees to undertake any manual handling operations at work which involve a risk of their being injured –
[304] (i) make a suitable and sufficient assessment of all such manual handling operations to be undertaken by them (...)
[305] (ii) take appropriate steps to reduce the risk of injury to those employees arising out of their undertaking any such manual handling operations to the lowest level reasonably practicable (...)
[306] Case unreported, although referred to in an article by Dominic Hayes, Woman receives £37,000 damages for injuries from restraining pupils, _Independent_ 17 April 2001

as to whether other councils provided that sort of training. Furthermore, it is doubtful that such training would have avoided the teacher incurring the back injury. The judge also mentioned the substantial financial strain being experienced by Croydon London BC.

This decision came out before the publication of the new DfES Guidance on Physical Intervention. In that guidance, paragraph 13.1 provides that 'staff who are expected to employ restrictive physical interventions will require additional, more specialised training. The nature and extent of the training will depend upon the characteristics of the people who may require a physical intervention, the behaviours they present and the responsibilities of individual members of staff.'

Moreover, the Guidance also stresses the point that any physical techniques used must be selected according to the characteristics and the needs of each individual who presents the challenging behaviour. Once trained, a carer must only use the techniques which he was taught in the manner which he was taught and cannot modify them (para 13.2).

5.3 Violence at work

5.3.1 Risk assessment   Breakwell[307] proposes a checklist that can help members of staff assessing whether there is a risk of violence before the violence actually occurs. She advocates that the list is a mental aid that should be run through regularly before entering into contact with an individual for whom care is to be provided.

In order for the checklist to be useful and effective, the carer must be able to answer the questions accurately. Therefore it is necessary that the carer has enough information concerning the person they care for, which supports the view expressed in the workbook on *Promoting Well-Being and Preventing Challenging Behaviour*[308] that knowing an individual can help anticipate challenging situations.

Here is a sample of the questions on the checklist to which a majority of positive answers would strongly suggest the presence of a risk of violence.

Before facing the person	When facing the person	Greater risk if answer yes
• Does the person have a history of violence? • Does the person have a history of criminal convictions? • Does the person have a history of psychiatric illness? • Does the person suffer from a medical condition which may result in loss of self-control?	• Is the person showing signs of atypical excitement or passivity? • Are there weapons or similar cues to violence in the room? • Is the person showing signs of atypical high arousal? • Is there a breakdown in the normal pattern of nonverbal communication?	• Am I alone and without back-up? • Are colleagues unaware of my whereabouts? • Am I without any means of raising the alarm if attacked? • Am I likely to be trapped without an escape route if the person becomes violent? • Am I unaware of how I react in violent situations?

---

[307] Breakwell GM, *Coping With Aggressive Behaviour, Personal and Professional Development*, published by The British Psychological Society, 1997
[308] supra, n.21, Lally

• Has the person verbally abused me in the past? • Has the person threatened me with violence in the past? • Has the person attacked me in the past?	• Is the person showing signs of rapid mood swings? • Is the person showing oversensitivity to suggestions or criticisms?	• Am I unaware of the assault cycle? • Am I unaware of the cultural norms which are likely to control this person's exhibition of violence? • Have I ever considered what I would do if attacked?

An employee, who fears for his safety when caring for an individual with a learning disability who also presents severe challenging behaviour, might find some protection under the law of contract. Indeed, a contract of employment implies that an employer has two obligations towards their employees, that is to provide them with a safe working environment in which the exposure to any risk is kept to a minimum; and an obligation to respect the principle of 'mutual trust and confidence', which is an implied term of the contract of employment.

In _Keys v Shoe Fayre Ltd_ [309] a part-time shop assistant who expressed her fears after a robbery occurred at the shop was told that no action could be taken in order to provide safety to staff. She eventually resigned after another robbery and set to look for another job. The court held that the resignation could be considered as a dismissal since the employer had failed to fulfil his obligation to provide his staff with a safe system of work and reasonably safe premises.

In _Courtaulds Northern Textiles Ltd v Andrew_, [310] the court stated that 'there is implied in a contract of employment a term that the employers will not, without reasonable and proper cause, conduct themselves in a manner calculated or likely to destroy or seriously damage the relationship of confidence and trust between employer and employee. (. . .) Any breach of that implied term is a fundamental breach amounting to a repudiation since it necessarily goes to the root of the contract.' This principle was reiterated in the more recent case of _BG Plc v O'Brien_. [311]

Based on these facts, it has been submitted that an employer who fails to consider his employees' fear of violence and to take action when violence is an actual occurrence in the course of the employee's work might be in breach of the employment contract. [312] Indeed, if an employee finds it difficult to carry on with his work due to a threat or actual violence in the workplace, they can resign. In these circumstances, the resignation is likely to be treated as a constructive and unfair dismissal.

> _'The practical implications are that the law requires employers to take seriously risks relating to violence and to develop a coherent and appropriate response, [which] would include:_
>
> • _Establishing a culture whereby concerns about threats and violence can be raised by employees openly and without prejudice, in confidence if necessary;_
>
> • _Providing an effective mechanism to investigate problems and explore possible options to remove or alleviate problems;_

[309] [1978] IRLR 476
[310] [1979] IRLR 84
[311] [2001] IRLR 496

- *Applying disciplinary procedures carefully and rigorously;*

- *Reviewing regularly overall incidence and nature of violent incidents and issues.*[313]

5.3.2 National Task Force on Violence against Social Care Staff[314] The Department of Health's website provides some guidelines to employers and care staff employees alike on the employer's responsibility as regards violence at work.

The website states that relevant legislation on that matter is as follows:

- Health and Safety at Work Act 1974;

- Management of Health and Safety at Work 1992;

- Reporting of Injuries, Diseases and Dangerous Occurrences Regulations 1995;

- Safety Representatives and Safety Committees Regulations 1977;

- Health and Safety (Consultation with Employees) Regulations 1996.

The Manual Handling Operations Regulations (MHOR) 1992 can also be added to this list.

The website provides employees with a checklist as to what their responsibility is as well as what their employer's position and responsibilities are:

The employer's primary responsibility includes that they must provide:

- a clear policy setting out the Code of Practice relevant to their organisation and their work;

- a clear risk assessment system;

- a clear procedure as to the actions that need to be taken in a risk situation;

- appropriate training;

- a safe working environment;

- support in dealing with issues of violence, threats or abuse;

- procedures that ensure the workability and the review of any precautions;

- support after an incident (eg de-briefing sessions).

The employee's responsibility is to familiarise himself with the organisation's policy, procedures, Code of Practice, and so on. The employee should also ensure that he is aware of what would trigger a risk situation in order to be prepared to deal and cope with it. Finally, the employee should have a knowledge and understanding of the procedures available for raising concerns with colleagues and managers.

For further detail, the reader can refer to the Department of Health's website.[314]

---

[312] Patricia Leighton, *Violence at Work: the legal framework*; Leather P, Brady C, Lawrence C, Beale D & Cox T (eds), *Work-related Violence – Assessment and Intervention*, Routledge 1999, pp. 19–33
[313] supra n.312, Leighton, *Violence at Work: the Legal Framework*, p. 26
[314] http://www.doh.gov.uk/violencetaskforce/card.htm

Chapter 6

Employer's responsibility in Scotland

Introduction

This chapter considers the liability of employers in Scotland in relation to the actions of their employees specifically in the context of the potential use of physical interventions. This is an important area of the law for any employee as well as for all employers. Those working with children and adults with learning disabilities and severe challenging behaviour should have a basic knowledge of the concepts of employer's responsibility in order to understand the arena of duties and responsibilities within which they work. What follows therefore is a brief indication of the relevant provisions applicable in Scotland.

6.1 Vicarious liability

An employer may face liability for the wrongful conduct of his employees, which has resulted in a third party being injured and which occurred during the course of the worker's employment. Similar to the principles established under English law, the employer-employee relationship and the commission of the act during the course of employment must be established in order to establish liability in the employer.

In order to determine whether an employer and a worker are bound by a contract of employment – in which case vicarious liability is actionable – rather than a contract for services, the courts will consider the control and economic relationship between employer and employee.

The 'control' test is set to determine the degree of control exercised by the employer on his employee: how much does the employer decide on <u>what</u> are and <u>how</u> the employee is to perform his employment duties? If it is proven that the employee is directed on which tasks he is to complete and the manner in which he is meant to perform them, then it is arguable that there is a sufficient degree of control by the employer, putting the latter in a position where he could be liable for the wrongful act of his employee.

In a similar fashion to the English approach, the Scottish courts will not merely consider the control element of an employee-employer relationship. They will also take other factors into account, such as the economic 'risk' borne by the parties.[315] In _Marshall v William Sharp & Sons Ltd_,[316] Lord Dunpark stated that 'one must have regard to all the relevant factors, which include the intention of the parties, power of selection, the method of payment and the reasons for that, the nature of the work and the power of dismissal'.

---

[315] _Ready Mixed Concrete (South East) Ltd v Minister of Pensions and National Insurance_ [1968] 2 QB 497
[316] [1991] SLT 114

In *United Wholesale Grocers Ltd v Sher*,[317] the defender had been contracted to perform some joinery and flooring work for the proprietors of a warehouse and had sub-contracted three other people to do the work. After the warehouse suffered damage due to a fire, the proprietors sued the defender, who denied being in an employer-employee relationship with two of the workers hired for the sub-contract.

It is to be understood from this case that in order to decide whether an individual is an employee or a contractor, the question to be asked is: 'is he *part and parcel of [the] business carried out by the [commissioner/employer]* or is the work performed merely *forming a part of what [he does] on [his] own account*?'. Lord Cullen held that 'in the absence of any determining principle which falls to be applied, the answer to the question depends upon *an assessment of all the factors which appear to be relevant to the particular case.*[318] The control exercised by the alleged employer over the way in which the work is done is obviously a very important consideration. However, there must be many cases in which such control is not exercised either because it was unnecessary or because the employer lacks the skill to exercise such control.'

Lord Cullen then concluded that the workmen in the *Sher* case were in an employee-employer relationship with the defender. Indeed, although the latter did not exercise any control *per se* over the workmen in directing their work, and they also brought their own tools with them, they were nonetheless paid for the work done on a daily basis rather than for the end product. Besides, the defender did provide them with the initial materials necessary to perform the work. He was thus held to be vicariously liable for the damages, 'although on any view that employment was on an extremely casual basis'.[319]

This statement appears to be particularly relevant in situations where a carer is employed by a care agency as bank staff and works as additional help in a residential home. It is argued that despite the casual nature of the work, in cases where a person with a learning disability incurs injury as a result of the wrongful act of a casual worker, the bank staff agency employing the casual worker and/or the residential home requiring the services of that worker might be held vicariously liable for damages.

After establishing that the parties are in an employee-employer relationship, it must be proven that the wrongful act was committed during the course of employment. This means that the employee must have acted while he was performing his contractual duties, and not while he was 'on a frolic of his own'.[320] However, determining what acts fall within or without the course of employment can be a difficult exercise. Indeed, Lord Pearce, in *Williams v A & W Hemphill Ltd*[321] stated that 'vicarious responsibility for the act of a servant will only attach to the master if the act of the servant is done within the scope of the employment. It is probably not possible, and it is certainly inadvisable, to endeavour to lay down an exhaustive definition of what falls within the scope of the employment. Each case must depend to a considerable extent on its particular facts.'

In *Angus v Glasgow Corporation*,[322] a lorry driver had been instructed to travel from point A to point B following the shortest journey possible. However, on his way to point B the driver

---

[317] [1993] SLT 284

[318] the authors' emphasis

[319] *per* Lord Cullen, at p. 287

[320] *Storey v Ashton* (1868–69) LR 4 QB 476, at p. 478

[321] [1966] SLT 33

[322] [1977] SLT 206

made a detour to his house to collect a spare pair of glasses, and was involved in a collision after leaving his house. Although his responsibility in the collision was recognised, it was nonetheless argued that the driver had acted outside the scope of his employment and on his own initiative as he went to his house for 'his own private purpose unconnected with his employment'. The driver argued in turn that he had needed the glasses in order for him to carry out his task 'comfortably and efficiently' after a first pair of glasses had been broken.

In this case, it was held that since the purpose of the deviation was to collect a pair of glasses, it was 'closely connected with the efficient execution of his duties. The onus was on the defenders to show that the journey was entirely unconnected with the employment'.

The Scottish courts have identified two situations in which an employer will be held vicariously liable, and two others in which he will not be liable for the act of his employee. This was illustrated in the case of _Williams v A & W Hemphill_,[323] in which Lord Pearce[324] stated the four different scenarios.

'... In the first place, if the master actually authorised the particular act, he is clearly liable for it'[325]

Thus, in _Neville v C & A Modes Ltd_,[326] a young girl had been accused of attempting to steal a dress by the employees of C & A Modes Ltd. After having been interrogated and searched, the girl sued the defenders for slander. The act to keep the girl under observation, follow her and finally bring her back into the shop for interrogation and search was recognised as being part and parcel of the duties of the employees. Therefore, it was held that the employers could not 'disclaim responsibility for what their employees [were] alleged to have done and said. That class of act being authorised, [the employers were] responsible for the manner in which in a particular case the act [was] performed.'[327]

'... Secondly, where the workman does some work which he is appointed to do, but does it in a way which his master has not authorised, and would not have authorised had he known of it, the master is nevertheless still responsible, for the servant's act is still within the scope of his employment'[328]

Thus, in the case of _Taylor v City of Glasgow District Council_,[329] the court re-stated the point that, on the issue of deciding whether an act is performed within the scope of employment or not, 'many words have been written in attempting to delimit the meaning of that phrase... [and] it is often difficult to say on which side of the line a particular set of facts falls'.

In this case the proprietors of flats situated in Glasgow, which had been purchased from a development company, sued the council for damages for the acts of an employee who had signed building warrants and completion certificates that were forgeries and that falsely stated that work had been undergone. The proprietors suffered financial losses as a result and argued that the council was vicariously liable despite the fact that the documents had actually been handed to developers before reaching the proprietors of the flat.

---

[323] [1966] SLT 233
[324] approving _Kirby v National Coal Board_ [1959] SLT 7
[325] _Williams v A & W Hemphill_ 1966, _per_ Lord Pearce, at p.260
[326] [1945] SLT 189
[327] extract from the Sheriff's notes, _Neville v C & A Modes Ltd_ 1945, at p.191
[328] _Williams v A & W Hemphill_ [1966], _per_ Lord Pearce, at p.260
[329] [1997] SLT 537

It was argued that if it was established that the employee had authority to issue such documents and to carry out any additional work so related, then this would be considered to be 'an improper mode of exercising his authority' and the council would therefore be vicariously liable. However, if the employee did not have the authority to issue such warrants and had a duty to refer applications to a supervisor, he was clearly acting outside the scope of his employment. On that basis, the court allowed the defender's reclaiming motion and therefore both parties would be able to provide proof supporting their arguments before a final answer was given on the matter.

'... On the other hand, in the third place, if the servant is employed only to do a particular work, or a particular class of work, and he does something outside the scope of that work, the master is not responsible for any mischief the servant may do to a third party'[330]

The issue here is to determine the ambit of the particular work, thus clarifying the scope of the employment. The court will consider the terms of the contract between the employee and the employer; however, these terms are not said to be conclusively indicative of the employee's duties.

In _Williams v A & W Hemphill Ltd_,[331] a 16-year-old boy, a member of the Boys' Brigade of Glasgow, had gone to a summer camp with the brigade and suffered injuries following a road accident on the way back to Glasgow, which had been caused by the driver's negligence. The driver had been instructed to drive the boys back to Glasgow on a direct route. However, he took a deviation after being persuaded by some of the passengers to take another route so they could meet with a party of the Girls' Guildry on the way.

The court held that, despite the deviation, the driver still acted within the scope of his employment, as he had not completed his duty to drive all the passengers back to Glasgow.

Lord Pearce in this case stated that the passengers' 'presence and transport is a dominant purpose of the authorised journey, and, although they are transported deviously, continues to play an essential part. . . . [T]heir transport and safety does not cease at a certain stage of the journey to be the master's business, or part of his enterprise, merely because the servant has for his own purposes chosen some route which is contrary to his instructions.'[332]

'... Lastly, if the servant uses his master's time or his master's place or his master's tools for his own purposes, the master is not responsible'[333]

This last scenario is best described in the leading Scottish case on vicarious liability _Kirby v National Coal Board_.[334]

In this case, eight miners suffered injuries following an explosion that was caused by one of the workers after he had taken a legitimate break and struck a match to light a cigarette in an unauthorised area. They argued that the employers were vicariously liable for illegal smoking in a non-ventilated area.

---

[330] _Williams v A & W Hemphill_ 1966, _per_ Lord Pearce, at p.260
[331] [1966] SLT 259
[332] _Williams v A & W Hemphill_ 1966, _per_ Lord Pearce, at p.260
[333] _Williams v A & W Hemphill_ 1966, _per_ Lord Pearce, at p.260
[334] [1959] SLT 7

It was stated that '. . . where the limits of the duty of the servant are not precisely defined it is easier to treat the act of the servant as a mode of doing his work, rather than to treat it as an independent act for which the master is not responsible'.

In this case, however, the miner went into an area where he had no right to be, not to perform any work duties, but for his own purposes. The court was of opinion that this conduct could not be regarded as 'an unauthorised mode of doing the work he was employed to do . . . [but as being] something which took him outside the scope of his employment'; therefore, the employers were not liable for his wrongful conduct.

6.2 Employer's liability

The concept of employer's liability, as in England, is concerned with the employer being held accountable for an injury suffered by his employee in the course of their employment. He has a personal duty to take reasonable care for the safety of his employee – 'personal' meaning that the duty is not delegable.[335]

The duty of care here is three-fold and includes the employer's obligation to provide his employees with proper plant and equipment and competent fellow workers, on both of which Scottish law largely follows the English common law, and a safe system of work.

A safe system of work means providing employees with any devices necessary to complete their work tasks safely. This includes such items as protective goggles, gloves or other clothes, or even stepladders, as was the case in _McGregor v AAH Pharmaceuticals Ltd_.[336] In this case, the duty to provide or devise a safe system of work is highlighted, and failure to do so will result in liability.

It is argued that, for carers, this implies that when they are faced with a challenging situation, they should benefit from an adequate system of personnel (eg enough staff) and material (eg appropriate environment) support. Moreover, this raises the issue of adequate training.

On this matter, the Scottish courts appear to be of opinion as stated in _McLeod v Aberdeen City Council_[337] (see 5.2.4) that it is an employer's duty to provide the means for their staff to protect themselves against physical violence, which is in contrast with the English courts' approach.[338]

This particular case illustrated the notion that an employer's obligation to provide all his employees with a safe system of work must also consider the specifics of an employee who might have certain health problems such as physical (eg back problems) or mental difficulties (eg nervous breakdown). For the employer, this implies that the degree of care he is under a duty to exercise might be slightly greater for this particular employee. If the employer has knowledge of these specifics, yet does not take reasonable care to protect the employee from incurring physical or psychological injury as a result of an unsound system of work, he may be facing liability.

---

[335] see _Hislop v Durham_ (1842) 4 D 1168
[336] [1996] SLT 1161
[337] (1999) GWD 23–1115
[338] See Chapter 5 on Employer's Responsibility in England and Wales at 5.2.4

Finally, in assessing the reasonableness of the steps taken by an employer in securing his employees' safety, the court will consider the *calculus of risk*,[339] which includes '... the magnitude of the risk, the seriousness of any injury which may result, and the difficulty and practicability of any measures required to eliminate it'.[340]

[339] Thompson J *Delictual Liability* Butterworths 2nd Edition at p. 206
[340] *per* Lord Coulsfield in *McErlean v J&B Scotland Ltd* [1997] SLT 1326

PART IV

The law in England and Wales

Introduction

It should be noted that this part of the report is not concerned with the responsibility in criminal or civil law of any person, under a disability, for any criminal or tortious act which they may have committed. The focus of this report is on the potential liability of those who use physical interventions on persons with learning disabilities who also present with severe challenging behaviour. This part of the report will therefore deal with the potential liability of those who may have to use physical interventions to respond to incidents of challenging behaviour under both the civil and criminal law of England and Wales. For definitions of the notion of civil and criminal liability, including definitions of a criminal offence and a civil wrong, see 2.6, 2.6.1, 2.6.2 and 2.6.3. This section is concerned with the potential offences that can occur as a result of the use of physical interventions.

Chapter 7

Criminal law

Introduction

This chapter considers in detail all the potential criminal offences which may be committed under the law of England, Wales and Northern Ireland by those who use restrictive physical interventions to respond to incidents of challenging behaviour. It goes on to consider in detail all the potential defences which may be raised by those charged with any such offences.

7.1 Offences against the person

7.1.1 False imprisonment False imprisonment consists of the unlawful and intentional or reckless restraint of a victim's freedom of movement from a particular place. However, merely preventing an individual from taking a certain direction when he can take another in order to reach his chosen destination will not amount to false imprisonment *(Bird v Jones*[341]*)*.

As regards the relationship between parent and child, the general rule is that a parent will rarely be found guilty of false imprisonment when confining their child since such conduct is considered to fall within the realms of reasonable parental discipline, which is therefore not unlawful. This would certainly be the case where the parent seeks to confine their child, who has learning disabilities and severe challenging behaviour, in their own house where there are really serious concerns about the safety of the child or young person outside the home. This would equally be the case in relation to an adult with learning disabilities and severe challenging behaviour.

In the case of *R v(MM) Rahman*,[342] however, a father who had kidnapped his daughter and forced her into his car in order to send her back to her native Bangladesh, was convicted of false imprisonment. The Court of Appeal expressed the view that such an act is deemed unlawful when (a) the parent has no parental responsibility over the child; or (b) the confinement is contrary to a court order; or (c) if the detention is for such a period of time and in such circumstances as to take it out of the realms of normal parental discipline.

In this case, the Lord Chief Justice quoted the statement of Bowen LJ in *re Agar-Ellis, Agar-Ellis v Lascelles*[343]: 'as soon as it becomes obvious that the rights of the family are being abused to the detriment of the interests of the infant, then the father shows that he is no longer the natural guardian – that he has become an unnatural guardian – that he has perverted the ties

---

[341] (1845) 7 QB 742
[342] *R v Mohammed Moqbular Rahman* (1985) 81 Cr. App. R. 349
[343] (1883) 24 Ch.D. 317

of nature for the purpose of injustice and cruelty. When that case arrives, the Court will not stay its hand.'

7.1.2 Common assault No statutory definition of assault is available. Section 39 of the Criminal Justice Act 1988 merely states that assault and battery are to be treated as summary offences (ie minor offences). The maximum sentence for this offence is six months' imprisonment or a fine.

> '*The term "assault" is frequently used to include both an assault and a battery (...). This leads to confusion between the two offences (...). Strictly, "assault" is an independent offence and should be treated as such (...). An assault is any act – and not a mere omission to act – by which a person intentionally – or recklessly – causes another to apprehend immediate unlawful violence (...).*
>
> *The act must be accompanied by a hostile intent calculated to cause apprehension in the mind of the victim. Where the hostile intent is not present, there will be no assault (...) unless, of course, it is proved that the alleged assailant was reckless as to whether the complainant would apprehend immediate and unlawful violence.*'[344]

This principle could be particularly important in cases where the victim has impaired understanding as a result of learning disabilities.

Assault is the act of causing a person to fear for their physical safety and to apprehend the application of immediate unlawful violence upon them, and if one is working with those with learning disabilities one must be aware of the possibility that they may have fears about particular courses of action which others without learning disabilities might not have.

An assault is not qualified by actual physical contact (as opposed to battery); however, the person committing the assault must either intend to apply physical touching, or be reckless as to whether they cause the victim to fear such an outcome (*Venna*[345]).

The elements constituting an assault are defined by case-law and are as follows:

- An assault must be committed by an act (eg shaking a fist, drawing an injection). An omission to do something is not enough. However, when the omission is part of a continuing act, then it can amount to an assault. In *Fagan v MPC*,[346] the defendant drove onto the foot of a police officer inadvertently but he then refused to move the car off the officer's foot as demanded of him once he realised what had happened. The court decided that the defendant's failure to remove the car amounted to an omission that here resulted in an offence of assault and battery.

- Words have also been recognised sufficient to constitute an assault (*Ireland*[347]). For instance, threatening a patient that he will be taken into seclusion or physically restrained can amount to an assault. However, the words used in the particular situation which indicate that no threat is being made can also negate the offence (*Tuberville v Savage*[348]).

---

[344] Richardson PJ, Thomas DA, Turner J, Shay S & Carter W, *Archbold*, Sweet & Maxwell 2003, 19–166, p. 1660
[345] [1976] QB 421
[346] [1969] 1 QB 439
[347] [1998] AC 147
[348] (1669) 1 Mod Rep 3

- The threat of unlawful force must be immediate, ie the victim must fear that the violence will occur at once, not at some point in the future.

7.1.3 Battery   The offence of battery will always include the offence of assault. However, the reverse is not always true as an assault does not necessarily include an offence of battery.

> 'When the term 'assault' is used to include a battery, it may be defined as an act by which a person intentionally or recklessly causes the complainant to apprehend immediate unlawful violence or to sustain unlawful personal violence (...). When, as is usually the case, the word 'assault' is used to mean a battery it simply means an act by which a person intentionally or recklessly applies unlawful force to the complainant (...). Provided those ingredients are proved, the offence will have been committed however slight the force.'[349]

Where assault merely implies the fear of violence, battery is concerned with the *actual application* of force upon a person, whether it is intended or reckless. Any unlawful physical contact, including the slightest touching, can amount to battery. Consequently there is no need to prove that harm or pain has been caused. Again, s.39 CJA 1988 states that the maximum sentence is six months' imprisonment or a fine.

Battery can occur even when the touching is not directly applied onto the physical body. As such, a carer can commit a battery just by touching or grabbing the clothes of the person they care for; whether the latter is aware of the touching or not is irrelevant. However, a distinction needs to be drawn between the kind of physical contact that is to be expected in the course of ordinary, everyday life (*Collins v Wilcock*[350]) – for instance, bumping into someone accidentally, touching somebody's back to get passed them in a crowded area – and touching that is socially unacceptable due to its hostile or inappropriate nature, which would be determined on a case-by-case basis (*Wilson v Pringle*[351]).

Another indirect application of force that can constitute a battery is when the act of a carer that is directed at one individual actually affects another, causing the latter to be subjected to unlawful personal violence upon them. For instance, in *Haystead v Chief Constable of Derbyshire*,[352] the defendant caused a child to fall onto the floor by punching the person holding that child.[353] In the context of the provision of care for those with learning disabilities and severe challenging behaviour, carers must therefore be careful that if they are having to manage a violent incident caused by one individual they do not cause another service user to be caught up in that violent incident themselves as this might then constitute battery.

As a general rule, an omission cannot constitute a battery. However, as explained previously (see paragraph on assault) it can amount to such an offence if it is part of a continuing act (*Fagan v MPC*[354]).

7.1.4 Section 47 OAPA 1861 – Assault Occasioning Actual Bodily Harm   Actual bodily harm (ABH) is described as any hurt or injury that has intentionally been inflicted on an

[349] supra, n.344, *Archbold*, 19–166a, p. 1660
[350] [1984] 3 All ER 374
[351] [1986] 2 All ER 440
[352] [2000] Crim LR
[353] [2000] Crim LR 758
[354] [1969] 1 QB 439

individual to affect their physical health and well-being (_Miller_[355]). ABH need not cause an injury that has permanent or serious consequences, nor is it necessary that ABH be proved by physical marks such as bruises. However, the injury must be significant, that is, it must cause sufficient pain or discomfort to the victim. Psychological harm can qualify as ABH (eg shock) provided it is not mere strong emotions (eg fear, distress, panic) nor states of mind that are not diagnosed as recognised clinical conditions (_Chan-Fook_[356]).

To find an accused guilty of causing ABH, technical assault must be proven. This means that there must be an intention or a reckless attitude on the part of the defendant as to whether he or she has caused the victim to fear being subjected to unlawful personal violence.

However such intention or recklessness as to whether harm is caused as a result of the assault is irrelevant to this particular offence. In _Savage and Parmenter_,[357] the defendant's intention was to throw a glass of beer at the victim but did not foresee that she would let go of the glass, which broke and injured the victim's wrist. Before the judges, the defendant argued that she had no intention to injure the victim; therefore she did not commit a criminal offence. However, the judges refused the argument since she did intend in the first place to apply unlawful force to the victim.

In other words, if a carer holds the person by the wrist, for instance, to stop a person with learning disability and challenging behaviour performing a dangerous act, and following this the person suffers from an injury, the carer would be guilty of a Section 47 offence unless he was able to raise the defence of self defence or defence of another.

7.1.5 Section 20 OAPA 1861 – Malicious Wounding or Inflicting Grievous Bodily Harm

> '_Whosoever shall unlawfully and maliciously wound or inflict any grievous bodily harm upon another person either with or without any weapon or instrument shall be guilty of an offence triable either way and being convicted thereof shall be liable to imprisonment for five years._'

It should be noted that the offence is written in the alternative and thus should be charged as either wounding or causing grievous bodily harm. Here, assault and battery need not necessarily be proven as an element of the s.20 offence. Indeed, although it is quite rare that grievous bodily harm (GBH) would be caused without an assault and battery leading to it, the judges recognised that it is possible that personal violence be absent from the offence. The word 'inflict', has a meaning which is allegedly narrower than 'cause', and actually suggests a detriment, including mental harm to which the victim is subjected. Therefore, offences where no physical contact is involved, such as psychiatric injury, are now covered by s.20 (_Burstow_[358]).

Although grievous bodily harm is to be understood as 'really serious harm' (_Smith_[359]) it does not mean that the harm has to be life-threatening. As for the meaning of 'wounds', this implies that there is a discontinuity in the whole of the skin. In other words, a cut will amount to GBH

---

[355] [1954] 2 QB 282
[356] [1994] Crim LR 432
[357] [1991] 1 AC 699
[358] [1998] AC 147
[359] [1961] AC 290

(*Moriarty v Brookes*[360]). Proof of such a wound can be inferred by the presence of blood from a cut, which can either be external or internal (eg a cut on or inside a cheek). On the other hand, if bleeding occurs without the presence of cut causing it, then this will not qualify as a wound (*C (a minor) v Eisenhower*[361]).

Another element that is required for this offence is intention or subjective recklessness on the part of the defendant, 'maliciously' implying that he or she was at least aware of the potential risk and consequences of applying unlawful force. In *Mowatt*,[362] Lord Diplock stated that: 'it is enough that [s/he foresaw]. . . that some physical harm to some person, albeit of a minor character, might result'.

7.1.6 Section 18 OAPA 1861 – Wounding/Causing Grievous Bodily Harm with Intent

> '*Whosoever shall unlawfully and maliciously by any means whatsoever wound or cause any grievous bodily harm to any person, with intent to do some grievous bodily harm to any person, or with intent to resist or prevent the lawful apprehension or detainer of any person, shall be guilty of an offence triable only on indictment, and being convicted thereof shall be liable to imprisonment for life.*'

Since the meaning of 'cause' is broader than that of 'inflict', it is sufficient for the act of violence to be proven substantial in causing the wound. Here, 'wound' and GBH have the same meaning as in s.20 OAPA 1861. As for the meaning of 'maliciously', this apparently adds nothing to the offence, as was stated in *Mowatt*.[363]

What distinguishes s.18 from the less serious s.20, is that in s.18 offences, it must be proved that the act is done with the specific intention of causing really serious harm.

7.2 Homicide – understanding the elements

A homicide is when a person causes the death of a human being. This definition contains the three elements necessary to such an offence:

Causation

The person must have caused the death of the victim.

The 'but for' test

This means that if it were not but for the person's act or omission, the victim would not have died the way and when they did. In *White*,[364] the defendant gave poison to his mother, intending to kill her, but she died of a heart attack before the chemical had any effect on her health. The poison was not the cause of her death, therefore, he was found not guilty.

---

[360] (1834) 6 C&P 684
[361] [1984] QB 331
[362] [1968] 1 QB 421
[363] [1968] 1 QB 421
[364] [1910] 2 KB 124

The *de minimis* rule

To induce someone's death, the act of the defendant must be more than just a minimal or trivial cause. It must be substantial in causing an early unnatural death.

In *R v Smith*,[365] a soldier was stabbed, then taken to the emergency unit, being dropped twice on the way, and left unattended for a long period of time once at the unit because the doctor wrongly believed that his situation was not so urgent. When the soldier finally received medical assistance, it was inappropriate and he later died. The court decided that despite these facts, the chain of causation between the stabbing and the resulting wound had not been broken, therefore the original wound was still an operative and substantial wound.

However, 'substantial' does not imply that the unlawful act has to be the sole cause of the victim's death. Indeed, the court in *Pagett*[366] stated that it was enough that the 'act contributed significantly' to the death.

It is also possible that the act of a third party, of the victim or a natural unpredictable event breaks the chain of causation. For example, if the victim's intervening act is such that it does not fall 'within the range of responses which might be expected from a victim placed in a [similar] situation'[367] and is so unpredictable that it could not have been foreseen, then the accused may be acquitted.

However, if it is reasonably foreseeable that the intervening act/event will occur, or that the intervening cause of the death is due to the victim's inherent weakness ('thin-skull' test) then the chain of causation will not be broken. The principle that the accused must take the victim as they find them was also extended to mental conditions and beliefs, as was stated in *Blaue*.[368]

As far as medical treatment is concerned, only abnormal treatment is said to be unforeseeable. Indeed, any treatment falling within the 'normal' range of incompetence that can be expected in such situations will be considered foreseeable. In *Cheshire*,[369] the defendant shot the victim in the leg and abdomen leading the latter to suffer from respiratory problems, which had to be dealt with by performing a tracheotomy. Complications occurred due to the tracheotomy, and the victim later died. Although the original gunshot wound did heal before the death, the court decided that the respiratory problem was a direct consequence of the shooting, and that the medical negligence did not break the chain of causation here.

Death

There is no legal definition of 'death'; therefore in *Malcherek and Steel*[370] the judges decided to look at the issue from a medical point of view and suggested that death occurs when the victim is brain-dead. Notwithstanding, the assessment of what death means and when it happens remains a matter to be decided on a case-by-case basis.

---

[365] [1959] 2 QB 35
[366] (1983) 76 Cr App R 279
[367] *R v Williams* [1992] 2 All ER 183, 191
[368] [1975] 1 WLR 1411
[369] [1991] 3 All ER 670
[370] [1981] 1 WLR 690

Interventions which result in death

In a very important piece of research[371] entitled *Deaths Associated with Restraint Use in Health and Social Care in the United Kingdom*, Patterson, Bradley, Stark, Saddler, Leadbetter and Allen released the results of a preliminary survey of such cases. This study reveals that there are very many more reported cases arising in health and social care settings in the USA than in the UK. Thus, leaving aside deaths occurring in the prison service, Patterson *et al* could find only 12 such cases as reported in the newspapers since 1979. In none of these 12 cases did the relevant authority pursue a prosecution. Disturbingly, however, the study revealed that a number of the deaths resulted from the varied use of a number of forms of restraint practised under the general heading of 'prone restraint'. The authors stress, however, that this term does not describe in any way a homogenous procedure but a wide range of situations in which the person is held generally 'face down'. A wide range of variations appeared to have been used in the cases described. This, say the authors, can be implied in the varying numbers of staff reportedly involved in the incidents, ranging from two to eight. The fact that no prosecutions resulted in these cases suggests that the prosecuting authorities had been satisfied that there was no intention to cause death or serious harm, which in the case of death resulting would have founded a charge of murder, nor was there any gross negligence which would have founded a charge of manslaughter. This is not to say that such circumstances would not arise and to that end the following discussion of those offences is offered.

Human being

The victim of a homicide must be a human being. By 'being', the courts understand that a person lives a life independent from that of the mother's; in other words, once a child is out of the womb and can function on its own, it is 'a being' capable of being the victim of a homicide.[372] In the case of a mother giving birth, the fact that the child might still be attached to her by the umbilical cord, or that it does not breath straight away does not negate its state of 'being'.[373]

7.2.1 Murder

> *'(...) [T]he crime of murder is committed where a person of sound mind and discretion unlawfully kills any reasonable creature and under the Queen's peace with intent to kill or cause grievous bodily harm.'*[374]

Although there is no statutory definition available, it is found in common law that a murder is an act by which a person takes the life/causes the death of another – a human being – with malice aforethought. Malice, here, means that there is an intention to kill or at least an intention to cause grievous bodily harm.

The intention is of a purely subjective nature. As stated in Section 8 of the Criminal Justice Act 1967:

> *'A court or jury in determining whether a person has committed an offence –*
>
> *(a) shall not be bound in law to infer that he intended or foresaw a result of his actions by reason only of its being a natural and probable consequence of those actions; but*

---

[371] Patterson B, Bradley P, Stark C, Saddler D, Leadbetter D and Allen D, Deaths Associated with Restraint Use in Health and Social Care in the United Kindom – The Results of a Preliminary Survey *Journal of Psychiatric and Mental Health Nursing*, 10, 3–15

[372] *Enoch* (1833) 5 C&P 539

[373] *Brain* (1834) 6 C&P 349

[374] supra n.344, *Archbold*, 19–1, p. 1612

(b) shall decide whether he did intend or foresee that result by reference to all the evidence, drawing such inferences from the evidence as appear proper in the circumstances.'

In other words, what matters is what the defendant actually foresaw and intended in the given situation as opposed to what he or she should have foreseen or intended – that is, from the 'reasonable man's' point of view (<u>*DPP v Smith*</u> [375]).

7.2.2 Voluntary manslaughter   Voluntary manslaughter is an act that can be described as murder, however, the court will look at mitigating circumstances that will serve as a partial defence and thus reduce the life sentence to a certain number of years of imprisonment.

'Voluntary manslaughter occurs when all the elements of murder are present, including an intent to kill or cause grievous bodily harm, but the crime is reduced to manslaughter by reason of (a) provocation; (b) diminished responsibility; or (c) death being caused in pursuance of a suicide pact.' [376]

Provocation

Section 3 of the Homicide Act 1957 provides:

> *Where on a charge of murder there is evidence on which the jury can find that the person charged was provoked (whether by things done or by things said or by both together) to lose his self-control, the question whether the provocation was enough to make a reasonable man do as he did shall be left to be determined by the jury; and in determining that question the jury shall take into account everything both done and said according to the effect which, in their opinion, it would have on a reasonable man.*

There are three points that need to be addressed here.

1. What can constitute 'provocation'?

Provocation can arise as the result of something either said or done, or both said and done at the same time. However, it cannot have been triggered by mere circumstances. For example, a support worker could not get any sleep the night before his shift and on his way to work had been shouting abuse at passers-by. Later that day he struck and killed a service user (who had a learning disability and also presented severe challenging behaviour) after the latter refused to do as he was asked. The support worker would not be able to plead provocation in his defence.

Words alone can constitute provocation. However, the provocative conduct need not be illegal nor wrongful (<u>*Doughty*</u> [377]); nor does it have to be directed exclusively at the defendant. Indeed, it is accepted that the provocative act could have been directed at a third party (<u>*Pearson*</u> [378]) or

---

[375] [1961] AC 290
[376] supra n.344, *Archbold*, 19–97, p. 1642
[377] (1986) 83 Cr App R 319
[378] [1992] Crim LR 193
[379] [1975] QB 691

that the defendant could have been provoked by a third party (_Davies_[379]) What matters is that it can be shown that the defendant was provoked to lose his or her self-control.

2. What is a loss of self-control?

Losing one's self-control is losing one's temper (_R v Cocker_[380]), which must be of a sudden and temporary nature. In _R v Duffy_,[381] Devlin J described provocation as 'some act, or series of acts, done by the dead man to the accused, which would cause any reasonable person, and actually causes in the accused, a sudden and temporary loss of self-control, rendering the accused so subject to passion as to make him or her for the moment not master his mind'.

The loss of self-control does not have to be complete. In other words, it is not necessary to prove that the defendant was not aware/conscious of his actions. In _Richens_[382] it was held to be sufficient for the accused to prove that he could not prevent himself from doing what he did.

3. Subjective and objective tests

The defence of provocation must be satisfied by the following questions:

Did the provocative act reasonably cause the defendant to lose his self-control?

The jury will be asked to decide the gravity of the provocation and whether the _defendant actually lost his self-control as a result_. If there is a lapse of time between the provocative act and the crime, it may be evidence of premeditation. In that case, the defendant may not be able to use provocation as a defence (_Ibrams_[383]) for premeditation negates the idea of a sudden and temporary loss of self-control (_Thornton_[384]).

Although the court will not recognise the principle of the slow-burn effect which was raised as part of the defence in the case of _R v Ahluwaliah_,[385] stating that it is an issue upon which Parliament should legislate, it was held in _R v Humphreys_[386] that the jury could take into account the 'cumulative' provocations in deciding whether the defendant was provoked. In _R v Thornton_ (No.2),[387] it was found that a minor incident could be considered a provocative act if it was the final straw in a long string of provocations over several years. (These three cases raise the issue of 'battered woman syndrome'.)

The factors which the jury needs to take into account can be summed up thus: the jury must look at all the facts, that is 'the whole picture, the whole story'. It must consider the issues of: time lapses; cumulative provocation; the impact of provocation directed at a third party and the characteristics of the defendant. The jury must then ask itself:

Would a reasonable person, showing the defendant's characteristics, have lost his self-control in the same circumstances?

[380] [1989] Crim LR 740
[381] [1949] 1 All ER 932n
[382] [1993] Crim LR 384
[383] (1981) 74 Cr App R 154
[384] [1992] 1 All ER 306
[385] [1992] 4 All ER 889
[386] [1995] 4 All ER 1008
[387] [1996] 1 WLR 1174

Once the jury has established that the defendant was provoked, it needs to look at whether a reasonable person would have reacted as the defendant did, that is, looking at the power of self-control expected from the reasonable person in similar circumstances.

The first issue is to determine the definition of the reasonable person. It is arguable that the reasonable person is predominantly 'an adult male or female'. Although in _Camplin_,[388] Lord Diplock stated that the reasonable man 'means an ordinary person of either sex, not exceptionally excitable or pugnacious, but possessed of such powers of self-control as everyone is entitled to expect that his fellow citizens will exercise in society as it is today'.

Physical characteristics that can be taken into consideration are primarily the sex and age of the defendant when it is deemed relevant to the issue. Other characteristics, such as those relating to the mental state or personality, must be sufficiently permanent to be relevant.

As regards intoxication, in the case of _R v Newell_[389] the court dismissed the defendant's appeal on the grounds that the loss of his girlfriend and hence his alcohol consumption were not permanent characteristics, but temporary ones. In contrast, in _Morhall_[390] the defendant's addiction to solvents was held to be a relevant characteristic that the jury should take into account since an addiction suggests a repetitive intake of such products and thus has more enduring mental consequences.

As regards depression, in _R v Smith (Morgan)_[391] the trial judge directed the jury that the defendant's severe depressive illness was 'neither here nor there'. However, the House of Lords held that it was not for the judge to decide what mental characteristics the jury should take into account or not when assessing the standard of self-control that is to be expected of the proverbial reasonable man.

Lord Hoffman argued that:

> _'judges should not be required to describe the objective element in the provocation defence by reference to a reasonable man, with or without attribution of personal characteristics. (...) The general principle is that the same standards of behaviour are expected of everyone, regardless of their individual psychological make-up. (...) But the jury should in an appropriate case be told (...) that this is a principle and not a rigid rule. It may sometimes have to yield to a more important principle, which is to do justice in the particular case. So the jury may think that there was some characteristics of the accused, whether temporary or permanent, which affected the degree of control which society could reasonably have expected of him and which it would be unjust not to take into account.'_

Diminished responsibility

Section 2(1) of the Homicide Act 1957 provides:

> _Where a person kills or is party to a killing of another, he shall not be convicted of murder if he was suffering from such abnormality of mind (whether arising from a_

---

[388] [1978] AC 705
[389] (1980) 71 Cr App R 331
[390] [1996] AC 90
[391] [2001] 1 AC 146

*condition of arrested or retarded development of mind or any inherent causes or
induced by disease or injury) as substantially impaired his mental responsibility for
his acts and omissions in doing or being a party to the killing.*

There are three major aspects of this defence that need to be considered which necessitates
consideration of the concept of an abnormality of the mind.

What is an 'abnormality of the mind'?

An abnormality of the mind encompasses not only the activities of the brain but also those of
the mind. In <u>R v Byrne</u>,[392] Lord Parker CJ stated that an abnormality of mind is:

> *'a state of mind so different from that of ordinary human beings that the reasonable
> man would term it abnormal. It appears to us to be wide enough to cover the mind's
> activities in all its aspects, not only the perception of physical acts and matters, and
> the ability to form a rational judgement as to whether an act is right or wrong, but
> also the ability to exercise will-power to control physical acts in accordance with that
> rational judgement.'*

However, an abnormality of the mind does not necessarily imply madness (<u>R v Seers</u>[393]) but it
does also cover severe shock, depression, pre-menstrual syndrome and 'battered woman
syndrome'.

What are the causes?

For the defence to succeed, the causes of the abnormality have to fall within the ambit of
Section 2(1), that is: arising from a condition of arrested retarded development of mind or any
inherent causes or induced by disease or injury (<u>King</u>[394]).

There are no legal or statutory definitions of what these causes are, only directions given by the
courts. It is argued that states such as hatred, jealousy and intoxication do not constitute an
abnormality. However, this is not a definite rule since there are cases where jealousy (<u>Miller</u>,[395]
<u>Asher</u>[396]) and rage (<u>Coles</u>[397]) have been found to count as an abnormality of mind.

When alcohol consumption is substantially persistent so as to be a chronic condition, it can be
considered as a disease incurring abnormality of mind. In <u>Tandy</u>,[398] the court stated that chronic
alcoholism is a disease if the brain is so affected by the chemicals that it induces an impairment
of the defendant's judgement and emotional responses. If the brain is not damaged, it must still
be proven that the defendant cannot exercise any control over her drinking addiction.

What are the effects?

The effect of an abnormality of mind must be such that the defendant's mental responsibility is
substantially impaired as regards his acts and omissions in doing or being a party to the killing.

---

[392] [1960] 2 QB 396
[393] (1984) 79 Cr App R 261
[394] [1965] 1 QB 443
[395] *The Times*, 16 May 1972
[396] *The Times*, 9 June 1981
[397] (1980) 144 JPN 528

'Substantially' does not mean that the lack of control has to be complete, but only that the defendant must find it really hard/difficult to exercise control over his acts or omissions (_Byrne_[399]). However, this will often be decided by the jury on a case-by-case basis.

7.2.3 Involuntary manslaughter Involuntary manslaughter is akin to murder. The difference, however, is that there is no intention to deprive the victim of his life. The homicide is due to an unlawful act but the offender did not intend to kill or impose grievous bodily harm on the victim; therefore, this offence covers 'accidental murders'.

> '_Involuntary manslaughter is unlawful killing without intent to kill or cause grievous bodily harm (...). Apart from intent, the elements of the offence are the same as in murder (...). The rules of causation, self-defence, etc, therefore apply (..)._
>
> _(...) [T]here are two classes of involuntary manslaughter, namely "unlawful act" manslaughter and manslaughter by gross negligence involving breach of duty._'[400]

Constructive manslaughter

An unlawful and dangerous act must be the cause of the victim's death. However, it is not sufficient that the act is unlawful for it must also and mainly be a criminal offence. In _Franklin_,[401] the defendant threw a box from a refreshment stall into the sea, which, unbeknownst to him, hit a person swimming by who died as a result. Although the defendant had committed a tort of trespass, the judges decided that a tort could not in itself give rise to manslaughter because there had to be an actual crime performed for that.

An omission by itself will not amount to an unlawful act, even when the omission is deliberate, as was stated in _R v Lowe_,[402] a case of child neglect which resulted in the death of the child.

The act must be dangerous in that one foresees it will incur an objective risk resulting in some kind of harm. The court in _R v Church_[403] stated that a dangerous act is what 'all sober and reasonable people would inevitably recognise must subject the other person to, at least, the risk of some harm resulting therefrom, albeit not serious harm'. The harm foreseen must be physical (_R v Dawson_[404]); but need not be aimed at the ultimate victim, it only needs to cause death. In _R v Goodfellow_,[405] the defendant was convicted of manslaughter for causing the death of his wife and children by setting fire to his house despite the fact that his intention was to force the council to re-house them, and not to harm his family (judgement confirmed in _Attorney-General's Reference_ No.3 of 1994[406]).

---

[398] (1988) 87 Cr App R 45
[399] [1960] 2 QB 396
[400] supra n.344, _Archbold_, 19–98, p. 1642
[401] (1983) 15 Cox CC163
[402] [1973] QB 702
[403] [1966] 1 QB 59
[404] (1985) 81 Cr App R 150
[405] (1986) 83 Cr App R 23
[406] [1996] 2 WLR 412

Gross negligence manslaughter

The definition of gross negligence manslaughter was given in the case of _Bateman_[407] by Lord Hewart CJ:

> '_In order to establish criminal liability the facts must be such that, in the opinion of the jury, the negligence of the accused went beyond a mere matter of compensation between subjects and showed such disregard for the life and safety of others as to amount to a crime against the state and conduct deserving of punishment._'

In other words, the act that led to the death is not unlawful per se, but the negligence is so gross that it can be considered a criminal offence.

The leading case in this area is _Adomako_.[408] In this case, the defendant was an anaesthetist who failed to recognise that his patient's oxygen tube was detached from the ventilator, which caused the death of the victim. Adomako was convicted of manslaughter. The House of Lords confirmed the fact that for a crime of gross negligence manslaughter to occur, a duty of care must be owed by the defendant to the victim, that duty must be breached, and the negligence must be such that the jury considers it criminal in nature.

7.3 Defences

7.3.1 Consent   As a general principle, when the victim has given consent then there is no offence. In cases where consent is given to an unlawful use of force which does not result in injury, the defence will be upheld. However, in _Donovan_,[409] it was held that an assault 'cannot be rendered lawful because the person to whose detriment it is done consents to it. No person can license another to commit a crime.'

The court will consider matters of public interest when deciding if consent can act as a defence for an unlawful act. In _Attorney-General's Ref.No.6_[410] two youths arguing in the streets decided to settle their disagreement by fist fighting each other. One of the youths suffered injuries as a result. The Court of Appeal held that, despite the consent of the victim, it was against public policy to consider his consent as a defence to assault. Lord Lane CJ stated that:

> '_it is not in the public interest that people should try to cause, or should cause, each other actual bodily harm for no good reason. Minor struggles are another matter. So, in our judgement, it is immaterial whether the act occurs in private or in public; it is an assault if actual bodily harm is intended and/or caused. This means that most fights will be unlawful regardless of consent._'

In cases where the defendant has a genuine mistaken belief that the victim did consent to the unlawful act, he will have a valid defence. In _Richardson_,[411] the defendant was a dentist who had been barred from the general dental practice; however, she still performed surgery on her patients, who consented to the treatment despite being unaware of her suspension. The court

---

[407] (1925) 19 Cr App R 8
[408] [1995] 1 AC 171
[409] [1934] 2 KB 498
[410] [1981] 2 All ER 1057
[411] [1999] Crim LR 62

held that the dentist had a genuine belief that her patients consented to the treatment; therefore she was not guilty of assault. The ground for this decision is that the consent would be vitiated only if the patients make a mistake as to the identity of the dentist, not as to the treatment they received.

7.3.2 Necessity   Here, the defendant has to make a choice between two courses of action, both of which would result in some kind of harm being caused. However, the choice of which course of action is best must take into consideration which of these would cause the lesser harm.

In _Re A (Children) (Conjoined twins: Medical Treatment)_,[412] doctors were faced with a situation of _ischiopagus tetrapus_ conjoined twin girls, who were joined at the abdomen. The twins had to be separated, for they would not have been able to survive in this way. However, the separation would ensure the death of the weakest twin. The family refused to make such a decision – allowing the killing of one of their children to save the other – and the hospital where the operation was to be performed sought a declaration from the judges allowing them to go ahead. The family appealed against the Family Division judge's decision that it was lawful for the hospital to perform such an operation. The appealed was dismissed.

Ward LJ stated that 'the law must allow an escape through choosing the lesser of two evils'. Brooke LJ agreed that the three requirements for the defence of necessity were covered: the act was done with the sole purpose of preventing a situation that could not be otherwise avoided and would cause inevitable and irreparable evil, the act performed was no more than reasonably necessary to tackle the danger, and the evil caused by the act was not disproportionate to the evil that would have resulted had the unlawful act not been carried out. Here, it was acknowledged that it would be in the best interest of the other twin, the stronger one, that the operation should be performed.

Necessity can be a defence in cases where a person has no choice but to act in such a way in order to protect themselves. For instance, there is an American case where a convict had to escape from the prison he was detained in because it was on fire. The judges accepted that it was _reasonable_ or at least understandable for the prisoner not to stay in the prison to get burnt.[413] Reference may be made by the courts in England to cases in the USA because it has a common law system based on that of England. This is more especially the case where they may be no comparable precedent in the English courts.

Necessity can also be a defence when the defendant performs an 'illegal' act to save someone's life. In _Bourne_,[414] an obstetric surgeon performed an abortion on a 14-year-old rape victim. He was acquitted because the jury recognised that the defendant had acted in good faith to save the girl's life.

This defence has also been used in other cases involving issues of mental capacity and consent, where a decision to save or assist someone's life without their consent has to be made.

In _Re F (Mental Patient: Sterilisation)_,[415] the sterilisation of a 36-year-old female patient with a severe mental disability was declared legal despite her lack of consent. It was considered to

---

[412] [2000] 4 All ER 961
[413] _US v Kirby_ (1869), referred to in Elliott C & Quinn F, Criminal Law, 3rd ed, p. 282, 2000
[414] [1938] 3 All ER 615
[415] [1990] 2 AC 1

be in her best interest to resort to such an extreme mode of contraception (all the others not being adequate to her situation) to avoid a pregnancy that could strongly affect her mental state.

Another case involved a pregnant woman who was advised by her doctors to give birth by Caesarean section, otherwise she would lose both her life and that of the unborn child. Although she was capable of giving consent, which she actually refused to give, the operation was still performed after the doctors were granted a declaration of legality by the judges, since it was held to be in her best interest.[416]

This principle of the best interest is the key to the doctrine of necessity; once necessity has been proven, the unlawful act is then justified.

In *R v Bournewood Community and Mental Health NHS Trust*,[417] L. was a 43-year-old man who was autistic, had some self-injurious tendencies, could not speak and therefore did not have capacity to consent to treatment. He was an inpatient at Bournewood Hospital for 30 years before moving in with a family, who were his carers. The hospital was still responsible for his care. One day at the day centre, L. showed agitation and a violent behaviour and he was given sedatives to calm down. He was then informally admitted to Bournewood Hospital's mental health behavioural unit where he remained.

The hospital argued before the House of Lords that L. had not been not detained because despite the fact that he could not consent, he did not object to his treatment as an in-patient. Furthermore, even if L. was actually detained, that there was no need to do so under Section 131(1) Mental Health Act 1983[418] as the common law doctrine of necessity, which was justified by the 'best interest' principle, would apply.

It was held that L. remained in the charge of the hospital despite being cared for in the community; that L.'s agitation and violent outburst was an emergency situation that called for intervention as a matter of necessity, in his best interests and to avoid danger to others. Their Lordships stated that 'all the steps in fact taken . . . were in fact taken in the best interests of L. and, in so far as they might otherwise have constituted an invasion of his civil rights, were justified on the basis of the common law doctrine of necessity'.

7.3.3 Duress of circumstances   This defence is not available for crimes such as murder and attempted murder (*Pommell*[419]).

A defendant may have to perform an act under the pressure of certain circumstances. This will be valid as a defence if it can be proven that the defendant acted in a reasonable manner, applying only the necessary amount of force to avoid a threat of injury or death.

In *Martin*,[420] the defendant drove his car while disqualified because his wife had threatened to commit suicide. This was recognised as sufficient duress of circumstances.

---

[416] *Mrs S* 1992, referred to in Elliott C & Quinn F, Criminal Law, 3rd ed, p. 282, 2000
[417] [1998] 1 AC 458
[418] Right to admit a patient informally
[419] (1985) 2 Cr App R 607
[420] [1989] 1 All ER 652

The case of _R v Graham_[421] suggested a two-fold test in order to establish whether there is duress of circumstances. The first question is concerned with whether the defendant was compelled to act as he did for fear of serious injury or death. If the answer to this question is yes, the second part of the test then asks whether a sober person of reasonable firmness, sharing the defendant's characteristics would have responded in the same manner.

In the case of _R v Abdul-Hussain (Mustafa Shakir)_,[422] an Iraqi family who had fled to Sudan feared that they would be deported back to Iraq where they would be punished and executed. Therefore they went on a plane going to Jordan and hijacked it. They pleaded duress of necessity and the court held that the defence was valid.

R v Abdul-Hussain (Mustafa Shakir) completes the _Graham_ test by adding that the threat of injury or death to the defendant or any person he might be responsible for must be imminent (although it need not be immediately carried out) and the danger must be playing on the defendant's mind at the time he performs the unlawful act.

7.3.4 Lawful correction   The Children and Young Persons Act 1933, s.1 provides that any adult who has responsibility for a child 'wilfully assaults, ill-treats, (. . .) or causes or procures [the child] to be assaulted, ill-treated (. . .) in a manner likely to cause [the child] unnecessary suffering or injury of heath (. . .)', that individual shall be guilty of a criminal offence.

The meaning of 'responsibility' in this context implies that an adult has 'custody, charge or care' of the child. In practice, it is often a question for the jury to decide.[423]

In the case of _R v Hopley_,[424] the defendant headmaster at a school had used a thick stick to strike a 14-year-old boy for approximately two and a half hours. After this ordeal the boy died. The court in that case set out the common law rule on corporal punishment in England and Wales.

Chief Justice Cockburn stated that:

> _'a parent or a schoolmaster (...) may for the purpose of correcting what is evil in the child inflict moderate and reasonable corporal punishment, always, however, with this condition, that it is moderate and reasonable. [However, if] the punishment is excessive, the violence is unlawful, and if evil consequences to life or limb ensue, then the person inflicting it is answerable to the law, and if death ensues it will be manslaughter.'_

He stressed that a punishment is not reasonable if is 'administered for the gratification of passion or of rage, or if it [is] immoderate and excessive in its nature or degree, or if it [is] protracted beyond the child's powers of endurance, or with an instrument unfitted for the purpose and calculated to produce danger to life or limb'.

Another element was introduced in the case of _R v Griffin_[425] in which a two-year-old girl died after having been belted by her father. The judge held that this treatment was not 'reasonable

---

[421]   (1982) 74 Cr App R 235
[422]   _The Times_, 26 January, 1999
[423]   supra n.344, _Archbold_, para.19–299, p. 1699
[424]   (1860) 2 F&F 202
[425]   Brown (1869) 11 Cox CC 400

chastisement'. The reasonableness of a chastisement is also measured by the fact that the child understands the punishment that is being administered.

The notion of corporal punishment, which denies a child's right to his or her own physical integrity, was challenged before the court in Strasbourg in the case of _A v United Kingdom_ 1999.[426]

In this case, a man who had beaten his nine-year-old step-son with a cane had been acquitted of a Section 47 OAPA 1861 charge, that is assault occasioning actual bodily harm after successfully pleading 'reasonable chastisement' at his trial. The boy's natural father made an application against that judgement, arguing that there was a breach of Article 3 of the Human Rights Act 1998 as he was submitted to inhuman and degrading punishment.

The European Court of Human Rights stated that 'ill-treatment must attain a minimum level of severity if it is to fall within the scope of Article 3. The assessment of this minimum is relative. It depends on all the circumstances of the case, such as the nature and context of the treatment, its duration, its physical and mental effects and, in some circumstances, the sex, age and state of health of the victim.' The court further added that British law fails to provide an adequate protection to children, which the British Government recognised to be true and accepted that there was a need for change.

This judgement was followed by _R v H (Assault of Child: Reasonable Chastisement)_[427] which elaborates on the notion of what is to be held 'reasonable' punishment.

In this case, a father was charged with assault occasioning actual bodily harm after belting his son. The father had used a belt to beat his son on his back several times because he refused or was unable to write his name as he was told to do.

Since the reasonableness of a punishment is assessed by a jury, the Court of Appeal conceded that standards of reasonableness change over the years and therefore a judge can take a different approach to the question of reasonableness according to the standards current at the time of trial when directing a jury.

The court stated that when assessing the reasonableness of a chastisement, a judge should in the light of the European Court of Human Rights decision in _A v UK_ (see Chapter 2 for a detailed discussion of this case) consider: the nature and context of the behaviour of the person inflicting the punishment; the duration of the punishment; its physical and mental consequences in relation to the child; the age and personal characteristics of the child; and the reasons given by the adult for administering punishment must also be taken into account.

The court finally held that for a chastisement to be classed as degrading and therefore in breach of Article 3 HRA 1998, (a) it had to reach a particular level of severity, (b) the degree of severity is to be assessed on a case-by-case basis, especially as regards the nature and extent of the punishment. The court also concluded that not all punishment would automatically be in breach of Article 3 HRA 1998.

---

[426] (1999) 27 EHRR 611
[427] [2002] 1 Cr.App.R.7

As regards the use of physical punishment in a schools setting, Section 131 of the Schools Standards and Framework Act 1998 stipulates that corporal punishment is now prohibited in all schools and nurseries, whether state or private, where the children receive education. Similar provision is made for Scotland by s.16 Standards in Scotland's Schools Act 2000.

The DfEE Circular 10/98 confirms in its introduction that 'Section 550A does not in any way authorise the use of corporal punishment with pupils in maintained schools or publicly-funded pupils in independent schools. For those pupils the law forbids a teacher to use any degree of physical contact which is deliberately intended to punish a pupil, or which is primarily intended to cause pain or injury or humiliation. That ban applies in all circumstances.'

Actions taken to avert an immediate danger of personal injury or an immediate danger to the property of any person (including the child himself) are not to be qualified as falling within the definition of corporal punishment.[428]

In brief, a teacher or any member of staff at a school cannot administer corporal punishment on any child.

7.3.5 Self-defence This defence encompasses actions taken to defend oneself as well as another from being the victim of an unlawful attack on their person (Section 3 Criminal Act 1967), although it will not be available if the force is used after all danger has disappeared.

The use of force must be reasonable as regards the danger; if it is disproportionate, ie excessive, then the defence will not be available. In _R v Clegg (Lee William)_[429] a British soldier in Northern Ireland was found guilty of murder for firing at the civilian driver of a stolen car who would not stop at the check point and killing him. The House of Lords concluded that the force used in this instance was excessive and unreasonable. Lord Lloyd of Berwick stated that 'the use of lethal force to kill or wound the driver of the car in order to arrest him was, in the circumstances, so grossly disproportionate to the mischief to be averted as to deprive [the defendant] of a defence under Section 3 [Criminal Act 1967]'.

Paradoxically, the belief in having to use force in self-defence need not be reasonable as the facts of the circumstances must be assessed in the light of what the defendant believed them to be.

In _DPP v Armstrong-Braun_[430] the defendant, an activist who wanted to protect the natural habitat of a protected species of newts from being destroyed by a building operation, struck a digger with a wooden stick and argued that he acted in self-defence because he feared the digger was about to hurt him. The Court of Appeal held that the force used was not reasonable in the circumstances and added that the reasonableness of an act of self-defence is to be assessed objectively in accordance with what the defendant believed them to be.

In other words, the court will consider the fact that the defendant acted honestly and instinctively, doing what he thought was necessary in the circumstances as strong evidence to support the defence. If based on the fact as seen by the defendant a reasonable person would have acted in the same way, then the defence is likely to succeed; if a reasonable person would not have acted in the same way, then the defence will fail.

---

[428] section 131(5)(a) and (b)
[429] [1995] 1 AC 482
[430] (1999) 163 J.P. 271

7.3.6 Mistake To work as a defence, the mistake must be based on the facts of the circumstances as the defendant saw them or believed them to be. If the mistake is genuine albeit unreasonable, the defendant will be granted the defence.

In _DPP v Morgan_,[431] deciding on a rape charge, the House of Lords held that as long as the defendants held the belief, the lack of reasonable grounds supporting that belief did not affect the defence of mistake.

In _R v Williams (Gladstone)_,[432] the defendant, charged with assaulting a police officer attempting to arrest a youth, believed that the officer was unlawfully assaulting the youth as he could not produce proof of his police status and so tried to prevent him from, as he saw it, assaulting the youth. The House of Lords held that the belief, however mistaken and unreasonable, was valid provided it was genuinely held by the defendant, who should therefore be judged on the facts as he believed them to be.

This approach was confirmed in _B v DPP_ [433] where the defendant, a 16-year-old boy, was charged with inciting a 13-year-old girl to perform oral sex on him. He argued that he honestly believed she was over 14. As the belief was genuine, however unreasonable, the defence of mistake was held operable in this case.

7.3.7 Common law and statutory power to detain the insane There is no power at common law to apprehend or detain a person suffering from mental disorder simply because he is so suffering.

In _Townley v Rushworth_ 1964,[434] it was held that where the provisions of the then Mental Health Act 1959 are not complied with, an individual has no authority to enter another's house so as to detain him; such an individual is said to be a trespasser.

But it is stated that a 'private person may without express warrant confine a person disordered in his mind who seems disposed to do mischief to himself or any other person.' (Bacon's Abridgement cited in Hoggett _Mental Health Law_)

What is meant by the term disordered in '[the] mind' is unclear especially in this context but Hoggett has argued that it is probably wider than the McNaughton Rules. The McNaughton Rules are used in criminal law as a guide to the viability of a plea of not guilty by reason of insanity. The Rules outline legal insanity as being:

> '_A disease of the mind which results in a defect of reasoning such that an individual does not know the nature and quality of what he is doing, or if he does know what he is doing he does not know it was wrong._'

Clearly, this test is restrictive since it was established to deal with situations under the criminal law where the defence needed to prove that the defendant was unfit to stand trial by reason of the fact that he was insane. It is suggested therefore, that when one is instead seeking to justify the detention of an individual because otherwise they would do either themselves or some other

---

[431] [1976] AC 182
[432] [1987] 3 All ER 411
[433] [2000] 2 AC 428
[434] (1964) 62 LGR 95

person a mischief and one is seeking to rely on this common law power it might be more appropriate to consider the various definitions provided in the Mental Health Act 1983. Such definitions are only to be deemed helpful in this context of trying to arrive at some sort of common law definition of insanity for the purpose of using the power and thus seeking to justify detaining the child, young person or adult. It is not here being suggested that the term insane is an appropriate one to use at all when discussing those with severe learning disabilities who also present severe challenging behaviour. If, however, one has to seek to rely on a common law power to detain the insane, bearing in mind that the origin of the power can be traced back for more than 100 years, the term insane at that stage would have covered those individuals whom we would now describe as people with learning disabilities who also present severe challenging behaviour. Thus, when defining insanity for these purposes, we would include persons suffering from a mental disorder within the meaning of s.1(2) MHA 1983, which includes those with arrested or incomplete development of the mind and those with mental impairment or severe mental impairment. On this basis it would be possible to seek to rely on the old common law power to detain the insane.

While it is accepted that this power derives from rather old judicial authority it is submitted that it would be untenable for the criminal law to provide no protection for an individual with severe learning disabilities presenting severe challenging behaviour.

In the case of _S v Airedale NHS Trust_[435] the lawfulness of seclusion was debated as regards a patient who was detained in a non-secure unit under the Mental Health Act 1983. The patient argued that it was an infringement of his Convention rights, in particular Article 3 (Prohibition of Torture), 5 (Liberty and Security) and 8 (Respect for Private and Family Life)[436] as he was secluded for a two-week period. The reason for his seclusion was his violent behaviour towards others, as he was suffering from a bipolar affective disorder, which could be displayed by aggressive, violent or sexually inappropriate behaviour.

The court stated that:

> '*seclusion is clearly not necessarily contrary to Article 3: it may be imposed for a very short time, in good conditions and with no negative impact on the patient. In such a case, it is not arguable that it reaches the level of severity involved in an infringement of Article 3. But the duration and conditions of seclusion, the reason for it and its effect on the patient may be such as to constitute an infringement of Article 3 and Article 8. It is clear that the use of seclusion must be minimised. Where, however, there is genuinely no sensible alternative to its use (...) there is not necessarily an infringement of Article 3, even if its use is not short term and an emergency measure: it does not necessarily reach the necessary level of seriousness.*'

The court went on to add that the Mental Health Act 1983 does not as such confer a power to seclude, as seclusion must be implicit in powers conferred by the Act such as the power to detain, which is justified by treatment purposes. The test to be applied in order to determine whether there is an implied power to seclude is whether there is 'a self-evident and pressing need' for the power. In other words, seclusion is an option only when the situation requires such an action to be taken.

---

[435] [2002] 1 WLR 1876
[436] The Human Rights Act 1998 is discussed at Chapter 9.

The judgement, however, mentions that, although seclusion of a patient does restrict an individual's freedom of movement, it does not necessarily amount to a violation of Article 5 HRA 1998 and does not always constitute an offence of false imprisonment, even when the seclusion is deemed unnecessary. Considering a judgement of the House of Lords in a similar case,[437] the court reiterates that although it affects the conditions of the detention, it does not become detention as such.

The view taken by the court in *S v Airedale NHS Trust* that there is a distinction to be made between the conditions surrounding detention and detention itself of 'a person of unsound mind', is supported by a previous judgement given by the European Court of Justice on the matter, in the *Ashingdane* case.

In *Ashingdane v United Kingdom*,[438] the European Court of Human Rights confirmed that Article 5(1) of the Convention means that any arbitrary detention is deemed unlawful.

Article 5(1)(e) provides that 'no one shall be deprived of his liberty save in the following cases in accordance with a procedure prescribed by law: (. . .) the lawful detention of persons for the prevention of the spreading of infectious diseases, of persons of unsound mind, alcoholics or drug addicts or vagrants'.

The European Court of Human Rights stated that a detention is lawful when it takes place within the confines of a hospital, clinic or other appropriate institution for that purpose. Otherwise, the court added that 'Article 5(1)(e) is not in principle concerned with suitable treatment or conditions'.

Following this judgement, the court in *S v Airedale NHS Trust* 2002 concluded that Article 5 of the Convention is not violated in a seclusion situation.

7.3.8 Prevention of a breach of the peace   A breach of the peace occurs in a situation where harm is either actually inflicted upon a person or property, or when there is a threat of such harm happening. It can also take place in circumstances where harm is feared due to an affray, riot, assault or other disturbance.

Prevention of a breach of the peace can be a defence to someone who has assaulted or imprisoned another individual if it can be argued that this individual was being either a physical threat to himself, to the offender or a third party, or was about to inflict damage to property.

In the case of *Albert v Lavin*,[439] it was suggested that the general rule is that detaining a man against his will without arresting him is unlawful as it contravenes the principle of citizen's liberty. Lord Diplock, however, stated that there is an exception to this rule in that:

> '*every citizen in whose presence a breach of the peace is being, or reasonably appears to be about to be, committed has the right to take reasonable steps to make the person who is breaking or threatening to break the peace refrain from doing so; and those reasonable steps in appropriate cases will include detaining him against his will.*

---

[437] *R v Deputy Governor of Parkhurst Prison, ex parte Hague* [1992] 1 AC 58
[438] (1985) 7 EHRR 528
[439] [1982] AC 546

At common law this is not only the right of every citizen, it is also his duty, although, except in the case of a citizen who is a constable, it is a duty of imperfect obligation.'

7.3.9 Prevention of a crime This defence, which is really only the justification for the commission of an unlawful act, can only be used for offences where some degree of force is employed.

Rules on reasonable force that apply to self-defence also apply for the prevention of crime defence. Section 3(1) of the Criminal Law Act 1967 stipulates that 'a person may use such force as is reasonable in the circumstances in the prevention of a crime. . .'. A crime, in this context, could be an unlawful act that is about or likely to incur physical damage to an individual or to property.

Chapter 8

Civil law

Introduction

This chapter considers the various torts (civil law wrongs) which may be committed by those who use physical interventions to deal with incidents of challenging behaviour and the potential defences which may be raised by those alleged to have committed such torts and from whom compensation by way of damages may be sought.

8.1 Assault

The definition for an assault here is similar to the criminal definition. Indeed, an assault is an act that makes the victim fear the application of immediate personal violence (_Smith v Superintendent of Woking_[440]).

The victim need not be touched or come to actual physical harm, nor is it important to determine what the defendant actually intends. It is enough that the victim is under the impression that they will be subjected to imminent violence (_Letang v Cooper_[441]).

The tort requires that the assault be an active behaviour as opposed to passive. However if the behaviour is any way threatening to the victim, then it will be considered an assault (_Read v Coker_), and so will a failed attempt at committing a battery (_Stephens v Myers_).

When it is clear that the threat of violence will not be carried out because the defendant would be unable to do so, then there will be no assault (_Thomas v National Union of Mineworkers (South Wales Area)_[442]). However, in cases where the defendant could not inflict violence but this would not be known or clear to the victim, then the threat of immediate violence is effective and will amount to assault (_R v St George_[443]).

Although words alone cannot constitute an assault in tort, they can nonetheless operate to negate the commission of the tort (_Tuberville v Savage_[444]).

Available defences: consent, self-defence and necessity. (For a full explanation of the defences see below at para 8.4.2.)

---

[440] (1983) 76 Cr. App. R. 234
[441] [1965] 1 QB 232
[442] [1986] Ch. 20
[443] (1840) 9 C & P 483
[444] (1669) 1 Mod Rep 3

8.2 Battery

The tort of battery occurs when a person intentionally and directly applies unlawful physical contact against another individual. Injury need not be a consequence of this act (*R v Chief Constable of Devon & Cornwall, ex parte Central Electricity Generating Board*[445]); nor is force a requirement – in medicine, for instance, a treatment that is imposed on a person without their consent will amount to a battery (*Re F*[446]).

The application of physical touch must be intentional (*Fowler v Lanning*[447]). In the absence of intention, the act becomes a matter of negligence (*Letang v Cooper*[448]).

The Court of Appeal in *Wilson v Pringle*[449] required an element of hostility for the tort to be complete. However, the House of Lords in *F v West Berkshire Health Authority*[450] did not deem the hostility requirement necessary.

For a battery to occur there must be a positive act – obstructing somebody's way in a passive manner will not be battery. Moreover, the force used need not involve personal violence or contact – indeed, battery can be committed by simply throwing water on the victim, pulling a chair under him or pulling an item from his grasp.

Available defences: consent, necessity, self-defence, inevitable accident, lawful arrest. (For a full explanation of the defences see below at para 8.4.2.)

8.3 False imprisonment

The tort of false imprisonment is committed when a person intentionally and directly restrains another's freedom of movement. This includes unlawful arrest and unlawful prevention of a person from leaving a particular place (eg room, open field) (*Collins v Wilcox* 1984[451]).

The infringement on the physical liberty must be total, ie there must be no exit available to the victim, no alternative (safe) direction that they could take, for however short or long a period of time (*Bird v Jones*[452]). The tort can still occur whether the claimant is unconscious (*Murray v Ministry of Defence*[453]) or unaware that they are being restrained at the time (*Meering v Graham White Aviation*[454]).

The restraint must be a direct consequence of a positive act; that is, it will not be false imprisonment if it is the result of a careless action (*Sayers v Harlow Urban District Council*).[455] Force is not required for this tort as words alone can give rise to a false imprisonment (*Davidson v Chief Constable of North Wales*[456]).

---

[445] [1982] QB 458
[446] [1990] 2 AC 1
[447] [1959] 1 QB 426
[448] [1965] 1 QB 232
[449] [1986] 2 All ER 440
[450] [1989] 2 All ER 545
[451] [1984] 1 WLR 1172
[452] (1845) 7 QB 742
[453] [1988] 2 All ER 521
[454] (1920) 122 LT 44 CA
[455] 1 WLR 623
[456] [1994] 2 All ER 597

Available defences: consent, mistaken arrest and lawful arrest. (For a full explanation of the defences see below at para 8.4.2.)

8.4 Negligence

Negligence can have different meanings, and thus different legal consequences, for the lawyer and the lay person.

Negligence can be first described as someone's inadvertent state of mind with regards to the consequences of a particular conduct; secondly, as a standard of behaviour (the 'reasonable person') against which a person's actions are measured; and finally, as the tort of negligence.

Lord Wright defined negligence as being a tort consisting of a legal duty to take care on the part of the defendant and a failure to do so; thus resulting in a breach of duty, which causes the plaintiff to suffer damages (_Lochgelly Iron Co v M'Mullan_[457]).

8.4.1 Elements of the tort of negligence
The four major components of negligence are that:

- the defendant owes a legal duty of care to the plaintiff; and

- the defendant has breached this duty by falling below the required standard of care demanded of him; and

- the plaintiff has suffered damage as a result of the breach of duty; and

- the damage suffered by the plaintiff was not too remote.

8.4.1.1 Duty of care
In _Donoghue v Stephenson_,[458] Lord Atkin explains when and how a duty of care arises. He thus stated what is known as the 'neighbour' principle:

> '_You must take reasonable care to avoid acts or omissions which you can reasonably foresee would be likely to injure your neighbour. Who, then, in law is my neighbour? The answer seems to be – persons who are so closely and directly affected by my act that I ought reasonably to have them in contemplation as being so affected when I am directing my mind to the acts or omissions which are called in question._'

In order to determine whether there is a duty of care owed by the defendant to the plaintiff, the court will thus apply the test of reasonable foresight. In other words, if a reasonable person would foresee that their careless action or omission is likely to cause injury or damage to an individual or group of individuals (_Haley v London Electricity Board_[459]), then there is a potential relationship between the parties based on that duty.

The House of Lords in _Caparo Industries plc v Dickman_[460] completed the test with two more elements: the notions of 'proximity' and the policy element; the latter being concerned with whether it is 'just and reasonable' to impose a duty on the defendant.

---

[457] [1934] AC 1
[458] [1932] AC 562
[459] [1965] AC 778
[460] [1990] 2 AC 605

Therefore, the full test implies that three questions must be answered for a court to find that there is indeed a duty of care on the part of the defendant, and a right to be taken care of in the claimant:

- Is the damage to the plaintiff reasonably foreseeable?
- Is the relationship between the parties sufficiently proximate?
- Is it 'just and reasonable' to impose such a duty?

It is arguable that these three components of the test are not separate from each other, but rather complete or simply reflect one another. In other words, it is like looking at the different facets of a diamond, exploring the various angles of an issue. Therefore, the courts can find a duty of care based on the positive answer to only one or all of the questions above. Yet, it also appears that not one of the elements is a sufficient criterion for the imposition of a duty of care. Indeed, although the element of foreseeability, or that of proximity may be satisfied, the courts can decide that there is no duty for policy reasons.

Reasonable foresight

Since the question of reasonable foresight revolves around what the reasonable person would have foreseen in the given circumstances, the idea of what is foreseeable is somewhat complex. Thus there is no fixed definition of foreseeability.

Judges resort to terms such as 'probability' or 'likely' and look both at the relationship between the parties and the nature and seriousness of the damage incurred to determine what ought to be foreseeable or not.

Proximity

Proximity is also referred to as the 'neighbour principle'; the term is not merely about physical contact or closeness. As Lord Oliver put it in _Caparo Industries v Dickman and Others_,[461] it is 'a convenient label to describe circumstances from which the law will attribute a duty of care'.

In cases where physical harm is incurred by the plaintiff as a result of the defendant's action, the court will often assume that there is reasonable foreseeability and that this will suffice to find a duty of care (_Murphy v Brentwood District Council_[462]).

Policy issues

'How wide the sphere of the duty of care in negligence is to be laid depends ultimately on the courts' assessment of the demands of society for the protection from the carelessness of others' (_Hedley Byrne & Co Ltd v Heller & Partners Ltd_,[463] per Lord Pearce).

The grounds on which a court can decide that it would not be just and reasonable to impose a duty of care on the defendant are for instance when:

---

[461] [1990] 2 WLR 358
[462] [1990] 2 All ER 908
[463] [1964] AC 465

- the claimant is responsible for his misfortune;

- there are other means of compensation;

- a duty of care would affect work done under statutory obligation (_X (minors) v Bedfordshire County Council_ 1995[464]);

- the award of damages would prove too heavy on public authorities' resources;

- a duty of care would impact on defendants' performance and quality of public service;

- a duty of care would impede on another course of action (_Calveley v Chief Constable of the Merseyside Police_[465]).

However, the judges, in making their decision as to whether a duty of care ought to exist or not, now have to take into account the Human Rights Act 1998. The courts must consider that excluding a duty of care on policy grounds might be an impeachment of the claimant's right to a remedial action for a breach of that duty.

Following the cases of _Osman v UK_ and _Z v UK_,[466] the national courts are less prone to readily dismiss a claim for a breach of a duty of care on policy grounds (_Barrett v London Borough of Enfield_[467]).

8.4.1.2 Breach of duty A breach of a duty of care occurs when a defendant's performance, action or omission has fallen beneath the required standard of care for the duty.

To decide whether a duty has been breached, the court applies the objective or 'reasonable man' test, ie 'the omission to do something which a reasonable man would do, or doing something which a prudent and reasonable man would not do' (_Blyth v Birmingham Waterworks_,[468] per Alderson B).

The test does not consider the weaknesses of the defendants, and the reasonable man is 'presumed to be free from both over-apprehension and over-confidence'. The courts will look at all the circumstances of the case as they presented themselves to the defendant (_Parkinson v Liverpool Corporation_[469]). However, the notion of what is reasonable will vary according the facts of the situation and the judges themselves – 'what to one judge may seem far-fetched may seem to another both natural and probable' (_Glasgow Corp. v Muir_,[470] per Lord Macmillan).

The elements taken into account when deciding whether there is a breach of duty include the plaintiff's special characteristics, the magnitude of the risk, the practicality of protection, common practice, social utility, and the professional factor.

In the case of _Paris v Stepney Borough Council_,[471] the court considered the disability of the plaintiff in deciding that the defendants owed him a duty of care due to his visual impairment that they did not owe to their other employees.

---

[464] [1995] 3 WLR 152
[465] [1989] AC 1228
[466] [1999] 1 FLR 193, _Osman v UK_ and _Z v UK_ [2001] 2 FLR 612
[467] [2001] 2 AC 550
[468] (1856) 11 Exch 781
[469] [1950] 1 All ER 367
[470] [1943] AC 448
[471] [1951] AC 367

The magnitude of the risk is a notion concerned with the likelihood of the damage occurring and the severity of that damage. If the chances of damage occurring are very slight despite a potential risk, it is argued that it would be reasonable for a man to accept that risk without being in breach of a duty to care if all precautions are taken to prevent it. In _Bolton v Stone_,[472] Lord Reid stated that 'what a man must not do . . . is to create a risk which is substantial'.

As for the potential damage, precautions must be taken in proportion to its seriousness. However, the defendant is under no obligation to take extraordinary measures of protection if the cost and trouble are deemed disproportionate to the risk (_Latimer v AEC Ltd_[473]). When responding to an emergency situation, the action of the defendant will be assessed in the light of how a reasonable man would have reacted in a similar situation, given the same circumstances and time limit.

In deciding on the reasonableness of the defendant's protection methods, judges will take into account what is considered common practice for others in the same field or situation. If the defendant has acted in accordance with that general practice, it is thought to be strong evidence that there is no negligent behaviour (_Morris v West Hartlepool Steam Navigation Co Ltd_[474]); except when that common practice is in itself considered negligent (_Thompson v Smith Shiprepairers (North Shields)_[475]). There is a duty to keep up to date with new knowledge and developing practices.

Some risks are 'worth' taking for the benefit of society if the alternative outcome for not taking it would result in greater damage (_Watt v Hertfordshire County Council_[476]). On the other hand, if there is no social utility to the defendant's action, the courts will expect him to show greater care to warrant any damage caused, however slight (_The Wagon Mound (No.2)_[477]).

In cases where professionals are involved, the defendant's action will be judged according to what a reasonable man with the defendant's skills would have done in the circumstances. 'The test is the standard of the ordinary skilled man exercising and professing to have that special skill. A man need not possess the highest expert skill at the risk of being found negligent. . . it is sufficient if he exercises the ordinary skill of an ordinary competent man exercising that particular art' (_Bolam v Friern Hospital Management Committee_,[478] per McNair J).

However some practices, though common, can be considered unacceptable and inappropriate (_Re Herald of Free Enterprise_[479]). Moreover, though a defendant can find an expert witness to support his course of action, judges can deem the opinion to lack reasonableness and logic and thus establish negligence:

> '_in the vast majority of cases the fact that distinguished experts in the field are of a particular opinion will demonstrate the reasonableness of that opinion. In particular, where there are questions of assessment of the relative risks and benefits of adopting a particular medical practice, a reasonable view necessarily presupposes that the_

---

[472] [1951] AC 850
[473] [1953] AC 643
[474] [1956] AC 552
[475] [1984] QB 405
[476] [1954] 1 W.L.R. 835
[477] [1967] 1 AC 617
[478] 1957] 1 W.L.R. 582
[479] 1989 WL 650794

relative risks and benefits have been weighed by the experts in forming their opinions. But if, in a rare case, it can be demonstrated that the professional opinion is not capable of withstanding logical analysis, the judge is entitled to hold that the body of opinion is not reasonable or responsible' (Bolitho v City and Hackney Health Authority [480]*).*

8.4.1.3 Damage and causation   Once the duty of care and its breach are established, it must be proven that there is a damage resulting from the negligent act or omission.

The test for determining the causal link is known as the 'but for' test: 'if the damage would not have happened but for a particular fault, then that fault is the cause of the damage; if it would have happened anyway, fault or no fault, the fault is not the cause of the damage' (*Cork v Kirby Maclean Ltd*,[481] per Lord Denning).

The defendant must take the plaintiff as he finds him – the courts will apply the 'thin skull' or egg-shell principle. This means that if the victim of a tortious act suffers from some weakness that the defendant may not have been aware of which then exacerbates the level of injury suffered eg the plaintiff has exceptionally brittle bones and when pushed over breaks several bones instead of just experiencing bruising, the defendant will be held liable for the full extent of the injuries instead of just those which he might reasonably have expected the plaintiff to suffer.

8.4.1.3.1 Nervous shock   The burden of proof lies on the plaintiff who must show that he is suffering from a physical injury or a recognised psychiatric illness as a result of the nervous shock incurred by the negligent act (*McLoughlin v O'Brian*[482]). The shock must be sudden and unexpected. The psychiatric conditions recognised include post-traumatic stress disorder or depression, as well as pathological grief. In the case of a person with learning disabilities who also presents challenging behaviour their parent or other family member taking the case on their behalf would have to obtain the relevant medical evidence to prove the suffering on the part of his child, parent or sibling.

8.4.1.3.2 Omissions   As a general rule, there is no obligation to act or help others, so a non-feasance (non-performance) will not give rise to liability. However, Lord Goff stated that there are exceptions to that rule where there is a contractual duty to act and a special relationship between the defendant and the plaintiff, for instance (*Smith v Littlewoods Organisation Ltd*[483]).

8.4.2 The defences which may be raised to an allegation that a tort has been committed
What is meant by the term defence when used in relation to the civil law? Howarth states that a defence is 'an argument that the defendant raises and has to prove which, if successful, means that the defendant wins the case'.[484]

8.4.2.1 Volenti non fit injuria   Also known as consent, this defence implies that a person cannot cause injury to someone who is consenting to the risk. However, this idea is tempered by the fact that consent is not just about knowing the risk, but also about understanding it – if

[480]   [1998] AC 232
[481]   [1952] 2 All E.R. 402
[482]   [1983] 1 AC 410
[483]   [1987] AC 241
[484]   Howarth D, Textbook on Tort (Butterworths, 1995) at p. 652

there is no understanding, then there is no consent. In *Stermer v Lawson*,[485] the plaintiff was a 17-year-old who borrowed a motorbike from the defendant, a 16-year-old. The plaintiff did not have any experience of motorbikes, so the defendant gave him some instructions; however, the plaintiff injured himself. It was held that that the plaintiff's consent to use the motorbike was vitiated by his ignorance of the dangers of such an activity and that the defendant had a duty to inform the plaintiff of those dangers.

When an individual gives consent to one specific act, the consent does not extend to another act being performed. In *Nash v Sheen*,[486] the victim suffered from a scalp injury after the hairdresser dyed her hair when she actually asked for a permanent wave. The court held that no consent was given to dye the hair and that the dyeing amounted to assault.

There is no consent when it is given under duress (*Smith v Baker*[487]). The issue of consent is most relevant in cases of medical treatment (see chapter 4.3 on medical treatment and consent).

8.4.2.2 Self-defence   An individual has a right to defend himself as long as the force used for that purpose is considered proportionate to the danger. What amounts to reasonable force is a question of fact that is assessed on a case-by-case basis.

In *Lane v Holloway*,[488] the plaintiff was a 63-year-old man who had an argument with the 23-year-old owner of a café in his neighbourhood after he insulted the owner's wife in reply to her verbal abuse. The plaintiff, believing that the owner was about to strike him, punched him on the shoulder. The owner reacted by hitting the plaintiff in his eye, which resulted in the plaintiff needing stitches, an operation and spending a month in hospital. The court held that the force used had been out of all proportion given the circumstances and that therefore self-defence did not apply.

8.4.2.3 Contributory negligence   Contributory negligence is not really a defence at all but it has to be proved by the defendant and then operates to reduce a claim for damages against a defendant by considering the plaintiff's role and contributing acts to their own injuries or damages. Thus s.1 (1) Law Reform (Contributory Negligence) Act 1945 states that:

> *'where any person suffers damage as the result partly of his own fault and the fault of any other person or persons, a claim in respect of that damage shall not be defeated by reason of the fault of the person suffering the damage, but the damages recoverable in respect thereof shall be reduced to such extent as the court thinks just and equitable having regard to the claimant's share in the responsibility for the damage.'*

In *Sayers v Harlow DC*,[489] the plaintiff was a woman who was trapped in a toilet cubicle due to a defective lock. She tried to get out of the cubicle by climbing over the door, which resulted in her falling and injuring herself. The Court of Appeal held that the local authority responsible for the operation of the public lavatory was negligent and the authority was therefore liable for damages. The plaintiff, however, also contributed to her injuries; therefore, the local authority was held to carry 75% of the blame, and the remaining 25% was the plaintiff's.

---

[485]   [1977] 5 W.W.R. 628
[486]   [1953] CLY 3726
[487]   [1891] AC 325
[488]   [1968] 1 QB 379
[489]   [1958] 1 W.L.R. 623

8.4.2.4 Necessity   The basis of the defence of necessity is 'a mixture of charity, the maintenance of the public good and self-protection, and it is probably limited to cases involving an urgent situation of imminent peril'.[490]

An action taken out of necessity must be justified by its reasonableness, which the court will assess on a case-by-case basis and will consider in the light of what is done, acceptable and deemed reasonable in this day and age given the circumstances.

In _R v Bournewood Community and Mental Health NHS Trust_,[491] the House of Lords held that necessity could justify detention when the individual detained represents a danger both to himself and to others.

It is thus submitted that (1) if there is no other safer and less damaging alternative to the unlawful act, then necessity could succeed as a defence. Also, once the danger has passed, there is no more necessity to perform the unlawful act.

8.4.2.5 Statutory authority   Some statutes will allow trespass to the person in certain situations. For instance, Section 3(1) and (2) Mental Health Act stipulates that a patient may be admitted to a hospital and detained there for the period allowed by the provisions of this Act if the patient is suffering from a mental illness or another mental disorder which demands medical treatment in a hospital; and if it is necessary for the patient's health and safety, as well as for the safety of others that he is detained under this Act.

In other words, where a statute authorises an act, which without consent would normally amount to an offence of assault, battery, or false imprisonment, this act, if performed within the ambit of the Act's provisions, will not be an offence as the statute will provide a valid defence.

8.4.2.6 Illegality   This defence works when the defendant causes injury to the plaintiff while the latter is performing an illegal action. 'The maxim _ex turpi causa non oritur actio_ can be roughly translated as meaning that no cause of action may be founded upon an immoral or illegal act'.[492] The general principle is that no one should benefit from a criminal enterprise.

In _Ashton v Turner_,[493] three men who had committed a burglary attempted to escape the scene of the crime by driving in one of the men's car. However they crashed and one of the offenders was injured. He claimed damages against both the owner of the car and the driver at the time of the crash.

Ewbank J stated 'the law of England may in certain circumstances not recognise the existence of a duty of care owed by one participant in a crime to another participant in the same crime, in relation to an act done in connection with the commission of that crime. That law is based on public policy, and the application of the law depends on a consideration of all the facts.' Considering that the three men were committing an illegal action, ie burglary, the judge held that there was no duty of care between the driver, the owner of the car and the victim of the accident. Therefore the victim could not claim damages.

---

[490]   Rogers W V H, _Winfield & Jolowicz on Tort_, 16th edition, London & Maxwell 2002, p. 872
[491]   [1998] 1 AC 458
[492]   _per_ Neil LJ in _Revill v Newberry_ [1996] QB 567
[493]   [1981] QB 137

However, there might some instances where the illegality of an act will not serve as a defence for damages. In <u>Revill v Newberry</u>,[494] the defendant shot the plaintiff with his shotgun as the plaintiff was trespassing on the defendant's land. The plaintiff suffered injuries and made a claim for damages in negligence. The court held that the force used in these circumstances was unreasonable, and stated that '. . . violence may be returned with necessary violence. But the force used must not exceed the limits of what is reasonable in the circumstances . . . the assailant or intruder may be met with reasonable force but no more; the use of excessive violence against him is an actionable wrong.'[495]

8.4.2.7 Inevitable accident   Where injury occurs as a result of an accident, ie an event that is beyond the defendant's control, the latter will not be held liable. An accident is defined as a situation that is 'not avoidable by any precautions as a reasonable man, doing such an act then and there, could be expected to take'.[496]

In <u>Stanley v Powell</u>,[497] the plaintiff was injured after the defendant, who was shooting at a pheasant, accidentally hit the plaintiff and wounded him. It was found that an act is wrongful if it is either negligent or wilful (intentional). If an act is neither, then there is no trespass to the person. Therefore, the defendant would have to prove that it was accidental, ie that the act was not intentional, and was 'not owing to neglect or want of due caution'.

8.4.2.8 Mistake   Mistake, that is a mistaken belief either of fact or law, is not a general defence and the significance of a mistake will vary from one case to another. A mistake that a reasonable man could have made in the same circumstances could be a defence.

---

[494] [1996] QB 567
[495] per Millet LJ, in <u>Revill v Newberry</u> 1996 QB 567
[496] Rogers W V H, *Winfield and Jolowicz on Tort*, London Sweet & Maxwell 2002, p. 868, quoting Sir Frederick Pollock (*Torts), 15th ed.*
[497] [1891] 1 QB 86

Chapter 9

Human rights law

Introduction

This chapter considers the potential impact of the various Articles of the European Convention on Human Rights now contained in Schedule 1 Human Rights Act 1998, implemented on October 2 2000, in relation to the use of physical interventions as a response to incidents of challenging behaviour.

9.1 Articles especially relevant to physical interventions (2, 3, 5, 7, 8, 10, 14 and 17)

Article 2 Right to Life

1. Everyone's right to life shall be protected by law. No one shall be deprived of his life intentionally save in the execution of a sentence of a court following his conviction of a crime for which this penalty is provided by law.

2. Deprivation of life shall not be regarded as inflicted in contravention of this Article when it results from the use of force which is no more than absolutely necessary:

    (a) in defence of any person from unlawful violence;

    (b) in order to effect a lawful arrest or to prevent the escape of a person lawfully detained;

    (c) in action lawfully taken for the purpose of quelling a riot or insurrection.

Article 3 Prohibition of Torture

No one shall be subjected to torture or to inhuman or degrading treatment or punishment.

Article 5 Right to Liberty and Security

1. Everyone has the right to liberty and security of person. No one shall be deprived of his liberty save in the following cases and in accordance with a procedure prescribed by law:

    (a) the lawful detention of a person after conviction by a competent court;

    (b) the lawful arrest or detention of a person for non-compliance with the lawful order of a court or in order to secure the fulfilment of any obligation prescribed by law;

(c) the lawful arrest or detention of a person effected for the purpose of bringing him before the competent legal authority on reasonable suspicion of having committed an offence or when it is reasonably considered necessary to prevent his committing an offence or fleeing after having done so;

(d) the detention of a minor by lawful order for the purpose of educational supervision or his lawful detention for the purpose of bringing him before the competent legal authority;

(e) the lawful detention of persons for the prevention of the spreading of infectious diseases, of persons of unsound mind, alcoholics or drug addicts or vagrants;

(f) the lawful arrest or detention of a person to prevent his effecting an unauthorised entry into the country or of a person against whom action is being taken with a view to deportation or extradition.

2. Everyone who is arrested shall be informed promptly, in a language which he understands, of the reasons for his arrest and of any charge against him.

3. Everyone arrested or detained in accordance with the provisions of paragraph 1(c) of this Article shall be brought promptly before a judge or other officer authorised by law to exercise judicial power and shall be entitled to trial within a reasonable time or to release pending trial. Release may be conditioned by guarantees to appear for trial.

4. Everyone who is deprived of his liberty by arrest or detention shall be entitled to take proceedings by which the lawfulness of his detention shall be decided speedily by a court and his release ordered if the detention is not lawful.

5. Everyone who has been the victim of arrest or detention in contravention of the provisions of this Article shall have an enforceable right to compensation.

Article 8 Right to Respect for Private and Family Life

1. Everyone has the right to respect for his private and family life, his home and his correspondence.

2. There shall be no interference by a public authority with the exercise of this right except such as is in accordance with the law and is necessary in a democratic society in the interests of national security, public safety or the economic well-being of the country, for the prevention of disorder or crime, for the protection of health or morals, or for the protection of the rights and freedoms of others.

Article 10 Freedom of Expression

1. Everyone has the right to freedom of expression. This right shall include freedom to hold opinions and to receive and impart information and ideas without interference by public authority and regardless of frontiers. This Article shall not prevent States from requiring the licensing of broadcasting, television or cinema enterprises.

2. The exercise of these freedoms, since it carries with it duties and responsibilities, may be subject to such formalities, conditions, restrictions or penalties as are prescribed by law and

are necessary in a democratic society, in the interests of national security, territorial integrity or public safety, for the prevention of disorder or crime, for the protection of health or morals, for the protection of the reputation or rights of others, for preventing the disclosure of information received in confidence, or for maintaining the authority and impartiality of the judiciary.

Article 14 Prohibition of Discrimination

The enjoyment of the rights and freedoms set forth in this Convention shall be secured without discrimination on any ground such as sex, race, colour, language, religion, political or other opinion, national or social origin, association with a national minority, property, birth or other status.

Article 17 Prohibition of Abuse of Rights

Nothing in this Convention may be interpreted as implying for any State, group or person any right to engage in any activity or perform any act aimed at the destruction of any of the rights and freedoms set forth herein or at their limitation to a greater extent than is provided for in the Convention.

9.2 Impact of each article

Article 2: right to life

This Article aims, on the one hand, to safeguard individuals against arbitrary deprivation of life by public authorities, and on the other hand, to impose upon the State a responsibility to protect individuals against unlawful killings. Indeed, the Commission stated in _X v UK_[498] that 'the concept that everyone's life shall be protected by law enjoins the State not only to refrain from taking life intentionally, but, further, to take appropriate steps to safeguard life'.

The reasonableness test will be used in order to find the State or a public body liable for not defending an individual's life. In _Osman v UK_,[499] the court stated that it is 'sufficient for an applicant to show that the authorities did not do all that could reasonably be expected of them to avoid a real and immediate risk to life of which they have or ought to have knowledge'. On the other hand, all the public body has to do is to prove or show that they acted reasonably regarding the circumstances of the situation.

When physical intervention is required by a situation, such as the prevention of unlawful violence, the force used should be 'no more than is necessary', which test was laid down in _Stewart v UK_.[500] The court stated that the force must be 'strictly proportionate to the achievement of the permitted purpose'.

In _Pretty v United Kingdom_[501] the European Court of Human Rights (hereafter the ECHR) stated that 'the Court's case-law accords pre-eminence to Article 2 as one of the most

---

[498] Application No 7154/75 (Rep), 12 October 1978, 14 DR 31 at 32
[499] [1999] 1 FLR 193
[500] (1985) 7 EHRR CD 453
[501] (2002) 35 EHRR 1 ECHR

fundamental provisions of the Convention. It safeguards the right to life, without which enjoyment of any of the other rights and freedoms in the Convention is rendered nugatory. It sets out the limited circumstances when deprivation of life may be justified and the Court has applied a strict scrutiny when those exceptions have been invoked by respondent Governments.'

The case concerned a 43-year-old woman who was suffering from motor neurone disease. The disease affects the muscles and eventually results in death as the breathing muscles weaken and the muscles controlling speaking and swallowing contribute to a respiratory failure and pneumonia. As her condition deteriorated, she wished to be able to choose the manner and the time of her death which would enable her to die with dignity and with a minimum of suffering. She could not commit suicide by herself, so this case was an attempt to make euthanasia legal in this particular circumstance.

On this point, the ECHR opined that it 'is not persuaded that "the right to life" guaranteed in Article 2 can be interpreted as involving a negative aspect'. It carries on explaining that Article 2 'is unconcerned with issues to do with the quality of living or what a person chooses to do with his or her life' as these rights would be guaranteed by other Articles of the Convention. The ECHR's conclusion is therefore that 'Article 2 cannot, without a distortion of language, be interpreted as conferring the diametrically opposite right, namely a right to die; nor can it create a right to self-determination in the sense of conferring on an individual the entitlement to choose death rather than life'.

Article 3: prohibition of torture

The State has a duty to protect people against the threat and/or infliction of torture and inhuman or degrading treatment or punishment. The leading case here is _A v United Kingdom_,[502] in which it was held that the UK had failed to protect a nine-year-old boy from being beaten by his parent, and thus violated the provisions of Article 3. This clearly establishes a positive duty on the part of the UK to help prevent an individual from suffering from degrading treatments or punishments. The United Kingdom has shown a willingness to follow this line of thinking; indeed, Article 6(1) of the HRA 1998 provides that 'it is unlawful for a public authority to act in a way which is incompatible with a Convention right'.

There are three branches in Article 3 and the main difference between them is the degree of suffering that they entail, or the purpose for which the ill-treatment is used.

A. Torture

The United Nations adopted the following definition of torture for the purposes of the Convention:

> '_Any act by which severe pain or suffering, whether physical or mental, is intentionally inflicted on a person for such purposes as obtaining from him or a third person information or a confession, punishing him for an act he or a third person has committed or is suspected of having committed, or intimidating him or coercing him or a third person, or for any reason based on discrimination of any kind, when such pain or suffering is inflicted by or at the instigation of or with the consent or_

---

[502] (1999) 27 EHRR 611

acquiescence of a public official or other person acting in an official capacity. It does not include pain or suffering arising from, inherent in or incidental to lawful sanctions.[503]

In the case of <u>*Aksoy v Turkey*</u>,[504] torture was held to be when one individual deliberately applies inhuman treatment to another thus causing very serious and cruel suffering for the purpose of obtaining information or inflicting punishment.

The torture threshold will be reached when the ill treatment attains a minimum level of severity. The judges will decide what amounts to the minimum level on a case-by-case basis. As stated in <u>*Ireland v UK*</u>,[505] 'the assessment of the minimum (. . .) depends on all the circumstances of the case, such as the duration of the treatment, its physical or mental effects and, in some cases, the sex, age and state of health of the victim, etc'.

While violations of Article 3 must be proved beyond reasonable doubt, once they have been established, they cannot be justified (<u>*Aksoy v Turkey*</u>).

Inhuman treatments that have psychological consequences can amount to torture (<u>*Aydin v Turkey*</u>[506]). In <u>*Denmark v Greece*</u>,[507] it was held that torture includes 'the infliction of mental suffering by creating a state of anguish and stress by means of other than bodily assault'.

B. Inhuman or degrading treatment

In <u>*Kudla v Poland*</u>,[508] it was held that for a treatment to be inhuman, it must have been 'premeditated, applied for hours at a stretch and caused either actual bodily injury or intense physical or mental suffering'. A treatment is degrading when 'it was such as to arouse in the victim feelings of fear, anguish and inferiority capable of humiliating and debasing them'. The suffering or humiliation endured by the victim must be so serious that it goes 'beyond that inevitable element of suffering or humiliation connected with a legitimate form of legitimate treatment or punishment'.

In the cases of <u>*X and Y v Netherlands*</u>, it was held that 'mental suffering leading to acute psychiatric disturbances falls into the category of treatment prohibited by Article 3 of the Convention'. This was confirmed in <u>*Kurt v Turkey*</u>.

C. Inhuman or degrading punishment

In the <u>*Tyrer v UK*</u>[509] case, the court found that degrading punishment ' – whereby (the victim) was treated as an object in the power of the authorities – constituted an assault on precisely that which it is one of the main purposes of Article 3 to protect, namely a person's dignity and physical integrity'.

---

[503] Article 1, paragraph 1 of the Convention against Torture and Other Cruel, Inhuman or degrading Treatment or Punishment
[504] (2003) 36 EHRR 6 ECHR
[505] ECHR, series A, no.25, 2 EHRR 25
[506] (1998) 25 EHRR 251 ECHR
[507] Case 3321–3/67; 3344/67
[508] (2002) 35 EHRR 11 ECHR
[509] (1979–80) 2 EHRR 1 ECHR

A degrading punishment could be inflicted both physically and mentally (anguish, fear, humiliation, feeling of inferiority). Breaking a victim's physical or moral resistance is enough to amount to degrading treatment provided the conditions of the ill-treatment are below a standard of acceptability.

Article 5: Right to liberty and security

This Article is concerned with protecting individuals against arbitrary arrest and detention (*Engel v Netherlands*[510]), as well as unlawful restriction of movement. However, this right is not absolute and is subject to the idea of public concern; that is, when an individual is a threat to himself or the community, restriction of liberty might be the only option.

The concept of the right to security is not separate from that of the right to liberty. The court held in *East African Asians v UK*[511] that 'security of person' and 'right to liberty' are both concerned with matters of physical liberty.

Detention is mainly when an individual is deprived of his liberty following an arrest. If the arrest is undertaken within the ambit of the Police and Criminal Evidence Act 1984 and the detention is based on one or several grounds covered by PACE, it can be said to be lawful and therefore will not be in contravention of Article 5. Indeed, Article 5 states that detention can only be carried out 'in accordance with a procedure prescribed by law'; and sub-paragraphs (a) to (f) of the Article provide an exhaustive list of exceptions to the right to liberty, such as after a conviction by a national court.

The issue of what constitutes a deprivation of liberty is a bit more complex. In the case of *Guzzardi v Italy*,[512] the court stated that it was difficult to establish a clear definition of 'deprivation of liberty' and that there was a grey zone within which mere restrictions can amount to full deprivation.

Article 8: Right to respect for private and family life

In *Botta v Italy*,[513] the ECHR stated that 'private life includes a person's physical and psychological integrity and the guarantee afforded by Article 8 of the Convention is primarily intended to ensure, without outside interference, development of the personality of each in his relations with other human beings'.

The court further added that:

> *'while the essential object of Article 8 is to protect the individual against arbitrary interference by the public authorities, it does not merely compel the State to abstain from such interference: in addition to this negative undertaking, there may be positive obligations inherent in effective respect for private or family life. These obligations may involve the adoption of measures designed to secure respect for private life even in the sphere of the relations of individuals between themselves. However, the concept of respect is not precisely defined. In order to determine whether such obligations*

---

[510] (1976) 1 EHHR 647
[511] (1973) 3 EHRR 76
[512] (1981) 3 EHRR 333 ECHR
[513] (1998) 26 EHRR 241

exist, regard must be had to the fair balance that has to be struck between the general interest and the interests of the individual, while the State has, in any event, a margin of appreciation.'

Article 10: Freedom of expression

In *Handyside v UK*,[514] the court stated that the concept of freedom of expression, for the purposes of Article 10:

> *'constitutes one of the essential foundations of [democratic] society, one of the basic conditions for its progress and for the development of every man. Subject to paragraph 2 of Article 10, it is applicable not only to "information" or "ideas" that are favourably received or regarded as inoffensive or as a matter of indifference, but also to those that offend, shock or disturb the state or any sector of the population. Such are the demands of that pluralism, tolerance and broadmindedness without which there is no "democratic society".'*

The scope of Article 10 includes the right to entertain ideas and express them, as well as the right to receive information (*Autronic AG v Switzerland*[515]). Although there is no such right as 'freedom of information' (*Leander v Sweden*[516]), one's right to be provided with information can nonetheless be protected by Article 10 (*Open Door and Dublin Well Woman v Ireland*[517]).

Article 10 does not discriminate between forms of expression and covers many, such as words, pictures, paintings, images, dress, actions... (*Stevens v UK*[518]).

The impact of this Article is that it can help an individual access information that he is entitled to receive but has been denied by the representatives of public bodies.

Article 14: Prohibition of discrimination

In *Botta v Italy*,[519] the court re-affirmed the position that 'Article 14 complements the other substantive provisions of the Convention and its Protocols. It has no independent existence, since it has effect solely in relation to enjoyment of the rights and freedoms safeguarded by those provisions. Although the application of Article 14 does not presuppose a breach of those provisions – and to this extent it is autonomous – there can be no room for its application unless the facts of the case fall within the ambit of one or more of the latter.'

The Lord's Chancellor Department Core Guidance on Human Rights explains that when there is an issue of discrimination debated before the ECHR, the court will 'consider whether there was an objective and reasonable justification for treating different categories of people in a different way, and whether any differential treatment was proportionate to the aim pursued'.[520]

[514] (1979–80) 1 EHRR 737 ECHR
[515] [1991] FSR 55 ECHR
[516] (1987) 9 EHRR 433 ECHR
[517] (1993) 15 EHRR 244 ECHR
[518] (1986) 46 DR 245
[519] (1998) 26 EHRR 241
[520] http://www.humanrights.gov.uk/guidance.htm

9.3 Application

9.3.1 Private individuals and public bodies The Human Rights Act 1998 provides a structure for the protection of individuals' rights before the national courts, and a procedure through which they can claim a remedy against the State or one of its representatives (public bodies) for breaches of Convention rights and/or duties. Actions under the Act can only be brought against a public authority, not against a private individual. However, the national courts are nonetheless under an obligation to interpret the law in accordance with the Convention, which means that Convention rights can be invoked (and thus must be respected) in an action involving private parties.

9.3.2 Public authority Section 6 does not define what a public authority is but only gives it a somewhat vague meaning. Sub-section (3) states that it includes (a) a court or tribunal, and (b) any person certain of whose functions are functions of a public nature.

However, the White Paper does give an indication of what a public body is (although this not an exhaustive list): central and local government, the police, immigration officers, prisons, and companies exercising public function and responsible for areas of activity which were previously within the public sector. Other instances of public bodies are schools and bodies in charge of nursing and residential homes.

Some private bodies can be considered as public authorities when they perform functions that are of a public nature. There is thus a distinction to be made between bodies that are 'pure' public authorities, those that are quasi-public authorities and those that are private.

Pure public bodies are under an obligation to act in accordance with the Convention rights; except when, for reasons of statutory duties, they have no choice but to perform an act that is incompatible with the Convention.

Quasi-public authorities are bodies whose actions are either of a public or a private nature. When the act is of a public nature, then a claim for breach of the Convention can be brought against them under the Act. However, if the action is of a private nature, ie in relation to their private purposes as opposed to public purposes, then they are not under an obligation to comply with the HRA.

Private bodies are 'immune' from claims for violation of Convention rights, for they are governed by private law, and not public law.

9.3.3 Victim Section 7(7) provides that only a victim can bring a claim under the Act and that the national courts are to understand 'victim' in the light of Article 34 of the Convention, which means any person (natural or legal), non-governmental organisation or group of individuals claiming to be the victim of a violation of Convention rights:

- someone who is actually or potentially directly affected by a violation of the Convention perpetuated by a public authority;

- a company/corporation, organisation, interest group or trade union, if it qualifies as a victim itself;

- any relative of a victim, if the complaint is about the death of the victim.

Public authorities cannot qualify as victims under the Human Rights Act.

9.4 Procedure and remedies

9.4.1 Procedure   There are two claims that can be brought before the UK courts: a claim for an alleged breach of human rights (this can either be an act or an omission that occurred after the coming into force of the Act on 2 October 2000), and one for judicial review proceedings.

The choice of which court or tribunal to go to will depend on the nature of the claim and will then obey the normal rules applied within the UK legal system; however, claims for judicial review are to be heard before the Administrative Court.

There is a time limit attached to any free-standing application as stated in section 7(5)(a)+(b). A claim for a breach of Convention rights must be brought before the courts within a year of its occurrence (although this limitation period can be extended on grounds of equity ie what the court will determine to be fair in all the circumstances of the case). A claim for judicial review has a shorter time limit of three months from when the grounds for review arose.

9.4.2 Remedies   The remedies available will depend upon the nature of the claim. In any case, the UK courts have a right to grant an effective remedy in compensation for a breach of Convention right.

Section 8(1) of the HRA provides that 'in relation to any act (or proposed act) of a public authority which the court find is (or would be) unlawful, it may grant such relief or remedy, or make such order, within its powers as it considers just and appropriate'.

However, section 8(2) adds that 'damages may be awarded only by a court which has power to award damages, or to order the payment of compensation, in civil proceedings'.

Section 8(3) carries on by providing that 'no award of damages is to be made unless (. . .) the court is satisfied that the award is necessary to afford just satisfaction to the person in whose favour it is made'. The concept of 'just satisfaction' is laid down in Article 41 of the European Convention of Human Rights and Fundamental Freedoms, and states: 'If the Court finds that there has been a violation of the Convention or the protocols thereto, and if the internal law of the High Contracting Party concerned allows only partial reparation to be made, the Court shall, if necessary, afford just satisfaction to the injured party.'

What amounts to 'just satisfaction' is not clearly defined. It appears from the court's case-law that it is to be determined on a case-by-case basis. However, we can say the test for the award of pecuniary damage is one of causality. In _Ferrarin v Italy_,[521] the court stated that 'according to its case-law, compensation of damage is recoverable only to the extent that a causal link is established between the violation of the Convention and the damage caused'. Thus, if there is no link, then there is no compensation. As for cases of a non-pecuniary nature, the court will look at the applicant's personal situation and at the circumstances of the case when deciding whether to award damages (_Kurt Nielsen v Denmark_[522]).

The ECHR does not seem to award a great deal of pecuniary compensation, nor does it grant any punitive damages. In terms of financial loss, the compensatory amount will usually not

[521] 26 April 2001, Application No. 34203/96
[522] 15 February 2000, Application No. 33488/96

exceed £15,000 (*Johnson v UK* 1997[523]) and the applicant will have to prove its loss in painstaking detail. Quite often, it appears that the court considers rendering a judgement in favour of the applicant a good enough remedy. On the other hand, the court might award compensation in cases of 'moral damage', that is where emotional distress, psychological damage and loss of social benefits are at stake.

The Act provides that the national courts are to follow as best they can the judgement of the ECHR. Indeed, section 8(4) states that in determining either to award damages and the amount of such a compensation, the UK court must consider the principles applied by the ECHR as regards the award of damages under Article 41 of the Convention.

Thus, for any violation of a Convention right, the national court may grant either damages, declarations, injunctions or relief; any remedy that is within the scope of its competence, bearing in mind the principle of 'just satisfaction' which will determine what is the remedy that is most adequate as regards the circumstances of the case.

9.4.3 The courts' interpretation In *R v DPP, ex parte Kebilene*,[524] Lord Hope stated that 'it is now plain that the incorporation of the European Convention on Human Rights into our domestic law will subject the entire legal system to a fundamental process of review and, where necessary, reform by the judiciary'.

Indeed, section 3(1) of the Act provides that 'so far as it is possible to do so, primary legislation and subordinate legislation must be read and given effect in a way which is compatible with the Convention rights'.

In other words, the UK courts have to interpret 'primary' and 'secondary' legislation in accordance with the Convention. However, the problem may arise when a piece of UK legislation is incompatible with the Convention. The Act does not affect the validity of such legislation, but puts a duty on the courts to find a middle ground.

The courts cannot diverge from the incompatible legislation. They can only do their best to interpret it as closely as possible in the light of the Convention. In the case of superior courts (ie House of Lords, Court of Appeal, High Court and Privy Council), they can make a declaration of incompatibility. This is not a remedy in itself since it does not affect the validity of the legislation against which it is issued, and it is not binding on the parties to the case (section 4(6)(a)+(b)).

The UK courts have to take into consideration the ECHR case-law, even though it is not binding on the UK courts. The latter are increasingly influenced by the Strasbourg Court's judicial reasoning and inspired to apply such doctrines as the principle of non-discrimination (ie that there should be no evidence of discrimination) or that of proportionality (ie that any intervention should be proportionate to the end intended to be achieved.)

Although the Act is primarily intended to provide a safety valve for individuals against violation perpetuated by the State, it is not clearly stated anywhere in the Act that it cannot be used in cases involving private parties. It has been argued by the Lord Chancellor that 'it is right as a

---

[523] 24 October 1997, Application 119/1996/738/937
[524] [2000] 2 AC 326

matter of principle for the courts to have the duty of acting compatibly with the Convention, not only in cases involving other public authorities but also in developing the common law in deciding cases between individuals. Why should they not?' (Hansard 24 November 1997, H. L. col.783).

PART V
The law in Scotland

Chapter 10

Criminal law

Introduction

The Scottish criminal law system is singular in that there is no code and few statutes which serve as a structure to determine a crime. The Scottish system functions mainly on common law, which is dictated by the High Court of Justiciary. The High Court has a declaratory power, which is described as an 'inherent power to punish every act which is obviously of a criminal nature',[525] and as such 'has the power to declare anything that has a tendency to corrupt public morals, and injure the interests of society, an indictable offence'.[526]

McCall Smith & Sheldon[527] argue that the Scottish criminal law, although close in nature to the English model (as regards statutes), is yet substantially different insofar as the requirements for an offence are involved. For instance, the mens rea[528] for murder in English law is defined as 'malice aforethought' which implies an intention to kill or an intention to cause grievous bodily harm. In Scottish law, the mens rea for murder is dual: it can either be intention or wicked recklessness.

This chapter aims to enlighten the reader on the law in Scotland with regard to the potential criminal liability arising from the use of physical intervention for control, restraint and caring purposes in relation to people with learning disabilities and challenging behaviours.

10.1 Non-sexual offences against the person

10.1.1 Assault   As explained earlier, in English criminal law 'assault' is an act that causes an individual to fear personal violence against him and does not involve physical contact. In contrast, in Scottish criminal law 'assault' is defined as an attack upon the person of another, which implies the possibility or likelihood of physical contact between the offender and the victim.

A person may commit an assault by applying direct physical force using either their body (eg kicking, punching, biting, hair pulling) or a weapon (eg throwing a chair at someone, using a stick to hit/beat a person). In _Codona v Cardle_[529] the defendant was charged with twisting the victim's arm while intending to perform a citizen's arrest. The High Court found that the

---

[525] Connelly C, _Law Basics, Criminal Law_, Edinburgh W.Greens/Sweet & Maxwell 2002, p. 2, [here, quoting Hume D, _Commentaries on the Law of Scotland Respecting the Description and Punishment of Crimes_. (2 vols, 1797) (reprinted 1986, Butterworths)]

[526] _per_ Lord Justice-Clerk Boyle, in _Bernhard Greenhuff_ (1838) 2 Swin 236

[527] McCall Smith R A A & Sheldon D, _Scots Criminal Law_, 2nd edition, Butterworths 1997

[528] ie the mental element behind the execution of a criminal act

[529] [1989] SLT 791

grounds for the citizen's arrest were not founded, but that even if they had been, the use of force deployed had not been reasonable and that therefore the defendant was guilty of assaulting the victim.

The victim need not be injured as a result of the attack and so in <u>*Jas Cairns*</u>[530] spitting at someone was found to constitute an assault.

An assault can occur indirectly, that is, the offender uses circumstances to inflict violence upon another person; there is thus no direct contact between the offender and the victim. In <u>*David Keay*</u>,[531] the victim was thrown off a horse, which reacted to being whipped by the defendant. More recently, in <u>*Quinn v Lees*</u>[532] the appellant was found guilty of assault for setting his dog onto three boys. Despite his arguing that this was meant as a joke, the High Court held the act was still to be considered deliberate since a dog could not differentiate between a joke and a command and so the consequences were foreseeable.

An assault is also committed by displaying physically threatening gestures. In <u>*Atkinson v HM Advocate*</u>[533] Lord Justice-Clerk Ross stated that an '*assault may be constituted by **threatening gestures** sufficient to produce alarm*.[534] For someone with a face masked to come into a shop and jump over a counter towards the cashier in the shop (. . .) could constitute assault according to the law of Scotland.'

The use of words alone, whether written or oral, cannot constitute an assault unless they convey a threat. The threat in question must be about performing an act that is by nature a crime. For instance, a threat will be criminal if its purpose and result are to intimidate a person causing them to fear for their physical safety (a threat to kill or injure) and to menace (threaten) the destruction of or serious damage to an individual's property.[535]

In Scottish criminal law, an assault is a crime of intent, which means that it cannot be committed accidentally or recklessly or negligently.

The mental element that is required to complete an offence of assault is 'evil intent'. There is no agreed precise definition of this concept. The jurisprudence has nonetheless come up with the following attempt at explaining it.

In <u>*Smart v HM Advocate*</u>[536] 'evil intent' is described as the 'intent to injure and do bodily harm'. The use of 'evil' here does not necessarily imply that the offender intends evil consequences. Rather, 'evil intent' actually stresses the fact that the act pertaining to the assault is deliberate.

From <u>*Lord Advocate's Reference (No.2 1992)*</u>,[537] it appears that 'evil intent' is more to do with the nature of the action rather than the motive that prompted it. The accused in this case attempted to rob a shop pointing an imitation gun at the cashier and asking the latter to hand

---

[530] (1837) 1 Swin 597
[531] (1837) 1 Swin 543
[532] (1994) SCCR 159
[533] (1987) SCCR 534
[534] The present authors' emphasis
[535] <u>*Jas Miller*</u> (1862) 4 Irv 238
[536] (1975) SLT 65
[537] (1993) SLT 460

over the cash contained in the till. The offender fled as soon as he realised that there were other people in the shop. He later argued in his defence that he only meant the attempted robbery as a joke.

Although meant as a joke, this motive was found to be irrelevant. The court considered the fact that the offender still showed a deliberate intention to go into the shop and use an, albeit fake, gun to threaten an individual in order to commit a crime. Lord Sutherland stated that '(. . .) intention means nothing more than wilful, intentional or deliberate as opposed to accidental, careless or even reckless (. . .)'.

However, the negligent or reckless causation of harm onto another person is still an offence in itself.

10.1.2 Culpable and reckless conduct   A reckless crime is committed when the offender causes injury or harm to another individual without intending to do so in the first place. Connelly[538] states that 'where the perpetrator has acted negligently or accidentally there will be no criminal responsibility. It is only where the actions involve a mens rea of recklessness that they will be categorised as a reckless conduct crime'.[539] Connelly gives three examples of such an offence:

10.1.2.1 Cruel and barbarous treatment and cruel and unnatural treatment   These offences occur when a person who has responsibility over another has neglected or cruelly treated the person for whom they care for.

10.1.2.2 Causing real injury   This offence occurs when an act does not amount to either assault or battery, or other recognised offences, yet it still incurs serious harm to the victim. It has been argued in _Khaliq v HM Advocate_[540] that it is just a new way of wording an already existing crime.

In _Khaliq_ two defendants supplied 'glue-snuffing kits' to children and were charged with _the culpable wilful and reckless supply to 18 named children and other unnamed children, all under 16 years of age, of solvents for the purpose of their abuse by these children._ It was argued that such an offence was not known to the criminal law of Scotland.

On the issue of what crime falls within the scope of the Scottish criminal law, Lord Avonside replied that 'the great strength of our common law in criminal matters is that it can be invoked to fill a need. It is not static. (. . .) It is alive today in dealing with the present age as it was in dealing with questions raised in the past'. Agreeing, Lord Emslie added that 'it would be a mistake to imagine that the criminal common law of Scotland countenances any precise and exact categorisation of the forms of conduct which amount to crime. It has been pointed out many times in this Court that such is not the nature or quality of the criminal law of Scotland.'

He further referred to Section 44 of the Criminal Procedure (Scotland) Act 1975, which 'provides that it shall not be necessary in any indictment to specify by any _nomen juris_ the crime which is charged but it shall be sufficient that the indictment sets forth facts relevant and sufficient to constitute an indictable crime'.

---

[538] supra, n.525, Connelly
[539] supra n.525, Connelly, refer to p. 39
[540] [1984] SLT 137

Lord Emslie then expressed the view that 'within the category of conduct identified as criminal are acts, whatever their nature may be, which cause real injury to the person. Does [the case of *Khaliq*], though never before occurring on its facts, fall within that general principle (. . .)? In my opinion it does, although the nature of the injury and the act alleged to be a cause of that injury may be new.'

This offence is not to be confused with the following 'reckless injury'. Indeed, 'causing real injury' does not imply recklessness on the part of the defendant; however, the act is still a culpable one, and as such is punishable in law.

10.1.2.3 Reckless injury   Reckless injury occurs when the defendant caused actual and severe injury to the victim as a result of a reckless conduct. This was discussed in <u>HM Advocate v Harris</u>,[541] in which a bouncer, Harris, assaulted a woman by getting hold of her and pushing her down some stairs, at the bottom of which she was then hit by a car and eventually suffered permanent disfigurement as a consequence.

Harris was charged with '*assault to severe injury and permanent disfigurement by seizing hold of his victim, pushing her on the body and causing her to fall down a flight of stairs and onto the roadway as a result of which she was struck by a motor vehicle*'. He was also subjected to an alternative charge stating that '*the accused culpably, wilfully and recklessly seized hold of his victim and did all of the acts libelled in the assault charge to her severe injury and permanent disfigurement*'.

The defendant was thus charged with either assault or reckless conduct causing actual injury. The question debated in this case was whether the second charge was a crime recognised in the law of Scotland, to which the High Court of Justiciary replied positively.

Lord Justice-Clerk Ross summarises the issue at the heart of the debate as follows:

'*the law draws a distinction between intent and recklessness (...). Accordingly, I am satisfied that the charges truly are alternatives. It will be for the jury to determine whether the accused acted in the manner described in the indictment, and if that is established, then although the accused was acting as a bouncer, the jury may conclude that when he seized hold of the complainer and pulled her, he had the intent necessary for assault; alternatively they may conclude that he lacked the intent necessary for assault but had displayed recklessness which caused her to fall and sustain injury. Of course, if the Crown fail to establish that the accused acted in the manner libelled or that he had the mens rea required for either of the alternative charges, they will acquit the accused.*'

On the alternative charge, Lord Prosser opined that:

'*it is not suggested that reckless conduct in itself, in the absence of either danger or injury to others, might be a crime. At the other extreme, it is not in doubt that reckless conduct causing death is a crime. That being so, if the same conduct has caused injury rather than death, I should expect it in principle to be regarded as a crime. (...) [Moreover] If reckless conduct causing injury is a crime, there is no need to libel danger, either to the person allegedly injured, or to others.*'

---

[541] [1993] SLT 963

10.1.2.4 Recklessly endangering the lieges (ie the subjects of the sovereign)

'This crime is distinguishable from reckless injury in that it will be charged where an accused has created a dangerous situation that may have placed the public in danger, even although no actual injury has been caused. The dangerous situation can be the result of the reckless performing of either a lawful or unlawful act.'[542]

'Liege' is a feudal term that was used to define the relationship between a vassal and his lord. Used in the plural sense, it means a subject.[543] One therefore understands that the reckless endangering the lieges is the reckless endangering of members of the public.

An individual who carries out an action, whether lawful or unlawful, which creates a situation where the public is or could be in serious danger, whether harm is caused or is threatened to be incurred, will be charged with recklessly endangering the lieges.

In _Gizzi v Tudhope_,[544] two men were charged and convicted by the Sheriff for 'reckless discharge of firearms' for firing shotguns at clay pigeons in an area where 'members of the public or children and others might come to be'. The High Court of Justiciary confirmed the two appellants' conviction (see also _Normand v Robinson_[545] and _Cameron v Maguire_[546]).

10.2 Homicide

10.2.1 Murder

'Murder is constituted by any wilful act causing the destruction of life, by which the perpetrator either wickedly intends to kill or displays wicked recklessness as to whether the victim lives or dies.'[547]

Wicked intention

It is suggested that 'wicked intention' will require that an intention to kill shall be either proven or admitted.[548] One could also argue that 'wicked intention' does not so much imply a wicked motive as a deliberate action that is the taking of someone's life. This trail of thought would follow the position of the court as regards the notion of 'evil intention' for the crime of assault, as discussed earlier. Therefore 'wicked' would add nothing to the homicide, but would merely stress the deliberate and wilful nature of the intention behind the commission of murder.

Wicked recklessness

In _HM Advocate v Cawthorne_[549] the Lord Justice General (Clyde) explained the difference between intention and recklessness in the crime of murder. He stated that 'in many cases it may

---

[542] supra n.525, Connelly, refer to p. 42
[543] *Oxford Concise English Dictionary* 1995
[544] 1983 SLT 214
[545] 1994 SLT 558
[546] 1999 SLT 883
[547] *per* Lord Justice General (Rodger) in _Drury v HM Advocate_ 2001 SLT 1013
[548] supra n.525, Connelly, p. 45, referring to Jones T & Christie M, *Criminal Law*, 2nd edition, W Green & Son, Edinburgh, 1996
[549] 1968 SLT 330

not be possible to prove what was in the accused's mind at the time, but the degree of recklessness in his actings as proved by what he did may be sufficient to establish proof of the wilful act on his part which caused the loss of life'.

An individual who acts recklessly towards another and shows no interest as to whether the victim dies or not as a result will be considered to have the necessary 'deliberate intent to kill', which will be proof enough that he intended to commit the homicide.

Wicked recklessness is present when the defendant intended to impose on the victim great bodily harm, which (1) might result in death and (2) shows an absolute and utter disregard as to whether the victim lives or dies.[550]

10.2.2 Culpable homicide   Culpable homicide, which is the Scottish version of the English 'manslaughter', is defined as:

> *'the killing of human beings in all circumstances, short of murder, where the criminal law attaches a relevant measure of blame to the person who kills. For instance, it covers cases where a person who is suffering from diminished responsibility intends to kill someone and does so. Even though the killing is intentional, the appropriate verdict is one of culpable homicide. Similarly, where the deceased has provoked the accused and the accused, under the influence of that provocation, kills him, the accused will be guilty of culpable homicide even though he intended to kill the deceased. (...) Since culpable homicide covers cases of intentional killing carried out under provocation, it must also cover cases where the assault displays a degree of recklessness which, but for the provocation, would lead to the inference that the accused had acted wickedly.'[551]*

10.2.2.1 Involuntary culpable homicide   An involuntary culpable homicide is a crime that has the physical element of murder but lacks the mental intention of taking someone's life. This crime can be committed by either a lawful or unlawful act which results in death.

Death that is the consequence of a criminal act such as an assault can qualify as an involuntary homicide. However, this will depend on the intensity and seriousness of the assault, as if the action is severe enough it could actually be proof that the defendant intended to commit the homicide or showed wicked recklessness as to whether the victim lives or dies as a result.

When death results from the performance of a lawful act, it is not enough that the defendant acted carelessly or negligently, it must be proven that he acted recklessly. In *Paton v HM Advocate*,[552] the defendant drove a car at an excessive speed and collided with the victim who consequently died. Although it was acknowledged that 'the driving was to some extent reckless', the High Court still concluded that 'there was an element of mischance in the case which played a part in the unfortunate result', therefore their Lordships downgraded a charge of culpable homicide to a minor one.[553]

---

[550] supra n.525, Connelly, p. 45, referring to Hume (above mentioned)
[551] supra n.547, *per* Lord Justice General (Rodger) in *Drury*
[552] [1936] SLT 298
[553] Section 11 of the Road Traffic Act 1930

10.2.2.2 Voluntary culpable homicide   In a case of voluntary culpable homicide, although the defendant has committed murder he was not in full control of himself and could therefore use the pleas of provocation or diminished responsibility (see Defences, below).

10.3 Defences

10.3.1 Reflex actions   This does not actually qualify as a defence per se; however it is not a defence to which the courts have paid much attention either. It is therefore judged relevant to include this particular notion of 'reflex actions' in this section dedicated to general and specific defences.

A reflex action was described in the case of _Jessop v Johnstone_[554] as a situation 'where a person instinctively reacts to violence in a reflex way, such as if a person is suddenly and without warning struck and turns round sharply so that he comes into contact with his assailant'.

In this particular case, the defendant was a teacher who was struck in the face by a teenage male pupil using a rolled-up school jotter. The teacher responded by hitting the pupil several times on the stomach and back and was charged with assault. The court decided that the teacher's response did not fall within the ambit of a 'reflex action' and that his behaviour was more likely to fall under the plea of provocation.

10.3.2 Self-defence   This defence can be used for both crimes of assault and homicide in circumstances where a person 'acts in order to defend [their] own person or in defence of persons other than [themselves]',[555] as well as occasionally in defence of property.

The defence works as a justification for the use of force to prevent injury or harm to occur, and as such, will result in acquittal of a defendant charged for assault, murder or even for breach of the peace.

The rules for a 'special defence' of self-defence to apply were laid out in _Fenning v HM Advocate_.[556] In this case, the accused struck the victim on the head several times with an air rifle and then got hold of the victim's head and struck him against a stone repeatedly. The victim died as a consequence of the act; the defender pleaded self-defence and alternatively, provocation. The High Court, quoting the trial judge, held:

> 'A special defence can only apply if the accused's own life has been put in danger or if he has reasonable grounds for apprehending such a danger, in other words, there must be **imminent danger to life**[557] and furthermore the actings of the accused **must be necessary** and, if he has a means of escape from the attacker, the plea of self defence simply will not do. And lastly (...) there must be **no cruel excess of violence** on the accused's part. If he goes further than is necessary for his defence and uses cruel excess that cannot in law constitute self defence (...).'

---

[554] [1991] SCCR 238
[555] _Jones (Francis Edward) v HM Advocate_ 1990 SLT 517
[556] [1985] SLT 540
[557] The present authors' emphasis

In other words, self-defence might be available as a 'special defence' if the following requirements are met:

There is an imminent danger to the defendant's life or to the life of others. The danger feared is not merely about physical safety or injury but actually implies the danger of imminent death. In _McCluskey v HM Advocate_,[558] Lord Justice-General Clyde stated that there is 'no justification at all for extending this defence to a case where there is no apprehension of danger to the accused's life, and indeed, very little evidence of any real physical injury done to the accused himself, but merely a threat pushed no doubt quite far, but nonetheless still only a threat of an attack on the appellant's virtue'.

There must be no other means of escape from the threatening situation. In _HM Advocate v Doherty_,[59] the accused, who was being attacked by the victim using a hammer, struck the latter with a bayonet and the victim later died as a result. From the facts of the case, it appears (1) that the defendant was handed the bayonet, which Lord Keith argued suggested the idea of a duel, and self-defence cannot apply there. (2) There was an open door and stairway just behind the defendant that he could have used to go out into the yard and thus escape the dangerous situation, but he did not do so.

Excessive force must not be used in the circumstances. Reasonable force to prevent or escape the threatening situation is what is required. However, the court will take into consideration the fact that it is not easy to assess the degree of reasonable force necessary in a given situation as other factors come into play. In _HM Advocate v Doherty_, Lord Keith stated: 'You do not need an exact proportion of injury and retaliation; it is not a matter that you weigh in too fine scales (. . .). Some allowance must be made for the excitement or the state of fear or the heat of blood at the moment of the man who is attacked (. . .).' In other words, excessive force might be allowed if it is considered 'reasonable' given the circumstances.

In the case where the accused has mistakenly assumed that his life is endangered and uses force as self-defence, the court held that the defence would function provided the belief is honest and reasonable.

In _Owens v HM Advocate_,[560] the defendant stabbed the victim with a pocket knife and argued self-defence as he believed the victim was trying to stab him with a kitchen knife. Even though this could not be verified, a kitchen knife was nonetheless found on the floor. Lord MacKay stated that 'self-defence is made out when it is established (. . .) that [the accused] believed that he was in imminent danger and that he held that belief on reasonable grounds. Grounds for such belief may exist though they are founded on a genuine mistake of fact.'

On the issue of self-defence as regards the protection of property, it is to be assumed from the case of _McCluskey v HM Advocate_ that the defence would not apply here as no life would be endangered.

10.3.3 Provocation   The line between self-defence and provocation was often said to be fine until the cases of _Crawford v HM Advocate_ and _Fenning v HM Advocate_. In _Crawford_, the court held that the difference between the two defences is that self-defence is a 'special defence'

---

[558]   1959 SLT 215
[559]   1954 SLT 169
[560]   1946 SLT 227

whereas provocation is a plea. The two defences are not inter-changeable as provocation can only be argued when the 'special defence' of self-defence was rejected by a jury. The other difference is that where a self-defence results in acquittal, provocation will reduce a charge for murder to one of culpable homicide.

Although a murder and a culpable homicide are identical in terms of the fatal act that killed the victim, the difference between these two crimes resides in the state of mind requirement and the sentencing. For murder, the state of mind required is either intention or wicked recklessness, and the charge carries a mandatory life sentence. The state of mind required for culpable homicide is recklessness as this crime implies a lack of intention on the part of the perpetrator. The sentence here is at the judge's discretion.

The defence of provocation includes that four elements must be present for it to be operable:

1. **Provocation must be brought about by some form of violence sustaining injury or harm. Words alone will be deemed insufficient to amount to a provocation**

In the case of _Cosgrove v HM Advocate_,[561] the defendant argued that he had been provoked to repeatedly punch and kick the victim as the latter admitted to interfering with a young girl and smirked as he made his statement.

In this case, the High Court confirmed the classic definition of provocation given by MacDonald in his Treatise on Criminal Law. Provocation is 'being agitated and excited, and alarmed by violence, I lost control over myself, and took life, when my presence of mind had left me, and without thought of what I was doing'.[562] It also follows that 'words of insult however strong or any mere insulting or disgusting conduct such as jostling or tossing filth in the face do not serve to reduce the crime from murder to culpable homicide'.[563]

In brief, the court decided that words, insult or smirks will not amount to provocation. Moreover, using a weapon in response to the threat of a wrist blow will not justify provocation either.

2. **There must be a total loss of self-control**

Not only does the accused have to prove that he lost his self-control, but that loss of self-control also has to be reasonable.

In _Low (Brian) v HM Advocate_,[564] the two defendants were charged with stabbing a man to death after he allegedly went to them with a knife and invited them to have sex. The first defendant pleaded provocation and the victim was found with over 40 stab wounds, ten of which were inflicted post-mortem. The High Court found that there was no evidence the defendant had suffered from a loss of self-control, therefore his particular case did not fit the description of provocation given by MacDonald as mentioned above.

---

[561] [1991] SLT 25
[562] MacDonald, G, _Practical Treatise on the Criminal Law of Scotland_, (1867), 4th edition at p. 135
[563] MacDonald, G, _Practical Treatise on the Criminal Law of Scotland_, (1867), 5th edition at p. 93
[564] [1994] SLT 277

3. The force used in response to the provocation must be proportionate to the provocative act

The High Court confirmed the view expressed in _Lennon v HM Advocate_[565] that another distinction between self-defence and provocation is that the former's use of force should not be in 'cruel excess' whereas for provocation, the retaliation should not be in 'gross disproportion' to the provoking act. The court stated in _Low (Brian) v HM Advocate_ that 'where a plea of provocation is taken, there must be some equivalence between the retaliation and the provocation so that the violence used by the accused is not grossly disproportionate to the evidence constituting the provocation'.

The test for evaluating whether the loss of control is reasonable is based on the reasonable person (objective) criterion. In _Drury v HM Advocate_[566] the defendant killed a woman with whom he had some sort of relationship. He attacked her with a claw hammer after she admitted having sexual intercourse with another man. She died as a result of the assault and the accused pleaded provocation.

The Lord Justice General (Rodger) in this case stated that:

> '_the law acknowledges that, even with the best will in the world, ordinary men and women will not always be able to adhere to the ideal path which it prescribes. So, when an accused overreacts in the way that ordinary men and women may tend to overreact, the law recognises that the accused is weak rather than wicked. (...) [However] if the killer reacts in a more extreme manner than the ordinary man or woman, he is not entitled to that strictly limited allowance which the law makes for the human frailty of ordinary men and women._'

In other words, there are two questions that need answering before deciding that a plea of provocation is actionable: (a) was there loss of self-control? And (b) would the ordinary man or woman have been liable to react in the same way in the same circumstances? If the answer is yes to both, then there is a good chance that the plea would be accepted.

4. The retaliation to a provocation must be immediate

The longer the lapse of time between the provocative act and the response to it, the less convincing the claim of loss of self-control would be accepted and thus premeditation would be presumed.

In _HM Advocate v Hill_[567] the defendant shot his wife and her paramour after they confessed to having an adulterous relationship. The judge stated that if an accused acts in the heat of the moment, provocation would be accepted. However, if the accused responded to the provocative act 'after an interval when his blood had cooled', this meant he acted 'from motives of revenge' and thus the plea of provocation would not be available to him.

The High Court has approached the issue of cumulative provocation in a very restrictive manner, especially in cases of domestic violence. In other words, cumulative provocation is not a valid concept unless there is a last provoking act or event that triggers the fatal response.

---

[565] [1991] SCCR 611
[566] [2001] SLT 1013
[567] [1941] SLT 401

In the case of _HM Advocate v June Greig_,[568] the defendant was a woman who killed her husband while he was asleep after he had verbally abused her. It appeared that they had had a violent and abusive relationship. The judge decided that self-defence did not apply there, and that there was no grounds for provocation. However, since the issue was left to the jury to decide, the latter went against the judge's directions and returned a verdict of culpable homicide, thus accepting the plea of provocation. This case shows how the notion of cumulative provocation can be applied by the jury in the circumstances of individual cases despite the High Court's very restrictive definition employed by the judges when directing a jury on the law.

Provocation, be it physical or verbal, may be a defence to a charge of assault. However, it will not lead to total acquittal but will help minimise the severity of a defendant's sentence.

10.3.4 Diminished responsibility Diminished responsibility is only a partial defence available for charges of murder and when successfully argued, this defence will reduce murder to a conviction of culpable homicide. 'The judge must decide whether there is evidence that, at the relevant time, the accused was suffering from an abnormality of mind which substantially impaired the ability of the accused, as compared with a normal person, to determine or control his acts.'[569]

The four requirements for a plea of diminished responsibility were laid out in the case _Savage v HM Advocate_.[570] There must be (1) an aberration or weakness of mind; (2) some form of mental unsoundness; (3) a state of mind bordering on, though not amounting to, insanity, and finally; (4) a mind so affected that responsibility is diminished from full responsibility to partial responsibility.

Connelly v HM Advocate,[571] which decided that all four elements had to be present together for a plea of diminished responsibility to succeed and that the mental element was to imply a mental disease, was overruled in _Galbraith (Kim Louise) v HM Advocate_.[572]

In _Galbraith_, the accused was a woman who had killed her husband. She pleaded diminished responsibility based on medical evidence that at the time of the murder, she was suffering from a post-traumatic disorder brought about by a previous two years of physical abuse by her husband.

In this case, the court held that _Connelly_ misinterpreted _Savage_ in that not all the criteria of the test in _Savage_ need to be met. On the issue of the 'mental disease', the court directed that this should not be interpreted narrowly and that diminished responsibility does not require that the abnormality of mind should border on insanity.

Although the mental illness requirement must be supported by medical expert opinion, diminished responsibility is a legal concept. It is thus the judge's prerogative to determine whether there is sufficient evidence that a charge of murder should become one of culpable homicide on the grounds of diminished responsibility.

[568] unreported, May 1979, HCJ
[569] _Galbraith v HM Advocate_ 2001 SLT 953
[570] [1923] SLT 659
[571] [1991] SLT 397
[572] [2001] SLT 953

An abnormality of the mind can take various forms. The High Court stated that:

> *'the abnormality may mean, for example, that the individual perceives physical acts and matters differently from a normal person. In some cases he may suffer from delusions. Or else it may affect his ability to form a rational judgement as to whether a particular act is right or wrong or to decide whether to perform it. In a given case any or all of these effects may be operating and may impair the accused's ability to determine and control his acts and omissions. (...) The law responds in this way, however, because it recognises that the individual is to be pitied since, at the relevant time, he was not as normal people are. (...) By contrast, the law makes no such allowance for failings and emotions, such as anger and jealousy, to which any normal person may well be subject from time to time. They do not call for the law's compassion. Rather, we must master them or else face the consequences.'*

10.3.5 Necessity The defence of necessity arises in cases where the accused is forced by circumstances to commit an illegal or criminal act in order to avoid another more dangerous or evil outcome than if he did not act at all.

There is little case-law on this particular defence, except where road traffic offences are concerned.

The case of _Moss v Howdle_[573] sets out the rules of the defence of necessity. In this case, the offender, Mr M. was convicted of driving in excess of the speed limit. He argued it was out of necessity since his passenger, Mr P., suddenly cried out in pain and seemed to have been taken seriously ill. Mr M. thought of using his mobile, but his batteries were flat. He could have pulled over on the roadside to determine the nature of Mr P.'s distress, but Mr M. decided to drive at 101.70 mph instead of 70 mph to a nearby service area in order to get some assistance. It was later found out that Mr P. had 'merely' suffered from an attack of cramp. The court found that:

- The accused must act in the face of immediate danger of death or great bodily harm;

- The danger may arise either from some contingency such as natural disaster or illness (including medical emergency) or from the deliberate threats of another;

- The defence may also be available either in cases of self-defence or 'in situations where the accused acts in an altruistic fashion to save a companion';

- The accused must be faced with no other choices but to break the law. If there is a possibility to act within the parameter of the law, the defence will not be available.

Once the danger has passed and the necessity to act in contravention with the law is no more needed, the accused must cease to perform the illegal act. This rule was laid down in _Ruxton v Land (Fiona Marjorie)_.[574]

In this case, the defendant was convicted for driving with excess alcohol. She was trying to get away from her boyfriend who had threatened her with a knife on her return from a night out. She started to drive to her brother's house some two miles away and was stopped by the police before she reached her destination. She pleaded necessity. The court, however, decided that

---

[573] [1997] SLT 782
[574] [1998] SCCR 1 (Sh,Ct)

although the defendant had clearly been in danger when she left her house, the danger had passed by the time the police stopped her, and so necessity for driving with alcohol in the blood stream had ceased to be a defence.

10.3.6 Coercion   Coercion occurs when the accused is forced by another person to commit a criminal act. S.78(2) of the Criminal Procedure (Scotland) Act 1995 specifies that it is a special defence.

The rules applying to this defence were spelled out by Hume in his commentaries on Crimes[575] and confirmed by the High Court. In _Thomson (Oliver) v HM Advocate_[576] Lord Hunter stated: 'a defence of coercion, in order to be successful, requires that the danger must be immediate and that the will and resolution of the accused must have been overborne by threats which he believed would be carried out so that he was not at the material time acting of his own free will'. These are the two basic requirements further explained below, which are followed by another two:

a) **The accused is in immediate danger of death or great bodily harm**

The threat in question must relate to present circumstances and not to the future ones;

b) **The accused is unable to resist the violence**

'The will and resolution of the accused must in fact have been overborne and overcome by the threats and the danger', which means that he was forced by the circumstances to act against his will. To decide whether a person's will was overwhelmed by a threat of danger, the court will apply the objective test and will ask whether an ordinary reasonable person of the same sex and age as the accused would have been unable to resist the violence in the same circumstances.

c) **The accused plays a backward and inferior part in the perpetration**

If the accused actually plays an active role in the perpetration of the crime, the court will not be lenient in accepting an argument of coercion. Lord Hunter added that 'it is clear that the criminal act committed by the accused must be in some reasonable balance with the threats and danger which confronted him'.

d) **The accused discloses the fact and/or gives the spoil back on the first safe and convenient**
   occasion

'To keep things secret for a period after the immediate danger has passed and to retain the stolen property may (. . .) indicate not something entirely against the will of the accused but something in which he has participated although it may be with some reluctance, depending on what view is taken of the evidence.'

10.3.7 Lawful force   This section concentrates particularly on the issue of physical chastisement of children by their parents or anybody else who has parental responsibility over them. The key legislation which relates to this issue are the Children and Young Persons

---

[575] supra n.525, (i, 51)
[576] [1983] SLT 682

(Scotland) Act 1937; the Criminal Justice (Scotland) Act 2003; the Standards in Scotland's Schools Act 2000 and the Regulation of Care (Scotland) Act 2001.

The law of Scotland still recognises a limited right of parents to inflict corporal punishment upon their child.[577] It has been said that 'parents may exercise over their children the degree of discipline and moderate chastisement upon them, which their perverseness of temper or inattention calls for'.[578]

Section 12(1) of the (Scotland) Act 1937 ensures protection against cruelty for children and young persons under the age of 16 providing that wilful assaults and ill-treatments will prompt criminal proceedings leading to a possible criminal conviction.

The law in Scotland has recently been changed in that the Scottish Assembly enacted section 51 of the Criminal Justice (Scotland) Act 2003, which came into force on 27 October 2003. This repeals[579] section 12 (7) of the Children and Young Persons Act 1937 which had provided parents or other persons having the care of the child charged with assault as a result of administering punishment to the child with the defence of 'reasonable chastisement'. Parents exercising their parental right to punishment now have to show that the use of such punishment amounted to a 'justifiable assault'[580] as defined in the law. In determining whether such action by the parent was a 'justifiable assault' the statute provides the court with a list of factors to which the court must have regard in determining whether a parent can claim that their action in punishing a child is a 'justifiable assault' carried out in exercise of a parental right or of a right derived from having care of the child. These factors are those which the European Court of Human Rights determined should be followed by UK courts in _A v UK_ in interpreting what could be regarded as 'reasonable' when considering the nature and degree of chastisement meted out by parents, and which are now followed by the courts in England and Wales. (See those set out above at para 2.9.3 (b) (iii).) In addition, section 51 (3) provides that the defence of 'justifiable assault' is not available to a parent or others having charge or care of a child where the action includes or consists of: a blow to the head;[581] shaking;[582] or the use of an implement.[583] These actions are therefore outlawed. Section 51 (4) also provides that children 16 and over cannot be the subject of the parental right to physical punishment.

Still, what amounts to 'reasonable' chastisement is left to argument, as can be shown in a 1999 case in which a 48-year-old 'conscientious and very good' father was convicted of assault for smacking his daughter in a dental surgery because she refused to have a tooth removed. The judge held that the father had gone beyond the bounds of 'reasonable chastisement'.[583]

Although corporal punishment may be legal when administered by a person with parental responsibility, provided there is compliance with section 51, section 16 of the Standards in Scotland's Schools Act 2000 prohibits any form of physical chastisement in the context of both public and private school education settings. Section 16(1) provides that 'corporal punishment given by, or on the authority of, a member of staff to a pupil (. . .) cannot be justified in any

[577] _R v Smith (David)_ (1985) 82 LSG 198
[578] Eskine (I, vi, 53) quoted by Spink P & Spink S in 'What is reasonable chastisement', _Journal of the Law Society of Scotland_, vol.44, No. 6, June 1999
[579] Section 51 (5) (b) Criminal Justice (Scotland Act) 2003
[580] _Ibid_ Section 51 (1)
[581] _Ibid_ Section 51 (3) (a)
[582] _Ibid_ Section 52 (3) (b)
[583] _Ibid_ Section 51 (3) (c)

proceedings on the ground that it was so given in pursuance of a right exercisable by virtue of having a position as a member of staff'.

A 'member of staff' includes teachers and 'any other person who works at that school or place; or otherwise provides services there, and has lawful control or charge of the pupil'.[584]

Section 16(4) provides an exception for steps which may have to be taken in certain situations but still does not sanction the administration of corporal punishment. Thus it stipulates that 'corporal punishment shall not be taken to be given to a pupil by virtue of anything done for reasons which include averting (a) an immediate danger of personal injury to; or (b) an immediate danger to the property of any person (including the pupil concerned)'.

10.3.8 Common law power to restrain a lunatic In contrast with the English common law, the Scottish case-law recognises private individuals' common law power to restrain a lunatic. In the words of Lord Griffiths, this power 'is confined to imposing temporary restraint on a lunatic who has run amok and is a manifest danger either to himself or to others – a state of affairs as obvious to a layman as to a doctor. Such a common law power is confined to the short period of confinement necessary before the lunatic can be handed over to a proper authority.'[585]

---

[584] Standards in Scotland Schools Act 2000, section 16(5)(i)+(ii)
[585] *B v Foresey* [1988] SLT 572

Chapter 11

Civil law in Scotland

11.1 Delictual liability

11.1.1 Introduction Delictual liability is the Scottish equivalent of the English law of tortious liability. Delict is thus defined as a wrongful action under civil law, committed by one person against another, rendering the wrongdoer liable to pay compensation, referred to as 'reparation', to the victim of the wrongful act. The law of delict comes under the Law of Obligations, which, along with the law of property, is an area of Scottish private law. Private law deals with matters concerning individuals taking legal actions against each other, as opposed to public law, which regulates the relationship between State bodies and private individuals.[586]

The law of obligations deals with the specific relationship, whether intentional or not, that 'binds' the private parties and looks at the legal duties and rights that arise from that relationship.

The duties and rights recognised in that particular relationship are not general. What can be understood as a duty is '. . . that a particular person will do, or will avoid doing a specific act'.[587] As for rights in this context, they are different from real rights (ie applicable to all in general) and are known as personal rights since '. . . they only relate to specific relationships. This means that certain individuals – usually those within that relationship – can enforce them [and] that these rights may only be enforced against other specific persons'.[588] For instance, in a care relationship, a service user who incurs injury as a consequence of the wrongful action of his carer can sue the latter for delictual assault or negligence. The carer could not be sued by someone else who is outside of this caring relationship and who has no vested interest; likewise, no other carer, ie a worker who is not part of the relationship, can be sued.

In brief, an obligation means that a person is obliged to another, whether voluntarily or involuntarily; in other words, an individual owes a duty towards another who has a right to have that duty/obligation enforced (as in the example above, to have the right to recover damages).

A voluntary obligation results from an agreement between the parties, such as a contract, where the free will of each individual is expressed into creating a 'conventional' obligation. In contrast, an involuntary obligation arises independently of the will of the parties as it is imposed by law and is also known as 'obediential'.

---

[586] Luiss: Liber Università Internazionale degli Studi Sociali, ErasmusLaw, Introduction to National Legal Systems – Scottish Legal System http://www.luiss.it/erasmuslaw/scozia/obligations.htm
[587] supra n.586, Luiss
[588] supra n.586, Luiss

This chapter will not deal with voluntary obligation (ie the law of contract) as this is outside the boundaries of this work but will instead focus on involuntary obligations, which look at issues of delictual liability.

11.1.2 The law of delict

> 'Delict is the area of the law which governs the obligation to refrain from wrongful conduct which may harm the interests of another, and the duty to compensate one who is harmed as a result of [another's] wrongful conduct.'[589]

Compensation in Scottish Delictual Law is referred to as 'reparation' and can only occur if and when harm was caused to the victim as a result of the wrongful act of another. In other words, for a claim in reparation to succeed there must be a delict, which occurs where 'harm to an interest protected by the law'[590] has arisen as a consequence of a wrongful act.

The harm suffered by the victim must be such that it is considered 'reparable' in law, and whether this is so will be determined in relation to the damage that affects an individual's personal interest, such as their physical integrity. Ultimately, it is the court's prerogative to decide when and whether such harm is reparable or not.

For instance, it is argued that the Scottish law of delict does not as yet recognise such personal interest as the right to privacy. Thompson[591] suggests that the protection of this particular right would be likely to be guaranteed through changes in the legislation. It would thus be of interest to keep sight of future developments in the Scottish case-law, in particular as regards the extent to which the Human Rights Act 1998 and the provisions of Articles 8 and 10[592] will impact on the protection of personal interests.

The wrongful act, or conduct, that causes the harm is fault-based, whether it is intentional or unintentional (through carelessness, recklessness and/or negligence). The element of fault is an important part of the law of delict – indeed, it is closely related to the question of whether an act is legally justified. Legal justification is provided either by statutes or by case law. As delict is an area largely based on common law, it is again the courts' prerogative to decide whether an act that results in harm to another individual is legally justified.

To summarise the issue in Thompson's words, 'the traditional Scottish law solution has been to restrict liability by insisting that it is triggered by the defender's fault and by refusing to recognise certain kinds of harm as reparable interests'.[593] This view is not necessarily restrictive in the construction of delictual liability from a moral stand; indeed, wrongful conduct devoid of intention can ground liability provided some degree of fault is present in the act.

'. . . However, in some areas it has been considered socially and economically desirable that persons should recover compensation for physical injury or damage to property without the need to establish fault on the part of the defender.'[594] This refers to delicts of strict liability, ie offences imposed by statutes.

---

[589] supra n.586, Luiss
[590] supra n.586, Luiss
[591] Thompson J, *Delictual Liability*, Butterworths 2nd ed. 2001, p. 2
[592] See Chapter 9 on Human Rights Law
[593] supra n.591, Thompson p. 6
[594] supra n.591, Thompson p. 6

The law of delict is further sub-divided through its categorisation of intentional delicts, unintentional delicts and delictual liability covering specific social and economic situations.

This section, like that in Chapter 8 on English Civil Law, will concentrate on issues of assault and injuries to liberty (intentional delict); negligence (unintentional delict), and finally on vicarious, employer's and professional liability.[595]

11.2 Intentional delicts

11.2.1 Assault As was the case for England, Wales and Northern Ireland, assault can either be a criminal offence and/or a delict. The latter is distinguished from the criminal offence as it lacks the element of 'evil' intent. However, intention is still an important element, and so there must be proof that the offender has an intention to invade the physical integrity of his victim. So even though criminal proceedings for assault would fail, it is still possible for the victim to claim damages for assault in the law of delict.

Assault here does not necessarily imply physical contact or damage – it also refers to an insult to the person suffered by an individual. Acting in a threatening manner towards an individual, such as shaking a fist, can be deemed to constitute an assault. Thus, physical injury is not a necessary requirement for a delictual assault to occur.

Contrary to the criminal offence of assault, the delict of assault is negated by consent, provided the victim has the capacity to consent. Indeed, delictual assault is based on the notion that an individual suffers a violation of their bodily integrity against their will, and so consent to such an action will render an otherwise wrongful act lawful.

Issues of assault and consent are largely raised in situations of medical treatment. Failure to obtain a capable patient's consent for the application of a particular medical treatment will result in the health professional facing delictual liability. This can also happen despite the fact that the procedure might be beneficial or even necessary to the life of the patient. As stated in *St George's Healthcare NHS Trust v S*:[596] 'even when [their] own life depends on receiving medical treatment, an adult of sound mind is entitled to refuse it'.

The Scottish law on delict has so far followed the English common law on matters of valid (ie informed) consent and the obligation to disclose information regarding the risks pursuant to a specific medical procedure.

It was held in *Sidaway v Board of Governors of the Bethlem Royal Hospital*[597] that a doctor is not under an obligation to disclose more information on the risks of a medical treatment than is deemed necessary by a responsible body of medical opinion. Therefore, a patient's right to informed consent is subjected to the opinion of a responsible body of medical professionals, which determines whether certain risks are to be mentioned or not to the patient before he gives his consent to a specific treatment. Moreover, a court of law can override such a medical opinion if it is found that there is a clear violation of the patient's fundamental right.

---

[595] see Thompson supra n.591
[596] [1998] 3 All ER 673
[597] [1985] 1 All ER 643

Any injury incurred by the patient must be the result of a risk inherent in the treatment and not due to the negligence of the health professional conducting the medical procedure. Such breach of a duty of care is dealt with under the notion of professional delictual liability.[598]

In brief, a patient *cannot* claim damages for delictual assault when appropriately informed consent has been given according to a responsible body of medical opinion. However, a patient *can* claim damages when a health professional has failed to provide him with appropriate information on the risks accompanying a certain medical procedure and the patient has suffered from a resulting injury. Thompson, however, argues such an action in delict is not so much about the assault itself but rather that it is an action for a breach of duty.

In _Moyes v Lothian Health Board_,[599] a female patient sued the Lothian Health Board for damages after incurring a stroke as a result of an operation. It was held that 'if a doctor contrary to established practice failed to warn the patient of the four special risks but did warn the patient of the standard risk and then the patient suffered complication caused physiologically by the standard risk factor rather than by one or other of the four special risks factors [he] should [not] escape the consequences of not having warned the patient of the added risks which that patient was exposed to',[600] provided the patient would not have consented to the procedure had she been told about the risks.

The Scottish courts do agree with the English view that the courts can intervene in deciding what constitutes a valid consent. Lord Caplan, however, stated in _Moyes_ that 'the risks inherent in a particular operation or procedure, the manner in which the operation may affect or damage a particular patient, the medical need for the operation and the ability of the patient to absorb information about his situation without adding damage to his health, are all matters where the doctor, with his own clinical experience and the benefit of the experience of other practitioners, is best able to form a judgement as to what the patient can safely be told in the exercise of medical care. Nor is it practical or necessary that the patient should be told of every risk.'[601]

Consent given to a particular conduct or treatment does not cover any other conduct or treatment. For instance, consent to being touched lightly on the arm in order to be directed to an area is not consent to being held tightly and forced into the area.

In the context of physical restraint for people with learning disabilities and severe challenging behaviour, self-defence, inevitable accident, necessity, provocation and duty of care could be explored. It is suggested that these defences follow the English common law principles.[602]

To conclude this section, it is worth mentioning that children who are subjected to corporal punishment by their parents cannot seek remedies for delictual assault. Indeed, parents have a right to impose physical force as a means of chastisement on their offspring, provided that the parent can show now that he or she is not in breach of section 51 of the Criminal Justice (Scotland) Act 2003.[603] (For a detailed examination of the new provisions, see above 10.3.7),

---

[598] supra n.591, Thompson p. 13
[599] (1990) SLT 444
[600] *Ibid per* Lord Caplan, at p. 447
[601] *Ibid* at p. 449
[602] See Chapter 8
[603] Implemented on 27 October 2003

a father smacking his daughter in response to her refusal to have a tooth removed by a dentist was deemed to constitute assault as the force was considered unreasonable.[604]

11.2.1.1 Defences The defences that apply as complete defences are: self-defence and unavoidable accident (ie an accident that could not be avoided). The principle of self-defence laid down in the English civil law would arguably also apply here; that is, only reasonable and necessary force should be used when it appears that the person acting in self-defence feels that her safety or that of a third party for whom she is responsible is at risk.

Necessity could possibly apply here as well, as a carer might be in a situation where he would need to use a degree of force in order to prevent: a service user from harming herself, a third party or the carer himself; or if the service user is about to commit a crime that cannot be stopped otherwise.

Consent will also negate a liability for delictual assault if it was given to accept the risk inherent in a specific situation. However, if the injury incurred is one that was outside the scope of the consent given then it will not serve as a defence.[605]

Provocation, as a partial defence, will also contribute to reducing the damages the defender will be liable to pay the victim if found guilty of delictual assault, if it is indeed proven that the defender acted on impulse due to the victim's provocation. Provocation can be either material or verbal, as the latter is considered 'a good ground for mitigating damages'.[606]

11.2.2 Injuries to liberty

'Next to life is liberty; and the delinquence against it are restraint and constraint. And though liberty be inestimable, yet the damages sustained through these delinquencies are reparable'.[607]

This section refers to issues of false imprisonment/detention and restraint. The loss of liberty experienced by a victim of unlawful detention or restraint is coupled with the fact that it is an affront to their person. Therefore, it is argued that 'a slight infringement of liberty is prima facie actionable'.[608]

In _Mackenzie v Cluny Hill Hydropathic Co_,[609] a lady was wrongfully detained on the defender's premises for 15 minutes and would not be released until she made an apology to the manager. The court held that such behaviour was an 'outrage'. Thus, there was cause for a delict in the wrongful detention of another.

On the matter of false imprisonment, the general rule that an individual cannot be detained against their will finds an exception where the detention is the result of legal proceedings, such a legal arrest, or is authorised by statutes. A relevant statute that grants the power to detain the mentally ill is the Mental Health (Scotland) Act 1984 (s.18: where the patient is a danger to himself or to others).

---

[604] see in Chapter 10 on Scottish Criminal Law
[605] supra n.591, Thompson p. 14
[606] _per_ Lord President Hope in _Anderson v Marshall_ (1835) 13 S 1130, at p. 1131
[607] supra n.591, Thompson p. 17, quoting Stair I, 9, 4.
[608] supra n.591, Thompson p. 17
[609] 1908 SLT 518

11.2.2.1 Defences

Lawful arrest

This includes 'citizens' arrest as well as arrest made by the police under a warrant.

Statutory power to detain the mentally ill

Under Section 18 of the Mental Health (Scotland) Act 1984, an individual suffering from a mental illness and presenting a danger to himself or to others can be put under compulsory detention in a mental hospital after appropriate recommendations by two medical professionals (including a psychiatrist) have been submitted to and accepted by a sheriff.

An order for detention will be issued for a period of six months, renewable, if deemed necessary, without recourse to the sheriff. The patient and/or his nearest relative have the right to challenge such a decision before the sheriff.

11.2.3 Fear and force This delict arises when an individual is a) pushed into committing or performing an act that they would not normally do, or b) when they are compelled into not doing something that they want to do or that they are, by law, entitled to do. This delict implies that an individual is intimidated, threatened or bullied by another, either verbally or physically, into acting in a manner that they would not were they to exercise their free will.

11.3 Unintentional delict

11.3.1 Negligence As mentioned in the section outlining the law of delict, for delictual liability to arise there must be an element of fault, which does not necessarily imply 'intention'. The careless conduct of a person, which causes harm to another, albeit unintended, can be deemed fault-based and therefore can result in a claim in negligence.

In the words of Thompson, 'if A acts in a careless manner, ie his conduct fails to meet the standard of care demanded by society of a person in his position, then prima facie A is liable to anyone who suffers harm as a result of A's careless conduct'.[610] For instance, a carer who acts in a wrongful manner – that is, in a way in which no other reasonable and ordinary carer in her position would have acted – and a client or patient suffers injury as a result of her careless or reckless conduct, the carer would be likely to face liability in negligence and the client could be awarded damages in reparation for the harm caused.

For a claim in negligence to be successful, the following elements must be present: there must be a duty of care owed by the wrongdoer towards the victim, that duty must have been broken, constituting negligence, and that breach must have caused harm. The first element is vital; indeed, if a duty of care is not established, then there can be no breach of such a duty, and so no harm done as a result of negligence.

11.3.1.1 Duty of care Before deciding whether there is a duty of care owed by one person to another in situations of potential physical harm, the court will look at the nature of their relationship. Indeed, a duty of care arises out of a special bond between the parties, and this

---

[610] supra n.591, Thompson p. 57

point is important as not every type of 'relationship' between people will suggest the presence of a duty of care owed by one to another. Ultimately, it is the court's prerogative to decide whether a particular relationship has given rise to a duty of care – the court has the power to extend or restrict the scope of a duty of care as not every '. . . act or omission which any moral code would censure cannot in a practical world be treated so as to give a right to every person injured by them to demand relief'.[611] In order to exercise this power, the courts have devised a test that is to be applied in order to establish the presence of a duty of care.

In _Donoghue v Stevenson_,[612] a friend bought the victim a bottle of ginger beer from a café shop. After having drunk some of the ginger beer, the friend poured the rest of the drink in a glass and found that there was a snail in a state of decomposition floating on the surface. As a result of this, the victim suffered from shock and illness and sued the manufacturer of the ginger beer, who was later found negligent.

In this case, the manufacturer was held liable in negligent as it was concluded that despite the lack of contractual relationship between the defender and the victim, there was a special relationship between them that was described as 'the neighbour' principle. This was explained by Lord Atkin, who stated[613]:

> '_The rule that you are to love your neighbour becomes in law, you must not injure your neighbour; and the lawyer's question, Who is my neighbour? receives a restricted reply. You must take reasonable care to avoid acts or omissions which you can reasonably foresee would be likely to injure your neighbour. Who, then, in law is my neighbour? The answer seems to be that "**persons who are so closely and directly affected by my act that I ought reasonably to have them in contemplation as being so affected when I am directing my mind to the acts or omissions which are called in question**"._'[614]

For instance, in a care situation, a person cared for would be closely and directly affected by the act of their carer. This would mean that these two people are 'neighbours' in the _Donoghue v Stevenson_ sense, or what is also known as a relationship of proximity. 'Proximity' does not necessarily imply physical closeness or nearness in time. It actually refers to the nature of a relationship between the parties.

The proximity factor, however, is not enough to find a duty of care. Indeed, the carer must keep in mind that his actions, during the course of his caring for the patient, could or would undoubtedly affect the latter and possibly cause her harm. This is what the court refers to as the element of foreseeability. In other words, one must consider the consequences of one's actions, including how one's actions could result in hurting one's neighbour.

In _Coleridge v Miller Construction Ltd_[615] the defenders' excavator truck, while digging a trench, struck and damaged an electric cable which resulted in the plaintiff's glassworks' electricity power being cut. The plaintiff sued the defenders for financial loss incurred as a result, both for the damaged glass and the cost of emergency repair that ensued the power cut.

---

[611] _per_ Lord Atkin in _Donoghue v Stevenson_ 1932 SLT 317, at p. 323
[612] [1932] SLT 317
[613] _Ibid_ at p. 323
[614] added emphasis
[615] [1997] SLT 485

In deciding whether there was a duty of care owed by the defender to the plaintiff, the Scottish court referred to the English case of *Caparo plc v Dickman* 1990[616] and stated, quoting from *Caparo* first, that:

> '... in addition to the foreseeability of damage, necessary ingredients in any situation giving rise to a duty of care are that there should exist between the party owing the duty and the party to whom it is owed a relationship characterised by the law as one of "proximity" or "neighbourhood" and that the situation should be one in which the court considers it fair, just and reasonable that the law should impose a duty of a given scope upon the one party for the benefit of the other.'

The Scottish court went on to state that:

> 'This last element completes the test for establishing a duty of care. Indeed, the court will consider the fairness of imposing a duty of care by examining the matter in the light of various policy issues that it might raise, such as allowing a claim in negligence on grounds of public policy, or refusing a claim in order to avoid any floodgates and unjust future legal proceedings.'

Notions such as 'proximity' and 'fairness' are not clearly defined, nor are they static concepts. Indeed, Lord Bridge, in *Caparo* adds that they '. . . amount in effect to little more than convenient labels to attach to the features of different specific situations which, on a detailed examination of all the circumstances, the law recognises pragmatically as giving rise to a duty of care of a given scope'.[617]

In *Coleridge*, the court expressed its doubt as to whether the parties were in a relationship of proximity. Indeed, the defenders did not seem to have any knowledge of any electrical cable on the site. Had they known about the lay-out of electrical cables where the excavation took place, it is likely that the judge would have found that there was sufficient proximity between the defenders and the plaintiff to imply a duty of care.

Furthermore, the defenders were not aware of the plaintiff's business and so it was not foreseeable for them that a power cut would damage the plaintiff's glassworks. The court finally decided, based on policy considerations, that it would not be fair, just and reasonable to impose a duty of care on the defenders for cutting the power supply.

It is argued that the tripartite test is to be applied in its entirety as the three elements – foreseeability, proximity and fairness – complete each other. However, although the first two elements might be present, the court will exercise its discretion in imposing a duty of care by considering the last element, namely whether it would be fair, just and reasonable to find a duty of care in a particular situation. On the other hand, it is also argued that such a three-fold test has made it possible for the courts to actually decide on cases presenting some new and sometimes challenging facts, and so the test allows for new precedent setting.[618] For instance, the test was applied in *Gibson v Orr*,[619] a case involving physical harm.

---

[616] [1990] 2 AC at pp. 617–618 and 628
[617] supra n.615
[618] supra n.591, Thompson p. 66

In this case, the police had coned off the north side of a collapsed bridge and placed a police vehicle on the south side. The police then drove off after an hour without having put any warning signs on the south side, from where a car later fell off the bridge. The passenger of the car suffered personal injury, and the court recognised that the police owed a duty of care to the victim. Lord Hamilton applied the tripartite test and thus stated[620] that 'although there is no authority directly binding . . . the three element test now falls . . . to be applied in Scotland in personal injury actions based on a duty of care as well as in other actions of damages so based'.

In brief, 'the important point is that the concept of a duty of care is used as a *threshold* device, enabling the courts to extend the scope of delictual liability or to refuse to do so, depending on policy considerations'.[621]

11.3.1.2 Breach of duty of care   Once it has been established that a person owes a duty of care to another, it must then be proved that such a duty has been breached.

An individual can be found negligent for an act or an omission; however, both must be voluntary – this means that the wrongdoer must have intended to act or omit to act as he did. For instance, a carer who is looking after a young child with learning disabilities, who is known for running away and so putting herself in danger when close to a busy traffic road, might be found negligent for failing to take reasonable precautions to avoid the child running towards the road and coming to potential harm.

The principle of a voluntary act or omission to act is illustrated by _Waugh v James K Allan Ltd_,[622] in which the victim was killed as result of a car accident after a lorry driver who suffered from a thrombosis failed to stop when he felt uncomfortable and later died at the wheel. The court found that the driver had not been negligent for carrying on driving as he believed he was only suffering from gastric discomfort, which thus implies that his death was involuntary and so there was no breach of duty.

Furthermore, it must be established that the harm caused by the negligent act was a natural consequence of that act. This was mentioned in _Muir v Glasgow Corporation_,[623] in which Lord Thankerton said that 'it has long been held in Scotland that all that a person can be held bound to *foresee* are the *reasonable and probable consequences of the failure to take care, judged by the standard of the ordinary reasonable man*[624]'.

The question is therefore an objective one which asks what a reasonable person in the defender's position would have foreseen as being a reasonable and probable consequence of a particular course of action.

The defender in this case was the manageress of a tea room and sweet shop situated in a park, who allowed a party of customers to have their picnic in the tea room. The customers carried an urn of boiling water past the sweet shop towards the tea room. However, the urn of boiling water was upturned near the sweet shop, where several children were standing and they suffered scalding injuries as a result. The court held that a reasonable person in her position

[619] [1999] SC 420
[620] supra n.591 at p. 431
[621] supra n.591, Thompson p. 67
[622] [1964] SLT 269
[623] [1944] SLT 60
[624] added emphasis

would not have foreseen such a situation occurring, therefore she had not breached the duty of care which she owed to the children.

It is thus necessary that a reasonable person would have foreseen harm as a reasonable and possible consequence of an act or omission. The principle does not, however, extend the requirement to foresee the full spectrum of a possible harm, nor does it mean that the defender should have foreseen all the details – ie 'features and developments' – of the accident which caused the injury.

In _Hughes v Lord Advocate_[625] a young boy suffered from burn injuries following an explosion in a manhole, which, along with a paraffin oil lamp, had been left unattended. Although the explosion, which was the result of the lamp falling into the manhole, was an unexpected accident that could not have been foreseen, the court found that it was a reasonable and probable consequence that a boy would attempt to inspect an unattended manhole and trip over the lamp that would then cause an explosion. Moreover, the unexpected gravity of the child's injuries did not negate the finding of a breach of duty of care.

As a general principle, an individual's act or omission will not be said to be in breach of a duty of care if harm is caused by an intervening third party, thus 'breaking' the chain of causation between the careless act and the damage.[626] Provided that there is a special relationship between the careless person and the third party, the latter's intervention might be deemed a reasonable and probable intervention following the former's careless act or omission, and this would thus amount to a breach of duty of care.

This is illustrated by the English case _Dorset Yacht Co Ltd v Home Office_[627] in which seven young boys, who were under the custody of three borstal officers on the Isle of Wight, stole a yacht and attempted to escape when the officers retired to bed for the night. They collided with another yacht, however, damaging it. The officers were found to have breached the duty of care towards the proprietor of the damaged yacht, as due to their special relationship with the boys – they were responsible for them – they should have foreseen that the boys would attempt to escape, stealing a yacht and damaging another in the process because of their lack of experience. This was therefore negligence on the part of the officers.

11.3.1.3 Standard of care   Negligence is evaluated against the standard of care that would be shown by the ordinary person in a given situation. If an individual fails to meet that level and another person suffers personal injury as a result, then he is said to have been negligent. On the other hand, if the act or omission, which is the cause of physical harm, is recognised as an act or omission that an ordinary and reasonable person would have engaged in the act or omission is not deemed negligent.[628] 'The law does not expect the defender to go beyond the standards of the reasonable person. The defender is only obliged not to be negligent: he is not expected to ensure that his acts or omissions never harm the [victim]'.[629]

In order to find a claim in negligence successful, the court will consider various elements that are said to characterise the steps that a reasonable person would have taken in the defender's position. If the latter did take these steps, then he would not be said to be negligent; however,

---

[625] [1963] SLT 150
[626] _Maloco v Littlewoods Organisation Ltd_ [1987] SLT 425
[627] [1970] 2 All ER 294
[628] see _Muir v Glasgow Corporation_ [1944] SLT 60, supra n.33
[629] supra n.591, Thompson p. 119

if he failed to take some or all of these steps, then prima facie, the defender would be found negligent.

The elements to be considered are the following: a) probability and seriousness of the injury, b) practicability and costs of precautions, c) utility of the defender's activities, and d) practice of other individuals in the defender's professional field.[630]

a) Probability and seriousness of harm

If it is improbable that a certain harm would be caused by the defender's action or omission to act in a certain manner, then even if harm has been caused, the element of foreseeability would not be satisfied if it is argued that a reasonable person would not have foreseen such a consequence as probable. This is illustrated by *Gillon v Chief Constable of Strathclyde Police*[631] in which it was held that 'the risk of a police officer being injured by a player at a football match was so small that a reasonable employer ... was not required to take any precautions'.[632]

As for the seriousness of an injury, the principle laid down in the English case *Paris v Stepney Borough Council*[633] also applies in Scottish negligence cases.[634] In the case of *Paris v Stepney Borough Council*,[635] the English court had taken into account the disability of the plaintiff in deciding that the defendants owed him a duty of care due to his visual impairment that they did not owe to their other employees.

b) Practicability and the costs of precautions

A defender is only required to take the reasonable precautions that are available to him at the time, and that are practicable in terms of installation and cost of taking such precautions to avoid potential harm.

In *Quinn v Cameron and Roberton Ltd*[636] iron foundry employers were found not to be negligent for not providing their employees with further precautionary measures to avoid harm from the inhalation of silica dust. Such danger from the dust had not been recognised at the time, and furthermore, the proper equipment for effective dust-extraction had not been made available to employers until 1950.[637]

'The hypothetical reasonable person in the position of the defender will take into account the cost of precautions and balance this against the probability of risk of harm and the seriousness of any injuries to be sustained.'[638] This statement is supported by the English case *Latimer v EC Ltd*[639] which sets out that when a defender has done all that is reasonable to avoid the

---

[630] supra n.591, Thompson p. 120
[631] [1997] SLT 1218
[632] supra n.591, Thompson p. 121
[633] [1951] 1 All ER 42
[634] for further details, see Chapter 8 on English Civil Law
[635] supra at n.633 and at [1951] AC 367
[636] [1956] SLT 2
[637] the action was brought by an employee who had worked for the defenders almost a decade prior to 1950
[638] supra n.591, Thompson p. 123
[639] [1953] 2 All ER 449

occurring of injury, in the manner which an ordinary and reasonable person would have done, then the defender will not be held to have been negligent even if harm does nonetheless occur.[640]

c) Utility of the defender's activities

It is argued that 'the social utility of the activities, which it is foreseeable may cause injury, must be taken into account'.[641] This is illustrated by the English case _Daborn v Bath Tramways Motor Co Ltd and Smithey_[642] in which an ambulance with a left-hand drive collided with a bus, despite the fact that the driver of the ambulance had put a sign at the back of the vehicle which read 'caution – left hand drive – no signal'. It was found that the ambulance driver had not been negligent, based on the considerations of the following factors: '. . . (i) the necessity in time of national emergency of employing all transport resources which were available and (ii) the inherent limitations and incapacities of this particular form of transport'.[643] The court concluded that the driver had acted reasonably in the given circumstances, considering the risk against the consequences of not taking such a risk.

d) Practice of other individuals in the defender's professional field

The standard of care required by an individual will be assessed against the standard of care to be expected from a person in that individual's position. So for instance, as explained further in the section on professional liability, the standard of care that a carer must show towards the person she cares for is different from that which is shown by the person's dentist or general practitioner. Indeed, the carer will be assessed according to what is expected of the reasonable carer in the same circumstances; similarly, the dentist will be assessed according to the ordinary dentist in the same circumstances.

Thus, in _Hunter v Hanley_,[644] Lord President Clyde stated[645] that 'the true test for establishing negligence in diagnosis or treatment on the part of a doctor is whether he has been proved to be guilty of such failure as no doctor of ordinary skill would be guilty of if acting with ordinary care'.[646]

11.3.1.4 Causation of harm   The principle that the harm incurred by a victim is the result of the defender's negligent act implies that if the victim suffers personal injury that is caused by another act or omission then the defender will be deemed to have been negligent as his actions would not be the cause of harm.

This is a notion analogous to the English 'but for' test, that is, if it was not but for the act or omission of the defender, the victim would not have suffered injury.[647]

In _McWilliams v Sir William Arrol & Co Ltd_[648] a widow claimed damages for the death of her husband, who worked as a steel-erector and fell from a tower crane, arguing that his employers had been negligent in failing to provide him with a safety-belt. It was found, on balance of

---

[640] For further details, see Chapter 8 on English Civil Law
[641] supra n.591, Thompson p. 122
[642] [1946] 2 All ER 333
[643] _per_ Asquith LJ, at p. 336
[644] [1955] SLT at p. 217
[645] _Ibid_ at p. 217
[646] For further details, see post section 11.4 on professional liability
[647] See Chapter 8 on English Criminal Law
[648] [1962] SLT 121

probabilities, that even if the husband had been provided with a safety-belt, he would not have worn it. Thus, despite acknowledging the employers' negligence, the court concluded that the widow could not prove that the negligence was the cause of the fatal accident.

11.3.2 Defences

11.3.2.1 Volenti non fit injuria (accepting the legal risk of harm)   In the words of Lord Nimmo Smith, 'the successful establishment of [volenti] means that the [victim] has accepted the risk of the defender's negligence in the exercise of his legal duties and has absolved the defender from the consequences arising from that negligence'.[649]

For instance, provided the individual is legally capable, this means that a person cared for can agree to a restraint procedure as part of her care plan, that she is aware of the risks involved in such a measure, and that she waives her right to sue the carers implementing that measure in negligence should she suffer from physical injuries that are an inherent risk of the restraint procedure. In other words, she willingly accepts to take the risk of incurring harm.

In *Sabri-Tabrizi v Lothian Health Board*[650] a woman claimed damages for becoming pregnant after a failed sterilisation. She underwent the operation in 1991, became pregnant in 1992 and terminated the pregnancy; however, she became pregnant a second time shortly after and later gave birth to a stillborn baby. It was argued that she had not accepted the risk that the sterilisation could possibly fail before it was carried out, as indeed she had not been told that this was a possibility. The court concluded that '. . . the acceptance of risk must occur either before or contemporaneously with the act or omission constituting the negligence, and not after it'.[651] Volenti did not occur in this particular case.

11.3.2.2 Contributory negligence   Section 1(1) of the Law Reform (Contributory Negligence) Act 1945 stipulates that 'where any person suffers damage as the result of his own fault and partly due to the fault of any other person or persons, a claim in respect of that damage shall not be defeated by reason of the fault of the person suffering the damage, but the damages recoverable in respect thereof shall be reduced to such an extent as the court thinks just and equitable having regard to the claimant's share in the responsibility for the damage'.

In other words, contributory negligence is not so much a defence but a means of reducing both one's liable responsibility and the financial cost of paying for reparation in negligence.

This defence might be of particular relevance in a situation where a person with learning disabilities runs towards a busy traffic road, and either suffers harm as a result of being hit by a car, or incurs minor injuries for being pulled back to safety by his carer or a passer-by. Prima facie, the driver of the car might be found negligent for the accident and the carer or passer-by might also be liable for injuring the individual. However, the circumstances are such that they could all clearly plead contributory negligence, as the individual engaged such a careless conduct. The burden of proving that the victim has been negligent seems to lie on the defender.[652]

---

[649] *Sabri-Tabrizi v Lothian Health Board* 1998 SLT 607, at p. 610
[650] [1988] SLT 607
[651] *Ibid, per* Lord Nimmo Smith, at p. 610
[652] supra n.591, Thompson p. 144

11.3.2.3 Joint fault   This 'defence' is particularly relevant to situations where a service user suffers harm as a result of several parties, which could include her carers (workers and managers), but also her general practitioner, occupational therapist and/or close relative; in other words, whoever is involved in caring for her and who is responsible for her well-being and her safety.

Joint fault, or joint wrongdoing, occurs when there is more than one defender who is in breach of a duty of care and whose action or omission has contributed to the same delictual negligence that caused personal injury to the person for whom care is provided.

This notion can be illustrated by the case of _Anderson v Ayr and South Ayrshire Local Committee of St Andrew's Ambulance Association, and The Western Scottish Motor Traction Company Limited_.[653] In this case, a nurse was returning to Ayr in an ambulance that collided with a bus. She suffered physical injuries as a result of the collision and sued both the ambulance and bus companies for reparation as the ambulance driver failed to stop at a 'halt' sign, whereas the bus driver failed to reduce speed at a 'slow' sign.

The court held that:

> '_there was on the part of each of these drivers a breach of a plain direction, and it seems ... that the breach of each contributed in equal degree to the damage which followed. There was a suggestion that it is a more heinous, or at any rate a more obvious, offence if you breach the direction to halt than if you breach the direction to go slow. These two directions are correlative, and the breach of one is just as serious as the breach of the other._'[654]

11.4 Professional liability

This section covers situations where a professional has wronged his client or customer. Although the client can sue the professional for breach of contract, if there is no contractual relationship between the parties, it is still possible for the professional to be sued for delictual liability.[655]

The notion of the duty of care is relevant to this delict, as a professional will be held negligent if it is proved that his course of action has fallen below the required standard of care that is to be expected of a reasonable person in his profession. In other words, if any other professional in the defender's position would not have acted as he did, in accordance with the opinion of the responsible body of professionals relevant to the sphere of activity concerned, then clearly, the defender will be said to be negligent.

On the other hand, if it could be proved that there exists another body of professionals, who are experts in the defender's field, who would actually have acted as the defender did, this implies that are two bodies of professionals having differing albeit valid, proper and reasonable expert opinions on the matter. In this case, the defendant would not necessarily be found

---

[653]   [1943] SLT 258
[654]   _per_ the Lord President (Normand), at p. 261
[655]   supra n.591, Thompson p. 149

negligent. This is so even though it might transpire that the defender's course of action is only rarely used by professionals in his discipline, or only practised by a minority of fellow experts.

This particular issue was raised in _Gordon v Wilson_.[656] In this case, a patient suffered from a brain tumour, which, she argued, should have been detected at an earlier stage than it was. She underwent an operation to have the tumour removed, but incurred nerve damage alleged to be a consequence of the time delay in diagnosing the tumour. The patient sued her doctor for professional negligence and provided expert evidence that the delay was the cause of harm. The defenders also provided expert testimony supporting the view that the delay had been harmless.

The court affirmed the principle that it was not within its ambit to voice a preference for one piece of expert evidence over another, finding that for a liability in negligence to arise, only the 'failure to exercise the ordinary skill of a doctor (in the appropriate speciality, if he be a specialist) is necessary'.[657] The court concluded that there was no evidence supporting the allegation that the delayed diagnosis had caused the harm suffered by the patient.

Gordon v Wilson follows the view expressed in _Hunter v Hanley_[658] that 'in the realm of diagnosis and treatment there is ample scope for genuine difference of opinion and one man clearly is not negligent merely because his conclusion differs from that of other professional men, nor because he has displayed less skill or knowledge than others would have shown'.[659] The basic principle being that when there are two professional bodies of opinion diverging (and possibly dissenting) on a normal course of action, the judges should not be concerned with establishing a preference for one body or the other.

In determining what amounts to a negligent act, the courts will consider whether there has been a breach of a duty of care. The standard of care required from a professional towards his client is not a general one but is a special one. Indeed, the standard of care required is that which would be expected from a person exercising a specific professional occupation. For instance, the standard of care a carer must show towards her service user is one that is specific to any carer in her field, and would not be the same standard of care to be expected from someone who is not a carer. Adapting the words of the court in _Hunter v Hanley_ to caring situations, 'the true test for establishing negligence in diagnosis or treatment on the part of a [carer][660] is whether he has been proved to be guilty of such failure as no [carer] of ordinary skill would be guilty of, if acting with ordinary care'.

In _Hunter v Hanley_, a doctor had given a series of injections of penicillin to his patient when at the twelfth injection the needle broke and the end of it was stuck in the patient's hip. She sued the doctor for professional negligence and claimed damages on the basis that he had failed to use appropriate equipment to perform the injections – alleging that the hypodermic needle was not strong enough. The issue at hand was to determine whether the needle used was part of a normal and usual practice in these circumstances.

Lord President Clyde stated that for liability in negligence for deviation from normal practice to be established, three elements must be proven, namely that a) there is actually a 'usual and normal practice'; b) the defender had not adopted that practice; and finally, the most important

---

[656] [1992] SLT 849
[657] Citing Lord Scarman in _Maynard v West Midlands Regional Health Authority_ [1985] 1 All ER 635
[658] [1955] SLT 213
[659] _per_ Lord President Clyde, at p. 217
[660] _Ibid_ The sentence, which should actually read 'doctor', has been changed for the purpose of this report

element, c) the action of the defender is one that no other 'professional man of ordinary skill would have taken if he had been acting with ordinary care'. Lord Clyde stressed that a plaintiff should be able to prove all three of these elements, as failure to do so would result in the claim being unsuccessful. His Lordship further added that 'if this is the test then it matters nothing how far or how little [the defender] deviates from the ordinary practice. For the extent of deviation is not the test. The deviation must be of a kind which satisfies the third of the requirements just stated.'[661]

11.5 Adults with Incapacity (Scotland) Act 2000

The Adults with Incapacity (Scotland) Act 2000[662] received the royal assent in May 2000 and came into force in July 2002. The Act provides guidelines on the decision-making process concerning the welfare, property and financial matters of adults classed as being legally incapable. AWI(S)A 2000 now includes a new system within which intervention orders are granted, and has given medical practitioners, who are involved with administering or regulating the medical treatment of the adult in question, the authority to assess the adult's incapacity and to decide on the best course of action to be taken.

11.5.1 Scope of AWI(S)A 2000 AWI(S)A 2000 seems to be aiming to provide a more thoughtful and effective legislative device that encourages, guarantees and protects, as much as is possible, the freedom and autonomy of people with mental incapacity in the running of their everyday lives. This is a more up-to-date approach to the issue of mental incapacity and the stigmas and abuses that have accompanied such a condition. If in the past, incapacity was a generic label that qualified an adult as incapable in virtually any circumstances, the new Act is innovative in acknowledging that there are various degrees of mental incapacity. Indeed, mental incapacity can be the result of either a mental or a communication impairment due to a physical disability; thus the Act 'recognises the great variety of intellectual disabilities and resulting impairments of capacity'.[663] This suggests that once an adult is recognised as incapable in one situation, he is not necessarily incapable in all situations.

Capacity in the context of the AWI(S)A 2000 is said to be task-/decision-specific, which means that when (in)capacity is assessed, the assessment focuses on 'specific areas or issues of decision making. [ie] An adult may be capable of making some types of decisions, but not others.'[664] When assessing, the medical practitioner will thus have to take into consideration the fact that (in)capacity will be affected by the 'time of day, adult's mood, distractions, time allowed to consider and decide their response, level of familiarity with surroundings, the way in which information is presented to the adult, eg using appropriate vocabulary and aids to communication'.[665]

The Act thus attempts to achieve a certain equilibrium between ensuring that necessary decisions for adults with mental incapacity are taken in consideration with their well-being, and avoiding an over-indulgence in controlling the physical, emotional, financial and material needs

---

[661] *Ibid* at p. 217
[662] From now on referred to as the AWI(S)A 2000, or 'the Act' in this section particular
[663] *Current Law Statutes 2000* vol.3, *asp*.4, <u>Adults with Incapacity (Scotland) Act 2000</u>, annotations by Ward Adrian D, MBE, LL.B, Solicitor, Turnbull & Ward, Barrhead, at pp. 4–5
[664] *Aide Memoire for Doctors*, issued by Chief Medical Officer (Dr. E.M. Armstrong), Scottish Executive Health Department. Weblink: <u>http://www.show.scot.nhs.uk/sehd/cmo/AWIaidememoire.pdf</u>, p. 3
[665] supra n.664, *Aide Memoire for Doctors*, p. 3

of these adults. The latter situation could lead to abuse and be construed as an overwhelming protective attitude on the parts of the decision makers. Indeed, 'there requires to be a balance between providing special measures where they are needed, but on the other hand not restricting, discriminating or disqualifying any more than necessary'.[666]

For that purpose, AWI(S)A 2000 establishes some general and fundamental principles, which are to be kept in mind whenever a decision is taken on behalf of an adult with mental incapacity.

Section 1 on 'General principles and fundamental definitions' stipulates that:

1) *The principles set out in subsections (2) to (4) shall be given effect to in relation to any intervention in the affairs of an adult under or in pursuance of this Act, including any order made in or for the purpose of any proceedings under this Act for or in connection with an adult.*

2) *There shall be no intervention in the affairs of an adult unless the person responsible for authorising or effecting the intervention is satisfied that the intervention will benefit the adult and that such benefit cannot reasonably be achieved without the intervention.*

3) *Where it is determined that an intervention as mentioned in subsection (1) is to be made, such intervention shall be the least restrictive option in relation to the freedom of the adult, consistent with the purpose of the intervention.*

4) *In determining if an intervention is to be made and, if so, what intervention is to be made, account shall be taken of –*

   (a) the present and past wishes and feelings of the adult so far as they can be ascertained by any means of communication, whether human or by mechanical aid (whether of an interpretative nature or otherwise) appropriate to the adult;

   (b) the views of the nearest relative and the primary carer of the adult, in so far as it is reasonable and practicable to do so;

   (c) the views of –

      (i) any guardian, continuing attorney or welfare attorney of the adult who has powers relating to the proposed intervention; and

      (ii) any person whom the sheriff has directed to be consulted,

      in so far as it is reasonable and practicable to do so; and

   (d) the views of any other person appearing to the person responsible for authorising or effecting the intervention to have an interest in the welfare of the adult or in the proposed intervention, where these views have been made known to the person responsible, in so far as it is reasonable and practicable to do so.

Another innovative and important principle is that, due to the various degrees of mental impairments that vary according to personal circumstances and the situations that require legal capacity or consent, the adult in question must be, 'in so far as is reasonable and practicable', encouraged to exercise her already existing skills and/or develop new ones as regards her decision-making on matters relating to her welfare, as is stated in Section 1(5) AWI(S)A 2000.

11.5.2 Key definitions In order to fully understand the scope of this Act, it is necessary to first establish the meaning of some important terms such as 'adult', 'incapable/incapacity', 'intervention' and 'medical treatment' in this context.

11.5.2.1 Adult An adult, for the purposes of this Act, is defined as a person who has attained the age of 16 years (Section 1(6) AWISA 2000). This follows the definition set out in the Age of Legal Capacity (Scotland) Act 1991 which provides, in Section 1(b), that 'a person of or over the age of 16 years shall have legal capacity to enter into any transaction'.

11.5.2.2 Incapable/incapacity Section 1(6) AWI(S)A 2000 then provides that:

'incapable' means that an adult is incapable of the following:

a) *acting; or*

b) *making decisions; or*

c) *communicating decisions; or*

d) *understanding decisions; or*

e) *retaining the memory of decisions,*

as mentioned in any provision of this Act, by reason of mental disorder or of inability to communicate because of physical disability. A person shall not fall within this definition by reason only of a lack or deficiency in a faculty of communication if that lack or deficiency can be made good by human or mechanical aid (whether of an interpretative nature or otherwise; and

'incapacity' shall be construed accordingly'.

Section 87 AWI(S)A 2000 describes 'mental disorder' as a 'mental illness (including personality disorder) or mental handicap however caused or manifested; but an adult shall not be treated as suffering from mental disorder by reason only of promiscuity or other immoral conduct, sexual deviancy, dependence on alcohol or drugs, or acting as no prudent person would act'.

11.5.2.3 Intervention There is no statutory definition available, as it was considered unnecessary to attempt to do so, as stated by the Deputy Minister for Justice, Angus MacKay.[667] However the Minister gave no further explanation as to why it was considered 'unnecessary'. 'Intervention' appears to be an umbrella term that covers an array of various and different situations within which a particular course of action would be required. It has been described as 'any legal means of intervening in an adult's life by removing powers from him or her and entrusting those powers in another person'.[668] The legal interventions covered by the AWI(S)A 2000 are: welfare and continuing powers of attorney, intervention orders and guardianship orders.

According to the Deputy Minister for Justice, in the context of medical treatment, 'intervention' would encompass both a positive and a negative act, which means that this covers situations where a decision has to be made to either act or to voluntarily refuse to do so, which would amount to a deliberate omission to act.[669]

Encapsulating the full spectrum of this term will thus require the involvement of the courts in future case-law to interpret it and give carers and professionals a clearer understanding of what an intervention is or can be. A broad interpretation of 'intervention' is to be expected, and would presumably include such actions as decisions to commence or end a treatment.

---

[666] supra n.663, Ward Adrian D, *Current Law Statues 2000*, vol. 3, *asp*.4, at pp. 4–5

[667] 29 March 2000, Scottish Parliament Official Report (SPOR), vol.5, no.11, col.1047

[668] Adults with Incapacity (Scotland) Act 2000 – *Guidance and Workbook for Social and Healthcare Staff*, Pack 1, Scottish Executive Publications, 2002. Weblink: http://www.scotland.gov.uk/library5/social/packnumber1.pdf

[669] *Per* Deputy Minister for Justice (Angus MacKay), SPOR, vol.5, no.11, col.1046

11.5.2.4 Medical treatment and physical intervention Section 47(4) provides that *'medical treatment' includes any procedure or treatment designed to safeguard or promote physical or mental health.*

It is argued that, for the purposes of this report, some type of physical interventions would probably come within the meaning of medical treatment or procedure, provided it is designed to 'promote or safeguard' the physical and mental welfare of the adult in question. Presumably, this could include the use of therapeutic devices, such as, for instance, a soft spinal jacket that is utilised as an alternative base for achieving and maintaining good trunk and head control for people who have no spine posture.

However, as set out in section 47(7) AWI(S)A 2000, the use of force or detention is not permitted *unless it is immediately necessary and only for so long as is necessary in the circumstances*. This provision is to be read in conjunction with the principle in section 1(3), which states that the use of force (which must be reasonable[670]) or the detention must only restrict an adult's freedom as little as possible. Therefore, only the minimum use of force reasonable, for the shortest time possible, should be used in a situation where there would be no other alternative available to safeguard and promote the adult's healthcare and welfare.

If a case requires an adult to be placed under detention to treat a mental disorder then the provisions of the Mental Health (Scotland) Act 1984 will apply here.

Finally, it is important to keep in mind that 'in addition to being difficult to achieve in practice, imposing a treatment on incapacitated adults where they refuse could obviously damage relationships with healthcare providers and undermine trust in carers'.[671]

11.5.3 Assessment of (in)capacity As a general rule, an adult is presumed to be competent to make decisions, act and give their consent, until and unless it is legally proven otherwise. This means that an adult does not have to prove their mental capacity, as the onus of proof lies on the individual claiming the adult to be incompetent.

The AWI(S)A 2000 gives medical practitioners authority as well as guidelines on how to assess an adult's mental (in)capacity in relation to a specific situation that would require the latter to exercise their judgement in a decision-taking situation. Thus, before reaching the conclusion that an adult is incompetent, the medical practitioner must ensure that the following principles are satisfied:

- the treatment is *beneficial* to the 'incapable' adult;

- it is also *necessary* as there is no other option to ensure the adult's welfare;

- it is the *least restricting* or violating measure on the adult's freedom.

Once it is established that the adult in question satisfies the definition of 'incapacity' provided in section 1 and the medical practitioner has ticked the boxes above, he must also consider the past and present wishes of the adult, as well as the views of relevant persons who have an interest in the adult's life, such as:

---

[670] For further details on the meaning of 'reasonable', see Chapter 7 on English Criminal Law
[671] Cox C, *Legal and Human Rights Issues Presented by the Management of Aggression and Use of Physical Intervention in Health and Social Care*, Royal College of Nursing, 2003, pp. 11 and 12.

- the adult's relative and primary care assistant;

- guardian, continuing or welfare attorney;

- any person appointed by the sheriff;

- any other person involved in or who has an interest in the adult's welfare.

The treatment is beneficial

A medical practitioner will consider an intervention, not so much because it is in the best interest of the adult – as this principle is not mentioned by the Act – but mainly because its aim is *to do what is reasonable in the circumstances, in relation to the medical treatment, **to safeguard or promote the physical or mental health of the adult***, as stated in section 47(4) AWI(S)A 2000.

The term 'benefit' has no statutory definition. It is argued that a treatment would be considered beneficial to an adult with mental incapacity if the latter is in need of such an intervention. Any measures on the adult's behalf must be taken in order to meet that specific need. Satisfying that need would arguably safeguard[672] or promote[673] the adult's healthcare or welfare; in other words, an *intervention cannot be taken to harm an adult*.

Again, future case-law will hopefully shed light on the meaning of 'benefit'. As for now, and 'with due caution, "benefit" can reasonably be interpreted as encompassing overcoming the limitations created by incapacity, so as to permit something which the adult could reasonably be expected to have chosen to do if capable'.[674]

The treatment is necessary

It is argued that this requirement in fact creates 'a positive obligation to take appropriate informal steps, if feasible and reasonable, where intervention would otherwise be necessary'.[675]

If a situation would be best served and resolved by taking informal steps, ie steps outside the scope of the Act (eg intervention orders, guardianship), it is argued that such a course would be preferable. Informal steps could take the form of mechanical devices that would facilitate communication; or a change of environment that would make the adult more comfortable and able to relax. It is argued that 'it may be possible to remove the problem rather than impose intervention upon the adult'.[676]

Similarly, if there is already a structure of formal measures in place for the adult's benefit, then on the face of it, it would not appear necessary to add to these already existing measures. Indeed, unless a new intervention is required to satisfy a need that cannot be satisfied otherwise, it would only be seen as a (potentially additional) hindrance to the adult's freedom.

However, if it appears that an intervention is paramount to safeguard and/or promote the adult's welfare, and that the latter cannot be achieved without the intervention in question, then it is argued that such a measure qualifies as necessary and should thus be enforced for the benefit of the adult.

---

[672] eg avoid or remove a discomfort or danger
[673] eg improve or develop well-being
[674] supra n.663, Ward Adrian D, *Current Law Statues 2000*, vol. 3, *asp*.4, at pp. 4–12
[675] supra n.663, Ward Adrian D, *Current Law Statues 2000*, vol. 3, *asp*.4, at pp. 4–12
[676] supra n.663, Ward Adrian D, *Current Law Statues 2000*, vol. 3, *asp*.4, at pp. 4–12

The treatment is the least restrictive

If the treatment is deemed necessary to the safeguarding and/or promotion of the adult's welfare, the intervention should not go beyond that which is necessary to achieve this goal. This means that an intervention on behalf of an 'incapable' adult should have the least restrictive consequences on the adult's freedom and generate the minimum disturbance possible in his or her life.

In commenting on the AWI(S)A 2000, Adrian D Ward[677] states that this principle operates at three levels, which include 'the choice of procedure; the choice of powers conferred; and the decisions and actions, on an ongoing basis, of appointees and others authorised to act'.

The choice of procedure would arguably refer to a measure which is not necessarily the simplest, but rather one that does not impede on the adult's freedom to too great an extent.

The choice of powers conferred would presumably suggest that there are different degrees of seriousness between the various modes of intervention covered by this Act – it is argued that guardianship is a more restrictive measure compared to intervention orders and powers of attorney. Indeed, a continuing power of attorney means that the adult has no or little control over decisions concerning his or her financial affairs and property. An intervention order, on the other hand, seems to be a more punctual response that focuses on a specific issue to which the adult lacks the mental capacity to apply his or her judgement – for instance, in relation to giving his or her consent to a medical treatment. Guardianship, by contrast, can be far more invasive into the adult's life as it can cover virtually all of these situations, ie financial affairs, consent to medical treatment, as well as decisions on general welfare issues.

Indeed, an individual applying for a guardianship order to the Sheriff Court will stipulate which powers, on behalf of the adult, they wish to be granted in the order. Each adult has an array of powers, rights and freedoms that they can exercise and enjoy, which are guaranteed and/or protected in law. This range of rights is also referred to as 'a menu of powers', from which an applicant for a guardianship order will select the ones that they believe they should exercise for and on behalf of the 'incapable' adult. 'These might range from control of aspects relating to the adult's financial affairs and property, to matters of personal welfare such as where the adult will live, how they will spend their time, aspects of consent to medical treatment, what type of services the adult will receive and so on'.[678]

The issue that arises here is therefore to determine the extent to which certain powers should be granted to an individual who will be acting for an 'incapable' adult. It is argued that 'the powers granted to a guardian should be limited to the minimum necessary'.[679]

As regards the appointees, in making their decisions in respect of the healthcare and welfare of the adult they represent, they should refer to the principle that any measure that they decide to take must be the least restrictive possible.

11.5.4 Liability under the AWI(S)A 2000

11.5.4.1 Limitation of liability Section 82 AWI(S)A 2000 provides that a person who has authority under an intervention or guardianship order, or a power of attorney, shall not be

---

[677] supra n.663, Ward Adrian D, *Current Law Statues 2000*, vol. 3, *asp*.4, at pp. 4–13
[678] supra n.668, *Guidance and Workbook for Social and Healthcare Staff* on AWI(S)A 2000
[679] supra n.663, Ward Adrian D, *Current Law Statues 2000*, vol. 3, *asp*.4, at pp. 4–13

liable for a breach of duty if their act or omission was performed in good faith, in accordance with the general principles of the AWI(S)A 2000, and was reasonable given the circumstances. Indeed, section 82 stipulates that there will be no liability if it is proven that they either a) acted reasonably and in good faith and in accordance with the general principles set out in section 1; or that they b) failed to act and the failure was reasonable and in good faith and in accordance with the said general principles.

There are thus three requirements that the defender would have to meet to escape liability:

1. They acted reasonably

It is argued that the test here would be an objective one, that is, reasonableness would be assessed according to what the reasonable and ordinary person in the defender's position would have done in the same circumstances.[680]

2. They acted in good faith

'Good faith' in this context has not been given any interpretation or statutory definition. Again, this means that 'good faith' will be assessed on a case-by-case basis, depending on the specific facts of each situation.

The principle of good faith has been used in contract and tort law cases, for instance. From this case-law, it is argued that the term 'good faith' suggests the presence of notions such as 'fairness', 'disclosure', 'misrepresentation' and 'advice'.[681] It could therefore be argued that acting in 'good faith' implies being aware of all the potential consequences inherent in a decision to intervene in the adult's life, that due consideration was given to the adult's feelings and wishes, and/or to any other individual who has an interest or is responsible for the adult's welfare; and that the defender, after assessing the situation, acted accordingly.

It could also be argued that in 'good faith' means that the defender did not have any ulterior motive in acting as he did, and that the sole reason for intervening was the safeguarding and promotion of the adult's welfare. This idea would tie in quite naturally with the following requirement that they must have acted in accordance with the general principles laid down in AWI(S)A 2000.

3. They acted in accordance with Section 1 AWI(S)A 2000

As stated before, these principles are that the intervention must be beneficial, necessary and the least restrictive invasion to the adult's life and freedom. Furthermore, an individual who has authority under AWI(S)A 2000 to act on behalf of an incapacitated adult must consult with the adult and other relevant people. In other words, a course of action would be discussed by the members of a multi-disciplinary panel who would consider the views, positions and options available although the responsibility to make a decision will ultimately lie with the person entrusted with the authority to act.

11.5.4.2 Section 83(1) AWI(S)A 2000 This section has created a new offence of **ill-treatment** and **wilful neglect**. This section provides that when a person has been found guilty of

---

[680] For further details, refer to section 11.3.1.3. on Standard of Care, in this chapter
[681] See, for instance, *Mumford/Smith v Bank of Scotland* [1994] SLT 1288

this offence in courts of summary jurisdiction, they shall be imprisoned for a maximum of six months or be subject to a fine; if they are charged and convicted on indictment in the higher courts, then their sentence could be a maximum of two years in prison or a fine, or both.

Again, there is no further explanation as to what ill-treatment and wilful neglect refer to in practical situations. It is argued, however, that this offence should be read in conjunction with Article 3 of the Human Rights Act 1998, which provides that 'no one shall be subjected to torture or to inhuman or degrading treatment or punishment'.[682]

11.6 Rights, Risks and Limits to Freedom – Guidance for the Use of Restraint[683]

'This guidance sets out a number of general principles that the Commission believes apply to the use of restraint in any setting. These general principles must be taken into account when restraint is being considered in the care of any person who has a mental impairment ... The guidance is intended to help care providers in the preparation of their own policies on restraint and should be considered alongside the standards produced in Scotland by the National Care Standards Committee.'[684]

The National Care Standards Committee (NCSC) was set up in 1999 in order to devise a general standard of care throughout Scotland, which includes the following principles: dignity, privacy, choice, safety, realising potential, equality and diversity for the people who are being cared for. The purpose of these standards is to enable service users to be recognised and accepted as individuals by improving the quality of care they receive, providing them with guidance on what to expect from care services, and promoting the awareness and respect of their rights and freedoms.[685]

The MCWS document focuses on the use of restraint that might be a daily occurrence or routine in care settings and are not always detected as such. So far, this report has focused on situations where there is no alternative to the use of physical interventions and they are used as a last resort. However, physical restraints can take many forms and the MWCS document deals with forms of restraints that are less apparent and that cover situations that are not necessarily synonymous with conflict *per se*, ie force is not always used, and restraint might be covert or indirectly performed.

11.6.1 Defining restraint The Guidance gives restraint the following definition: 'in its broadest sense, restraint is taking place when the planned or unplanned, conscious or unconscious actions of care staff prevent a resident or patient from doing what he or she wishes to do and as a result is placing limits on his or her freedom'.[686] It is thus to be understood that restraint here is about limiting an individual's freedom of choice and action by performing an act that goes against the individual's wishes; the situations here do not particularly involve risk of violence to staff, but rather risk of injury or self-harm to the patient.

---

[682] For further details, refer to Chapter 9 on Human Rights Law

[683] Mental Welfare Commission for Scotland (MWCS), November 2002 – *Principles and Guidance on Good Practice in Caring for Residents with Dementia and Related Disorders and Residents with Learning Disabilities where Considerations is Being Given to the Use of Physical Restraint and Other Limits to Freedom*

[684] supra n.683, MWCS, p. 4

[685] See Scottish Executive weblink: http://www.scotland.gov.uk/health/standardsandsponsorship/default.asp for further information

[686] supra n.683, MWCS, p. 2

The Guidance draws a difference between the direct use of force in restraint situations, and indirect, 'softer' restraint methods that also affect incapacitated people in a care setting.

While overt restraint can be achieved by directly interfering with the bodily movement of an individual through physical contact, mechanical devices or medical treatment, there are other less evident forms of intervention that can amount to restraint. As stated in the Guidance:

> '... *verbal control and psychological pressure can have as much a restraining effect on a person's behaviour as direct physical intervention ... Brusque or bullying attitudes by staff do not encourage residents or patients to ask for help, for example, to go to another room or to the toilet and can be seen as having a restraining effect on the freedom of movement of the resident concerned. Actions such as not providing someone with a walking aid, or not providing assistance with stairs are, in effect, restraint by default'.*[687]

Verbal control is discussed in the Guidance under the title of 'indirect limits to freedom'.[688] It is also referred to as *restraint as a result of interpersonal control by staff*, which means that the resident is being 'guided' without physical contact. 'These interventions may be the least restrictive interventions and may be preferable to more restrictive methods of controlling behaviour. However, where such interventions are regularly used then they should be considered as a form of restraint and be fully assessed and discussed as part of that resident's plan of care.'[689]

The concept of *restraint by default* can be particularly relevant to cases where mechanical devices and bodily interventions are used therapeutically. For instance, the use of a hip abduction splint could be argued to constitute a form of restraint on the individual wearing it, although it is usually qualified as therapeutic holding. However, since the device hinges at the hip and enables the bearer to either stand or sit, it is also argued that not providing the individual with this mechanical help could amount to a restraint by default, as it would deprive them of their autonomy. It is clearly in the interest of the individual in question to be as mobile and independent as possible. Indeed, Section 59(3) of the Regulation of Care (Scotland) Act 2001 provides that 'the independence of [the people using care services] is to be promoted'.

However, if staff are of the opinion that the individual may be at a greater risk of physical harm if 'allowed' to be mobile within the care setting, it is suggested that this position be supported by strong evidence relevant to the patient's characteristics and situation. Restraint of mobility cannot be justified by the fact that there is a shortage of staff, which means that the patient cannot be watched and there is thus a risk that they could, for example, fall and incur injury.

The MCWS states that life is not risk-free. Many activities, whether they are for professional, sport or leisure purposes, involve implicit or explicit risk-taking. Risks are quite relative in that their nature will vary according to the specifics of a situation and of the people involved. One cannot monitor every activity and every risk inherent that it carries, nor can one regulate people's risk-taking. For instance, everyone drinks fluids; however there is always a risk that one might choke on that fluid – does this mean that drinking should be restricted?

There is a suggestion that any person is entitled to take some kind of risk in their life. The issue therefore is 'if people have a right to take risk how do care staff strike the right balance between

---

[687]   supra n.683, MWCS, p. 2
[688]   supra n.683, MCWS, section 9, p. 20
[689]   supra n.683, MCWS, section 9, p. 20

freedom and harm and when should they intervene?',[690] considering that, under Section 59(2) of the Regulation of Care (Scotland) Ac 2001, they have a responsibility to ensure that 'the safety and welfare of all persons who use, or are eligible to use, care services are . . . protected and enhanced'.

It is argued that staff should assess and recognise what constitutes an acceptable risk and keep in mind that a restraint is not aimed at rendering a carer's job easier. 'When assessments of risk are made as part of a resident's care plan it is the risk to the resident that is paramount, not the risk to the establishment in which they are being cared for.'[691] Restraint should be kept to a minimum level and can only be used 'when there is a clear and unequivocal benefit to the resident'.

11.6.2 General principles The Guidance provides eight main principles that are to be observed in any care setting and which apply to any situation where restraint of 'adults with a mental impairment' is being considered.

1. Considering the use of restraint

> *'Self-determination and freedom of choice and movement should be paramount unless there are compelling reasons why this should not be so.'* [692]

Residents should be allowed and encouraged to participate in any decision concerning the potential use of restraint on them. Establishing a policy on the use of restraint is a requirement. The policy should clearly stipulate in what circumstances staff can resort to restraint, consideration must be given to the resident's right to take some degree of risk in their life, and restraint should be avoided whenever possible.[693]

2. Initial assessment

> *'When an individual resident's behaviour is such that restraint is contemplated, the first step should be to assess why the person is acting in the way that is causing concern', therefore, 'assessment of any risks should be a normal part of care planning for each resident with mental impairment. These care plans should include strategies to anticipate and manage future risks.'* [694]

When devising such strategies, an establishment should consider the health and safety risk issues, as well as recognise and acknowledge the resident's normal level of daily activities, cultural and ethnic background, and any other specific characteristics. Moreover, people who are on the outside and have an interest in the welfare of the resident should also be consulted when appropriate.

An assessment of the benefit that restraint might or will bring to the resident should also be mentioned in the care plan. 'It is highly undesirable to restrain a resident in a way which causes greater distress than the original problem.'[695]

---

[690] supra n.683, MCWS, p. 2
[691] supra n.683, MCWS, p. 3
[692] supra n.683, MCWS, section 1.2, p. 5
[693] supra n.683, MCWS, p. 5
[694] supra n.683, MCWS, section 1.5, p. 5
[695] supra n.683, MCWS, section 1.12, p. 6

3. Acceptable risk

As mentioned before, everybody has a right to take some risks. In the case of 'adults with mental impairment', staff must allow them a certain degree of freedom in this risk-taking provided the risk is acceptable. Staff must therefore weigh the pros and cons of restraining or not restraining a resident based on the acceptability of that risk: if the risk is greater if the resident is not properly restrained than if he was, then prima facie, restraint would be considered to be for the benefit of the resident.

Any discussion on the possibility of resorting to restraint must include a multi-disciplinary panel, including members of staff, the resident in question, his significant relatives, guardians, or other relevant representatives.[696]

4. Alternatives

> 'Alternatives to physical restraint should always be considered first. These may include medical, psychological or other treatments, and/or modifications of observation policy, care regimes, the resident's activities, or even of buildings.'[697]

5. Applying restraint

'If restraint is considered necessary it should be the minimum required to deal with the agreed risk, applied for the minimum possible time.'[698] When intervening in a restraining manner in the resident's life, staff must ensure that the latter is given a clear explanation, in terms that he easily understands, as to why, how and for how long the restraint shall be performed.

If a resident requires a more permanent, ie regular, use of restraint in his life, then staff should consider legal provisions such as a welfare guardianship under AWI(S)A 2000, or detention under the Mental Health (Scotland) Act 1984.[699]

'Restraint procedures should only be used by staff who have been fully trained in non-restrictive methods of care and also in the methods of restraint. A carer properly trained in restraint procedures should be less likely to feel the need to use them.'[700]

6. Continuous reassessment

> 'Any restraint used must be a considered part of the resident's individual care plan. Its use should be based on a multi-disciplinary discussion, which should be fully described in the care plan, together with the decisions taken and the arrangements for regular reviews _within specified periods of time._'[701]

> 'Each episode of restraint must be recorded in a clear standard format and must include a record of the time for which the restraint was applied.'[702]

---

[696] supra n.683, MCWS, see sections 1.13 and 1.14, p. 6
[697] supra n.683, MCWS, section 1.15, p. 7
[698] supra n.683, MCWS, section 1.15, p. 7
[699] supra n.683, MCWS, section 1.20, p. 7
[700] supra n.683, MCWS, section 1.21, p. 7
[701] supra n.683, MCWS, section 1.22, p. 7
[702] supra n.683, MCWS, section 1.23, p. 7

7. Unplanned restraint

'*If restraint has been applied in an emergency, without time to explain its use, it is most important that a full explanation and support is offered to the resident as soon as reasonably possible after the event.*'[703]

The incident should also be recorded in the care plan and the establishment's incident book.

8. Monitoring the use of restraint

'*Managers of care homes or hospitals should audit patterns of restraint use and relevant incidents or accidents. Such audit should inform local policy and practice and must be recorded.*'[704]

11.6.3 Direct physical restraint

Definition

Restraint is 'the actual or threatened laying of hands on persons to stop them from embarking on some movement or activity or following it through'.[705] Restraint is resorted to in situations where there is danger to the person in question and/or to third parties.

Duty to care

'*... Staff are expected to behave as professionals, not neglecting their charges nor putting them at unnecessary risk.*'[706]

For further details on duty of care, refer to Chapter 11.3.1.1 on Scottish Civil Law.

Guidelines

'*Direct physical restraint must only be applied under clear guidelines with careful monitoring and review, accessible to outside observers including relatives and inspection teams ... Policies on restraint should always be discussed with individual residents where possible and certainly with the immediate family when available.*'[707]

Restraint in non-health settings

'*Care staff in homes and the community should recognise ... that their duty to care effectively for their charges and not put them unnecessarily at risk is, in fact, not greatly different from the duty of nursing staff to care for informal residents.*'[708]

Informal residents are people who join in the daily activities of a residential home; however, they live in the community.

---

[703] supra n.683, MCWS, section 1.24, p. 8
[704] supra n.683, MCWS, section 1.26, p. 8
[705] supra n.683, MCWS, section 2.1, p. 9
[706] supra n.683, MCWS, section 2.3, p. 9
[707] supra n.683, MCWS, section 2.4, p. 9
[708] supra n.683, MCWS, section 2.5, p. 9

Training

> 'Restraint techniques require to be taught effectively with regular refreshers courses ... Recognised training in such techniques should therefore be an essential part of all nurse and care staff education, to ensure that the least restrictive methods are always used.'[709]

The issue raised by this statement is to determine how training in physical intervention is classed as 'recognised'. It can be argued that such recognition is synonymous with accreditation, which means that the body accrediting training organisations and programmes is nationally recognised. In this instance, the reader might refer to the BILD list of accredited organisations.[710]

It is acknowledged that accreditation, recognition and physical intervention training form an issue that would command further discussion; however this does not fall within the ambit of the present report.

11.6.4 Direct mechanical restraint

> 'The commonest form of direct mechanical restraint in use is the restraining chair for people who are mobile, or think they are mobile, but are liable to fall or otherwise injure themselves when they walk or attempt to walk. Other forms of mechanical restraint sometimes considered include limb restrictions for those who repeatedly harm themselves, and cot sides or secure sleeping bags for those who are restless at night.'[711]

When considering using mechanical restraint on a resident, staff should consider the following issues[712]:

- The resident's normal activity;
- An assessment to identify the resident's needs and consider any physical disability;
- Any alternative to using such an intervention (eg safety clothing, such as padded clothing, knee pad, helmets, etc);
- Providing an exercise programme to help improve the resident's mobility;
- Increasing staff numbers;
- Environmental factors and potential safety risk;
- The use of night attire, trays, limb restrictions and bed rails to restrict the resident's movement should be carefully assessed and discussed; alternatives should always be sought and envisaged before resorting to any of the above mentioned interventions.

11.6.5 Locking the doors
The general principle is that every individual benefits from the freedom to move and a violation or restriction of this right might have legal consequences.

[709] supra n.683, MCWS, section 2.6, p. 9
[710] weblink: http://www.bild.org.uk/physical_interventions/accredited_organisations.htm
[711] supra n.683, MCWS, section 3.1, p. 10
[712] supra n.683, MCWS, for further details, see section 3 at pp. 10–13.

Therefore, rules apply here, and an intervention restricting someone's mobility is subjected to satisfying strict criteria that there is a risk to the person in question, to staff and/or to other parties.

Shortage of staff does not justify the locking of doors, nor should a resident's restless wandering be penalized if there is no risk involved. The use of mirrors, alarms, tagging[713] and CCTV[714] might be considered instead of more direct physical restraints. Although these electronic interventions can also be seen as a violation of one's freedom, it is argued that these might be the least restrictive means of monitoring a resident's whereabouts and of supervising and ensuring his safety – provided an assessment concludes that the risks to the resident of not using these devices outweigh the risks and discomfort that might ensue by using them.

The Guidance adds that staff should consider the following issues when contemplating locking doors as a means of physical restraint[715]:

- Types of locked doors and use of double handles, code number pads, etc;

- Balance of duty between the resident's right to self-determination and the staff's duty to care for the resident's safety;

- Other residents, ie the situation of those who do not need locked doors within the establishment must be given due consideration;

- Policy on locking doors must be made available to all staff, visitors and residents;

- If a resident needs to have doors locked on a permanent basis due to repeated attempts to walk out, then provisions under the Mental Health (Scotland) Act 1984 might be considered;

- The rights of a resident to lock themselves away in his or her room;

- The design of the wards and homes within whose walls the residents circulate must be spacious enough to a) enable staff to supervise and observe residents easily, and b) allow people to walk about. Potential modifications to the design should also be envisaged as an alternative to locking doors, if arguably that is feasible and reasonable.

11.6.6 Medication restraint   Medication, in this context, refers to the use of drugs, such as sedatives and tranquilizers, *for purely symptomatic treatment of restlessness or other disturbed behaviour*.[716] A multi-disciplinary assessment of these symptoms and their causes should be conducted, and alternatives sought, before deciding on imposing a medication restraint.[717] The assessment should look into issues of monitoring, side-effects, medical responsibility, individual variation and consent.

---

[713] supra n.683, MCWS, section 5, p. 15
[714] supra n.683, MCWS, section 6, p. 16
[715] supra n.683, MCWS, sections 4.5 to 4.12, at pp. 13 and 14
[716] supra n.683, MCWS, section 8.1, p. 18
[717] supra n.683, MCWS, sections 8.2 & 8.3, p. 18

Chapter 12

Human rights law in Scotland

Introduction

The Scotland Act 1998 created a Scottish Parliament and enacts the structures, duties and powers of the Scottish Executive, the Scottish Parliament and the institutions thereby.

The Scotland Act refers explicitly to the European Convention on Human Rights and puts an obligation upon both the Scottish Parliament and the Scottish Executive to comply with the Convention Rights, therefore they cannot enact any legislation that would contravene those rights. (These provisions came into force on 1 July 1999.)

Section 29 (1) provides that 'an Act of the Scottish Parliament is not law so far as any provision of the Act is outside the legislative competence of the Parliament'. Section 29(2)(d) thus stipulates that 'a provision is outside that competence so far as any of the following paragraphs apply (. . .) if it is incompatible with any of the Convention rights or with Community law'.

Section 57(2) provides that 'a member of the Scottish Executive has no power to make any subordinate legislation, or to do any other act, so far as the legislation or act is incompatible with any of the Convention rights or with Community law'.

(Thus if any provision of any Scottish statute is in conflict with any Convention or Community rights that law gives way to the rights conferred under the Convention or under European Economic Community law.)

This chapter examines the potential impact in Scottish law of the various Articles of the Convention contained in Schedule 1 Human Rights Act 1998 (which was implemented on October 2, 2000) on the liability of those who use physical interventions in response to challenging behaviour.

12.1 Human rights and criminal law

Connor A Gearty, in *The Human Rights Act and the Criminal Law: An Overview of the Early Case-Law*,[718] observes that at first glance, there has not been much of a change in the substantive criminal law of Scotland since the introduction of the Human Rights Act 1998.

However, Gearty concedes that there might be some indirect effect on the substantive criminal law, as the case of <u>*ADT v United Kingdom*</u>[719] seems to prove.

---

[718] In Boyle A, Himsworth C, Loux A & MacQueen H (eds), *Human Rights and Scots Law*, Hart Publishing, Oxford and Portland Oregon, 2002, at pp. 293–306

[719] (2001) 31 EHRR 33

In this case, a man was convicted of gross indecency when after a police search at his home, videos and photographs of his homosexual practices with more than one partner were recovered. The man applied to the European Court of Justice and claimed that there was a violation of his private life under Article 8 of the Human Rights Act 1998, as well as a breach of Article 14 which prohibits discrimination on the grounds of sexual orientation, amongst others.

The ECHR did not question the validity of section 13 of the Sexual Offences Act 1956 which renders unlawful any homosexual activities happening in private between more than two men. The court found that:

> '*at some point, sexual activities can be carried out in such a manner that State interference may be justified, either as not amounting to an interference with the right to respect for private life, or as being justified for the protection, for example, of health or morals. However, the facts of the present case do not indicate any such circumstances. The applicant was involved in sexual activities with a restricted number of friends in circumstances in which it was most unlikely that others would become aware of what was going on. It is true that the activities were recorded on video tape, but the applicant was prosecuted for the activities themselves, and not for the recording or for any risk of it entering the public domain. The activities were therefore genuinely 'private' and the Court's approach must be to adopt the same narrow margin of appreciation as it found applicable in other cases involving intimate aspects of private life.*'

The court thus held that there had been a breach of Article 8 and 14 of the HRA 1998.

However covert this change might be, Gearty argues that 'the [Convention] does not set out to reform the criminal law: any changes that might occur are incidental to the procedural rights guaranteed in the document'.[720] Indeed, it seems that most of the changes brought about by the Act affected the criminal procedure system.

In the case of _Starrs v Ruxton_,[721] two accused persons appeared on trial before a temporary Sheriff Court. The accused appealed to the High Court arguing that there was a breach of their right to 'a fair and public hearing within a reasonable time by an independent and impartial tribunal', under Article 6 HRA 1998. Their Lordships held that a prosecution that contravenes Article 6 of the European Convention is deemed unlawful under Scottish Law.

Lord Reed thus stated:

> '*the effect given to the European Convention by the Scotland Act and the Human Rights Act in particular represents, to my mind, a very important shift in thinking about the constitution. It is fundamental to that shift that human rights are no longer dependent solely on conventions, by which I mean values, customs and practices of the constitution which are not legally enforceable. Although the Convention protects rights which reflect democratic values and underpin democratic institutions, the Convention guarantees the protection of those rights through legal processes, rather than political processes. It is for that reason that art 6 guarantees access to*

---

[720] supra n.610, Gearty, p. 295
[721] 2000 SLT 42
[722] supra n.718, _Human Rights and Scots Law_, pp. 245–274 and pp. 343–344

independent courts. It would be inconsistent with the whole approach of the Convention if the independence of those courts itself rested upon convention rather than law.'

12.2 Human rights and medical law

Graeme Laurie, in *Medical Law and Human Rights: Passing the Parcel Back to the Profession?*,[722] explains that medical law is a fairly new field that has been developing for the past three decades or so. The main feature of this discipline is that there is no clear and precise protection of certain 'fundamental rights' that a patient should be able to enjoy.

Rights, such as the right to life, the right to respect for personal autonomy, the right to privacy and the right to reproduce and found a family, which are paramount to any individual in a democratic society, are nonetheless subjected to a paternalistic attitude from the medical professional panels and the judges alike.

Scottish medical law has so far followed the same trend as in the rest of the UK. Laurie argues that this trend can be summarised thus:

- *'grudging acceptance of the right to self-determination, including the right to refuse treatment;*

- *dominance by the 'best interests' test where patient competence is in doubt;*

- *undue deference by the courts to the medical profession to determine what should be meant by 'best interests';*

- *serious reluctance on the part of the courts to intervene in the assessment of best interests; and,*

- *(...) the rarely qualified surrender by the courts of the responsibility for deciding the scope of duty of care of the medical profession to its patients, and the linking of this with the assessment of best interests.'[723]*

This view can be supported by the case of <u>*Re T (Adult: Refusal of Treatment*</u>[724] in which the patient had been involved in a car accident when she was 34 weeks pregnant. She signed a form refusing blood transfusion and was told that there was an alternative treatment. She underwent a Caesarean section; however the baby was still-born, and her condition subsequently worsened. The hospital was eventually granted a declaration that the transfusion necessary to save her life was lawful, as it was an emergency situation.

It was acknowledged that the patient's mental capacity was not impaired, and that her refusal to receive the blood transfusion was a conscious and voluntary one. Despite this, the judge considered the fact that the patient had been influenced by her mother. He then concluded that the circumstances of the case were such that her refusal did not extend to the situation as it had developed and granted the declaration sought.

Graeme further states that Scottish medical law could very well undergo some change with the enactment of the Scotland Act 1998 re-establishing the Scottish Executive.

---

[723] supra n.718, Laurie, p. 248
[724] [1993] Fam.95

PART VI

Case studies

Chapter 13

Case studies

Introduction

The basic facts of the case scenarios submitted below have been kindly provided by various sources such as care organisations (eg Voice UK), carers, parents, therapists and other professionals and bodies who wish to remain anonymous. The authors of this report have then followed these facts with the advice potentially applicable in each situation.

Reminder: The use of reasonable force in restricting the mobility of an individual can only be justified when it is reasonable to do so in a 'There Is No Alternative' situation. A TINA situation can occur either for therapeutic reasons, as part of an individual care plan or in emergency circumstances.

NB: Disclaimer

Every effort has been made to ensure that the information contained in this section is correct, or at least that it is a reasonable interpretation. However, the reader should bear in mind that a report of this nature is likely to contain some errors; that the law changes and is anyway subject to inherent uncertainties; and that individual cases possess their own unique circumstances and facts.

Cases involving the application of the law in England and Wales

13.1 Carer and employer's legal position

Jacquie is a support worker newly employed in a residential home (the home) caring for adults with learning disabilities. Some of the residents have severe challenging behaviours that are manifested through violent outbursts.

She is directed to do an observational session[725] with one particular resident, Ronan, who has cerebral palsy. Ronan is said to often become agitated and throw himself on the floor, flailing his arms and legs around and shouting.

Jacquie clearly indicates to the care manager that she is not trained in physical intervention techniques and asks for support guidelines on manual handling concerning Ronan. The only verbal instruction given to her is to stay away if and when an incident occurs, as Ronan's bedroom floor is covered with padded mats.

---

[725] This means to sit in a room and observe the person, answering to his needs (eg drinks, food)

What are the possible liabilities of Jacquie and the home if:

Jacquie stands aside while Ronan throws himself on the floor and eventually hurts himself by banging his head on the end foot of the bed?

As Jacquie would be following the care manager's instructions, she would not be personally liable for omitting to act but the home, represented by the care manager, would be vicariously liable for the injury.

The home has a duty of care towards Ronan; therefore it could be held vicariously liable in negligence. In order to avoid this, the employer could argue that although there might be breach of duty, the breach did not fall below the required standard of care demanded of them. In other words, the home would have to satisfy the 'reasonable man test', showing that it acted in a way a reasonable employer would do in the given circumstances.

The reasonableness of an action will be assessed by taking into consideration the following factors: Ronan's special characteristics, the magnitude of the risk involved when he displays a challenging behaviour, the practicality of the protection offered by the home, what is known to be common practice in this regard, social utility and the professional factor.

As regards the professional factor, if it can be proven that a responsible body of skilled professionals, ie other care homes, would find the practice deployed by the latter as proper, even if it can also be argued that a body of opinion would have used a different technique, then the home could escape liability in negligence.

If standing back while Ronan displays challenging behiour would not be recognised as proper and/or common practice, it could be deemed to be an omission to act. An omission in itself would not give rise to liability. However, in a situation where there is a contractual duty to act or a special relationship between the parties, as is the case between a care staff employer and residents, the courts might find that there is a breach of duty (see _Smith v Littlewoods Organisation_ (1987)).

If Jacquie, ignoring the guidelines, intervenes in an attempt to prevent injury occurring to Ronan?

If Ronan sustains injury, Jacquie could be charged with assault and battery. However she could plead necessity based on the facts as she believed them to be and rely on the 'best interest' principle if she believed that Ronan's physical integrity was at risk. She must show that the force she used was reasonable in the circumstances.

If in hindsight it appears that Jacquie's intervention with Ronan was not necessary, she could plead mistake; that is, she mistakenly believed that the circumstances were such that she felt compelled to intervene.

Jacquie could also possibly be liable for negligence against which she could plead necessity.

The employer can be held vicariously liable for the physical intervention performed by Jacquie even if the intervention was wrongfully performed and despite the fact that it was forbidden by the care manager. Following the reasoning in _Lister and others v Hesley Hall Ltd_ (2001) and _Mattis v Pollock_ (2002), there is a clear connection between Jacquie's intervention and the nature of her employment, and the home owes a duty of care towards Ronan, which was delegated to Jacquie. Therefore, the courts are likely to find that there was a breach in the performance of the duty of care for which the home would be held vicariously liable.

Finally, the employer might be liable for failure to provide Jacquie with a safe system of work, which could include the duty to provide training in physical intervention techniques. However, as seen in _Daws v Croydon London Borough Council_ (2001),[726] it is questionable whether a court would find the employer negligent in this respect, especially if it is argued that the physical intervention training might not have prevented the worker's injuries.

If Jacquie sustains injuries, the home could be held liable in damages for failure to provide her with:

a) a safe place of work. The home cannot discharge its duty of care by delegating to Jacquie the responsibility to take safety measures (_McCafferty v Receiver for the Metropolitan Police District_ 1977);

b) a safe system of work. As stated in _Speed v Thomas Swift & Co Ltd_ (1943), a safe system of work would cover the physical lay-out of a job and the issue of special instructions to perform it.

Jacquie could argue that she was not given proper instructions on the course of action she should take if Ronan was at risk of injuring himself.

Under this heading, Jacquie could also argue that she was not provided with appropriate physical intervention training. However, the court would have to consider liability in negligence very carefully. Based on the case of _Daws v Croydon London Borough Council_ (2001), it is submitted that a court could find the home negligent provided that (1) it is an accepted common practice to provide physical training in these circumstances, (2) that it is a measure that a reasonable employer would take and (3) the physical intervention technique would have helped Jacquie avoid incurring injury.

The courts would also have to consider the DfES Guidance on the use of physical intervention. Paragraph 4.2 provides that employers should assess the risks to both employees and service users arising from work activities, which includes the use of physical interventions. 'Employers should also establish and monitor safe systems of work and ensure that employees are adequately trained.'

13.2 Medical treatment, consent and human rights

Twenty-two-year-old Lorna has a learning disability and mental illness and refuses to eat because she says it is the only way she can exercise some control over her general behaviour. For her, it is a form of either self-privation or self-punishment for acting in a particular way.

Marie, her carer, owes Lorna a duty of care due to their special relationship. An omission to act in these circumstances by summoning appropriate help and assistance, which would mean that Lorna could starve to death, could be held negligent.

---

[726] supra, Chapter 5, Employer's Responsibility section

If Marie decides to intervene and to administer a treatment to Lorna against her will despite the fact that it would protect and maintain her health and life, Marie could face a charge of assault and battery.

Before administering the treatment to Lorna, Marie must first seek to obtain a court order rendering the proposed treatment lawful.

In _Re T (Adult: Refusal of Treatment)_,[727] in a situation where doctors who cared for an individual whose life was in danger and believed her refusal to consent to a treatment that might save her was not an informed refusal, the court held the doctors should seek a declaration acknowledging the legality of the recommended treatment before intervening.

The court is likely to overrule Lorna's refusal to consent to treatment since it would be in her best interest to save her life. This position would be the same if Lorna was a minor. It should be made clear that the doctrine of medical necessity might be used to justify emergency treatment if to do otherwise would lead to Laura's imminent death.

In _Re W (a minor) (Medical Treatment: Court's Jurisdiction)_,[728] a sixteen-year-old girl under the care of the local authority suffered from _anorexia nervosa_. The local authority and the girl's aunt made an application under s.100 of the Children Act 1989 before the court. They sought to be allowed to give her medical treatment recommended by her doctors despite her refusal to consent to the treatment. The Court of Appeal allowed the local authority to go ahead with the treatment taking into account the girl's wishes, yet finding it in her best interest that her refusal to consent should be overruled.

Although it could be argued that such an order could contravene art.3 HRA 1998 as it would constitute an inhuman and degrading treatment, the fact that Lorna is refusing to eat could amount to a delayed suicide attempt. An omission to intervene could infer that Marie is 'assisting' Lorna in her suicide attempt. According to the ECHR in _Pretty v United Kingdom_ 2002, Article 2 (right to life) of the Convention cannot be interpreted as conferring a right to die, nor does it create 'a right to self-determination' that would entitle Lorna to choose death over life.

13.3 Carer victim of assault, self-defence

Michael, who is twenty five years old, and who has a learning disability, bites his carer Alan's forearm.

Alan pinches Michael's nose in order to impede on his breathing and pull his arm out of the bite.

Alan could be charged with assault and battery. However he could plead self-defence as he was himself victim of an assault and battery.

---

[727] [1993] Fam.95
[728] [1993] Fam.64

Prima facie, such a defence would work provided the degree of force deployed by Alan is reasonable. In considering the reasonableness of Alan's reaction, it is important to bear in mind that as the carer of a vulnerable person, he owes Michael a duty of care.

If Alan reacted instinctively and believed that pinching Michael's nose was necessary to disengage himself, and if Alan did not wilfully attempt to inflict undue pain on Michael, then this would be strong evidence in support of his claim of self-defence. For the defence to succeed though, it must be an action that a reasonable person in Alan's particular circumstances would have taken (*DPP v Armstrong-Braun* 1999).

It is thus submitted that if pinching is considered excessive in the circumstances in that a reasonable carer would have taken a different and less drastic measure, then Alan will not benefit from the defence. In assessing the reasonableness of the pinching it might also be relevant to consider the degree of psychological harm and physical injury that Michael might incur.

Alan forces Michael's mouth on his forearm so as to exercise a pressure on the mouth and make the bite difficult to hold for Michael.

The same reasoning and principle of reasonableness apply here. However, it is relevant to mention that forcing the forearm in the mouth in order for the bite to release the arm is likely to cause injuries such as damage to teeth, jaw, nose area, possible laceration, risk of infection if the skin is broken, and anoxia.[729]

This method is quite controversial. It is actually taught by some organisations. Others suggest that this method is too dangerous and is not in the best interest of an individual with a learning disability who presents severe challenging behaviour. Some training organisations are against the use of such a technique and suggest other methods of dealing with cases of biting.

Alan could be charged with assault and battery, and possibly a Section 47 OAPA 1861 offence if it appears that Alan intended to inflict some degree of harm to Michael. Alan could plead self-defence. It is submitted that if there are indeed other more appropriate methods of disengaging from a bite, then the defence would work only if these methods do not work and forcing the arm into the mouth is a last resort.

It can be argued that in a situation where Michael is known to bite his carers, the care team should be able to devise an appropriate course of action in response to his biting and settle for a physical technique that is not damaging to Michael. It is important to remember that there is a special relationship between Alan and Michael as Alan owes Michael a duty of care. That duty implies doing what is in Michael's best interest.

Ultimately, the decision will lie on the judges who will have to assess what was the best course of action and whether it was in the best interests of both parties to use this specific technique. It must be understood that judges know that they have the benefit of calm consideration of circumstances after the event. They would be slow to impose liability on a person doing no more than that which he honestly thought was in the best interests of the person with learning disabilities presenting severe challenging behaviour.

---

[729] *Positive Behavioural Management – Preventing & Responding to Aggressive Behaviour in Persons with Intellectual Disabilities*, Trainer's Manual, PRT, 1999, unit 10 – Crisis, Self Protected Strategies, (10.30 section 6).

13.4 Parental right to reasonable chastisement

Angus, who is fifteen years old and who has learning disabilities, has made repeated allegations that he is being beaten by his parents. Rose, his mother, admits that he is smacked as a reprimand for his behaviour. The practice of smacking is carried out with all her three children and she does not differentiate between her son with learning disabilities and her other children who do not have learning disabilities.

The European Court of Human Rights found that for corporal punishment to contravene Article 3 (prohibition of torture) of the Convention, the force used must reach a certain degree of severity (_A v United Kingdom_ 1999[730]).

The degree of severity will vary from case to case as one punishment might be deemed too severe in one case, and yet not so severe in another. One must consider the nature and extent of the punishment according to the individual upon whom it is inflicted.

This means that a court would look at the physical and mental effect of the smack on Angus. It would also consider Angus' learning disability and his age. The English case-law provides added guidance in that Angus must be able to understand the nature of the smack and the reason for the punishment (_R v Griffin_ (1869) and _R v H_ (2002)).

Furthermore, for Rose to avoid a charge of assault, she has to ensure that she does not use excessive force in administering the punishment to Angus and that her intention was to punish her son (_R v H (Assault of Child: Reasonable Chastisement)_ 2002). If Rose inflicted a harsher punishment than a smack onto Angus 'for the gratification of passion or rage', thus causing him unnecessary suffering, this would amount to an assault.

Whether Rose applied reasonable chastisement or assaulted her son, this case would most certainly be investigated by either the police and/or social services.

13.5 Incident recording

Jo, a 10-year-old boy with autism living in a residential special school, has sustained a number of physical injuries and bruising over a period of two years, some of which were accounted for and others which were unexplained. His mother has made formal complaints to the local authority that placed her son and to the local authority where the child resides.

Such a case would need to be investigated. If it transpires that Jo is being physically abused by members of staff, the local authority would be held in breach of a duty of care.

Following _Lister and others v Hesley Hall Ltd_ (2001), the local authority would be held vicariously liable for failing to take reasonable steps to protect and safeguard Jo in his physical, moral and educational development at the school.

If Jo is presenting the staff with challenging situations which lead them to use physical force the staff would have to justify using physical interventions and ensure these are reasonable in view of the circumstances.

[730] (1999) 27 EHRR 611

The fact that Jo has been physically marked by these interventions would suggest that he was victim of an assault and battery. This suggestion would be supported by the lack of incident recording in an incident book. Paragraph 11.3 of the DfES Guidance on Physical Interventions stipulates that whether they are planned or unplanned, these physical interventions 'should always be recorded as quickly as practicable (in any event within 24 hours of the incident) by the person(s) involved in the incident in a book with numbered pages'.

If Jo is being bullied at the school, the local authority could be held to be in breach of its duty of care for failing to take appropriate steps to stop the bullying.

13.6 Physical restraint and assault

Jack, a 12-year-old boy with autism, is living in a residential school. It is reported to his mother Mrs T. that the school has had to restrain him. His nose has been broken and there are marks where ropes have cut into him. Jack has also made allegations that he has been held down and punched.

It is submitted that the individual members of staff could be charged with the offence of assault occasioning actual bodily harm under section 47 of the Offences Against the Person Act 1861. The school may be liable in damages to Jack, for the tortious act of their employees as well damages for the potential infringement of Articles 3 (prohibition of torture) and 8 (respect for private and family life) of the Convention.

The court would need to look at the reason why, and the circumstances in which, Jack was being restrained. However, the fact that Jack sustained a nose injury and that the school has had to use rope to restrain him would be evidence of an excessive and possibly abusive use of force.

Assuming that Jack's hands were tied up and he was then held down on the floor, and subsequently punched (which might be the reason for the broken nose), the school would be held vicariously liable for its staff carrying out the assault. In these circumstances, it would be difficult to argue that the action was necessary.

It should also be remembered that teachers or other members of staff at a school do not have the right to inflict corporal punishment (s.131 SSFA 1998 and DfEE Circular 10/98).

The assault would also be in direct contravention of Article 3 HRA 1998 if is proven to be a premeditated action that has been applied for hours at a stretch and caused actual bodily injury. This would be particularly the case if the suffering and humiliation endured by Jack goes beyond what is deemed to be legitimate and reasonable when administering a punishment (*Kudla v Poland* 2000).

The assault may also be in violation of Article 8 HRA 1998 since this Article covers a person's right to physical integrity.

In order to avoid liability, the local authority would need to record the incident carefully and accurately, giving all the information including the names of the staff involved, the reason for using the physical restraint, the type of restraint employed, the date and the duration of the intervention and finally a record of any injury that staff or the child might have incurred.[731]

---

[731] DfES Guidance on the Use of Physical Interventions, para.11.3

This would support any plea of necessity, self-defence, prevention of a breach of the peace or prevention of a crime (assuming that Jack might have attempted to commit either) as a defence justifying their action.

13.7 Physical restraint, therapeutic purposes

Dennis is a five-year-old-boy with epilepsy and cerebral palsy, whose hips are being monitored for potential risks of dislocation. His parents ask the physiotherapist for some night-time splinting for their son. The parents say that such splinting is essential to prevent their son's hip position deteriorating. Previously the mother had asked the PT for a bed with high sides because the child wouldn't stay in bed at night. This had been declined because there was no therapeutic indication for this. Advice had been given on making the bedroom environment safe and a stair gate was in place at home.

If it can be medically proved that the splinting would prevent Dennis dislocating his hip, then it can be said that the splinting is for therapeutic use and as such would be in the child's best interests. It appears from the facts of this case though that the motive for Dennis' parents in asking for splinting is to restrict his movement at night time. The DfES Guidance on Physical Interventions provides that any devices usually used for therapeutic purposes cannot be used as a method of behaviour control.

On the other hand, if Dennis' parents can argue and produce evidence that Dennis is at risk of significant harm at night time, that the therapist's suggestions to make the bedroom safer have failed, then the Guidance provides that 'a decision to use therapeutic devices to prevent problem behaviour must be agreed by a multi-disciplinary team in consultation with service users, their families and advocates (. . .)'.[732]

It is submitted that the therapist cannot simply dismiss the parents' concerns. They would have a right to be heard and have their case properly assessed and eventually discussed in a multi-disciplinary meeting.

13.8 Therapeutic treatment, Article 3 HRA 1998

Colin, an eight-year-old boy with cerebral palsy affecting mainly his legs, has a home programme. The programme includes the use of some firm pressure to maintain the ranges of movement in the child's ankle joint to prevent further deformity and loss of function and also some difficult exercises. The exercises and degree of pressure required for the passive movements have been demonstrated by the physiotherapist, and the ability of Colin's father to perform these appropriately has been checked and recorded. It has been explained to the father that cerebral palsy is a permanent condition and that therapy aims to improve function not 'cure'. The challenge and difficulty of the therapy programme for the child has been explained and the need for gentle encouragement over time has been emphasised.

However, at the next appointment Colin's father says that the child is lazy and cries at anything and has to be pushed all the time. He reports that he makes the child do the exercises until he

---

[732] para 5.3

(the father) is satisfied. The father tells the therapist that she is too soft and he knows his child best.

Paragraph 8.1 of the DfES Guidance on Physical Interventions provides that 'occasionally, it may be considered in the best interests of the child or adult to accept the possible use of a restrictive physical intervention as part of a therapeutic or educational strategy that could not be introduced without accepting that reasonable force might be required'.

Although the exercises appear to be in Colin's best interests, pushing him to perform them, until his father is satisfied, to the point where Colin cries due to pain clearly is not.

It could be argued that the State is in breach of Article 3 of the Convention in failing to protect Colin from his father (see _A v UK_ [1998] 2 FLR 583; and _Z v UK_ [2002] 2 FLR 585]. It is argued that Colin is being exposed to undue and unnecessary suffering, causing him significant harm, which under Section 47 of the Children Act 1989, implies that he is suffering from ill-treatment or an impairment of his health and development.

This could amount to assault in that the father demonstrates an intention to force Colin to carry on with the exercises despite his discomfort and pain. This would also qualify as a violation of Colin's right not to be subjected to inhuman and degrading treatment (_Kudla v Poland_ 2000).

13.9 Physical intervention, policies and prevention

Mark is a 14-year-old boy who attends a residential school for children with special needs from Monday to Friday. On Wednesday morning, Mark tells his carer Damien that he is going to his mother's that evening to attend her birthday party. Damien is sceptical as the residents usually only allowed to go home at the weekend. Damien suggests that Mark calls his mother to wish her a happy birthday. Then Damien talks to his mother on the phone and she confirms that Mark is not going to the party.

Mark becomes upset when he realises that he is not going to his mother's and starts kicking and punching the walls and doors. No real damage could be caused since the building was designed for that kind of situation. However, the care manager decides to take action and to restrain Mark. Damien refuses to do so, so other carers are called to get hold of Mark and hold him down on the floor for 15 minutes until he calms down.

Damien refused to perform the physical restraint as he believed that the intervention did not meet the criteria set out in the school's policy document.

First, the policy sets out that minimal physical restraint using reasonable force may be employed to prevent or control only in cases where a pupil presents a risk or imminent danger of (a) causing physical injury to themselves, other pupils or member of staff; (b) causing damage to property, or (c) refusing to follow a reasonable request from an adult or behaving in a manner that directly challenges the order and discipline of the school.

Mark was kicking the walls and the doors. He did not try to hurt himself, or anybody else in the vicinity. The residential school is built with such events in mind so the premises could not be damaged. Mark was not asked to calm down, nor was there evidence that other pupils were in his presence. Given these facts, it is arguable that Mark should not have been held down on the floor for 15 minutes. The use of force here seems unreasonable and excessive, especially as other options were available, such trying to calm him down with soothing words considering that he was clearly upset at not being able to go to his mother's. The action by the staff was disproportionate both to the nature of the challenging behaviour and to the risk that it presented.

Second, the school policy also stresses that physical interventions should never be used to punish, cause pain, injure or humiliate a pupil. Before using a physical restraint, staff should attempt to defuse the aggressive behaviour through calm reasoning, which would give the child the chance to manage their personal conflict and work on their self-control.

In this case, there is no evidence that preventative action was even considered by the head of care, as she took the decision to intervene without looking at alternative options.

It can be concluded that the use of force in this instance was inappropriate, unreasonable, unnecessary and could qualify as an assault and battery, a breach of Articles 3 (prohibition of torture), 5 (right to liberty and security) and 8 (respect for private life) HRA 1998.

13.10 Environmental changes, seclusion, false imprisonment

Joanne, who is 32 years old and has an autistic spectrum disorder, recently moved into a residential home. When she is upset, she starts attacking people around her, trying to kick them. Physical restraint, such as trying to hold her, only leads to her screaming.

After making some observations and assessing the risks posed by the use of other measures, the staff came to the conclusion that seclusion works better for Joanne as she would calm down easily and more rapidly.

This method, however successful, cannot be inserted into an individual care plan as part of a treatment programme since it is an emergency method, only to be used as a last resort for the shortest time possible.

It could be argued that Joanne calms down when she is moved into another environment, possibly where she is alone and has no other stimuli that would make her upset. In this light, moving Joanne into another room or another area of the residence would be an appropriate measure. It would allow Joanne time and space to deal with her emotions and inner conflicts. Joanne, however, should never be put into a locked room, as this would amount to false imprisonment.

Case studies illustrating the application of the law in Scotland

13.11 Violence against carer and defences

Douglas, who is twenty five years old and has a learning disability, bites his carer Alistair's forearm.

- Alistair pinches Douglas' nose in order to impede on his breathing and pull his arm out of the bite. Or,

- Alistair forces Douglas's mouth on his forearm so as to exercise a pressure on the mouth and make the bite difficult to hold for Douglas.

Alistair would be in breach of art.3 (prohibition of torture and inhuman or degrading treatment/punishment) of the Human Rights Act 1998.

In both cases, in criminal law, Alistair could be charged with assault, if his intentions were to inflict injury or serious bodily harm upon Douglas (presence of 'evil intent'). However, if Alistair lacked the wilful intention to cause Douglas any harm by pinching his nose, then he may be charged with culpable and reckless conduct. Also, as Alistair has a responsibility towards Douglas as his carer, he could also be charged with cruel and barbarous treatment and cruel and unnatural treatment. If Douglas suffers injury as a result of Alistair's conduct, the latter could also face a charge of reckless injury.

Given the circumstances, Alistair could plead the following defences: reflex actions, self-defence and necessity due to the fact that Douglas attacked him.

If Alistair reacts instinctively in pinching the nose or in applying pressure of his forearm on Douglas' mouth, the defence of reflex action could be available (_Jessop v Johnstone_[733]). However, if his action is intentional (intention to apply physical force, not to cause harm), then it is arguable that the defence would not succeed and self-defence might be more appropriate.

If Alistair reacts as he does in order to avoid further harm to happen to him, ie to protect himself, then self-defence might be raised as a defence (_Jones (Francis Edward) v HM Advocate_[734]). The defence might work if the nose pinching or the forearm pressure are the only alternative to Douglas' behaviour and if it is recognised that the degree of force used by Alistair is reasonable in the circumstances (_HM Advocate v Doherty_[735]). It is understood that the force used must be proportionate to either the actual or potential danger.

The defence of necessity will only be available if it is recognised that Alistair's nose pinching or forearm pressure are the only alternative to a more dangerous course of action or outcome. The immediacy of the danger posed by Douglas' behaviour towards Alistair might support a claim of necessity (_Moss v Howdle_[736]) provided the use of force does not carry on after the danger has passed, for this would cancel the notion of necessity (_Ruxton v Land (Fiona Marjorie_[737]).

In civil law, Douglas (or a person acting on his behalf) could make a claim for damages for assault (intentional delict), negligence (unintentional delict) or professional liability (ie the carer has wronged his client).

On the claim for assault in civil law, Alistair could plead self-defence (if he acted for his safety), necessity (to prevent further harm to himself occurring) or provocation (reducing the amount of damages). Alistair might be liable to pay damages if found guilty: _Anderson v Marshall_[738]).

---

[733] [1991] SCCR 238
[734] [1990] SLT 517
[735] [1954] SLT 169
[736] [1997] SLT 782
[737] [1998] SCCR 1 (Sh, Ct)
[738] [1835] 13 S 1130

On the claim for negligence, Alistair could plead contributory negligence if Douglas suffers harm from Alistair's action, which was brought about by Douglas' own initial action/fault (section 1(1) Law Reform (Contributory Negligence) Act 1945 – which would reduce Alistair's responsibility and the amount of damages to pay if found guilty).

On the claim for professional liability, if Alistair can prove that his action has not fallen below the general standard of care that is to be expected from a professional in Alistair's situation, therefore, that is no breach of duty, he will not be found liable for being negligent (_Gordon v Wilson_[739]).

13.12 Parental right to reasonable chastisement

Duncan, who is 15 years old, has learning disabilities and has made repeated allegations that his parents are beating him. Caitlin, his mother, admits that he is smacked as a reprimand for his behaviour. The practice of smacking is carried out with all her three children and she does not differentiate between her son with learning disabilities and her other children who do not have learning disabilities.

Caitlin would be in breach of art.3 (prohibition of torture and inhuman or degrading treatment/punishment) of the Human Rights Act 1998.

On the face of it, Caitlin could be charged with criminal assault or under Section 12(1) Children and Young Person's (Scotland) Act 1937, Caitlin could be charged with wilful assault and ill-treatment.

As a result of the limited reform of Scots law in relation to the parental right to use physical punishment,[740] Caitlin may raise the defence of justifiable assault as provided for in the Criminal Justice Scotland Act 2003. If she raises this defence in any proceedings which may result in court, then the court has to decide: the nature of what was done, the reason for it and the circumstances in which it took place; its duration and frequency; any effect (whether mental or physical) which it has been shown to have had on Duncan; the child's age; and the child's personal characteristics, including the child's sex and state of health at the time the punishment was administered.[742] The court may also have regard to such other factors as it considers appropriate in the circumstances of the case.[743] Caitlin must ensure that the smacking does not include or consist of a blow to Duncan's head, shaking him or the use of an implement as the court will then not allow the defence of justifiable assault to be raised.

13.13 Physical restraint and assault

Sean, a 12-year-old boy with autism, is living in a residential school. It is reported to his mother that the school has had to restrain him. His nose has been broken and there are marks where ropes have cut into him. Sean has also made allegations that he has been held down and punched and that several members of staff have been involved in the incident.

---

[739] [1992] SLT 849
[740] see section 51 Criminal Justice (Scotland) Act 2003 generally
[741] Section 51(1) Criminal Justice (Scotland) Act 2003
[742] _Ibid_ section 51(1)(a) to (e)
[743] _Ibid_ section 51(2)

The school and the staff would be in breach of Articles 3 (prohibition of torture, inhuman and degrading treatment/punishment) and 8 (respect for private life) Human Rights Act 1998.

The school, as the staff's employers, could be held liable for vicarious liability in negligence if it is proven that the staff acted in the course of their employment (_Williams v A & H Hemphill Ltd_[744]). If Sean had been an adult, the school could also have been held liable for ill-treatment and wilful neglect under Section 83(1) AWI(S)A 2000.[745]

The school should have a policy document stating in what circumstances physical intervention may be employed. This document should provide staff with clear guidelines as to which techniques they can and should use and what the general procedure is to be followed in a situation which requires their physical intervention. In _Rights, Risks and Limits to Freedom_[746] guidance is provided on what such policy documents should contain.[747]

If the actions taken by the staff were not authorised by the school, the school might not be found vicariously liable for negligence (_Neville v C & A Modes Ltd_[748]). However, if the school policy on physical restraint authorises staff to physically intervene, but the intervention is not done/performed properly (perhaps due to a failure to comply with the guidelines), the school can still be held vicariously liable (_Taylor v City of Glasgow District Council_[749]). Finally, if the members of staff acted out of a personal interest which can be dissociated from their employment duties, the school will not be found vicariously liable for their actions (_Kirby v National Coal Board_[750]).

In criminal law, members of staff, who can be identified for having committed the actions against Sean, could be charged with assault (if 'evil' intent is present), culpable and reckless conduct, cruel and barbarous treatment and cruel and unnatural treatment, reckless injury and/or with wilful assault and ill-treatment under Section 12(1) Children and Young Person's (Scotland) Act 1937.

To the charge of assault, the staff could plead self-defence if they were attempting to protect themselves or a third party from harm, or Sean from injuring himself. They could also plead necessity if the circumstances in which they have to use force on Sean are such that physical intervention is the only alternative.

Under Section 16(A) Standards in Scotland's Schools Act 2000 where members of staff act in a way that is unlawful in order to prevent 'immediate danger of personal injury; or immediate danger to the property of any person', then such staff could not benefit from pleading this as a justification for their action. Only if the action taken to prevent immediate danger can be shown to be lawful ie not using corporal punishment in any form, will the defence under the statute be available.

However, the broken nose and the rope cuts on Sean's wrists suggest that the use of force was far from reasonable or proportionate to any danger arising in a school setting. The response from the staff appears to be unlawful and would be very difficult to justify.

[744] [1966] SLT 33
[745] Adult With Incapacity (Scotland) Act 2000
[746] See Guidance n.683 supra
[747] See Chapter 11, Civil Law in Scotland, para. 11.6.2
[748] [1945] SLT 33
[749] [1997] SLT 537
[750] [1959] SLT 7

Staff cannot plead lawful defence as, under Section 16 Standards in Scotland's Schools Act 2000, physical chastisement in a school setting is prohibited; and section 16(1) stipulates that any form of corporal punishment by members of staff cannot be justified.

In civil law, the identified members of staff could be liable for assault and/or injuries to liberty (intentional delicts); for negligence and/or professional liability (unintentional delicts).

As regards liability for assault, staff could plead self-defence, necessity and possibly provocation. However, again, the extent and nature of the injuries suffered by Sean seem to indicate that the use of force was excessive. It is therefore doubtful that any of these defences would be successful.

As regards liability for injuries to liberty (restraint), staff could plead lawful arrest (if Sean was committing or about to commit a crime/offence/delict) or statutory power to detain the mentally ill under Section 18 Mental Health (Scotland) Act 1984 (if Sean presented a danger to himself, staff or third parties). Again, the same doubts on the viability of these defences arise due to the apparently excessive (and most probably inappropriate) use of force on Sean.

As regards the liability for negligence, the school and staff could plead contributory negligence (if Sean acted in such a way as is similar to Douglas's case above (see para 13.11) or joint fault (ie the failure of both the school and staff contributed to the negligent act causing harm to Sean. (_Anderson v Ayr and South Ayrshire Local Committee of St Andrew's Ambulance Association, and The Western Scottish Motor Traction Company Limited_[751]).

As regards professional liability, if both the school and staff can demonstrate that they have not acted in a manner which falls below the general standard of care expected of professionals in their field, they might avoid liability (_Gordon v Wilson_[752]).

---

[751] [1943] SLT 258
[752] [1992] SLT 849

Appendix A

Feedback on physical intervention training with a physical intervention training organisation

Introduction

The purpose of the Appendix is to set out the experiences of one of the researchers in attending one course run by one of the co-funders of the report in the techniques of managing challenging behaviour. This is an organisation which is formally accredited by BILD and the organisation has given permission for this account to be reproduced here so that all can learn from the comments and observations made.

Feedback on physical intervention training with a physical intervention training organisation

The lack of staff training in Physical Intervention is a major problem, both for the individual with a learning disability and challenging behaviour and the carers. There are several issues here that need to be addressed:

(1) The lack of formal training and accreditation;

(2) The absence of cohesion and consensus between the various P.I. training organisations;

(3) The lack of clear, precise and engaged legal guidance and structure about the application of physical intervention.

One of the researchers went on a three-day course with a specialist training organisation in the techniques of 'Management of Challenging Behaviour' in August 2002.

The first session was concerned with the 'Law in Relation to Assault' and the view was formed that this would need more emphasis and clarity in the future. This section covered assault & battery, self-defence, reasonable force, health and safety, duty of care, acting in good faith, best practice and the paramountcy principle.

Although the session did attempt to explain the issue of assault, the view was that there was confusion about the difference between assault and battery. This particular part of the training would need to lay out clearly what exactly the offences of battery, assault, negligence and other relevant ones are in order to give the participants a full perspective of the importance of the law in relation to the use of physical restraints.

The handout given after the training does mention that clear guidelines and policies are needed for staff to be protected. However, the training should also be a tool to make the participants aware of the legal implications and responsibility of using force in dealing with challenging behaviours – in these particular situations, ignorance of the law is no excuse. Hopefully, this report will bring some backbone to this particular part of the programme.

The participants were told that in TINA situations they could possibly use reasonable force. However, very little information was given as to what amounts to reasonable force. This is an important issue as the carer must be able to assess whether the force used is commensurate to the situation. More guidance on the concept of force and of what is reasonable seemed necessary.

The session also stressed the importance of the paramountcy principle, which is concerned with the individual's best interest, the use of less aversive physical interventions in dealing with challenging behaviours and the desire to proceed with the most reasonable course of action.

The other two days of the training were devoted to learning about techniques of management of challenging behaviours, which meant opening the participants' minds to alternative interpretations of challenging situations. Participants were encouraged to think before reacting to a situation. They were led to question the function or reason behind the challenging behaviour instead of assuming that the behaviour or violence happened unexpectedly and for no obvious reason. As stated in the handout, 'we should always be attempting to understand human behaviour no matter how confusing or complicated it would appear on the surface. Challenging behaviours are by nature complicated and difficult to understand'.

The training organisation used pertinent observation skills to understand the possible 'why/ what for' behind a challenging situation, and simple language to convey it to participants. When a carer is in a position where he or she feels under an obligation to use force in order to deal with what he or she perceives as a violent situation, the training organisation argues that it is possible to have an alternative perspective on the reasons for this situation. The carer may then realise that (1) the 'challenging' behaviour is misinterpreted, thus (2) the physical intervention is not always needed, and (3) could be disproportionate in the circumstances of the case.

The training organisation gave a list of some of the common causes for challenging behaviours:

Being unable to communicate a need

Inability to communicate one's needs can lead to violence.

Being confused

Certain demands are made on people with a learning disability that can be too demanding or misunderstood by the service user. Misunderstanding often generates confusion and fear which can then be expressed through violent outbursts.

Being in pain

Expressing how one feels by behaving in a challenging manner can be due to problems communicating pain.

Medication changes

'Medication changes are often routine and well intentioned, but lack of adequate explanation may lead to a sequence of events that a person with learning difficulties may not understand. This may lead to confusion and can occasionally precipitate aggression and violence.'

Inactivity

Inactivity contributes to boredom and dwelling on one's problems, which can lead to a need for change, stimulation, and action translated into aggressive behaviour.

Attention-seeking behaviour

Although not so common, when this is the case, the participants were encouraged to wonder about the reasons why the individual with a learning disability is seeking attention.

Changes in routine

This can create a situation of confusion and fear, leading to violence, in particular for people with an autistic spectrum disorder.

Environmental effects

This is concerned with how the individual with a learning difficulty relates to his/her environment, including other people, the layout of furniture, the colour scheme, the lights, the noise, personal space, etc.

Delusional thoughts

Often related to people with a mental illness, delusional thoughts are explained by paranoia, thoughts or voices heard by the individual that either tell them to do something or that a danger to their life is imminent.

When explaining each of these possible causes, the training organisation also attempted to make these more real to the participants by asking them to try to identify with what it would feel like to be in a situation where they would be unable to communicate their needs. For instance, what their reaction would or could be in these circumstances, and how frustrated they would be. For example, picture a situation when one is working on a PC and something goes wrong – all the work is lost and cannot be retrieved, or so it seems. One's reaction can be frustration for all the work lost, powerlessness at not being able to get it back, and possibly anger, which can be expressed by cursing at and banging on the computer. Could this be interpreted as a challenging behaviour? How would this be dealt with by onlookers?

The techniques taught by the training organisation are gentle, non-aggressive and non-invasive. Their aim is to help the carer not to react to a situation on an impulse that could precipitate violence, but to act in a positive and safe manner in order to keep a situation steady, to diffuse a possible problem and to protect oneself and the other individual. The technique is about keeping calm and in control of a situation that should not get out of hand.

Throughout the training, the participants were made aware of their role in inducing or diffusing a possible challenging situation, in (in)voluntarily contributing to a specific behaviour, and in keeping or failing to keep an open and unbiased view of a situation. The participants are also reminded that dealing with a challenging behaviour is not a battle of will between the carer and the person cared for; it is about caring for the needs of the latter, which implies understanding these needs and how they are expressed.

An example of a scenario played out during the training was that of a person with a learning disability who attempts to touch a carer's head. The movement might be brusque, and may even seem threatening to the carer. Whether the service user's intention is to stroke the carer's head or to pull their hair, the action recommended was not to grab at the service user's hand, but to gently push it away so as to redirect it without causing distress to them. Grabbing the client's hand or wrist can contribute to a violent outburst which will result in a battle of strength, which is not the desired outcome.

Covering the training in just three days did not seem to be adequate. There was quite a lot to take in and to digest for the participants, particularly if they came for the first time and most of the philosophy of the training organisation represented a new concept to them.

Not only should the training be spread over a longer period of time for the participants to fully understand the importance of the law, to integrate the ideas behind the techniques of behaviour management, and to remember and practise these techniques more thoroughly, but there should also be follow-up training. Refreshing people's minds after a certain time is essential if the training is to be effective in providing the participants with long-term benefits, up-to-date skills and coping strategies.

The case of one of the participants illustrates this point. She had attended a previous training course some time before coming back on this particular one. She was attending a second P.I. training course because she had been involved in a situation where she was faced with a violent behaviour from a service user, a situation in which she felt she had no control. In shock, she totally forgot what she learned in training in order to be able to defuse such a situation. She was also physically injured. The view was that the second time she came for the training it was as much about managing challenging behaviour as it was about learning how to protect herself in the future.

However, since it is the responsibility of the employing services to arrange for such P.I. training to be provided, it is also up to them to ensure that follow-ups are also offered. Besides the fact that on-going training, or at least regular refresher sessions, is recommended, it also appears that the carers themselves would welcome some form of counselling, support or de-briefing session. Indeed, there is a need for emotional release after carers have had to deal with a challenging situation – carers need to unwind, to talk about their experience so that they can free their mind of tension and any emotional burden.

Appendix B

Glossary of terms

Abuse

The notion of abuse is defined in the DoH Guidance *No Secrets* as 'a violation of an individual's human and civil rights by any other person or persons'.[753]

Adult

Although there is no specific statutory definition of this term, the Family Law Reform Act 1969 provided in England and Wales for the reduction of the age of majority from twenty-one to eighteen. Section 1 (1) of that Act provides that, since 1971, a person attains 'full age' on attaining the age of eighteen instead of on attaining the age of twenty-one. Generally, the same is true for Northern Ireland and Scotland, but the law in Scotland provides that an adult, for the purposes of the Adults With Incapacity (Scotland) Act, is defined as a person who has attained the age of 16 years (Section 1(6) AWISA 2000). This follows the definition set out in the Age of Legal Capacity (Scotland) Act 1991 which provides, in section 1(b), that 'a person of, or over the age of, 16 years shall have legal capacity to enter into any transaction'.

Section 1(6) AWI(S)A 2000 provides, however, that:

'an adult may be deemed "incapable" where he or she is incapable of the following:

a) *acting; or*
b) *making decisions; or*
c) *communicating decisions; or*
d) *understanding decisions; or*
e) *retaining the memory of decisions,*

as mentioned in any provision of this Act, by reason of mental disorder or of inability to communicate because of physical disability. However a person shall not fall within this definition by reason only of a lack or deficiency in a faculty of communication if that lack or deficiency can be made good by human or mechanical aid (whether of an interpretative nature or otherwise) and "incapacity" shall be construed accordingly'.

Assault

In both civil and criminal law, an assault occurs when a person intentionally or recklessly does an act which causes another to apprehend immediate and unlawful personal violence ie when a person is in fear of being attacked by another.

---

[753] Section 2, para 2.5, at p. 9 – DoH 2003 http://www.doh.gov.uk/pdfs/nosecrets.pdf

Capacity

In relation to the criminal law there is a presumption in England, Wales and Northern Ireland that a person aged ten or over is capable of committing a crime whereas in Scotland there is a lower age limit of eight. This presumption may, however, be rebutted by the presenting of evidence as to a lack of mental capacity due to disability or mental illness. Under the law of torts, or in Scotland, delict, there is no defence of minority available to children. A child is therefore as likely to be sued as an adult in tort or delict, although the same defences will be available.

In relation to medical treatment, capacity is the right to express one's mind by determining what is the best or chosen course of action to be taken in a given situation. The concept of capacity implies that a person has the ability to:

- comprehend the nature of their condition and the proposed treatment;

- understand the information and the possible consequences of consenting or not to such a treatment, in terms of the principal benefits and risks; and

- make a decision based on the understanding of the information provided. The level of capacity required depends upon the seriousness or gravity of the decision which needs to be taken, and so capacity is reviewed on an individual case-by-case basis.

The basic principles of capacity in relation to those whose position may be dealt with under the mental health legislation are laid out in paragraph 15.10 of the Mental Health Act 1983 'Code of Practice' and broadly cover the same issues as those outlined above.

Carer

A **parent carer** is a parent who cares for their disabled child, who may of course be an adult.[754] Where the child is still chronologically a child, and therefore a child under the relevant legislation then under section 2(9) Children Act 1989, (Article 5(8) C(NI)O 1995, and s.3(5) C(S)A 1995) a person with parental responsibility may arrange for some or all of this responsibility to be met by one or more persons on their behalf. Thus, the carer does not have parental responsibility as such, although the parent has delegated some aspects relating to the care, control and safety of their child to the carer.

A **carer, other than a parent or other person with parental responsibility**, in the context of this work is a person who is involved in providing for the care, control and safety of children, young people and adults with learning disabilities presenting severe challenging behaviour. 'Carer' could thus encompass day-centre workers, residential workers, paid respite carers, health workers, employees of voluntary organisations and of local authority social services departments, and many would thus be defined under the Care Standards legislation as 'social care workers' (see at page 281 of this *Glossary of Terms* for a full explanation.)

An **unpaid carer**. This may well include parents and other relatives, who may thus qualify for assistance under the Carers (Recognition and Services) Act 1995 which also applies to Scotland. An unpaid carer is someone who has not entered into a contract to care for another, or is not

---

[754] Caring About Carers, http://www.carers.gov.uk/whatis.htm

providing such care as a volunteer for a voluntary organisation. Under s.1(1) of that Act, a carer is someone who provides or intends to provide (on an unpaid basis (ss3)which excludes those who are contractually providing care or doing so as a volunteer on behalf of a voluntary organisation) a substantial amount of care on a regular basis for the relevant person (ie the person in need of care). An unpaid carer has also been described in DoH Guidance as someone who looks after 'a relative or friend who needs support because of age, physical or learning disability or illness, including mental illness'.[755]

A care worker is defined in Section 80(2) Care Standards Act 2000 as:

'(a) *an individual who is or has been employed in a position which is such as to enable him to have regular contact in the course of his duties with adults to whom accommodation is provided at a care home;*

(b) *an individual who is or has been employed in a position which is such as to enable him to have regular contact in the course of his duties with adults to whom prescribed services are provided by an independent hospital, an independent clinic, an independent medical agency or a National Health Service body;*

(c) *an individual who is or has been employed in a position which is concerned with the provision of personal care in their own homes for persons who by reason of illness, infirmity or disability are unable to provide it for themselves without assistance.'*

A **care provider for adults** is defined in Section 80(7) Care Standards Act 2000 as:

'(a) *any person who carries on a care home;*

(b) *any person who carries on a domiciliary care agency;*

(c) *any person who carries on an independent hospital, an independent clinic or an independent medical agency, which provides prescribed services; and*

(d) *a National Health Service body which provides prescribed services.'*

Carers' and local authorities' responsibilities

Duties of, and to, carers in general

The Department of Health White Paper, *Valuing People*, sets out four key principles in a programme to help improve, safeguard and guarantee the rights of children, young people and adults with learning disabilities, which are: rights, independence, choice and inclusion.[756]

Rights: 'People with learning disabilities have the right to a decent education, to grow up to vote, to marry and have a family, and to express their opinions, with help and support to do so

---

[755] Caring About Carers, http://www.carers.gov.uk/whatis.htm, April 2003, DoH. According to this website, there are approximately 5.7 million people who fit this definition in Great Britain today, although the General Household Survey referred to in debates on the 1995 Act, put the figure at 6.8 million. (See Hansard, H.C. Vol 258 col 426). In Caring about Carers the Government makes a commitment to providing details of the services or benefits affecting carers on the Internet.

[756] *Valuing People*, Chapter 2, pp. 23–26, DoH 2001

where necessary.' The overall aim is to ensure the promotion and safeguarding of people with learning disabilities' civil and legal rights and to eradicate social discrimination.

Independence: 'while people's individual needs will differ, the starting presumption should be one of independence, rather than dependence, with public services providing the support needed to maximise this. Independence in this context does not mean doing everything unaided.'

Choice: '. . . everyone should be able to make choices. This includes people with severe and profound disabilities who, with the right help and support, can make important choices and express preferences about their day to day lives.'

Inclusion: 'inclusion means enabling people with learning disabilities to do . . . ordinary things, make use of mainstream services and be fully included in the local community.'

As part of the Government's objectives, carers and local authorities have a responsibility a) to increase and promote disabled children's chances to benefit from adequate educational, social and health care; and b) to enable people with learning disabilities to reach a certain level of independence and autonomy which would allow them more control over their own day-to-day lives, including the planning of their person-centred care plan.

Furthermore, carers should benefit from help and support from all relevant 'local agencies in order to fulfil their family and caring roles effectively'. In addition, unpaid carers have an entitlement to the assessment of their needs for care or the provision of services themselves under the terms of the Carers (Recognition and Services) Act 1995, which also applies to Scotland. Alternatively, the assessment under s.1(2) of the Act might conclude that they are not fit themselves to take on such burdensome responsibilities and that the person for whom they are caring must be provided instead with services under the National Health Service and Community Care Act 1990.

Carers who look after children and young people

A local authority has certain rights and duties towards carers of disabled children. Section 2(1) Carers and Disabled Children Act 2000 provides that 'the local authority must consider the assessment and decide a) whether the carer has needs in relation to the care which he provides or intends to provide; b) if so, whether they could be satisfied (wholly or partly) by services which the local authority may provide; and c) if they could be so satisfied, whether or not to provide services to the carer'.

Those carers over the age of 16 looking after children, in whatever context, would be expected to do all that is necessary to prevent the child harming him/herself or others, or exposing him/herself or others to harm with due respect to the child's functional ability rather than chronological age. (Statutory authority for this duty of care can be found in Section 1 Children and Young Persons Act 1933, which provides for the imposition of criminal liability on parents or those over 16 looking after children who fail to protect them from ill treatment, neglect or abuse; and Section 3(5) Children Act 1989, which provides for the civil standard of care, which if breached could, under the provisions of s.31 Children Act 1989, result in the removal of the child from wherever she is being cared for and the possible institution of care proceedings on the basis that the child 'is suffering or likely to suffer significant harm').

Very importantly, section 3(5)(a) and (b) (Article 6(5) C(NI)0 1995 and section 5(1) CSA 1995) provide that: 'A person who does not have parental responsibility for a particular child may (subject to the provisions of this Act) do what is reasonable in all circumstances of the case for the purpose of safeguarding or promoting the child's welfare'.

Challenging behaviour and severely challenging behaviour

The term 'challenging behaviour' is used in an attempt to designate an individual's behaviour which represents a 'challenge' to themselves, their environment (both people and property) and/or society in general. Such behaviour may be classified as 'seriously challenging' where there is perceived to be a greater risk of the individual's behaviour potentially harming himself, others, or damaging property, or where it is perceived as representing a greater challenge to the capacities of those who have to deal with both the behaviour and its consequences. The use of such terms, however, does not refer to an intrinsic 'wrongness' with the person presenting the challenge, but is rather reflective of a situation which is defined and interpreted by social factors.

Emerson *et al* (1987) defined severe challenging behaviour in the Mansell Report (1993) as:

> *'behaviour of such intensity, frequency or duration that the physical safety of the person or others is placed in serious jeopardy or behaviour which is likely to seriously limit or deny access to the use of community facilities. Ordinarily it would be expected that the person would have shown the pattern of behaviour that presents such a challenge to services for a considerable period of time. Severely challenging behaviour is not a transient phenomenon.'*

This was modified by Emerson in 1995, where he defined challenging behaviour as:

> *'culturally abnormal behaviours of such an intensity, frequency or duration that the physical safety of the person or others is likely to be placed in serious jeopardy, or behaviour which is likely to seriously limit use of, or result in the person being denied ordinary access to ordinary community services.'*[757]

The Committee on Services for Children with a Learning Disability and Severely Challenging Behaviour, established by the Mental Health Foundation in 1993 and which finally reported in 1997,[758] adopted a rather more expanded working definition of severely challenging behaviour. Thus, this Committee defined severely challenging behaviour as:

> *'Behaviour of such an intensity, frequency, or duration that the physical safety of the person or others is likely to be placed in serious jeopardy, or behaviour which is likely to seriously limit or deny access to and use of ordinary community facilities or impair a child's personal growth, development and family life. It should be emphasised that such behaviour represents a challenge to services and that definitions are therefore based on social judgements (what challenges one service or institution may not challenge another) and definitions must be considered in context.'*

---

[757] Emerson E, *Challenging Behaviour Analysis and Intervention in People with Learning Disabilities*. Cambridge: Cambridge University Press 1995

[758] The Mental Health Foundation, *Don't Forget Us – Children with Learning Disabilities and Severe Challenging Behaviour*, 1997, p. 12

The authors of this guide consider that a challenging behaviour can be more precisely or particularly described by the actual forms it can take – in other words, a challenging behaviour is arguably situation-based and socially-defined.

Child

The law in England, Wales and Northern Ireland adopts an essentially chronological approach to the definition of 'child', ie as someone who has not attained the age of majority of eighteen as provided for in s.1 Family Law Reform Act 1969 (and s.1 Age of Majority (Northern Ireland) Act 1969). When the term 'child' is used, however, it is either used specifically to denote the legal capacities attributable to such a person or to denote a relationship between two persons. For these purposes, therefore, the definition provided by both the FLRA 1969 and the CA 1989 together with the C(NI)Order 1995 has been used. Section 105(1) CA 1989 and Article 2 C(NI)O 1995 define a child as being a person under the age of 18. In Scotland, identical provision to s.1 FLRA 1969 was made by the provisions of ss 1 (1) and (2) Age of Majority (Scotland) Act 1969. In Scotland, however, changes were effected to the law on capacity of minors to enter into transactions by the Age of Legal Capacity (Scotland) Act 1991.This provided that generally children under 16 would have no capacity to enter into binding transactions. This was subject to certain major exceptions such as the power to make a will, consent to adoption and consenting to medical treatment. The Act provided, however, that those over 16 would have such general capacity to enter into transactions of a more legally binding nature such as contracts for the supply of goods and services. This approach of assuming that those over the age of 16 had general capacity to enter into transactions in Scotland was then subsequently adopted in the Adults with Incapacity (Scotland) Act 2000.

Children in need

Section 17 CA 1989 and Article 17 C(NI)O 1995 define children in need as a child who is:

- unlikely to achieve or maintain, or to have the opportunity of achieving or maintaining, a reasonable standard of health or development without the provision for him of services by a local authority;

- his health or development is likely to be significantly impaired or further impaired without the provision for him of such services;

- he is disabled.

These provisions are repeated for children in Scotland by s.93 (4) (a) C(S)A 1995 but with the addition that 'in need' is further defined as being 'in need of care and attention'. In addition, as well as the three categories of need defined in the legislation of the other jurisdictions, a fourth category of need is laid down consisting of being in need if he is adversely affected by the disability of any other person in his family.

Sections 17A and 17B Children Act 1989, (Arts 17A and B) make special provision for the making of direct payments to cover the provision of services to parents looking after disabled children, to disabled young people themselves of 16 and 17 and to any disabled person with parental responsibility for a child, where the individual wishes to choose for themselves the providers of such services to the child in need.

Similar provision is made for children in Scotland by virtue of amendments to the C(S)A 1995.

Civil law

The civil law is concerned with the regulation of conduct between individuals on a one-to-one basis and thus requires that if any person is aggrieved or injured by the conduct of another, then they must individually take action against that other person in respect of the civil wrong (sometimes referred to as a 'tort') which the conduct discloses.

A tort is defined as 'a wrongful act or omission for which damages can be obtained in a civil court by the person wronged'.[759] Civil law is concerned with actions between private individuals; assuming that there is proof of the existence of a duty of care between the two individuals, the breach of such duty by one of them (the wrongdoer, referred to in legal terms as the 'tortfeasor') will entitle the other (the person who has suffered the wrongdoing referred to in legal terms as the 'plaintiff') to bring an action against the other for damages (ie monetary compensation). Damages, however, are not the only remedy available. Depending on the issue, a plaintiff may ask for an injunction, which is an order of the court forbidding the tortfeasor from acting in a certain manner or ordering him to perform a certain act so as to avoid or prevent harm from happening to the plaintiff.

The same circumstances, which give rise to the possible prosecution of an individual under the criminal law, may also amount to the commission of a civil wrong. This means that an offender can be charged by the Police and prosecuted by the Crown Prosecution Service, (or in Scotland by the Procurator Fiscal) and may also be sued by his victim in a civil court of law. An offender can thus be convicted in the criminal court for assault and battery, and may also have to pay civil law damages to the victim in reparation for the injury that the latter has incurred. However, a civil claim for damages does not necessarily depend on a criminal conviction to succeed. Indeed, a civil action can still be brought against an offender even though the act causing the injury may not be so serious as to amount to a criminal offence, which would thus lead the Crown Prosecution Service (or the Procurator Fiscal in Scotland) not to pursue the matter before a court of criminal law.

The torts of particular relevance to those caring for adults and children with challenging behaviour include: assault, battery, false imprisonment and negligence.

Civil law defences excepting Scotland

Contributory negligence   is only a partial defence which reduces a claim for damages against a defendant by considering the plaintiff's role and contributing acts in the latter's injuries or damages.

Illegality can be raised as a defence when the defendant causes injury to the plaintiff while the latter is performing an illegal action. The general principle is that no one should benefit from a criminal enterprise.

Inevitable accident is a defence that will negate an offender's liability when the victim suffers injury as a result of an accident; ie an event that is beyond the defendant's control. An accident can be defined as a situation that cannot be avoided by any means or precautions that a reasonable person might be expected to take in the circumstances.

[759] Martin E A (ed), *Oxford Dictionary of Law*, Oxford University Press 2002

Mistake, ie a mistaken belief either of fact or law, is not a general defence and the significance of a mistake will vary from one case to another. A mistake that a reasonable man could have made in the same circumstances could be a defence.

Necessity is 'a mixture of charity, the maintenance of the public good and self-protection, and [the defence of necessity] is probably limited to cases involving an urgent situation of imminent peril'.[760] An action taken out of necessity must be justified by its reasonableness, which the court will assess on a case-by-case basis and will consider in the light of what has been done in the individual circumstances of the case, what might be deemed to be an acceptable action in the given situation and what might be deemed to be a reasonable course of action in this day and age given the circumstances.

Self-defence An individual has a right to defend himself as long as the force used for that purpose is considered proportionate to the danger. What amounts to reasonable force is a question of fact which is assessed on an individual case-by-case basis.

Statutory authority where a statute authorises an act, which without consent would normally amount to an offence of assault, battery, or false imprisonment. Such an act, if performed within the ambit of the Act's provisions, will not be an offence as the statute will provide a valid defence. (For instance, the statutory power to detain the mentally ill provided by Section 3 Mental Health Act 1983 justifies the detention of people with a mental illness who represent a threat to themselves or to the public – without this provision, the detention would amount to the criminal offence and civil tort of false imprisonment and to unlawful deprivation of liberty contrary to Article 5 (right to liberty and security) Human Rights Act 1998).[761]

Volenti non fit injuria, also known as consent, implies that a person cannot cause injury to someone who is consenting to the risk. However, this idea is tempered by the fact that consent is not merely about knowing the risk, it is also about understanding it – if there is no real understanding of the risk then there can be no consent.

Civil law defences Scotland

Compensation in Scottish Delictual Law is referred to as 'reparation' and can only occur if and when harm was caused to the victim as a result of the wrongful act of another, to which there is no valid defence. In other words, for a claim in reparation to succeed there must be a delict, which occurs where 'harm to an interest protected by the law has arisen as a consequence of a wrongful act to which there is no valid defence'. The harm suffered by the victim must be such that it is considered 'reparable' in law, and whether this is so will be determined in relation to the damage that affects an individual's personal interest, such as their physical integrity. Various defences may be raised, however, in relation to the different delicts. Ultimately, it is the court's prerogative to decide when and whether such harm is reparable or not.

Defences to assault The defences that apply to the intentional delict of assault as complete defences are: self-defence and unavoidable accident. The principle of self-defence laid down in the English civil law would arguably also apply here; that is, only reasonable and necessary force should be used when it appears that the person acting in self-defence feels that her safety or that of a third party for whom she is responsible is at risk. Necessity could possibly apply

---

[760] Rogers W V H, *Winfield & Jolowicz on Tort*, 16th edition, London & Maxwell 2002, p. 872
[761] See bibliography for full details of the article

here as well, as a carer might be in a situation where he would need to use a degree of force in order to prevent a client from harming herself, a third party or the carer himself; or if the client is about to commit a crime that cannot be stopped otherwise. Consent will also negate a liability for delictual assault if it was given to accept the risk inherent to a specific situation – if the injury that is incurred is one that was outside the scope of the consent given then it will not serve as a defence. Provocation, as a partial defence, will also contribute to reducing the damages the defender will be liable to pay the victim if found guilty of delictual assault if it is indeed proven that the defender acted on impulse due to the victim' provocation. Provocation can be either material or verbal, as the latter is considered 'a good ground for mitigating damages'.[762]

Defences to claims of 'injuries to liberty' including false imprisonment or wrongful detention:

The defence of lawful detention   On the matter of false imprisonment, the general rule that an individual cannot be detained against their will finds an exception, and thus grounds a defence, where the detention *is the result of legal proceedings,* where such a detention would constitute a legal arrest, *or if the detention is authorised by statute.* A relevant statute granting the power to detain the mentally ill is the Mental Health (Scotland) Act 1984. Under Section 18 Mental Health (Scotland) Act 1984, an individual suffering from a mental illness and presenting a danger to himself or to others, can be put under compulsory detention in a mental hospital after appropriate recommendations by two medical professionals (including a psychiatrist) have been submitted to, and accepted by a sheriff. An order for detention will be issued for a period of six months, renewable, if deemed necessary, without recourse to the sheriff. The patient and/or his nearest relative have the right to challenge such a decision before the sheriff.

Lawful arrest   the defence of lawful arrest can arise in relation to allegations of false imprisonment or wrongful detention. This includes 'citizens' arrest as well as arrest made by the police under a warrant.

Defences to negligence   Volenti non fit injuria – As has been stated by the courts, 'the successful establishment of [volenti] means that the [victim] has accepted the risk of the defender's negligence in the exercise of his legal duties and has absolved the defender from the consequences arising from that negligence'.[763]

For instance, provided the individual is legally capable, this means that a person being cared for can agree to a restraint procedure as part of her care plan, that she is aware of the risks involved in such a measure, and that she waives her right to sue the carers implementing that measure in negligence shall she suffer from physical injuries that are an inherent risk of the restraint procedure. In other words, she willingly accepts to take the risk of incurring harm. The courts have also concluded that '. . . the acceptance of risk must occur either before or contemporaneously with the act or omission constituting the negligence, and not after it'.[764]

Contributory negligence   Section 1(1) of the Law Reform (Contributory Negligence) Act 1945 stipulates that 'where any person suffers damage as the result of his own fault and partly due to the fault of any other person or persons, a claim in respect of that damage shall not be

---

[762] *per* Lord President (Hope) in <u>*Anderson v Marshall*</u> (1835) 13 S 1130, at p. 1131
[763] <u>*Sabri-Tabrizi v Lothian Health Board*</u> 1998 SLT 607, at p. 610
[764] *per* Lord Nimmo Smith, at p. 610

defeated by reason of the fault of the person suffering the damage, but the damages recoverable in respect thereof shall be reduced to such an extent as the court thinks just and equitable having regard to the claimant's share in the responsibility for the damage'. In other words, contributory negligence is not so much a defence as it is a means of reducing both one's liable responsibility and the financial cost of paying for reparation in negligence. The burden of proving that the victim has been negligent seems to lie on the defender.[765]

Joint fault   This 'defence' is particularly relevant to situations where a patient suffers harm as a result of several parties, which could include her carers (workers and managers), but also her general practitioner, occupational therapist and/or close relative; in other words, whoever is involved in caring for her and who is responsible for her well-being and her safety. Joint fault, or joint wrongdoing, occurs when there is more than one defender who is in breach of a duty of care and whose action or omission has contributed to the same delictual negligence that caused personal injury to the person cared for.

Consent (in relation to medical treatment)

'"Consent" is the voluntary and continuing permission of the patient to receive a particular treatment, based on an adequate knowledge of the purpose, nature, likely effects and risks of that treatment including the likelihood of its success and any alternatives to it.'[766] Consent is sought and should be given before any medical care, treatment or examination is performed on a patient. A person who administers medical treatment to a patient who has not given consent, or who has clearly refused to give their consent, could be liable under both civil and criminal law. The rules for valid consent will vary according to the nature of the condition that needs treating, ie whether it is treatment for a physical or mental disorder (the latter being covered by the Mental Health Act 1983). However, in general, for consent to be valid, three elements are required:

a)   *Generally, the person giving the consent must have the capacity*[767] *to do so.* Once it is established that the patient understands the particular situation, ie has capacity, their decision to consent or not is valid, whether the reasons behind the decision are (un)reasonable, (ir)rational, (un)known or (non)existent.

b)   *Generally, the person must be sufficiently informed as to the nature, purpose, potential risks and consequences of the proposed treatments, as well as to any alternative therapeutic methods available.* For those whose situations may be covered by the provisions of the Mental Health Act 1983, para. 14.13(a) *Code of Practice – Mental Health Act 1983* provides that in relation to consent to treatment 'the patient must be informed, in terms which he is likely to understand, of the nature, purpose and likely effects of the treatment proposed'.

c)   *Generally, the consent must be given freely and voluntarily.* For those whose situations may be covered by the provisions of the Mental Health Act 1983, para. 15.12 *The Code of Practice – Mental Health Act 1983* provides that 'permission given under any unfair or undue pressure is not "consent"'. Moreover, patients must be advised of their right to withdraw their consent to a treatment at any time before it is undergone.

---

[765]   supra n.586, Thompson p. 144
[766]   Department of Health and Welsh Office, *Code of Practice, Mental Health Act 1983* (MHA'83), published August 1993, para.15.12
[767]   See definition of Capacity supra

Consent and children

Under s.8(1) Family Law Reform Act 1969, the consent to surgical, medical and dental treatment of a child of 16 years of age is presumed to be an effective consent at law and no parental consent is necessary. Since _Gillick v West Norfolk and Wisbech AHA_ in 1986,[768] it is recognised that a child under 16 can be legally capable of giving consent to a treatment if they show enough maturity, intelligence and comprehension as to the nature and implications of such a treatment.

Although it is also acknowledged that parents are often the best judges as to what is in the best interest of their child, in some rare cases, the doctor might be the one best qualified to make that judgement. Where the parents refuse the treatment felt by the doctor to be in the child's best interests and the child is not deemed capable of providing the relevant consent, then the doctor must seek a court order known as a 'specific issue' order under s.8 Children Act 1989 to sanction proceeding with the treatment in the absence of such consent. The court in such circumstances will hear all the evidence and will decide the case on the basis of what is in the child's paramount interests (s.1(1) Children Act 1989).

Criminal law

A developed, civilised society will generally provide that certain type of conduct will not be acceptable and will provide that conduct to be unlawful through its criminal law. The criminal law of all the UK jurisdictions is made up of offences to be found either in statutes passed by Parliament or in Judge-made or customary law referred to as the 'common law'. In broad, general terms, the criminal law requires that before a person can be convicted it must be proved _beyond reasonable doubt_ that the person has acted in a way which is deemed criminal (the deed of _actus reus_) _and that the person has acted intentionally_ or _recklessly_ as to the consequences (the mental element or the _mens rea_). There are criminal offences, offences of _strict liability_, which do not require proof of a mental element, but these do not relate to any of the actions described in this Guide.

In contrast with civil law where a private individual may take the initiative to present an action before the courts, in criminal law the Police will consider charging the alleged offender and the Crown Prosecution Service in England and Wales, and the Public Prosecution Service in Northern Ireland or in Scotland the Procurator Fiscal (the Government Departments responsible for prosecuting an offence through the courts on behalf of the State), will consider bringing a prosecution against any individual who has committed an unlawful criminal act. If found guilty in the courts after trial or after a plea of guilty, the offender will then be sentenced. The sentence can be one of imprisonment, a compensation order, a fine or a community rehabilitation or punishment order.

Where any person therefore engages in any sort of conduct which has been designated a 'criminal offence', if the Police are notified they will then investigate and consider charging the individual concerned with the particular criminal offence. If the Police encounter some difficulties in, for instance, the investigation of a suspected false imprisonment, or assault and/or battery against a child, young person or adult with a learning disability and presenting severe challenging behaviour, they may want to refer the case to the Crown Prosecution Service,

---

[768] [1986] AC 112

the Public Prosecution Service for Northern Ireland or in Scotland the Procurator Fiscal for advice. The Crown Prosecution Service, the Public Prosecution Service, or the Procurator Fiscal's office will then consider all the circumstances of the case and will pay special attention to whether the facts disclosed that give rise to possible charges by the Police are actually justified by such defences as lawful excuse, for instance.

Criminal law offences include: false imprisonment, common assault, battery, assault occasioning bodily harm, s.18 OAPA 1861 malicious wounding/inflicting grievous bodily harm with intent to cause grievous bodily harm, s.20 OAPA 1861 wounding/causing grievous bodily harm without intent to cause grievous bodily harm, murder, voluntary manslaughter and involuntary manslaughter.

Criminal law defences excepting Scotland

1) Common Law and Statutory Power to Detain the Insane   Common Law Power – There is no power at common law to apprehend or detain a person suffering from mental disorder simply because he is so suffering. But it is stated that a 'private person may without express warrant confine a person disordered in his mind who seems disposed to do mischief to himself or any other person'.[769] While it is accepted that this power derives from a rather old judicial authority (more than a 100 years) it is submitted that it would be untenable for the criminal law to provide no protection for an individual with severe learning disabilities presenting severe challenging behaviour.

Statutory Power – Section 3(1) and (2) of the Mental Health Act 1983 stipulates that a patient may be admitted to a hospital and detained there for the period allowed by the provisions of this Act if the patient is suffering from a mental illness or another mental disorder which demands medical treatment in a hospital; and if it is necessary for the patient's health and safety, as well as for the safety of others that he is detained in under this Act.

2) Consent   As a general principle, when the victim has given consent then there is no offence. In cases where consent is given to an unlawful use of force which does not result in causing injury, the defence will be upheld. However, in _Donovan_ 1934,[770] it was held that an assault 'cannot be rendered lawful because the person to whose detriment it is done consents to it. No person can license another to commit a crime'.

3) Duress of circumstances, which is not available as defence for murder or attempted murder, otherwise implies that a person may have to perform an act under the pressure of certain circumstances. This will be valid as a defence if it can be proven that the defendant acted in a reasonable manner, applying only the necessary amount of force to avoid a threat of injury or death.

4) Lawful correction is a defence available to parents in England, Wales and Northern Ireland who have the right to dispense corporal punishment to their child, for whom they have parental responsibility. The defence will be valid provided the punishment is reasonable. These standards of reasonableness have changed over the years, with judges adopting a different approach to the question of reasonableness according to the standards current at the time of trial. When directing a jury, at present as influenced by the decisions of the European Court of Human

---

[769] Bacon's Abridgement cited in Hoggett _Mental Health Law_
[770] [1934] 2 KB 498

Rights, a reasonable punishment will imply that a) it is not immoderate and excessive; b) it is not for the satisfaction of a parent's personal gratification; c) it is not beyond the child's endurance; c) it is not administered by an inappropriate instrument likely to threaten the child's life and integrity of limbs; and d) the child understands the nature of the punishment.

In accordance with a judgement of the European Court of Human Rights,[771] in _R v H (Assault of Child: Reasonable Chastisement)_ 2002[772] it was held that when assessing the reasonableness of a chastisement, a judge in giving directions to the jury or in determining sentence in the case of a plea of guilty should consider: the nature and context of the behaviour of the person being chastised; the duration of the punishment; its physical and mental consequences in relation to the child; the age and personal characteristics of the child; and the reasons given by the adult for administering punishment.

5) **Mistake** In order for mistake to succeed as a defence, it must be based on the facts of the circumstances as the defendant saw them or believed them to be. If the mistake is genuine, albeit unreasonable, the defendant will be allowed to raise it as a defence.

6) **Necessity** could be described as a situation where a person has to make a choice between two courses of action, both of which would result in some kind of harm being caused. However, the choice of which course of action is best must take into consideration which of these would cause the lesser harm. Necessity can be a defence in cases: a) where a person has no choice but to act in such a way in order to protect themselves; b) when the defendant performs an 'illegal' act to save someone's life; and c) involving issues of mental capacity and consent, where a decision to save or assist someone's life without their consent has to be made.

7) **Prevention of a breach of the peace** In a caring situation, a carer could use this defence where a person with learning disabilities she cares for is restrained because they are likely to cause harm to other individuals or property in the immediate future, or where harm is feared in the immediate future as a result of an affray, a riot, assault or other disturbance. It would not make a restraint lawful where it is used to prevent the person with learning disabilities harming themselves. A situation where there is public alarm or general excitement will not constitute a breach of the peace unless there is an actual or potential threat of violence that is likely to occur in the near future.

8) **Prevention of crime** Section 3(1) of the Criminal Law Act 1967 stipulates that 'a person may use such force as is reasonable in the circumstances in the prevention of a crime. . .'. A crime, in this context, could be an unlawful act that is about or likely to incur physical damage to an individual or to property. This defence, which is really only a justification for the commission of an unlawful act, can only be used for offences where some degree of force is employed.

9) **Self-defence** This defence encompasses actions taken to defend oneself as well as another from being the victim of an unlawful attack on their person (Section 3 Criminal Act 1967), although it will not be available if the force is used after all danger has disappeared.

The use of force must be reasonable as regards the danger; so if it is disproportionate, ie excessive, then the defence will not be available. Paradoxically, the belief in having to use force

---

[771] _A v United Kingdom_ (1999) 27 EHRR 611
[772] [2002] 1 Cr.App.R.7

in self-defence need not be reasonable, as the facts of the circumstances must be assessed in the light of what the defendant believed them to be. In other words, the court will consider the fact that the defendant acted honestly and instinctively doing what he thought was necessary in the circumstances as strong evidence to support the defence. If, based upon the facts as seen by the defendant, a reasonable person would have acted in the same way, then the defence is likely to succeed. If a reasonable person would not have acted in the same way, then the defence will fail.

Criminal law defences in Scotland

1) **Reflex actions** This does not actually qualify as a defence *per se*, however it is not a crime to which the courts have paid much attention either. It was therefore judged relevant to include this particular notion of 'reflex actions' in this section dedicated to general and specific defences.

A reflex action has been described in case-law as a situation 'where a person instinctively reacts to violence in a reflex way, such as if a person is suddenly and without warning struck and turns round sharply so that he comes into contact with his assailant'.

2) **Self-defence** Scottish case-law has provided that this defence can be used for both crimes of assault and homicide in circumstances where a person 'acts in order to defend [their] own person or in defence of persons other than [themselves]', as well as occasionally in defence of property. The defence works as a justification for the use of force to prevent injury or harm to occur, and as such, will result in acquittal of a defendant charged for assault, murder or even for breach of the peace.

The rules for a 'special defence' of self-defence were laid down in case-law where the High Court, quoting the trial judge, held:

> '*A special defence can only apply if the accused's own life has been put in danger or if he has reasonable grounds for apprehending such a danger, in other words, there must be* **imminent danger to life**[773] *and furthermore the actings of the accused* **must be necessary** *and, if he has a means of escape from the attacker, the plea of self defence simply will not do. And lastly (...) there must be* **no cruel excess of violence** *on the accused's part. If he goes further than is necessary for his defence and uses cruel excess that cannot in law constitute self defence (...).'*

In other words, self-defence might be available as a 'special defence' if the following requirements are met: 1) there is an imminent danger to the defendant's life or to the life of others; 2) the danger feared is not merely about physical safety or injury but actually implies the danger of imminent death; 3) there must be no other means of escape from the threatening situation; and 4) excessive force must not be used. Reasonable force to prevent or escape the threatening situation is required here; however, the court will take into consideration the fact that it is not all that easy to assess the degree of reasonable force necessary in a given situation as other factors come into play. On the issue of whether self-defence could be raised with regard to the protection of property, it is to be assumed from case-law that the defence would not apply as no life would be endangered.

---

[773] The present authors' emphasis

3) **Provocation**   In Scottish law the line between self-defence and provocation was often said to be fine until the courts held that the difference between the two defences is that self-defence is a 'special defence' whereas provocation is a plea. The two are not inter-changeable as provocation can only be argued when the 'special defence' of self-defence has been rejected by a jury. The other difference is that where the defence of self defence can result in acquittal, provocation will only operate to reduce a charge for murder to one of culpable homicide.

The defence of provocation requires four elements to be present for it to be raised. Provocation must be brought about by some form of violence sustaining injury or harm. Words alone will be deemed insufficient to amount to a provocation. There must be a total loss of self-control. Not only does the accused have to prove that he lost his self-control, but that loss of self-control also has to be reasonable. The force used in response to the provocation must be proportionate (reasonable) to the provocative act. The test for evaluating whether the loss of control is reasonable is based on the reasonable person (objective) criterion. In other words, there are two questions that need answering before deciding that a plea of provocation can be entered: (a) was there loss of self-control? And (b) would the ordinary man or woman have been liable to react in the same way in the same circumstances? If the answer is yes to both, then there is a good chance that the plea would be accepted.

Provocation, be it physical or verbal, may be a defence to a charge of assault. However, it will not lead to total acquittal but will help minimise the severity of a defendant's sentence.

4) **Diminished responsibility**   Diminished responsibility is only a partial defence available for charges of murder and when successfully argued, this defence will reduce murder to a conviction of culpable homicide. 'The judge must decide whether there is evidence that, at the relevant time, the accused was suffering from an abnormality of mind which substantially impaired the ability of the accused, as compared with a normal person, to determine or control his acts.'[774]

The four requirements for a plea of diminished responsibility have been laid down in case-law. There must be (1) an aberration or weakness of mind; (2) some form of mental unsoundness; (3) a state of mind bordering on, though not amounting to, insanity, and finally; (4) a mind so affected that responsibility is diminished from full responsibility to partial responsibility.

5) **Necessity**   The defence of necessity arises in cases where the accused is forced by circumstances to commit an illegal/criminal act in order to avoid another more dangerous or evil outcome than if he did not act at all. There is little case-law on this particular defence, except where road traffic offences are concerned. Such cases have established the criteria required to be able to raise the defence of necessity. The courts have directed that:

- The accused must act in the face of immediate danger of death or great bodily harm;

- The danger may arise either from some contingency such as natural disaster or illness (including medical emergency) or from the deliberate threats of another;

- The defence may also be available either in cases of self-defence or 'in situations where the accused acts in an altruistic fashion to save a companion';

- The accused must be faced with no other choices but to break the law. If there is a possibility to act within the parameter of the law, the defence will not be available.

---

[774] *Galbraith v HM Advocate* 2001 SLT 953

Once the danger has passed and the necessity to act in contravention with the law is no longer needed, the accused must cease to perform the illegal act.

6) Defence of coercion   The defence of coercion is available when the accused is forced by another person to commit a criminal act. S.78(2) of the Criminal Procedure (Scotland) Act 1995 specifies that it is a special defence. The courts have established that 'a defence of coercion, in order to be successful, requires that the danger must be immediate and that the will and resolution of the accused must have been overborne by threats which he believed would be carried out so that he was not at the material time acting of his own free will'. The two basic requirements are subject to two additional elements, which are that the accused plays a backward and inferior part in the perpetration and that the accused discloses the fact and/or gives the spoil back on the first safe and convenient occasion.

7) Defence of lawful force   This notion relates to the issue of physical chastisement of children by their parents, teachers or anybody else who has parental responsibility over them. The key legislation on this issue is: the Children and Young Persons (Scotland) Act 1937; the Children (Scotland) Act 1995; the Standards in Scotland's Schools Act 2000; and the Regulation of Care (Scotland) Act 2001 and the Criminal Justice (Scotland) Act 2003. The law of Scotland still recognises the right of parents to inflict corporal punishment upon their child. But it has recently been changed in that the Scottish Assembly enacted section 51 of the Criminal Justice (Scotland) Act 2003, which came into force on 27 October 2003. This repeals[775] Section 12 (7) of the Children and Young Persons Act 1937 which had provided parents or other persons having the care of the child charged with assault as a result of administering punishment to the child with the defence of 'reasonable chastisement'. Parents exercising their parental right to punishment now have to show that the use of such punishment amounted to a 'justifiable assault'[776] as defined in the law. In determining whether such action by the parent was a 'justifiable assault' the statute provides the court with a list of factors to which the court must have regard in determining whether a parent can claim that their action in punishing a child is a 'justifiable assault' carried out in exercise of a parental right or of a right derived from having care of the child. These factors are those which the European Court of Human Rights determined should be followed by UK courts in _A v UK_ in interpreting what could be regarded as 'reasonable' when considering the nature and degree of chastisement meted out by parents, and which are now followed by the courts in England and Wales. (See those set out above at para 2.9.3 (b) (iii).) In addition, section 51 (3) provides that the defence of 'justifiable assault' is not available to parents or others having charge or care of the child where the action includes or consists of: a blow to the head;[777] shaking; or the use of an implement.[778] These actions are therefore outlawed. Section 51 (4) also provides that children 16 and over cannot be the subject of the parental right to physical punishment.

Although subject to the provisions outlined above corporal punishment is legal when administered by a person with parental responsibility, Section 16 Standards in Scotland's Schools Act 2000 prohibits any form of physical chastisement in the context of both public and private school education settings. Section 16(1) provides that 'corporal punishment given by, or on the authority of, a member of staff to a pupil (. . .) cannot be justified in any proceedings on the ground that it was so given in pursuance of a right exercisable by virtue of having a position

---

[775] Section 51 (5) (b) Criminal Justice (Scotland) Act 2003
[776] _Ibid_ section 51 (1)
[777] _Ibid_ section 51 (3) (a)
[778] _Ibid_ section 51 (3) (b) and (c)
[779] Standards in Scotland Schools Act 2000, section 16(5)(i)+(ii)

as a member of staff'. A 'member of staff' includes teachers and 'any other person who works at that school or place; or otherwise provides services there, and has lawful control or charge of the pupil'.[779] Section 16(4) provides an exception and stipulates that 'corporal punishment shall not be taken to be given to a pupil by virtue of anything done for reasons which include averting (a) an immediate danger of personal injury to; or (b) an immediate danger to the property of any person (including the pupil concerned)'. Parents with parental responsibility cannot delegate their power to administer corporal punishment to members of staff at a school, any other educational establishment, day or residential care provision.

8) **Common law power to restrain a lunatic**   In contrast with English common law, Scottish case-law recognises that private individuals have the common law power to restrain a lunatic. In the words of Lord Griffiths, this power 'is confined to imposing temporary restraint on a lunatic who has run amok and is a manifest danger either to himself or to others – a state of affairs as obvious to a layman as to a doctor. Such a common law power is confined to the short period of confinement necessary before the lunatic can be handed over to a proper authority'.[780]

Delict

Delict is the area of Scottish law which equates to the English law of torts or civil wrongs and which governs the obligation to refrain from wrongful conduct which may harm the interests of another, and the duty to compensate one who is harmed as a result of [another's] wrongful conduct. Delicts are divided into intentional delicts eg assault, and unintentional delicts eg negligence.

Disability

Section 1(1) Disability Discrimination Act 1995 provides that 'a person has a disability for the purposes of this Act if he has a physical or mental impairment which has a substantial and long-term adverse effect on his ability to carry out normal day-to-day activities'. A disabled person, therefore, means someone who has a disability.

Employer's responsibility

In tort law, an employer can be found liable for the act of his employees even though he is not the tortfeasor, ie the person actually committing the wrong. Vicarious liability involves imposing liability on the employer for the act of his employees, done in the course of their employment. Employer's liability is concerned with rendering the employer accountable for any breach of his duty of care towards his employees.

False imprisonment

False imprisonment has been defined as 'an act of the defendant which directly and intentionally or negligently causes the confinement of the plaintiff within an area delimited by the defendant'. In Scotland, the issues that arise in relation to the intentional delict of false imprisonment/detention and restraint are the loss of liberty experienced by a victim of unlawful detention or restraint coupled with the fact that it is an affront to their person; therefore, it is argued that 'a slight infringement of liberty is prima facie actionable. Case-law has established

[780]   *B v Foresey* [1988] SLT 572

that detaining a person on one's own premises until an apology is made is outrageous and constitutes the delict of wrongful detention.

Human Rights Act 1998

The Human Rights Act 1998 has, since its implementation on 2 October 2000, provided a structure for the protection of individuals' rights before the national courts, and a procedure through which they can claim a remedy against the State or one of its representatives (public bodies) for breaches of provisions of the European Convention on Human Rights. Actions under the Act can only be brought against a public authority, not against a private individual. However, the national courts are nonetheless under an obligation to interpret the law in accordance with the Convention, which means that Convention rights can be invoked (and thus must be respected) in an action involving private parties.

Lawful excuse

There will be many situations in which parents or carers of children and young people or even the adult children of adults with learning disabilities who also present severe challenging behaviour technically commit criminal and/or civil offences. This may come about in an attempt to provide adequate care, control and safety of their children, be they under 18 or adults, or for their parents, or to provide for the safety of other persons.

The notion of 'lawful excuse' is referred to in cases where a carer's conduct is justified in the eyes of the law. Without this lawful excuse, the carer's conduct would normally constitute a criminal offence or civil wrong. A lawful excuse thus acts as a defence to a potential criminal or civil liability.

There is, however, no statutory and clear definition of what constitutes a lawful excuse. The general essence remains that a lawful excuse justifies a conduct, which would otherwise be unlawful and would give rise to a liability. However, a lawful excuse will vary according to situations to which it applies.

For instance, in a UK Parliament session, the Lords discussed the issue of defining 'lawful excuse/authority' with regards to an Animal Health Bill. Lord Plumb argued that it 'should . . . be defined in the legislation in order for anyone to go to court and use it as a defence'. Lord Whitty stated '*Lawful authority* is normally powers given by statute; a *lawful excuse* is one which could be legally proven in court as a reason for not complying with an order. If we go back to *reasonableness*, *mitigating circumstances* and so on, that is what *excuse* means. But *authority* would be something that is statutorily based. . .'.

With regards to the Criminal Damage Act 1971, s.5(2) provides that a person who has damaged someone else's property would have a lawful excuse if it is believed that the owner of the damaged property actually consented to the destruction of his property or that the offender acted in that way in order to protect another property that is his own or somebody else's.

For details on the various lawful excuses, see the various chapters on the civil and criminal law defences operative in England, Wales and Northern Ireland and the separate chapters on Scotland.

Learning difficulty

Section 312 of Part IV Education Act 1996 provides that

> '*a child has a learning difficulty if:*
>
> *(a) he has a significantly greater difficulty in learning than the majority of children of his age,*
>
> *(b) he has a disability which either prevents or hinders him from making use of educational facilities of a kind generally provided for children of his age in schools within the area of the local education authority, or*
>
> *(c) he is under the age of five and is, or would be if special educational provision were not made for him, likely to fall within paragraph (a) or (b) when of or over that age.*'

Learning disability

There is no statutory definition of learning disability; however, this expression is seen by some as equating with the term 'mental impairment', defined further below.

Medical treatment

Certain 'psychoactive' and 'anti-psychotic' medications are used in the treatment of challenging behaviours. There are various forms of psychotropic drugs, such as antipsychotics, anxiolytics, anti-manics, anti-depressants, anti-epileptics, stimulants and opiate antagonists, which were originally used in cases of mental illness such as schizophrenia.[781]

These drugs have been progressively and widely used to manage challenging situations despite some studies showing that they are not very effective in this domain as it is argued that there is a lack of relation between challenging behaviour and mental illness. Nevertheless, psychotropic drugs are still used, either as part of a therapeutic treatment or in an emergency situation. In the case of a therapeutic treatment, the issue of consent is raised, and with it, the question of capacity. In the case of an emergency use of the medication, the possible offence of battery becomes an issue.

Mental impairment

Section 1 Mental Health Act 1983 provides a definition for 'mental impairment', which is a 'state of arrested or incomplete development of mind which includes significant impairment of intelligence and social functioning'.

Parent

The parents of a child are either the biological parents, ie the child was produced from the female's egg and male's sperm and carried by the female, or they are people who are treated as

---

[781] Kennedy C H & Meyer K A, The Use of Psychotropic Medication for People with Severe Disabilities and Challenging Behaviour: current status and future directions, *Journal of the Association for Persons with Severe Handicaps*, 23, 1998, pp. 83–97

the mother and father as defined by the Human Fertilisation and Embryology Act 1990. (The provisions of this Act apply across all of the jurisdictions).

Section 27 (1) defines a mother as: 'the woman who is carrying or has carried a child as a result of the placing in her of an embryo or of sperm and eggs and no other woman is to be treated as mother of the child'.

Section 28(2) states that a father is 'a man who is married to the mother and did not object to the placing in her of the embryo or the sperm and eggs or to her insemination'.

Section 28(3) makes the same provision as above but for an unmarried couple. No other man is to be treated as the father of the child.

Parental responsibility

The CA 1989 (for England and Wales) and the C(NI)O 1995 (Art 6) provide that parents have *responsibilities*, not rights. However Section 3(1) CA 1989 and Art 6(1) C(NI)0 1995 defines parental responsibility as: 'All the rights, duties, powers, responsibilities and authority which by law a parent of a child has in relation to the child and his property'. The Acts do not actually define these rights, duties, powers and responsibilities. The Department of Health's Introduction to the Children Act 1989 points out that 'that choice of words emphasises that "the duty to care for the child and to raise him to moral, physical and emotional health and it is the fundamental task of parenthood and the only justification for the authority that it confers".'

Who holds parental responsibility?

- *Married parents:* both mother and father

- *Unmarried parents:* mother alone unless father has taken formal legal steps to acquire, and has acquired parental responsibility

- *Divorced:* both even if child lives with one parent

- *Persons holding a s.8 CA 1989 residence order:* but only for the duration of the order (s.12(2) Children Act 1989)

Who does not hold parental responsibility?

- *Unmarried fathers:* unless he applies for a court order or makes a formal agreement with the mother on a special form lodged with the appropriate court offices. (Since the implementation of the relevant provisions of the Adoption and Children Act 2002, (December 1, 2003) unmarried fathers have been able to acquire parental responsibility if they register the child's birth together with the mother).

- *Step parents:* unless conferred through Section 8 residence order under the Children Act or adoption (NB After the implementation of the relevant provisions of the Adoption and Children Act 2002 (as yet no date has been set) step-fathers will be able to apply for parental responsibility orders under the newly-inserted Section 4A Children Act 1989.)

In Scotland, however, there is a limited attempt in s.1 CSA 1995 to define what is meant by 'parental responsibility' by reference to: safeguarding and promoting the child's welfare, providing appropriate direction and guidance, maintaining personal relations and direct contact with the child, and acting as the child's legal representative. Somewhat confusingly, given that the intention of the legislation was to move over to an emphasis on the concept of parental responsibility and away from the notion of parental rights, there is in s.2 CSA 1995 another limited attempt this time to define 'parental rights' by reference to: the right to have the child living with him or her or otherwise to regulate the child's residence; controlling, directing or guiding the child's upbringing; maintaining personal relations and direct contact with the child; and acting as the child's legal representative. All of these provisions are examined in some detail hereafter, and consideration is also given to the issue of how the notion of parental responsibility may be interpreted when focusing on the actions of parents or other carers seeking to provide for the care, control and safety of children and young people under the age of 18 with learning disabilities who also present challenging behaviour.

Parental responsibility (revoking of)

Parental responsibility can be revoked in all jurisdictions on the following grounds: a) death of child; b) adoption; c) freeing for adoption; d) the court revoking a parental responsibility order and e) the discharge of a residence order held by someone other than a parent.

Exercise of parental responsibilities

Parental responsibility including, for example the responsibility to give consent for medical operations or the administration of medication, *can* be exercised by one parent possessed of parental responsibility unless it is consent for: a) adoption; b) marriage; and/or c) freeing for adoption, in which case both parents, where they both have parental responsibility will have to give consent or their consent will have to be dispensed with. Parents, or those with parental responsibility, *cannot* act in a way which is contrary to or which undermines an order made under the CA 1989 or the C(NI)O 1995 or C(S)A 1995, ie if an order has been made that a child must go to a special therapy unit, the father cannot stop the child going. Parents in all the jurisdictions *can delegate responsibility* to, for example, childminders, carers and/or schools. *However* parents may be found to be negligent if, knowing their child to be prone to severe challenging behaviour and capable of sudden destructive outbursts, they place the care of their child in the hands of a person lacking sufficient skill, experience or qualifications to look after such a child. If any injury befell the child of a third party (eg another child) caused by the inexperience of the carer, parents may bear responsibility and thus may be sued for damages. In practice, most parents would not be insured against such risks and therefore it would not be considered worthwhile bringing an action against them, more particularly if the action were being considered on behalf of their own child. However, the parents of another child to whom injury has been caused, may feel that it is worth their while pursuing legal action in anticipation of recovering even a small award for damages to compensate their child for any injuries received and any consequential additional costs.

Physical intervention

A physical intervention can be described as an action taken which may involve the employment of a certain degree of force to deal with an individual's challenging behaviour, or it may involve the person physically blocking a person's pathway, or it may involve the carer in providing manual guidance to assist a person in walking. Where force is used to restrict, limit or re-direct a person's movement, the idea is that sometimes some kind of resistance may exercised by the person to whom the force is applied. 'Restrictive physical interventions' are defined in the

Guidance issued by the DfES and the DoH and this definition is set out under that heading below.

A working definition of physical intervention which appears to concentrate more on the notion of a 'restrictive physical intervention' is also to be found in the *National Minimum Standards for Care Homes for Younger Adults* where it is provided that 'physical intervention is a method of responding to violence or aggressive behaviour, which involves a degree of direct force to limit or restrict movement or mobility'.[782]

Positive handling and positive handling plans

Positive handling is a term used by some to describe a whole plan which has been devised for the child, young person or adult which may incorporate physical intervention strategies and which may also include other systems of rewards as reinforcement of good behaviour. It is also clear that it is used by others simply as an alternative term to the expression 'physical intervention' because it does not have the same negative connotations as the latter term and therefore may be more acceptable both to those dealing with children and young people with learning disabilities and severe challenging behaviour and to their parents.

Although 'positive handling' is mentioned in paragraph 8.2 of the DfES *Guidance on the Use of Restrictive Physical Interventions for Staff Working with Children and Adults who Display Extreme Behaviour in Association with Learning Disability and/or Autistic Spectrum Disorders*[783] – in which is stated that 'in schools, the possible use of restrictive physical interventions, as part of a broader educational or therapeutic strategy, will be included within the pupil's *Positive Handling Plan*' – there is no definition of this term anywhere in the guidance.

Team-Teach has defined Positive Handling Plans as 'the agreed strategies (non-verbal verbal and physical) that aim to support the individual, providing them with a sense of security, safety and acceptance, allowing for recovery and repair, facilitating learning and growth for all involved'.[784]

Restrictive physical intervention

A 'restrictive physical intervention' as set out in para 3.1 of the 'Guidance on physical Intervention' is described as a restrictive form of intervention, designed to prevent movement or mobility or to disengage from dangerous or harmful physical contact and is distinguished from non-restrictive methods.

'Restrictive physical interventions' are defined there as involving 'the use of force to control a person's behaviour and can be employed using bodily contact, mechanical devices or changes to the person's environment'.

---

[782] DoH, 2002

[783] Referred to in this report as the 'Guidance on physical intervention'. Department for Education and Employment, SEN (Special Educational Needs), July 2002, http://www.dfes.gov.uk/sen/documents/PI_Guidance.pdf

[784] InTeam-Teach training manuals since 1997 as advised by George Matthews of Team-Teach in an email 29 June 2003

Risk assessment

Under Health and Safety legislation employers are required to conduct a 'suitable and sufficient' assessment of risks to the health and safety of employees when they are at work, and of people who are not in employment and who might be affected by the employers'/employees' actions or work activity. According to para 1.5 of the 'Guidance on Physical Interventions' similar risk assessments must be carried out in relation to pupils who present challenging behaviour not only in relation to other employees but also in relation to others. For example, assessments should be carried in relation to the risks posed to other pupils as well as to visitors.

Social care worker

Section 55(2) of the Care Standards Act 2000 provides that a:

'social care worker' is a person who: '

(a) engages in relevant social work (referred to in this Part as a "social worker");

(b) is employed at a children's home, care home or residential family centre or for the purposes of a domiciliary care agency, a fostering agency or a voluntary adoption agency;

(c) manages an establishment, or an agency, of a description mentioned in paragraph (b); or

(d) is supplied by a domiciliary care agency to provide personal care in their own homes for persons who by reason of illness, infirmity or disability are unable to provide it for themselves without assistance.

Section 55(3) also stipulates that the following people are to be treated as:

'social care workers':

(a) a person engaged in work for the purposes of a local authority's social services functions, or in the provision of services similar to services which may or must be provided by local authorities in the exercise of those functions;

(b) a person engaged in the provision of personal care for any person;

(c) a person who manages, or is employed in, an undertaking (other than an establishment or agency) which consists of or includes supplying, or providing services for the purpose of supplying, persons to provide personal care;

(d) a person employed in connection with the discharge of functions of the appropriate Minister under Section 80 of the 1989 Act (inspection of children's homes etc.);

(e) staff of the Commission or the Assembly who –

(i) inspect premises under Section 87 of the 1989 Act (welfare of children accommodated in independent schools and colleges) or Section 31 or 45 of this Act; or

(ii) are responsible for persons who do so;

and staff of the Assembly who inspect premises under Section 79T of that Act (inspection of child minding and day care in Wales) or are responsible for persons who do so;

(f) a person employed in a day centre;

(g) a person participating in a course approved by a Council under Section 63 for persons wishing to become social workers.'

Finally, Section 55(4) defines 'relevant social work' as 'social work which is required in connection with any health, education or social services provided by any person'; and Section 55(5) describes a 'day centre' as a place where nursing or personal care (but not accommodation) is provided wholly or mainly for persons mentioned in Section 3(2).

Supply worker

Section 80(5) of the Care Standards Act 2000 defines a supply worker as someone who:

'(a) in relation to an employment agency, means an individual supplied by the agency for employment in a care position or for whom the agency has found employment in a care position;

(b) in relation to an employment business, means an individual supplied by the business for employment in a care position.'

Vulnerable adult

Section 80(6) of the Care Standards Act 200 defines a vulnerable adult as:

'(a) an adult to whom accommodation and nursing or personal care are provided in a care home;

(b) an adult to whom personal care is provided in their own home under arrangements made by a domiciliary care agency; or

(c) an adult to whom prescribed services are provided by an independent hospital, independent clinic, independent medical agency or National Health Service body'.

No Secrets which is of course not law but strong guidance, which has to be abided by unless there are exceptional reasons why it should not be adhered to, defines a vulnerable adult as 'someone over the age of 18' 'who is or may be in need of community care services by reason of mental or other disability age or illness and who is or may be unable to take care of him or herself, or unable to protect him or herself against significant harm or exploitation'.[785]

There is, as yet, no comparable definition of a vulnerable child.

---

[785] DoH, May 2000 drawing extensively on *Who Decides* – A Lord Chancellor's Consultation Paper (1997) and see also *Making Decisions* – a report issued in the light of responses on the Law Commission's document Mental Incapacity (1996)

Bibliography

⊠ Guidance Documents

▤ Journals/Articles

✐ Literature

☝ Electronic/Internet Resources

Guidance Documents

(Includes print and electronic resources)

☝ *A guide to consent for examination or treatment*, http://www.ucht.cwc.net/uchtweb/medicolegal/consent.htm (downloaded in January 2003)

☝ *A guide to Risk Assessment Requirements – Common provisions in health and safety law*, http://www.hse.gov.uk/pubns/indg218.pdf (downloaded in June 2003)

⊠ Scottish Executive Publications *Adults With Incapacity (Scotland) Act 2000 – Guidance and Workbook for Social and Healthcare Staff, Pack 1,* April 2002, http://www.scotland.gov.uk/library5/social/packnumber1.pdf

⊠ *BILD Code of Practice for Trainers in the Use of Physical Interventions*, BILD, 2001

☝ Charity Commission for England & Wales *Operational Guidance – Human Rights Act 1998, Article 8 – to respect for private and family life*, http://www.charity-commission.gov.uk/supportingcharites/ogs/g0/1c002.asp, September 2000

⊠ *Clear Expectations, Consistent Limits – Good practice in the care and control of children and young people in residential care* prepared for the Social Work Services Inspectorate by the Centre for Residential Child Care, 1997

☝ Department of Health, *Reference Guide to Consent for examination or treatment*, includes sections on seeking consent for people with learning disabilities, http://www.doh.gov.uk/consent/guidance.htm

⊠ Hughes A & Coombs P, *Easy Guide to the Human Rights Act 1998 – implications for people with learning disabilities*, BILD, 2001

☝ *Guidance on the Use of Restrictive Physical Interventions for Staff Working with Children and Adults who Display Extreme Behaviour in Association with Learning Disability and/or Autistic Spectrum Disorders*, Department for Education and Employment, SEN (Special Educational Needs), July 2002, http://www.dfes.gov.uk/sen/documents/PI_Guidance.pdf

☝ *Guidelines for Mental Health and Learning Disabilities Nursing – a guide to working with vulnerable clients*, UK Central Council for Nursing, Midwifery and Health Visiting, 1998, http://www.nmc-uk.org/cms/content/publications/Guidelines%20for%20MH. .pdf

⊠ *Guidance on Section 550A of the Education Act: The Use of Reasonable Force to Control or Restrain Pupils, Circular 10/98*, Department for Education and Employment, July 1998

⊠ *Guidance Notes for the use of force to control or restrain pupils – Model policy for the control and restraint and physical contact with pupils* attached to a letter from Jim Carlsen, School Employment Advisory Team to all headteachers and chairs of governors, the City of Liverpool City Council, Education and Lifelong Learning Service, 1 May 2002

⊠ *Guidance on Child protection for Staff within the Education Directorate*, The City of Liverpool, Education Directorate, January 1996

⊕ Health & Safety Executive, *Five Steps to Risk Assessment*, HSE Books, http://www.hse.gov.uk/pubns/indg163.pdf (downloaded in June 2003)

⊕ Health & Safety Executive, *Getting to grips with Manual Handling – A short guide for employees*, http://www.hse.gov.uk/pubns/indg143.pdf (downloaded in June 2003)

⊠ Lyon C *Legal Issues Arising from the care and control of children with learning disabilities who also present severe challenging behaviour, Main Research Report and the Guide for Parents and Carers*. The Mental Health Foundation, 1994

⊕ Mental Welfare Commission for Scotland, *Restraint of People with Mental Impairment in care Homes and Hospitals – Principles and Guidance on Good Practice in Caring for Residents with Dementia and Related Disorders and Residents with Learning Disabilities*, April 1998 http://www.markwalton.net/scotland/restraint.pdf

⊕ NUT (National Union of Teachers), *Law on restraint – Legal Provisions* http://www.suffolk.org.uk/restraint.htm (downloaded in February 2003)

⊕ *National Care Minimum Standards for Care Homes for Younger Adults* Department of Health, http:/www.doh.gov.uk April 2002

⊠ *No Secrets: Guidance on developing and implementing multi-agency policies and procedures to protect vulnerable adults from abuse*, Department of Health, 2000

⊕ *Protection of Vulnerable Adults – Implementing the 'In safe Hands' Guidelines for the protection of Vulnerable Adults in Wales, Inter-agency policy & procedures for responding to alleged abuse and inappropriate care of vulnerable adults in South Wales, Section 8 'Capacity and Consent'* http://www.neath-porttalbot.gov.uk/downloads/swapforum/08_capacity_consent.pdf (downloaded January 2003)

⊕ *Rights, Risks and Limits to Freedom – Guidance for the use of restraint*, Mental Welfare Commission for Scotland, *Good Practice Guidance*, http://www.mwcscot.org.uk/publications/goodpractice/rights.pdf, 2002

⊠ *Taking Care – Taking Control*, video and booklet guide, Hawkshead Production & Department of Health, Crown Copyright 1996

⊠ *The Control of Children in the Public Care: Interpretation of the Children Act 1989*, letter from Sir Herbert Laming CBE, Chief Inspector, Social Services Inspectorate, Department of Health, 20 February 1997

⊕ The Lord Chancellor's Department (LCD) Human Rights, *Human Rights Come to Life*, Human Rights Act – **Core guidance for public authorities: a new era of rights and responsibilities**, http://www.humanrights.gov.uk/coregd.htm, 2000-2001

⊕ The Royal College of Psychiatrists, *OP41. Management of Imminent Violence – Clinical practice guidelines to support mental health services*, Gaskell, March 1998, http://www.rcpsych.ac.uk/publications/op/op41.htm (quick reference guide), http://www.rcpsych.ac.uk/publications/guidelines/violence_full_b.htm (full version)

⊕ Schwehr B, *A Guide to the Human Rights Act 1998*, Rowe & Maw Offices, Public Law Group, 2001, www.schwehrcare.co.uk

⊠ *Violence to Employees – Departmental Guidelines and Procedures*, City of Nottingham, January 1999, Nottingham City Council Social Services Department, 1999

⊠ *Violence and Aggression to staff in health services – guidance on assessment and management*, Health & Safety Commission, Health Services Advisory Committee, 1997

Journals/Articles

(Includes print and electronic resources)

⊕ Association of Child Abuse Lawyers (ACAL), *Council not liable for abuse by teacher*, 10 September 1998, (in relation to *T v North Yorkshire County Council*), http://www.childabuselawyers.com/trotman.htm

Adults with learning difficulties' involvement in health care decision-making, Findings October 1999, Joseph Rowntree Foundation

BBC News, *Law change plea after smacking trial*, 19 May 1999, http://news.bbc.co.uk/1/hi/uk/347853.stm

BBC News, *Human Rights: The European Convention*, 29 September 2000, http://news.bbc.co.uk/1/hi/uk/948143.stm

Boyle P, *Fatal Hugs: The Most Dangerous Moves*, Youth Today, September 2000, p.43, http://www.ytyt.org/infobank/document.cfm/parent/1133

Cooper J, *John Cooper's Legal Focus – Defence of reasonable chastisement by a parent upon a child*, Justis, 17 May 2001, http://www.justis.com/news/jc_01051/.html

Enright S, Special Educational Needs, Disability Focus, *NLJ* (New Law Journal) Practitioner, 1 March 2002, p.311

Greig R, The real challenged in Valuing People, in *Managing Community Care*, The Journal for Social Care, Health and Housing, pp.3-5, vol.9, issue 3, June 2001

Harney N, *Vulnerable Adult Abuse – Recent Development In The Law*, AbuseLaw.co.uk, Stewarts Solicitors http://www.abuselaw.co.uk/default.ihtml?step=4&pid=49 (downloaded February 2003)

Hayes D, *Woman receives £37,000 damages for injuries from restraining pupils*, Independent.co.uk – *Education*, 17 April 2001, (referring to *Daws v Croydon London Borough Council* 2001, unreported) http://education.independent.co.uk/news/story.jsp?story=66967

Hewitt D, *An end to compulsory psychiatric treatment?* New Law Journal, 8 February 2002, pp.194195

How not to stop a child – DoH advice, Childright, October 1992, No.90, p.7

Medical treatment – Refusal of Treatment – Capacity of adult patient – *Ms B v An NHS Hospital Trust*, Law Reports, *NLJ* (New Law Journal) Practitioner, 29 March 2002, p.470

Mahenda B, Facing up to a child's dilemma (. . . issues when a parent refuses treatment for a child), *New Law Journal*, 22 March 2002, p.426

Marchant S, Increasing accountability for mental health professionals – how human rights law is affecting non-consensual treatment of competent patients' options available to a patient when challenging past treatment, *New Law Journal* (NLJ), 12 July 2002, p.1062 and 1074

McDonnell A, Reeves S, Johnson A & Lane A, Managing Challenging Behaviour in Adults with Learning Disabilities: The Use of Low Arousal Approach, *Behavioural and Cognitive Psychotherapy*, 1998, 26, pp.163-171 (OUP)

Murphy G, Self-Injurious Behaviour: What do we Know and Where are we Going? *Tizard Learning Disability Review* vol.4, issue 1, January 1999, Pavilion Publishing (Brighton) Limited

McCreadie C, No Secrets: guidance in England for the protection of vulnerable adults from abuse, Policy Overview, *The Journal of Adult Protection*, vol.2, issue 3, September 2000, Pavilion Publishing (Brighton) Limited

Middleton-Roy P, *Vicarious liability and Child Abuse: The Impact of Lister v. Hesley Hall Ltd*, Abuselaw.co.uk, Stewarts Solicitors, downloaded in February 2003, http://www.abuselaw.co.uk/default.ihtml?step=4&pid=50

NAMI (The Nation's Voice on Mental Illness), *Comments on Interim Final Rule on the Use of restraint and seclusion in Psychiatric Residential Treatment Facilities*, Health Care Financing Administration Department of Health and Human Services Attention, 20 March 2001 http://web.nami.org/pressroom/testimony/20010320_restraint_seclusion.html

Patterson, B, Stark, C, Saddler, D, Leadbetter, D, Allen, D, Deaths Associated with Restraint Use in Health and Social Care in the United Kingdom: The Results of a Preliminary Survey, *Journal of Psychiatric and Mental Health Nursing*, Vol 10, No 1, Feb 2003

Peterkin T & Martin N, *Prison for smacking a toddler*, Telegraph.co.uk, 7 September 2001, http://www.telegraph.co.uk/news/main.jhtml?xml=/news/2001/09/07/nhit07.xml

Rt Hon Lord WOOLF, *Human Rights: Have the Public Benefited?* The British Academy, 2002, http://www.britac.ac.uk/pubs/src/tob02/woolf.html

Scottish Executive, *The law commissions review Strasbourg case-law on the award of damages under ECHR*, press release issued on behalf of the Scottish Law Commission, http://www.scotland.gov.uk/news/2000/10/se2599.asp, 3 October 2000

Stein R & Swaine F, *Ms B v An NHS Trust: the patient's right to choose*, New Law Journal, 26 April 2002, pp.642-643

Tobin JW, Time to remove the shackles: the legality of restraints on children deprived of their liberty under international law *The International Journal of Children's Rights*, 9:213-239, 2001 (2002 *Kluwer Law International*)

Wheeler R, Medical manslaughter: why this shift from tort to crime? *New Law* Journal, 19 April 2002, pp.593-594

Legal resources

(Includes print and electronic resources)

Circular 10/98 – Section 550A of the Education Act 1996: The Use of Force to Control or Restrain Pupils, Department for Education and Employment, July 1998, http://www.dfes.gov.uk/publications/guidanceonthelaw/10_98/summary.htm

Circular 56/94 – The education of Children with Emotional and Behavioural Difficulties, Welsh Assembly Government, Learning Wales, http://www.wales.gov.uk/subieducationtraining/content/special/5694-cnts-e.htm, downloaded in November 2003

Court Service, *Human Rights Act 1998 – Information for court users*, www.courtservice.gov.uk

Adults with Incapacity (Scotland) Act 2000, annotated by Ward Adrian D, *Current Law Statutes* 2000 vol.3, *asp.4*

European Convention of Human Rights and Fundamental Freedoms, Rome, 4.XI.1950, Council of Europe European Treaties, Registry of the European Court of Human Rights, http://www.echr.coe.int/Convention/webConvenENG.pdf, February 2003

Mental Health Act 1983 – Code of Practice, Department of Health and Welsh Office, August 1993

Richardson PJ, Thomas DA, Turner J, Shay S & Carter W, *Archbold – Criminal Pleading, Evidence and Practice,* Sweet 7 Maxwell, 2003

Valuing People – A New Strategy for Learning Disability for the 21st Century, A White Paper, Department of Health, March 2001

Literature

(Includes print and electronic resources)

Adults with incapacity (Scotland) Act 2000 – Aide memoire for doctors, downloaded in June 2003 http://www.show.scot.nhs.uk/sehd/cmo/AWIaidememoire.pdf

Alaszewski H, Parker A & Alaszewski A, *Empowerment and Protection – The development of policies and practice in risk assessment and risk management in services for adults with learning disabilities*, The Foundation for People with Learning Disabilities, 1999

Allen D, Mediator analysis: an overview of recent research on carers supporting people with intellectual disability and challenging behaviour, *Learning Disability Bulletin* 117/2, BILD, June 2000

Allen D, *Training carers in Physical interventions – Research towards evidence-based practice*, BILD, 2001

Allen D, *Ethical approaches to physical interventions – Responding to challenging behaviour in people with intellectual disabilities*, BILD, 2003

Allen MJ, *Textbook on Criminal Law*, Blackstone Press, 6th edition, 2001

Baker C, *Human Rights Act 1998: A Practitioner's Guide*, Sweet & Maxwell, 1998

Bates P, *Legal Responsibility and protection of Mentally Disordered People in English Law*, POL.it *Psychiatry on line*, 1998, http://www.pol-it.org/ital/bates.htm

Behind Closed Doors – Preventing sexual abuse against adults with a learning disability, Home Office, July 2000

Bell L & Stark C, *Measuring Competence in Physical Restraints skills in residential Child Care*, *Social Work Research Findings No.21*, The Scottish Office, Home Department: Social Work Services Group, downloaded in February 2003, http://www.scotland.gov.uk/cru/documents/re-fin21.htm

Breakwell GM, *Coping with Aggressive Behaviour*, Personal and Professional Development, The British Psychological Society, 1997

Breggin PR, *Principles for the Elimination of Restraint*, report, Centre for the study of Psychiatry and Psychology, 25 April 1999, http://www.breggin.com/jcah.html

BILD Factsheet No.10, on Physical Interventions http://www.bild.org.uk/factsheets/physical_interventions.htm (downloaded August 2002)

BILD Physical interventions Accreditation Scheme Handbook, BILD, 2002

Breakaway Training services (BTS) *Managing Violence & Aggression (MV&A) within the Workplace – Developing Quality Practice* http://www.doh.gov.uk/violencetaskforce/breakaway.pdf (downloaded December 2002)

Brown L, *Challenging and inappropriate Sexual Behaviour in People with Learning Disabilities: A literature Review*, Central Research Unit, The Scottish Office, 1998

Brusca R, Nieminen G, Carter R & Repp A, The relationships of staff contact and activity to the stereotypy of children with multiple disabilities, *Journal of the Association for Persons with Severe Handicaps*, 1989.14, pp.127-136.

Carr E, The motivation for self-injurious behaviour: a review of some hypotheses, *Psychological Bulletin* 1977, 84, 4, 800-816.

Carr EG, Levin L, McConnnachie G, Carlson JI, Kemp DC & Smith CE, *Communication-Based Intervention for Problem Behaviour. A User's Guide for Producing Positive Change*, Baltimore (1994)

Carr, EG; Horner, RH; Turnbull, AP; Marquis JG; McLaughlin DM; McAtee, ML; Smith CE: Ryan KA; Rueff, MB & Doolabh, *Positive behaviour Support for people with Developmental Disabilities: A research Synthesis*. American Association on Mental Retardation, Washington (1999)

Childs P, *Criminal Law*, Sweet & Maxwell, 1999

Children are unbeatable! Alliance Scotland – Response to 'The Physical Punishment of Children in Scotland' – a consultation, April 2000 http://www.childreninscotland.org.uk/polresp/CAUScotlandresponse.pdf

Clarke D, *What is Learning Disability?* Chapter 1 in *An Introduction to Learning Disability Psychiatry*, edited by Roy M, Clarke D, Roy A. West Midlands Learning Disability Group, http://www.ldbook.co.uk/Chapter_1.htm, 2000

Connelly C, *Law Basics – Criminal Law, Student Study Guides*, Edinburgh, W.green/ Sweet & Maxwell, 2002

Cullen C, *A Review of Some Important Issues in Research and Services for People with Learning Disabilities and Challenging Behaviour*, October 1999, http://www.scotland.gov.uk/ldsr/cullen.pdf

Cullen C, Brown JF, Combes H & Hendy S, *Working with People who have Intellectual Impairments; What is Clinical Psychology*, J.Mazillier & J.Hall (eds), 3rd edition 1999

Daw R, *The Impact of the Human Rights Act on Disabled People*, The Disability Rights Commission, 2002

Donnellan AM, LaVigna GW, Negri-Shoultz N & Fassbender LL, *Progress without punishment: effective approaches for learning with behavioural problems*, Columbia University, 1988

Don't forget Us – Children with Learning Disabilities and Severe Challenging Behaviour (Report of a Committee set up by the Mental Health Foundation), The Mental Health Foundation, 1997

Elliot C & Quinn F, *Tort Law*, Longman, 2nd edition, 1999

Elliot C & Quinn F, *Criminal Law*, Longman, 3rd edition, 2000

Emerson E & Hatton C, *Violence Against Social Care Workers Supporting People with Learning Difficulties: A Review*, downloaded in December 2002, http://www.doh.gov.uk/violencetaskforce/emersonhatton.pdf

Emerson, E, *Challenging Behaviour: Analysis and Intervention in People with Intellectual Disabilities*, Cambridge University Press, 2nd edition 2001

Emerson E, Hatton C, Felce D & Murphy G, *Learning Disabilities – The Fundamental Facts*, The Foundation for People with Learning Disabilities, 2001

Federation of Families for Children's Mental Health (FFCMH), *The Use of Restraint and Seclusion with Children* http://www.ffcmh.org/new%20site/factsheet_restraints.htm (downloaded January 2003)

Feldman D, *Civil Liberties and Human Rights in England & Wales*, 2nd edition, Oxford University Press (OUP), 2002

Felce D, Repp A, Thomas M, Ager A & Blunden R, The relationship of staff-client ratios, interactions, and residential placement, *Research in Developmental Disabilities*, 1991.12, pp.315–331.

Fenwick A, *On attribution theory: challenging behaviour and staff beliefs*, *Clinical Psychology Forum*, 79, pp.29–31.

Glendinning R, Buchanan T, Rose N & Hallam A, *Well? What do you think? A National Scottish Survey of Public Attitudes to Mental Health, Well Being and Mental Health Problems*, Health and Community Care, Analytical Services Division, Scottish Executive Social Research, 2002

Gournay K & team from the Department of Health Services Research Institute of Psychiatry and South London and Maudsley NHS Trust, *The Recognition, Prevention and Therapeutic Management of Violence in Mental Health Care – A Consultation document*, prepared for the UK Central Council for Nursing, Midwifery and Health Visiting, http://www.doh.gov.uk/violencetaskforce/ukcc.pdf (downloaded January 2003)

Harris J, Allen D, Cornick M, Jefferson A & Mills R, *Physical Interventions – A Policy Framework*, BILD, 2000

Hastings R, Understanding factors that influence staff responses to challenging behaviours: an exploratory interview study, *Mental Handicap Research,* BILD, 1995, 8, 4, pp.297–320. http://www.nau.edu/ihd/positive/library/hastings15.pdf

Harborne A, *Challenging behaviour in older people: nurses' attitudes*, research, Nursing Standard. 11, 12, 39-43, http://www.nursing-standard.co.uk/archives/vol11-12/research.htm

Hastings R & Remington B, Staff behaviour and its implications for people with learning disabilities and challenging behaviours, *British Journal of Clinical Psychology* 1994, 33, pp.423–438.

Hastings R & Remington B, The emotional dimension of working with challenging behaviours, *Clinical Psychology Forum*, 1995, 79, pp.11–16.

Human Rights and Scottish Law, edited by Boyle A, Himsworth C, Loux A & MacQueen H, Hart Publishing, 2002

Hyland S, *Physical Intervention and Restraint Procedures*, Synergy Child Service Ltd (SCS), 2002

Introduction to the Scottish Law of Obligations, in *Introduction to National Legal Systems – Scottish Legal System*, Liber Università Internazionale degli Studi Sociali (Luiss), ErasmusLaw, http://www.luiss.it/erasmuslaw/scozia/obligations.htm, (downloaded June 2003)

John P, *Physical Intervention: Policy into Practice – A report on the one day conference held at Whitbrook Training Unit, Manchester on 22 July 1998*, North West Training & Development Team, http://www.nwtdt.com/pdfs/pipi.pdf

Jones MA, *Textbook on Torts*, 7th edition, Blackstone Press Limited, 2000

Keywood K, Flynn M, *Best Practice? Health Care Decision-Making By, With and For Adults with Learning Disabilities*, National Development Team, 1999

Lally J, *Promoting Well-Being and Preventing Challenging Behaviour, series: How you can help people who use learning disability services*, Manchester Learning Disability Partnership, 2002

Lyon CM, *Legal issues arising from the care, control & safety of children with learning disabilities who also present severe challenging behaviour*, The Mental Health Foundation, 1994

Lyon CM, *Loving Smack or Lawful Assault – A Contradiction in Human Rights and the Law*, Institute for Public Policy Research (IPPR), 2000

Lyon CM, *Child Abuse* (3rd Edition) Jordans Family Law, 2003

Mandelstam M, *Manual Handling in Health and Social Care – An A-Z of Law and Practice*, Jessica Kingsley Publishers (JKP), 2002

Martin J, *Criminal Law – Key Facts*, Hodder Stoughton, 2001

Martin G & Pear J, *Behaviour modification: what it is and how to do it*, Prentice-Hall, 1992

Mental Health Policy: the challenges facing the new Government, a briefing by The Sainsbury Centre for Mental Health, July 2001

Mitchell G & Hastings R, Learning disability care staffs' emotional reactions to aggressive challenging behaviours: development of a measurement tool, *British Journal of Clinical Psychology* 1998, 37, pp.441–449. http://www.nau.edu/ihd/positive/library/mitchell3.pdf

More W, Norman G & Wornham D, *Disengagement, Breakaway and Self-Defence*, PEPAR Publications, 1998

Morgan G & Hastings R, Special educator's understanding of challenging behaviours in children with learning disabilities: sensitivity to information about behavioural function, *Behavioural and Cognitive Psychotherapy*, 1998, 26, pp.43–52. http://www.nau.edu/ihd/positive/library/morgan1.pdf

McDonnell A, *Staff Training in The Management of Challenging Behaviour*, Studio 3 Training Systems, 1995

McGill P, Teer K, Rye L & Hughes D, paper on *The relationship between aspects of the service environment and challenging behaviour in people with learning disabilities*, project completed in September 1996, http://www.doh.gov.uk/research/rd3/nhsrandd/timeltdprogs/pcd/funded/co. . ./a5013htm

Obligations: The Law of Tort, Lord Templeman & Pitchfork ED, Old Bailey Press, 1997

Patterson B, Bradley P, Stark C, Saddler D, Leadbetter D & Allen D, Deaths Associated with Restraint Use in Health and Social care in the United Kingdom – The Results of a Preliminary Survey, *Journal of Psychiatric and Mental Health Nursing*, 10.1 Feb 2003

Positive Behavioural Management – Preventing & Responding to Aggressive Behaviour in Persons with Intellectual Disabilities – Trainer's Manual, Positive Response Training Ltd (PRT), 1999

Reed T & Watts M, Community staff causal attributions about challenging behaviour in people with intellectual disabilities, *Journal of Applied Research in Intellectual Disabilities* 1997, 10.3, pp.238–249.

Rogers WVH, *Winfield and Jolowicz on Tort*, Swett & Maxwell, 16th edition, 2002

Regional Advisory Group for Learning Disabilities, *Physical interventions – How we work with people who are considered at times to be in need of physical restraint*, North Western Training & Development Team (NWTDT), 1993

Sailas E & Fenton M, *Seclusion and restraint for people with serious mental illnesses (Cochrane review)*, The Cochrane Library, issue 1, 2003, Oxford: Update Software Ltd, http://www.update-software.com/abstracts/ab001163.htm

Smith, McCall RAA & Sheldon D, *McCall Smith & Sheldon: Scottish Criminal Law*, Butterworths Tolley, 1997

Scottish Executive, *The Physical Punishment of Children in Scotland: A Consultation*, The Scottish Executive Justice Department, February 2000, http://www.scotland.gov.uk/library2/doc11/ppcs-00.asp

Scottish Parliament Official Report, vol. 5, No.11, *Adults With Incapacity (Scotland) Bill: stage 3* (col.1038 to col.1054) http://www.scottish.parliament.uk/S1/official_report/session-00/or051102.htm

Simpson S & Freeman M, *Addressing the Prone Position in Control and Restraint – examining the Literature*, May 2000, http://swacri.cornwall-nhs.net/article.htm

Slevin E, Challenging Behaviour in people with learning disabilities, *Learning Disability Bulletin 117/1*, BILD June 2000 and/or *Mental Health Care*, 2, 7, March 1999, 242-245.

Smith F & Lyon CM, *Personal Guide – The Children Act 1989 in the context of the Human Rights Act 1998*, Children act Enterprises, 2nd edition, 2002

Spencer M & Spencer J, *Nutshells – Human Rights*, Sweet & Maxwell, 1st edition, 2001

Studio 3 Training Systems, *Draft Template on the Management of Challenging Behaviour for Staff Working at (name your service)*, January 2001

The Loddon school, *PROACT-SCIPr-UK – Physical intervention Schedule*, for further details, refer to the web site: http://www.loddon-school.demon.co.uk/

The Prevention and Management of Aggression – A Good Practice Statement, Working Group on Mental Illness, July 1996, NHS – Quality Improvement Scotland

The Scottish Parliament (Information Centre), *Physical Chastisement of Children*, Research Note, RN 00/11 (Revised), 6 September 2001 http://www.scottish.parliament.uk/S1/whats_happening/research/_pdf_res_notes/rn00-11.pdf

The Scottish Parliament (Information Centre*), Criminal Justice (Scotand) Bill: Children*, SPICe Briefing, 02/52, 13 May 2002, http://www.scottish.parliament.uk/S1/whats_happening/research/pdf_res_brief/_sb02-52.pdf

Thompson J, *Delictual Liability*, 2nd edition, Butterworths, 2001

Turner C, *Tort – Key Facts*, Hodder & Stoughton, 2001

Weiner B, An attribution theory of achievement and motivation, *Psychological Review*. 92.4.pp.548-573.

Work-Related Violence – Assessment and Intervention, Leather P, Brady C, Lawrence C, Beale D & Cox T (eds), Routledge, 1999

Wright J, *Tort Law and Human Rights*, Hart Publishing, 2001

Zarkowska E and Clements J *Problem Behaviour and People with Severe Disabilities: the Star Approach*, Chapman Hall (1996)

Internet Resources (General)

AbuseLaw.co.uk, *Human Rights Factsheet*, Stewards Solicitors, downloaded in April 2003, http://www.abuselaw.co.uk/humanRights/default.ihtml?step=2&id=4

Additional Needs Net, *What is Challenging Behaviour?* 2001 http://www.additionalneeds.net/Challenging_Behaviour/whatis.htm

BluePsy – online professional psychological advice and counselling: http://www.bluepsy.com/challenging.htm

British Institute of Learning Disabilities, http://www.bild.org.uk/

Centre for Family Development, *Informed Consent to Treatment*, www.center4familydevelop.com.Informed_Consent.htm, 2000-2003

Crescent Life, **Learning Disability** http://www.crescentlife.com/disorders/learning_disabilities.htm (downloaded November 2002)

Contact a Family, *Contact a Family Factsheet: Caring for Children with Disabilities and Special Needs – A guide for Students and Professional Workers*, http://www.cafamily.org.uk/students.html (downloaded January 2003)

Contact a Family – *An Introduction to Behavioural Phenotypes:* http://www.cafamily.org.uk/behaviou.html (downloaded 7 November 2003)

🌐 *Employee Checklist*, National Task Force on Violence Against Social Care Staff, Department of Health, http://www.doh.gov.uk/violencetaskforce/card.htm

🌐 End All Corporal Punishment of Children, *Key Judgements*, http://encorporalpunishment.org/pages/hrlaw/judgements.html (downloaded in December 2002)

🌐 End All Corporal Punishment of Children, *UK responses to European Court Judgement on parental corporal punishment*, November 2001, http://www.endcorporalpunishment.org/pages/news/uk.html

🌐 *Findings, Consulting with disabled children and young people*, http://www.jrf.org.uk/knowledge/findings/socialcare/741.asp, July 2001

🌐 Lambeth Teacher with Lambeth NUT, *NUT advice to divisions on negotiating issues with LEAs on positive handling strategies for pupils with severe behavioural difficulties*, http://www.lta.demon.co.uk/circ_physical_restraint.pdf, 2001

🌐 Law Teacher.Net, *The English Law Website of Asif Tufal*, http://www.lawteacher.net/

🌐 Mencap Briefing, *Valuing People: Implementation Guidance*, September 2001, http://www.mencap.org.uk/download/implementation_guidance.pdf

🌐 Mind, *Factsheets – Mind Legal Briefings – The Human Rights Act 1998*, Mind Publications, downloaded in April 2003 http://www.mind.org.uk/NR/exeres/AA286E1F-35BA-40DE-B481-10CD76E86A43.htm?NRMODE=Published&wbc_purpose=Basic&WBCMODE=PresentationUnpublished

🌐 NHS National Electronic Library for Health *Learning Disabilities*, *Challenging Behaviour*, http://www.minervation.com/ld/challenging/ 2002

🌐 Roach T & Eslea M, *Quality of Life In Children With Severe Learning Disabilities: What Factors Predict Challenging Behaviour?* Department of Psychology, University of Central Lancashire, downloaded in December 2002 http://www.uclan.ac.uk/facs/science/psychol/bully/files/blackpool1.pdf

🌐 Royal National Institute for the Blind (RNIB), *Challenging behaviour in visually and learning disabled adults*, http://www.rnib.org.uk/multdis/chall.htm (downloaded December 2002)

🌐 The Health Evidence Bulletin (Wales), *9: Staff Training*, 31 December 1999 http://hebw.uwcm.ac.uk/learningdisabilities/chapter9.htm

🌐 The Scottish Office, *Human Rights in Scotland* http://www.scotland.gov.uk/library/documents-w9/huri-01.htm (downloaded April 2003)

🌐 University of Central England in Birmingham Faculty of Health and Community Care webpage on Challenging Behaviour: http://www.hcc.uce.ac.uk/cpsu/Packs/LD/challeng.htm

Index

Please note that all Statutes and Regulations are in **bold** print

ABH (Actual Bodily Harm) 147–148
abnormality of mind 155–156, 202
abuse
   defined 259
   of rights, prohibition (HRA Article 17) 179
   risk of 73–74
   vulnerable adults 24
accident, inevitable (negligence defence) 176, 265
ACRT (Audit Commission Review Team) 9
Actual Bodily Harm (ABH) 147–148
actus reus 94
Additional Needs Net 17, 56
Adoption Act 1976 36
adoption, agreement to 36
Adoption and Children Act 2002 26, 35, 36, 39,
   40, 41
Adoption NI Order 1987 36
Adoption (Scotland) Act 1978 36
adults
   care provider for 45
   definition of 'adult' 13, 223, 259
   legal capacity, assumption of 78
   vulnerable, abuse of 23–24, 282
Adults with Incapacity (Scotland) Act 2000 *see*
   **AWI (S) A (Adults with Incapacity
   (Scotland) Act 2000**
age of children, and control/restraint 90–91
Age of Legal Capacity (Scotland) Act 1991 13,
   33, 34, 223, 264
Age of Majority Act (Northern Ireland) 1969 13,
   264
Age of Majority (Scotland) Act 1969 13, 264
agencies, impact of law on practice/policy 10–11
aggressive behaviour 56
*Agreeing Procedures for the Use of Physical
   Force on Pupils* 20–21
Allen, David 127
anti-social behaviour 56
applied behaviour analysis, challenging behaviour
   prevention 66, 67–68, 70
Area Child Protection Committees 20
Ashworth Hospital, control and restraint
   techniques 84
assault
   actions 146
   bodily harm *see* Actual Bodily Harm (ABH);
      Grievous Bodily Harm (GBH)

civil law (England and Wales) 167
common, criminal law (England and Wales)
   146–147
as crime of intent 192
criminal law (Scotland) 191–193
defined 259
gestures 192
intentional delicts (Scotland) 208–210
   defences 210, 266–267
justifiable 30, 204, 274
physical contact 146
physical restraint and 247–248, 252–254
words 146
Association for Persons with Severe Handicaps in
   North America 55
Audit Commission Review Team (ACRT) 9
authorised staff, identity 95
autistic spectrum disorders
   challenging behaviour 58
   guidance *see Guidance on Use of Restrictive
      Physical Interventions for Staff Working
      with Children and Adults who Display
      Extreme Behaviour in Association with
      Learning Disability and/or Autistic
      Spectrum Disorders 2002*
**AWI (S) A (Adults with Incapacity (Scotland) Act
   2000**
   acting in accordance with 227
   definitions 13, 222–223, 259, 264
   ill-treatment/wilful neglect (s 83(1)) 227–228
   incapacity assessment 224
   liability limitations 226–227
   scope 221–222

battered woman syndrome 153
battery 147, 168
behavioural therapy 67
best interests principle 78–80, 159
BILD (British Institute of Learning Disabilities)
   19, 20
**Births, Deaths and Marriages Registration
   (Northern Ireland) Act 1956** 29
Births and Marriages Registration Act 1953 29
births, registration of (parental responsibility) 29
Bolam test 82
breach of duty, criminal law 171
breach of peace, prevention 165, 271

breakaway techniques 101
British Institute of Learning Disabilities (BILD)
    19, 20
Broadmoor Hospital, control and restraint
    techniques 84
'but for' test, homicide 149, 217

CA 1989 *see* **Children Act 1989**
CAFCASS (Children and Family Courts Advisory
    and Support Service) 35
capacity
    basic principles 78
    consent, giving of 77–82
    defined 260
    medical treatment and 76–77
care and control, assessment 49-50
care givers (belief, perceptions and behaviour) 61-
    64
care provider for adults, defined 46, 261
carers
    of children, duties of 38, 262–263
    and employer's legal position (case study)
        241–243
    natural 63
    parent 260
    responsibilities 261–264
    standard of care 217
    terminology 45–47, 260
    unpaid 45, 260–261
Carers and Disabled Children Act 2000 262
Carers (Recognition and Services) Act 1995 45,
    260–261, 262
Care Standards Act 2000 9, 13, 24, 46, 261, 291
Care Standards authorities 6
care worker, defined 46, 261
challenging behaviour
    applied behaviour analysis 66, 67–68, 70
    best practice 70
    biological causes 57–58
    care giver's belief, perceptions and behaviour
        61–64
    case study 60
    communication, means of 61
    defined 15, 263–264
    problems 17
    ecological causes 59–61
    feeling-based model 66
    forms 55–56
    interactional challenge contrasted 17
    learnt 58–59
    management 67
    prevention strategies 66–68
    reactive management strategies, legal
        implications 70
    risk assessment 125, 127–130
    staff training 64–65
chastisement, reasonable 29, 204, 205
    case studies 246, 252
child
    adoption, agreement to 36
    age, understanding and competence 90–91

care of, without parental responsibility 44
defined 12–13, 264
each, focus on needs of 10
parental responsibility for *see* parental respon-
    sibility
Child Abduction Act 1984 34
Children Act 1989
    children in need 264
    criminal liability 262–263
    defects 4
    impact 8
    justifications 22
    lawful excuse 22
    mythology (England and Wales) 10
    parental responsibility 25, 26, 27, 28, 29, 32,
        34, 35, 38, 39, 40, 41, 42, 44, 47, 48, 49,
        288
    residential care 87
    significant harm 23
    terminology 4, 5, 13
    Children Bill 2004 10
Children with Disabilities 23
Children and Family Courts Advisory and
    Support Service (CAFCASS) 35
children in need 264
Children (Northern Ireland) Order 1995
    child, defined 23, 264
    children in need 264
    impact 8
    parental responsibility 22, 25, 26, 28, 32, 35,
        38, 39, 40, 41, 42, 44, 47, 48, 49, 262,
        288
    significant harm 23
    terminology 4, 5, 13
    UK jurisdictions 4
Children (Scotland) Act 1995
    children in need 264
    impact 8
    lawful force defence 204, 274
    parental responsibility 3, 22, 25, 26, 28, 32,
        36–37, 38, 39, 40, 41, 44, 47, 48, 49,
        288, 289
    significant harm 23
    terminology 4, 13
    UK jurisdictions 4
**Children (Secure Accommodation (No. 2))
    Regulations 1991** 87
**Children (Secure Accommodation) Regulations
    1991** 87
**Children and Young People (Northern Ireland
    Order) 2003** 9-10
Children's Commissioner for Wales Act 2001 9
Children's Homes Regulations 1991 87, 88, 92
Children's Homes Regulations 2002 87, 88, 92
children's legislation 8-9, 49–51
    see also specific statutes eg **Children and Young
        Persons Act 1933**
Children's Rights Commissioner for Wales 9
Children's Rights Director for England 9-10
Children and Young Persons Act 1933 22, 29,
    32, 42, 44, 160, 262

Children and Young Persons (Scotland) Act 1937
22, 29, 30, 32, 44, 203–204, 252, 253,
274
Child Support Agency (CSA) 36
Circular 9/94 (*Education of Children with
Emotional and Behavioural Difficulties*) 7
Circular 10/95 (*Protecting Children from Abuse*)
99
Circular 10/98 (*Section 550A of Education Act*)
94–100
Circular 93/13 (*Guidance on Permissible Forms
of Control in Children's Residential Care*)
(DoH) 7, 8, 85–92
circulars, defined 6
civil law (England and Wales) 167–176
assault 167
battery 168
definitions 265
false imprisonment 145–146, 168–169, 250
negligence *see* negligence
civil law (Scotland) 206–234, 266–269
Adults with Incapacity (Scotland) Act 2000 *see*
**AWI(S) A (Adults with Incapacity
(Scotland) Act 2000**
delicts *see* delictual liability (Scotland); delicts,
intentional; delicts, unintentional
professional liability 219–220
restraint, guidance for use *see* restraint
(Scotland)
civil liabilities, employers *see* employer's civil
liabilities
civil vicarious liability *see* vicarious liability
civil wrong/tort, defined 21
*Clear Expectations, Consistent Limits - Good
Practice in the care and control of children
and young people in residential care* 100
C(NI)O 1995 *see* **Children (Northern Ireland)
Order 1995**
Code for Employers of Social Care Workers 7
Codes of Guidance 3–4
Code for Social Care Employees 7
Codes of Practice 6, 51, 122
coercion defence, Scotland 203, 274
**Commissioner for Children and Young People
Act 2003** 9
Commission for Social Care Inspection (CSCI) 9,
88
Committee on Services to Children with a
Learning Disability and Severely
Challenging Behaviour (MHF) 16–17, 263
common law
criminal offence, defined 21
defined 4
employer's duties 114
insane, statutory power to detain 163–165,
205, 270
Community and Mental Health Support teams 43
complaints, Education Act 1996 (s 550A) 99
consent defence 157–158, 210, 270
consent to medical treatment
best interests principle 78–80

Bolam test 82
capacity to give 77–82, 268
case study 243–244
children and 269
England, Wales and Northern Ireland 32–33
forms 83
free and voluntary requirement 82, 268
HRA 1998 and 83–84
information requirements 81–82, 268
medications 76–77
parental responsibility 32–34
Scotland 33–34
constructive manslaughter 156
contributory negligence 174–175, 218, 265,
267–268
control, and restraint
see also restraint; restraint (Scotland)
breakaway techniques 101
detention of pupils 103–105
expectations 101–102
force, use of *see* **Education Act 1996 (s. 550A)**
garment, restraining 85
limits, consistent 101–102
residential care, permissible forms of control
(DoH Guidance) 7, 8, 85–92
taking care/control 100–101
verbal control 229
Cornelia de Lange syndrome 58
corporal punishment 30, 94, 204, 205
Council of Europe 27
country, leaving of by child (parental responsibility) 34
CPS (Crown Prosecution Service) 21, 265, 270
crime prevention defence 166, 271
Criminal Act 1967 271
Criminal Justice Act 1967 151–152
Criminal Justice (Scotland) Act 2003 204, 209,
252, 274
Criminal Law Act 1967 93, 166
criminal law (England and Wales)
defences
breach of peace prevention 165, 271
consent 157–158
crime prevention 166, 271
duress of circumstances 159–160, 270
insane, statutory power to detain 163–165,
270
lawful correction 160–162, 270–271
lawful excuse 22, 276–277
mistake 163, 266, 271
necessity 158–159, 175, 266, 271
self-defence 162, 174, 271–272
homicide *see* homicide
offences against the person *see* Offences
Against the Person
criminal law (Scotland)
assault 191–193
cruel and barbarous treatment/cruel and
unnatural treatment 193
defences
coercion 203, 274

criminal law (Scotland) *(Cont.)*
  diminished responsibility 201–202, 273
  lawful force 203–205, 274–275
  lunatics, common law power to restrain 205,
    275
  necessity 202–203, 210, 273–274
  provocation 198–201, 273
  reflex actions 197, 272
  self-defence 197–198, 272
  human rights and 235–237
  lieges, recklessly endangering the 195
  real injury, causing 193–194
  reckless injury 194
criminal liability, concept 22
criminal offence, defined 21
Criminal Procedure (Scotland) Act 1975 193,
  203, 274
criminal vicarious liability 109
Crown Prosecution Service (CPS) 21, 265,
  270
cruel and barbarous/unnatural treatment
  (Scotland) 193
CSA 1995 *see* **Children (Scotland) Act 1995**
CSCI (Commission for Social Care Inspection) 9,
  88

death, and homicide 150–151
deceased child, burying or cremation (parental
  responsibilities) 36
delegated legislation, defined 4, 5
delicts, intentional
  assault 208–210
  defences 210
  fear and force 211
  lawful arrest 211, 267
  liberty, injuries to 210
  defences 211
  mentally ill, statutory power to detain 211
delicts, unintentional
  negligence
  see also negligence
  breach of duty of care 214–215
  causation of harm 217
  duty of care 211–214
  standard of care 215–217
delictual liability (Scotland)
  see also delicts, intentional; delicts,
    unintentional
  law 207–208
dementia 58
de minimis rule, homicide 150
detention of pupils, outside school hours
  103–105
diminished responsibility defence 154–156,
  201–202, 273
disability, defined 275
Disability Discrimination Act 1995 275
discipline of child, parental responsibility 29–30
discrimination, prohibition of (HRA 1998,
  Article 14) 179, 183, 236
  consent to medical treatment 83

**Domestic Proceedings Magistrates' Courts Act
  and Matrimonial Causes Act 1978** 36
Don't Forget Us (MHF) 11, 18
doors, locking 90–91, 233–234
drugs *see* medication
duress of circumstances defence 159–160, 270
duty of care
  see also standard of care
  breach of 171–173, 214–215
  causation 173
  damage 173
  defined 4, 105
  Donoghue v Stevenson case 212
  negligence 169–171, 211–214
  policy issues 170–171

ECHR (European Convention for the Protection
  of Human Rights and Fundamental
  Freedoms)
  see also **HRA (Human Rights Act) 1998**
  consent to medical treatment 83
  discipline of children 29
  education, right to (First Protocol) 31
  impact 6, 177
  religious upbringing, parental power to
    determine 31
  remedies, violation of rights 185, 186
  Scotland Act 1998 and 235
Education Act 1996 14–15, 30, 103, 277
Education Act 1996 (s. 550A) 92–100
  application of force 97–98
  authorised staff, identity 95
  Circular 10/98 94–100
  complaints 99
  corporal punishment 94
  further guidance 94
  history/provisions 7
  incident planning 94–95
  incident recording 98–99
  incident types 96
  physical contact with pupils, circumstances
    other than force 99–100
  practical considerations 97
  provisions 95
  reasonable force, defined 96–97
  residential homes 86
  school policy, necessity to have 94
  self-defence 95
Education Act 1997 7, 103
Education Act 2002 105
Education (Scotland) Act 1980 30
emergencies, actions in 95
employer's civil liabilities 109–132, 275
  see also vicarious liability
  carer and (case study) 243-244
  common law duties 114
  competent staff 114–115
  Health and Safety at Work Act 1974 121
  health and safety matters 121–122
  P.I. training, responsibility to provide 130–132
  plant and equipment 115–116

risk assessment 125–130
safe place of work 115
safe system of work 117–120
Scotland 139–140
statutory duties 120–130
vicarious 110–114
England and Wales
  Care Standards authorities 6
  Children's Rights Director/Commissioner 9
  civil law *see* civil law (England and Wales)
  consent to medical treatment, parental responsibility 32–33
  criminal law *see* criminal law (England and Wales)
  homicide *see* homicide
  parental responsibility, statutory definition 28
environmental changes 90, 250
epilepsy 58
European Convention on Human Rights *see* ECHR (European Convention for the Protection of Human Rights and Fundamental Freedoms)
European Court of Human Rights 30, 161, 165, 204, 274
Evaluating a training package for staff working with people with learning disabilities prior to hospital closure 65
evil intent, assault 192
extinction 58
ex turpi causa non oritur actio 175

false imprisonment 145–146, 168–169, 267, 275–276
  case study 250
Family Law Reform Act 1969 13, 264
Family Support, Day Care and Education Provision for Young Children 43
fathers, unmarried 41, 288
fear and force delict 211
feeling-based model, challenging behaviour prevention 66
force
  positive handling concept 20
  proportionate 198-201
  reasonable 92, 96–97, 198
  unplanned use 72
  use of to control/restrain pupils *see* **Education Act 1996 (s. 550A)**
foresight, duty of care 170
fostering, secondary legislation 5
Fostering Services Regulations 2002 87
Foundation for People with Learning Disabilities 24, 57, 74, 126
freedom of expression, HRA 1998 (Article 10) 178–179, 183

GBH (Grievous Bodily Harm) 148–149
General Social Care Council for England 6
'Gillick competence' 81
good faith principle 227
Government of Scotland Act 1998 6

Government of Wales Act 1998 6
Grievous Bodily Harm (GBH) 148–149
  with intent 149
gross negligence manslaughter 157
guardian ad litem, defined 35
guardian, power to appoint 35
Guidance, defined 5–6
Guidance on Model Behaviour Policies for Pupils in Special Schools 85
Guidance on the Use of Restrictive Physical Interventions for Pupils with Severe Behavioural Differences 8, 85
Guidance on Use of Restrictive Physical Interventions for Staff Working with Children and Adults who Display Extreme Behaviour in Association with Learning Disability and/or Autistic Spectrum Disorders 2002 8, 20, 71–73, 290
Guide for Parents and Carers 16

harm
  see also Actual Bodily Harm (ABH); Grievous Bodily Harm (GBH)
  causation (standard of care) 217
  defined 23
  probability/seriousness 216
  significant *see* significant harm
hazards, risk assessment 125–126
Health Evidence Bulletin (Wales) 64
Health and Safety at Work Act 1974 121, 122
Health and Safety Commission (HSC) 121
Health and Safety (Consultation with Employees) Regulations 1996 130
Health and Safety Executive (HSE) 121
Health and Social Care (Community Health and Standards) Act 2003
  adults and children, coverage 3–4
  Commission for Social Care Inspection and 9
  documents 11
  terminology 4-6
  UK jurisdictions 4
Health and Social Services Boards (Northern Ireland) 4
home, outside (care and control of children) 89–90
homicide
  'but for' test 149, 217
  causation 149–150
  culpable
    involuntary 196
    voluntary 197
  death 150
  interventions resulting in 151
  de minimis rule 150
  England and Wales 149–157
  human being as victim 151
  involuntary manslaughter 156–157
  murder 151–152, 195–196
  Scotland 195–196
  thin-skull test 150
  voluntary manslaughter 152-156
  wicked intention 195

Homicide Act 1957 152, 154–155
HRA (Human Rights Act) 1998
  Articles 177–179
  see also abuse of rights, prohibition;
    discrimination, prohibition of; freedom of
    expression; inhuman or degrading
    treatment, prohibition; liberty and security,
    right to; life, right to; private and family
    life, right to; torture, prohibition of;
  impact 179–183
  challenging behaviours 71
  European Convention and *see* ECHR
    (European Convention on Human Rights)
  impact 6
  medical treatment consent 83–84
  private individuals, and public bodies 184
  purpose 276
  therapeutic treatment, case study 248–249
HSC (Health and Safety Commission) 121
HSE (Health and Safety Executive) 121
human being, as victim 151
Human Fertilisation and Embryology Act 1990
  26, 288
Human Rights Convention *see* ECHR (European
  Convention for the Protection of Human
  Rights and Fundamental Freedoms)
human rights law
  see also ECHR (European Convention for the
    Protection of Human Rights and
    Fundamental Freedoms); **HRA (Human
    Rights Act) 1998**
  court's interpretation 186–187
  criminal law and 235–237
  medical law and 237
  private individuals/public bodies 184
  procedure 185
  public authority 184
  remedies 185–186
  Scotland (criminal/medical law) 237
  victim requirement 184
Hypomelanosis of Ito 58

illegality, negligence defence 175–176, 265
ill-treatment offence 227–228
incapable, defined 223
incapacity
  assessment 224–226
  best interests 78–80
  children under 16 years old 13
  defined 81, 223
incident planning 94–95
incident recording 98–99, 246–247
incident types 96
inhuman or degrading treatment, prohibition
    (HRA 1998 Article 3) 181–182, 228
  case studies 246, 247, 248–249, 250, 251,
    252
injury 193–194
insane, statutory power to detain (common law)
    163–165, 205, 211, 270
intentional wrongdoing, vicarious liability 112

intervention
  control, maintaining 91
  defined 223
  medication use as 76–84
  primary/secondary 72
involuntary manslaughter 156–157

Jefferson, Alan 10
joint fault, negligence defence 218–219, 268
Joint Social Services Inspectorate (JSSI) 9
justifications, criminal liability 22
just satisfaction, human rights remedies 185

King's Fund Centre 55

Law Commission 27, 80
lawful arrest 211, 267
lawful correction defence 160–162, 270–271
lawful detention 267
lawful excuse defence 22, 276–277
lawful force defence 203–205, 274–275
Law Reform (Contributory Negligence) Act 1945
    218, 252
learning difficulty, defined 14–15, 277
Learning Disabilities - Fundamental Facts 18, 57
Learning Disabilities Sub-Committee Working
    Party (1993), Mental Health Foundation
    90
learning disability 14, 71–73, 277
*Learning disability care staff's emotional
    reactions to aggressive challenging
    behaviours* 65
learnt behaviour 58–59
*Legal issues arising from the care control and
    safety of children with learning disabilities*
    (MHF 1994) 3
legal proceedings, representation of child 35
legislation, defined 4
Lesch-Nyhan syndrome 58
liberty
  injuries to (intentional delicts) 210
  defences 211, 267–268
  restriction of 87–88
  methods of care and control falling short of 91
liberty and security, right to (HRA 1998, Article
    5) 177–178, 182
  case study 250
life, right to (HRA 1998, Article 2) 83, 177,
    179–180
likely to suffer significant harm, defined 4
local authority accommodation, children
    remanded/detained within 87
Local Authority Inspection Units 8–9
Local Authority Social Services Act 1970 5, 6
lunatic, common law power to restrain 205, 275

McNaughton Rules 163
maintenance of child (parental responsibility) 36
Making social care better for people (Stakeholder
    Information Pack) 9
malicious wounding 148–149

Management of Health and Safety at Work Regulations 1999 121, 123
management responsibilities, children's residential homes 91–92
management strategies, challenging behaviour prevention 66
Mansell Report (1993) 11, 263
manslaughter
    see also murder
    constructive 156
    depression 154
    diminished responsibility 154–156
    gross negligence 157
    intoxication 154
    involuntary 156–157
    provocation 152–154
    self-control, loss of 153
    subjective/objective tests 153
    voluntary 152–156
Manual Handling Operations Regulations 1992 121, 124–125, 131, 134
Marriage Act 1949 34
marriage of children, parental consent to 34
mechanical restraint, direct 233–234
medical law (Scotland) 237
medical treatment
    see also medication
    beneficial 225
    capacity 76–77
    consent *see* consent to medical treatment
    least restrictive 226
    necessary 225
    and physical intervention 224
medication
    anti-psychotic 76, 277
    as intervention 76–84
    psychoactive 76, 277
    psychotropic 77
    as restraint 234
mens rea 93–94, 191
mental disorder, defined 223
mental handicap/retardation 14
Mental Health Act 1983 3–4
    consent/capacity 77, 78, 79, 80, 81, 82, 260, 268
    insane, statutory power to detain 164, 266
    learning disability 14
    necessity principle 159
    time-out 76
Mental Health Foundation
    Committee on Services to Children with a Learning Disability 16–17, 263
    Learning Disabilities Sub-Committee Working Party (1993) 90
    publications 3, 10, 11, 49
Mental Health (Scotland) Act 1984 224, 254, 267
mental impairment 14, 277
mentally ill persons
    common law power to restrain 205
    diminished responsibility 154–156, 201–202, 273

medications 77
statutory power to detain 163–165, 205, 211, 270
Mental Welfare Commission, Scotland 19
MHF (Mental Health Foundation) *see* Mental Health Foundation
MHOR (Manual Handling Operations Regulations) 1992 121, 124–125, 131, 134
mistake defence 163, 176, 266, 271
Model Policies for Local Education Authorities and for Special Schools on the Use of Physical Interventions for Pupils with Severe Behavioural Difficulties 3
multi-element behavioural support 67
murder 151–152, 195–196

name, giving to child (parental responsibility) 28
National Care Standards Commission (NCSC) 9
National Care Standards Committee (Scotland) 228
National Electronic Library for Health (NHS) 18
National Health Service and Community Care Act 1990 262
National Minimum Standards for Children in Residential Care 87, 290
National Minimum Standards for Fostering 87
National Task Force on Violence Against Social Care Staff 134
NCSC (National Care Standards Commission) 9
necessity defence 158–159, 175, 266, 271
    Scotland 202–203, 210, 273–274
negligence
    see also negligence defences
    causation of harm 217
    contributory 174–175, 218, 265, 267–268
    defined 169
    duty of care *see* duty of care
    standard of care 215–217
    statutory duties contrasted 120
negligence defences
    contributory negligence 174–175, 218, 265, 267–268
    illegality 175–176, 265
    inevitable accident 176, 265
    joint fault 218–219, 268
    mistake 163, 176, 266, 271
    necessity 158–159, 175, 202–203, 210, 266, 271, 273–274
    self-defence *see* self-defence
    statutory authority 175, 266
    volenti non fit injuria 174, 217–218, 266, 267
neighbour principle, duty of care 169
nervous shock 119, 173
Northern Ireland
    see also **Age of Majority Act (Northern Ireland) 1969; Births, Deaths and Marriages Registration (Northern Ireland) Act 1956; Children (Northern Ireland) Order 1995; Children and Young People (Northern Ireland Order) 2003**

Northern Ireland *(Cont.)*
 parental responsibility, statutory definition 28
 Public Prosecution Service 4, 21
 Social Care Council 6
Northern Ireland Act 1998 5
No Secrets 24, 49, 74

OAPA (Offences Against the Person Act) 1861
 Actual Bodily Harm (s.47) 147–148
 case studies 245, 247
 Grievous Bodily Harm (s.20) 148–149
 Grievous Bodily Harm with intent (s 18) 149
 offences 270
 wounding (ss.18 and 20) 148–149
Offences Against the Person
 see also **OAPA (Offences Against the Person
  Act) 1861**
 assault *see* assault
 battery 147
 false imprisonment 145–146, 168–169, 250,
  267
 homicide *see* homicide

PACE (Police and Criminal Evidence Act) 1984
 182
paramountcy principle, welfare 3, 33, 47
parental responsibility
 children's legislation, influence on 50-51
 concept/definition 25, 26, 38–39, 46
 delegation 43
 matters encompassed within 43-44
 holding 39, 288
 independent exercise of 41–42
 exceptions 42-43
 jurisdictions 25
 listed, statutory provisions 28–36
 other person acquiring, effect 39–40
 persons without but with care of child 44
 revoking 289
 statutory definition 27–28
 step-parents 40-41, 288–289
parental rights
 defined 26
 reasonable chastisement 29, 205
 case studies 246, 252
parent carer, defined 260
parent, meaning 26, 288
Parents and Carers Guide 3
*Permissible Forms of Control in Children's
  Residential Care* (Circular 93/13) 7, 8,
  85–92
physical intervention
 see also control, and restraint; intervention;
  physical restraint; restraint; restraint
  (Scotland)
 abuse risk 73–74
 autistic spectrum disorders, guidance *see
  Guidance on Use of Restrictive Physical
  Interventions for Staff Working with
  Children and Adults who Display Extreme
  Behaviour in Association with Learning*

 *Disability and/or Autistic Spectrum
  Disorders 2002*
 death, resulting in 149-157
 description 70–71, 289–290
 learning disability 71–73
 medical treatment and 224
 methods 75–76
 policies and prevention, case study 249–250
 restrictive/non-restrictive 18–19, 290
 situations, examples 74–75
 use of 74–76
physical restraint
 assault and 247–248, 252–254
 direct 232–233
 good practice 102–103
 guidelines 232
methods falling short of 91
 residential care guidance 88–89
P.I. training 130–132
 feedback 255–258
plant and equipment, safety aspects 115–116
Police and Criminal Evidence Act 1984 182
Positive Behavioural Management 74
positive handling concept/plans 7, 20–21, 290
PPSNI (Public Prosecution Service for Northern
  Ireland) 4, 21, 270
Prader-Willi syndrome 58
precautions, standard of care 216
primary legislation, defined 4
private and family life, right to respect (HRA
  1998, Article 8) 83, 178, 182–183, 236
 case studies 247, 250, 252
Procurator Fiscal, Scotland 21, 265, 269, 270
professional liability 219–220
*Promoting Well-Being and Preventing
  Challenging Behaviour* 18, 61, 66, 132
property administration (parental responsibility)
  35
proportionate force 198-201
protection of child (parental responsibility) 29
provocation defence 152–154, 198–201, 210,
  273
proximity, duty of care 170
public authority 184
Public Prosecution Service for Northern Ireland
  (PPSNI) 4, 21, 270

reasonable chastisement 29, 205
 case studies 246, 252
reasonableness test
 see also force: reasonable
 duty of care 171
 manslaughter 153
 murder 152
 provocation 200
 reasonable force 96–97, 198
recklessness
 Actual Bodily Harm 148
 culpable and reckless conduct 193–195
 injury 194
 wicked 196

recording of incidents, case study 246–247
Reference Guide to Consent for Examination and Treatment 33, 78
reflex actions defence 197, 272
Registration of Births Deaths and Marriages (Scotland) Act 1965 28
Regulation of Care (Scotland) Act 2001 204, 274
reinforcement 58
religious upbringing (parental responsibility) 31–32
reparation 266
Report on Guardianship and Custody (Law Commission) 26
Reporting of Injuries, Diseases and Dangerous Occurrences Regulations 1995 130
Residence Order 41, 42
residential care, permissible forms of control (DoH Guidance) 7, 8, 85–92
responsible parenthood concept 91
restraint
 see also control, and restraint; physical intervention; restraint (Scotland)
 applying 231
 assault and, case study 247–248
 considering use of 230
 continuous re-assessment 231
 default, by 229
 defined 228–230, 232
 force, use of *see* **Education Act 1996, s 550A**
 garment, restraining 85
 initial assessment 230
 law relating to children 87
 monitoring of use 232
 in non-health settings 232
 physical *see* physical restraint
 terminology 19
 therapeutic purposes, case study 248
 training 233
 unplanned 232
restraint (Scotland)
 definition of 'restraint' 228–230
 direct mechanical 233–234
 direct physical 232–233
 general principles 230–232
 locking doors 233–234
 medication 234
retaliation, immediate 200–201
Review of Some Important Issues in Research and Services for People with Learning Difficulties and Challenging Behaviour 65
risk assessment
 acceptable risk 231
 challenging behaviours 127–130
 civil liabilities 125–130
 definition of risk 126
 requirements 281
 violence at work 132–134
RNIB (Royal National Institute for the Blind) 17–18
Royal College of Nursing 76
Royal College of Psychiatrists 76, 84

Royal National Institute for the Blind (RNIB) 17–18

Safeguarding Children – Child Protection: Guidance about Child Protection Arrangements for the Education Service 99, 105
safe place of work 115
safe system of work 117–120
Safety Representatives and Safety Committees Regulations 1977 130
school age, defined 30
school attendance (parental responsibility) 30–31
school policy, necessity to have 94
School Standards and Framework Act 1998 30, 31, 93, 162
Scotland
 see also under particular legislation, eg **Children and Young Persons (Scotland) Act 1937**
 civil law *see* civil law (Scotland)
 consent to medical treatment, parental responsibility 33–34
 criminal law *see* criminal law (Scotland)
 employer's civil liabilities 139–140
 homicide 195–196
 Mental Welfare Commission 19
 National Care Standards Committee 228
 Office of the Procurator Fiscal 21, 265, 269, 270
 primary legislation 4
 Social Services Council 6
 vicarious liability 135–139
Scotland Act 1998 235
Scottish Office Social Work Research Findings 18
seclusion 75–76
 case study 250
secondary legislation, defined 4, 5
Secretary of State for Health 5
secure accommodation 87
self-control, loss of 153, 199
self-defence 95, 162, 174, 197–198, 266, 271–272
 case study 244–245
self-injurious behaviour 56
severely challenging behaviour 15, 263–264
severe mental impairment 14
Sexual Offences Act 1956 236
significant harm 22–24
Smith-Magenis syndrome 58
social care worker 6, 46, 281–282
Social Services Inspectorate (SSI) 22–23
Special Development Team, University of Kent 55
Special Hospital Authority 3
staff
 competent 114–115
 violence towards 130, 250–252
standard of care 215–217
Standards in Scotland's Schools Act 2000 30, 93, 204, 205, 253, 274–275

statutory authority, negligence defence 175, 266
step-parents, position of 40, 288–289
supply worker 282

Taking Care, Taking Control 100
Team-Teach, Positive Handling Plans 20
therapeutic treatment, human rights legislation
      case study 248–249
thin-skull test, homicide 150
time-out 76
TINA situations 19, 66, 241
tort, defined 21, 265
torture, prohibition of (HRA 1998 Article 3), 29,
      83, 177, 180–181
  case studies 246, 247, 248–249, 250, 251, 252
training
  challenging behaviour 64–65
  control 91
  P.I., responsibility to provide 130–132
  feedback 255–258
  restraint 233

United Nations Convention on the Rights of the
      Child 1989 4, 25
University of Kent, Special Development Team 55
unpaid carer 45, 260–261
upbringing of child (parental responsibility) 29
utility of defender's activities, standard of care
      216–217

Valuing People (White Paper) 14, 261
vicarious liability 110–114, 275
  in course of employment test 111–112
  economic reality test 111
  employee, act committed by 110
  of employers 112

financial risk test 111
  integral part of the business test 110–111
  organisation test 110–111
  Scotland 135–139
  tort, act as 110
victim requirement 151, 184
violence
  see also Offences Against the Person
  aggressive behaviour 56
  assault and 167
  at work
    National Task Force on Violence Against Social
      Care Staff 134
    risk assessment 132–134
    staff, towards 130, 250–252
    provocation 199
*Violence and Aggression to Staff in Health
    Services* 130
volenti non fit injuria, negligence defence 174,
    217–218, 266, 267
voluntary manslaughter 152–156
vulnerable adult 23–24, 282

welfare, children's, safeguarding 49–51
welfare principles
  checklist 3, 48–49
  paramountcy 3, 33, 48
Wells, Chris 20
Welsh Assembly, *see also* England and Wales
Welsh Assembly, legislation 4–5, 9-10
West Midlands Learning Disability Group 18
wicked intention 195
wicked recklessness 196
wilful neglect offence 227–228
wounding 148–149
wrongful detention 267